THE WAR ON TERROR AND THE LAWS OF WAR

The War on Terror and the Laws of War

A MILITARY PERSPECTIVE

Second Edition

Geoffrey S. Corn

James A. Schoettler, Jr.

Dru Brenner-Beck

Victor M. Hansen

Richard B. "Dick" Jackson

Eric Talbot Jensen

Michael W. Lewis

Foreword by Major General Charles J. Dunlap, Jr.
United States Air Force

OXFORD
UNIVERSITY PRESS

OXFORD
UNIVERSITY PRESS

Oxford University Press is a department of the University of Oxford. It furthers the University's objective of excellence in research, scholarship, and education by publishing worldwide.

Oxford   New York

Auckland   Cape Town   Dar es Salaam   Hong Kong   Karachi   Kuala Lumpur   Madrid
Melbourne   Mexico City   Nairobi   New Delhi   Shanghai   Taipei   Toronto

With offices in

Argentina   Austria   Brazil   Chile   Czech Republic   France   Greece   Guatemala   Hungary
Italy   Japan   Poland   Portugal   Singapore   South Korea   Switzerland   Thailand
Turkey   Ukraine   Vietnam

Oxford is a registered trademark of Oxford University Press in the UK and certain other countries.

Published in the United States of America by
Oxford University Press
198 Madison Avenue, New York, NY 10016

Library of Congress Cataloging-in-Publication Data
The war on terror and the laws of war : a military perspective / Geoffrey S. Corn [and six others]; foreword by Major General Charles J. Dunlap, Jr., United States Air Force. — Second edition.
    pages cm. — (Terrorism and global justice series)
    Includes bibliographical references and index.
    ISBN 978-0-19-994145-2 ((hardback) : alk. paper)—ISBN 978-0-19-022141-6 ((pbk.) : alk. paper)
1. War on Terror, 2001-2009. 2. Terrorism—Prevention—Law and legislation. 3. War (International law)
I. Corn, Geoffrey S.
    KZ6795.T47W37 2014
    341.6—dc23

                                                                              2014020388

9 8 7 6 5 4 3 2 1

Printed in the United States of America on acid-free paper

Note to Readers
This publication is designed to provide accurate and authoritative information in regard to the subject matter covered. It is based upon sources believed to be accurate and reliable and is intended to be current as of the time it was written. It is sold with the understanding that the publisher is not engaged in rendering legal, accounting, or other professional services. If legal advice or other expert assistance is required, the services of a competent professional person should be sought. Also, to confirm that the information has not been affected or changed by recent developments, traditional legal research techniques should be used, including checking primary sources where appropriate.

(Based on the Declaration of Principles jointly adopted by a Committee of the American Bar Association and a Committee of Publishers and Associations.)

> **You may order this or any other Oxford University Press publication by visiting the Oxford University Press website at www.oup.com**

Disclaimer

The views or opinions expressed in this book are not attributable to the U.S. Department of Defense or the U.S. military services, but are strictly the views and opinions of the authors. All statements are based on information drawn from the public record.

Author Biographies

Geoffrey S. Corn is The Presidential Research Professor of Law at South Texas College of Law in Houston Texas, who retired in 2004 from the U.S. Army as a Lieutenant Colonel. Professor Corn's teaching and scholarship focuses on the law of armed conflict, national security law, criminal law and procedure, and prosecutorial ethics. He has appeared as an expert witness at the Military Commission in Guantanamo and the International Criminal Tribunal for the Former Yugoslavia, and in federal court. He is the lead author of THE LAW OF ARMED CONFLICT: AN OPERATIONAL PERSPECTIVE and the first edition of THE LAWS OF WAR AND THE WAR ON TERROR, and a coauthor of PRINCIPLES OF COUNTER-TERRORISM LAW. His Army career included service as the Army's senior law of war expert advisor; tactical intelligence officer in Panama; supervisory defense counsel for the Western United States; Chief of International Law for U.S. Army Europe; Professor of International and National Security Law at the U.S. Army Judge Advocate General's School; and Chief Prosecutor for the 101st Airborne Division.

James A. Schoettler, Jr. is an Adjunct Professor of Law at the Georgetown University Law Center. He is a retired U.S. Army Colonel, with 30 years of service as a Judge Advocate on active duty and in the Army Reserve. His most recent assignments prior to retirement were as Assistant Chief (Individual Mobilization Augmentee), International and Operational Law Division, Office of the Judge Advocate General, U.S. Army, and Deputy Counsel and Staff Judge Advocate, U.S. Army Element (Individual Mobilization Augmentee), Defense Prisoner of War/Missing Personnel Office at the

U.S. Department of Defense. Since leaving active duty in 1987, he has been in private practice in the Washington, DC area (with a one-year posting to the Czech Republic), practicing international commercial law and trade regulation. He is a coauthor of THE LAW OF ARMED CONFLICT: AN OPERATIONAL APPROACH and the first edition of THE LAWS OF WAR AND THE WAR ON TERROR. He is a graduate of The Johns Hopkins University (BA), the Georgetown University Law Center (JD), and the Georgetown University School of Foreign Service (MSFS).

Dru Brenner-Beck is an attorney in private practice in Littleton, Colorado, and consults on international law matters. She served in the U.S. Army initially as a Military Intelligence officer, and then as a member of the Judge Advocate General's Corps from 1992 to 2004, retiring with the rank of Lieutenant Colonel (LTC). As a Judge Advocate, LTC (Ret.) Brenner-Beck served worldwide as a prosecutor, an administrative law attorney, and an Army litigator, and as Deputy General Counsel for the Department of the Army Inspector General. After retirement, she served as a Law Clerk to the Honorable Carlos F. Lucero of the U.S. Court of Appeals for the Tenth Circuit. She is a graduate of Georgetown University's School of Foreign Service and of Boston University's School of Law, and earned an LLM in military law from The Judge Advocate General's Legal Center and School. She is also the current president of the National Institute of Military Justice.

Victor M. Hansen is Associate Dean and Professor of Law at New England Law Boston. Professor Hansen holds a JD, magna cum laude, from Lewis and Clark Law School. He is a coauthor of THE LAW OF ARMED CONFLICT: AN OPERATIONAL APPROACH and the first edition of THE WAR ON TERROR AND THE LAWS OF WAR. He previously served as a Lieutenant Colonel in the U.S. Army Judge Advocate General's Corps.

Richard B. "Dick" Jackson is the Special Assistant to the U.S. Army Judge Advocate General for Law of War Matters. He is a retired U.S. Army Colonel, with over 30 years of experience as an Infantryman and Judge Advocate in such far-flung places as Panama, Haiti, Bosnia, Kosovo, and Iraq. Dick Jackson retired from the Army in 2005, having served the previous 10 years as a Staff Judge Advocate (the senior legal advisor) at the NATO Joint Forces Command in NATO, the U.S. Army, Pacific, Multinational Division North in Bosnia, the 25th Infantry Division in Hawaii, and the U.S. Army Special Operations Command, in Fort Bragg, North Carolina. He was also the Chair of the International and Operational Law Department at the U.S. Army Judge Advocate General's Legal Center and School. Mr. Jackson has written extensively and frequently lectured on law-of-war matters. Mr. Jackson is a coauthor of THE LAW OF ARMED CONFLICT: AN OPERATIONAL APPROACH and the first edition of THE LAWS OF WAR AND THE WAR ON TERROR.

Eric Talbot Jensen is an Associate Professor at Brigham Young Law School in Provo, Utah, where he teaches Public International Law, U.S. National Security Law, Criminal Law, and the Law of Armed Conflict. Prior to his current position, he spent 20 years in the U.S. Army, serving in various positions including as the Chief of the Army's International Law Branch; Deputy Legal Advisor for Task Force Baghdad; Professor of International and Operational Law at The Judge Advocate General's Legal Center and School; legal advisor to the U.S. contingent of U.N. Forces deployed to Skopje, Macedonia; and legal advisor in Bosnia in support of Operation Joint Endeavor/ Guard. Professor Jensen is a graduate of Brigham Young University (BA, International Relations), University of Notre Dame Law School (JD), The Judge Advocate General's Legal Center and School (LLM) and Yale Law School (LLM). He is a coauthor of THE LAW OF ARMED CONFLICT: AN OPERATIONAL APPROACH and the first edition of THE LAWS OF WAR AND THE WAR ON TERROR.

Michael W. Lewis is a professor of law at Ohio Northern University School of Law. He has written extensively on various aspects of the laws of war and the conflict between the United States and al-Qaeda and is a coauthor of the first edition of THE LAWS OF WAR AND THE WAR ON TERROR. He has testified before Congress on the legality of drone strikes in Pakistan and Yemen and on the civil liberties trade-offs associated with trying some al-Qaeda members or terrorist suspects before military commissions. He earned a BA from Johns Hopkins and a JD from Harvard Law School, cum laude, in 1998. Prior to entering law school he served in the U.S. Navy from 1987 to 1995 where he flew F-14s from the aircraft carrier USS *Independence*. He graduated from the Navy's Topgun fighter weapons school in 1992.

Table of Contents

Acknowledgments

THE AUTHORS WOULD like to first collectively acknowledge all the great leaders who mentored and shaped them as officers and legal professionals. Our collective experiences serving the United States as members of the armed forces—although in often divergent circumstances—provided a common bond that made working together on this project a genuine pleasure. Our service has also offered us the opportunity to consider these complex issues through an important and in many ways unique lens.

We would each also like to thank our research assistants. Without these devoted and exceptional students, this project could never have come to fruition as efficiently as it did.

Finally, we would like to thank the editors at Oxford University Press. The polish they put on our work will undoubtedly make the experience of reading these pages much more pleasant.

List of Treaties and Sources Frequently Cited in this Book

AP I Protocol Additional to the Geneva Conventions of 12 August 1949, and Relating to the Protection of Victims of International Armed Conflicts (Protocol I), June 8, 1977, 1125 U.N.T.S. 4.

AP II Protocol Additional to the Geneva Conventions of 12 August 1949, and Relating to the Protection of Victims of Non-International Armed Conflicts (Protocol II), June 8, 1977, 1125 U.N.T.S. 610.

AP Commentary INT'L COMM. RED CROSS, COMMENTARY ON THE ADDITIONAL PROTOCOLS OF 8 JUNE 1977 TO THE GENEVA CONVENTIONS OF 12 AUGUST 1949 (1987).

CCW Convention on Prohibitions or Restrictions on the Use of Certain Convention Weapons Which May Be Deemed to Be Excessively Injurious or to Have Indiscriminate Effects, Oct. 10, 1980, 1342 U.N.T.S. 163.

Declaration of St. Petersburg Renouncing the Use, in Time of War, of Explosive Projectiles Under 400 Grammes Weight, Nov. 29, 1868 (Dec. 11), 18 MARTENS NOUVEAU RECUEIL (1e ser.) 474, translated and reprinted in 1 AM. J. INT'L L. SUPP. 95 (1907).

GCIV Geneva Convention Relative to the Protection of Civilian Persons in Time of War, August 12, 1949, 6 U.S.T. 3516.

GCIV Commentary INT'L COMM. RED CROSS, COMMENTARY: IV GENEVA CONVENTION RELATIVE TO THE PROTECTION OF CIVILIAN PERSONS IN TIME OF WAR (1958).

Geneva Protocol Protocol for the Prohibition of the Use in War of Asphyxiating, Poisonous or Other Gases, and of Bacteriological Methods of Warfare, June 17, 1925, 26 U.S.T. 571, 94 L.N.T.S. 65.

GPW Geneva Convention Relative to the Treatment of Prisoners of War, August 12, 1949, 6 UST 3316.

GWS Geneva Convention for the Amelioration of the Condition of the Wounded and Sick in Armed Forces in the Field, August 12, 1949, 6 U.S.T. 3114.

GPW Commentary INT'L COMM. RED CROSS, COMMENTARY: III GENEVA CONVENTION RELATIVE TO THE TREATMENT OF PRISONERS OF WAR (1960).

GWS Commentary INT'L COMM. RED CROSS, COMMENTARY: I GENEVA CONVENTION FOR THE AMELIORATION OF THE CONDITION OF THE WOUNDED AND SICK IN ARMED FORCES IN THE FIELD (1952).

GWS-Sea Geneva Convention for the Amelioration of the Condition of the Wounded, Sick and Shipwrecked Members of the Armed Forces at Sea, August 12, 1949, 6 UST 3217.

Hague IV Hague Convention (IV) Respecting the Law and Customs of Law on Land with annex of regulations, October 18, 1907, 36 Stat. 2277, 1 Bevans 631.[1]

Hague IX Hague Convention (IX) Concerning Bombardment by Naval Forces in Time of War, October 18, 1907, 36 Stat. 2351, 1 Bevans 681.

---

[1] In this book, references to articles of Hague IV are references to the regulations annexed thereto.

Foreword to the Second Edition

CICERO FAMOUSLY OBSERVED that "In times of war, the law falls silent." However true that may have been in ancient Rome, it is certainly not so today. The events of 9/11 kicked off a robust and ongoing debate about the law applicable to the transnational nonstate terrorist groups who pose such a serious threat not just to the physical security of the citizenry of the United States and other nations, but to the efficacy of the rule of law itself.

The dangerousness of these terrorists groups has in many instances necessitated the resort to armed forces organized, trained, and equipped for a different kind of opponent. Aligning the law to the array of new activities the military finds itself performing brings to mind the metaphor of "building the airplane while flying it." Rather than being silent, the law in the time of today's conflicts literally "shouts." The question becomes: Is it shouting the right answers?

Unsurprisingly, the legal debates initiated by 9/11 have hardly diminished since the publication of the first edition of this book. Nations around the globe struggle to reconcile a legal architecture drafted largely with state-on-state conflicts in mind. Even when one considers such treaties as Additional Protocol II to the Geneva Conventions, which was aimed at non-international armed conflicts, we are still confronted with law that mainly contemplates belligerents different from the most dangerous transnational nonstate terrorist groups who bedevil security forces today.

The harsh truth is that unlike traditional conflicts—international and non-international alike—there is no end of terrorism in sight. Indeed, the melancholy reality is that there may not *ever* be an end. This produces a legal environment that if not completely unprecedented, is nevertheless fraught with a myriad of legal questions.

The fact is that despite the evolution of the law since 9/11, practitioners continue to be faced with complex legal issues many of which are—still—of first impression. Unfortunately, many practitioners lack the time to do the kind of in-depth research and thinking that these intricate issues require. Naturally, they frequently will look to the academy and other nongovernmental entities to build the intellectual infrastructure that they know they need to solve the legal dilemmas they face.

Therein, however, we find the critical issue: Do these "legal infrastructure builders" really have a sufficiently robust understanding of people, weaponry, and warfighting contexts to address the issues in such a way that they will have the legitimacy and logic that resonates with consumers of legal advice?

Too often the answer is no. In fact, as these issues have gained greater prominence, an increasing number of international law scholars have entered the fray. Some have educated themselves to the all-important context, but many of them are not as conversant as they need to be of the environment in which the legal issues play out. Put another way, some do not know what they do not know.

The second edition of this book is meant to carry on the critical mission of providing an unabashedly *military* perspective to the ongoing dialogue about the law. This is not to say, necessarily, that this unique perspective carries the imprimatur of infallibility simply because of the soldier-scholar status of this volume's authors; rather, it is to suggest that the absence of consideration of the military perspective means that any legal analysis is, by definition, incomplete.

Decision-makers and, especially, the executors of decisions deserve better. Even if one were to consider and reject the approaches these authors suggest, the final product nevertheless would be better for the intellectual rigor that consideration of their views would mandate.

What is more is that polls show that the American public evinces more trust in the armed forces than any other institution in our society, so it is vitally important that the perspective this book uniquely provides be taken into account as legal policies and interpretations are produced. Only in this way can we ensure that in the years ahead we provide advice that holds firm to our values and principles, yet also solves the real-world needs of those we send in harm's way as well as meeting the expectations of the American public writ large.

Charles J. Dunlap, Jr.

Foreword to the First Edition

HISTORIANS LIKE TO speak of revolutions in military affairs to describe the dramatic evolutions in warfare that technology and other developments produce at various points in warfare. While the remarkable rise in the prominence of law in war in recent years might not be quite as impressive as, say, the invention of gunpowder on armed conflict, the effect of law in twenty-first century conflicts is nevertheless quite extraordinary, a reality understood by the military profession. An iconic example of this recognition came from General James L. Jones, USMC, then the commander of NATO, and now in retirement heading the United States' National Security Council. In 2003, he remarked that going to war was once a task focused on leading combat forces, but now "you have to have a lawyer or a dozen. It's become very legalistic and very complex."[1]

Why is this? As I have noted for many years, the reasons are manifold. The rise of globalized commerce with its insistence on legally binding arrangements—not to mention an ever-expanding number of international legal forums to resolve disputes—all serve to normalize law as a feature in international affairs to an unprecedented degree. Add to this the emergence of information technologies that enable the near instantaneous communication around the world of incidents that raise legal issues and it is readily apparent how law gets the attention it does these days. Indeed, that such developments infuse law

---

[1] Lyric Wallwork Winik, *A Marine's Toughest Mission (Gen. James L. Jones)*, PARADE MAG., Jan. 19, 2003 *available at* http://www.parade.com/articles/editions/2003/edition_01-19-2003/General_Jones.

into almost every aspect of modern war much as it has penetrated virtually every other aspect of contemporary life, is hardly surprising.

Clearly, evaluating the propriety of twenty-first century military operations requires a sophisticated understanding of the law of war, an understanding made all the more complicated by the rise of nonstate actors who operate transnationally and use terrorism as their principal weapon. Of course, there are a significant number of experts skilled in the history of the development and delineation of the meaning of the law of war. Moreover, a growing body of scholarship seeks to discuss the conceptual application of the law of war to terrorists in various situations.

However, in practice, the law of war—like other legal disciplines—much depends upon the ability to appreciate the factual context in which the law must operate. For the practitioner, understanding the "facts" of military operations can be quite daunting. The military "client" is engaged in a "business," so to speak, that is fundamentally unlike most human endeavors. It involves extraordinarily intricate and unique technologies, as well as complex psychological interactions all designed, in the final analysis, to facilitate—when necessary and unavoidable—the melancholy task of killing other human beings.

The volume you are holding aims to bring to the discussion the perspective of lawyers who have served in what the Supreme Court in *Parker v. Levy*[2] calls the "specialized society separate from civilian society" that is the armed forces. By virtue of their military service in this "specialized society," these attorneys bring a unique perspective to the law of war questions that bedevil decision-makers at every level attempting to deal with the threat of terrorism. This mindset is derived not only from the academic exploration of the law, but perhaps more importantly from years spent developing expertise in the context in which the law is intended to apply. This context, I submit, is an essential component in developing a genuine appreciation for the purpose and objectives of the law, which in turn is essential to critically analyzing the role of this law in the emerging realities of warfare. In short, the collective experience of these authors in the art of war—understanding the weapons, tactics, and, especially, the psychology of warriors on a nontraditional battlefield—enables the authors to provide an often overlooked perspective on these increasingly complex and important legal issues.

The linkage of a technical understanding of the law of war with the actual practice of war is vital. I can well recall a symposium of highly regarded civilian international lawyers convened in the aftermath of the Kosovo conflict. Almost to a person, these law-of-war experts were critical of what they understood to be the American practice of conducting air operations at altitudes no lower than 15,000 feet. They were convinced that what they thought was "high-altitude" bombing was the cause of what they took to be excessive civilian casualties.

---

[2] Parker v. Levy, 417 U.S. 733, 744 (1974).

What was striking is that for all their legal erudition, virtually none of these lawyers had a real understanding of the technology of modern warplanes. They simply did not comprehend that lower altitude strikes were typically less precise than those conducted at altitudes that optimized sophisticated targeting equipment. In addition, they did not appreciate that lower altitudes not only unnecessarily increased risk to the pilot, but also to those on the ground who could find themselves in the path of a 20-ton, fuel- and weapons-laden aircraft shot out of the air to tumble out of control into whatever happened to be in its way.

This is not to suggest that only those with military service should advise the military and the civilian authorities on law-of-war matters. On the contrary, the explosion of interest in this field has produced a rich landscape of critically important scholarship, debate, and commentary. However, it has and will remain critically important that those who wade into these murky waters remain cognizant of the reality that their conclusions will ultimately inform the development of law that must be applied by belligerents. Because of this, a keen understanding of how the law of war is implemented by warfighters in today's battles against terrorists and extremists, a heretofore underrepresented viewpoint in the contemporary scholarly landscape, can only contribute to the advancement of the law. This book seeks to provide a military perspective on the difficult task of ensuring adherence to the law under circumstances hardly imaginable only a decade ago.

The practical impact of law on the war on terror is also well understood today. No observer of the post-9/11 era fails to recognize that the most serious setbacks for the American military involve not an adversary's battlefield successes, but rather alleged violations of the law by the United States' own forces. But this was no revelation for the profession of arms. For members of the American military profession who came of age in the era between Vietnam and September 11th, the significance of legal legitimacy at the strategic, operational, and tactical levels had become virtually axiomatic. These professionals understood what Professors Michael Reisman and Chris T. Antoniou rightly pointed out in their 1994 book *Law of War*—that popular modern democracies will not support military operations "no matter how worthy the political objective, if people believe that the war is being conducted in an unfair, inhumane, or iniquitous way."[3] Professor William G. Eckhardt articulated a similar view in terms intuitive to the military professional: the legality and morality of military operations are, in strategic terms, a "center of gravity" for the United States and other nations who embrace the rule of law.

The first line of defense of such a center of gravity is to ensure that one's own forces follow the law, and to be able to prove such observance. And the first "fighting position" in that line of defense is to ensure that a pragmatic understanding of when, why, and

---

[3] W. Michael Reisman & Chris T. Antoniou, The Laws of War xxiv (1994).

how the law applies to combat operations—an understanding informed by the realities of military operations—drives the evolution of the law.

The War on Terror and the Laws of War: A Military Perspective is especially timely and apt because it squarely addresses some of the thorniest issues of recent years. While it will be a prized refresher for many military practitioners, its greatest value may be as a source for those without a military background who may nevertheless wish to inform their analysis with a complete range of views. Because it does not shrink from tackling the toughest topics, some assertions in this book may generate strong dissents from the reader (including the reader in uniform). Yet as everyone steeped in the advocacy system appreciates, truth emerges from the reasoned analysis of conflicting views well presented and skillfully articulated. This book gives you just such a presentation of the military perspective.

Major General Charles J. Dunlap, Jr.
United States Air Force
April 2009
Washington, DC

Introduction

THIRTEEN YEARS AFTER the United States initiated a military response to the terrorist attacks of September 11th, 2001, the nation continues to prosecute what it considers an armed conflict against al-Qaeda. During this time, interpretations of legal authorities related to every aspect of this armed conflict have evolved substantially. Nonetheless, the core premise has remained constant: an armed conflict exists between the United States and al-Qaeda–associated forces.

This premise is itself highly controversial. To this day, a large number of states and many international legal experts contest the validity of characterizing a struggle against a terrorist organization (if that label is even legitimate), even when operating transnationally, as an armed conflict. There is little dispute that the struggle against the Taliban in Afghanistan qualifies as an armed conflict, and that therefore operations against terrorist belligerents *in that domain* fall within the scope of that recognized armed conflict. However, it is clear that the United States neither considers its armed conflict with al-Qaeda to be derivative of the distinct armed conflict against the Taliban, nor restricted to the geographic boundaries of Afghanistan.

Nonetheless, it is clear that the term "war on terror" is legally and operationally overbroad and misleading. President George W. Bush and his senior administration officials used that characterization in the aftermath of September 11th, but it is doubtful that even in the early days of this struggle the scope of this armed conflict was conceived so broadly. Instead, it is more likely that the terminology was initially used to signal a fundamental shift in the way in which the United States would respond to this terrorist threat, by overtly leveraging the military component of national power to disrupt, degrade, and ideally defeat it. Since that time, a much more refined conception of the nature of this armed conflict has emerged: it is not an armed conflict consuming within its scope every suspect terrorist or terrorist group around the globe. It is instead an armed conflict against a specific armed organized belligerent terrorist threat to the United States—al-Qaeda and its associated co-belligerent groups—an armed conflict conducted pursuant to the 2001 Congressional Authorization for Use of Military Force (AUMF), and "informed" by the law of war.

Still, this more refined conception of armed conflict has in no way eliminated controversy and criticism of the legal foundation upon which U.S. policy is constructed. Indeed, it has in many ways crystalized and focused this criticism on issues related to the so-called "geography of armed conflict," the permissible duration of what seems to be a conflict with no definable endpoint, the authority to target individuals based on their "status" as members of an organized belligerent group when neither the group itself or its members manifest anything close to the traditional indicia of "combatant" status, and the credibility of using military tribunals—tribunals traditionally understood as forums of necessity in the context of traditional armed conflicts—as the forum of choice to criminally sanction captured operatives of these groups.

All of this indicates that the topic of this book—the application of the law of armed conflict to this armed conflict against transnational nonstate terrorist groups—is as important today as it was in September 2001. It also indicates that the evolution of legal analysis related to this issue requires an update to the first edition; hence this new one. Still, the continued relevance of the core legal foundation for this struggle renders our original introduction equally relevant, and so it is offered below.

Introduction to Our First Edition

This book is about commitment, commitment to a tenet that has animated the development of the laws and customs of war since their inception centuries ago. That tenet is that the authority of war must be tempered by limitations that mitigate the suffering inevitably caused by war. Many might consider this premise intuitive. Certainly from the warrior perspective—the original source of the laws of war—conflict without regulation is almost oxymoronic, for it is through the regulation that the moral legitimacy of that endeavor is preserved. But as will be revealed in the chapters that follow, the intersection of a post-September 11th decision to characterize the struggle against transnational terrorism as "armed conflict" with the law-triggering paradigm that evolved from the ashes of the Second World War challenged this tenet as never before.

On September 10, 2001, virtually every law-of-war expert in the world, including the members of the U.S. military legal profession—a profession that had grown to unprecedented strength and had made expertise in the law related to the planning and execution of military operations a core competency—assumed that the laws of war could apply only in two distinct situations. The first was inter-state warfare, where the armed forces of two opposing states engaged with each other to accomplish a national purpose. The second was intra-state conflict in which the armed forces of a state battled against an internal opposition group that had attained military-type capabilities. These two law-triggering situations were understood through the ubiquitous characterization derived from common articles 2 and 3 of the four Geneva Conventions of 1949: the common article 2 international (inter-state) armed conflict and the common article 3 non-international (intra-sate) armed conflict. This two-part paradigm was so pervasive that it formed the foundation of law-of-war education for an entire generation of military lawyers.

But these lawyers had also learned firsthand the operational limits of this paradigm. This education began well before the events of September 11th, originating with the Vietnam conflict. In response to the uncertainty associated with determining the locus within this law-triggering spectrum of operational decisions related to that conflict, the Department of Defense adopted what became its bedrock law-of-war mandate: that U.S. forces would comply with the principles of the law of war during any military operation no matter how that operation was legally characterized. This policy was intended to ensure that operational planning and execution would be based on the well-established principles of the law most suited for such a purpose: the laws of war. The policy was also intended to provide military commanders and the staffs that advised them essential predictability by providing a consistent standard of operational regulation, and by ensuring that every soldier, marine, sailor, and airman was trained to one standard of operational conduct.

This policy "gap filler" proved remarkably effective during the years between Vietnam and September 11th, and was particularly essential during the era of "peace operations" that dominated the 1990s. During that era, U.S. armed forces conducted countless military operations that by definition failed to trigger the laws of war, by then referred to as the law of armed conflict (LOAC). Yet these operations nonetheless necessitated an operational, regulatory framework. Thus, LOAC principles guided operational decision-making for detention in Kosovo, medical treatment obligations in Haiti, the use of combat power in Bosnia, and detainee interrogations in Somalia.

A somewhat ironic, second-order consequence of this policy extension of the law was that it inhibited any consideration of whether these principles should be applicable in such third-category situations not just as a matter of policy, but as a matter of law. When the United States initiated military action against al-Qaeda in response to the terror attacks of September 11th, the limits of this policy mandate were quickly exposed, and military lawyers throughout the Department of Defense were finally forced to contemplate this long-overlooked issue. This was the result of a simple reality: the U.S. government had invoked the power of war to address the challenge of transnational terrorism. Thus, the United States has and continues to consider the military component of the struggle against transnational terrorism as an "armed conflict." While all the authors acknowledge that this determination was and remains controversial, it is also indisputable. As a result, U.S. military combat power was unleashed against this nonstate transnational enemy. Thus, military legal advisors confronted a genuine anomaly: military operations designated by the nation as "war" or "armed conflict" that failed to fit neatly within the accepted common article 2 or 3 law-triggering paradigm.

The initial response to this anomaly seemed logical: apply LOAC principles in accordance with Department of Defense policy. This method had provided an effective response to similar uncertainty in the past, and rendered the uncertainty as to whether the LOAC was applicable as a matter of law essentially transparent at the operational level. However, almost as soon as these military operations began, another reality entered into the equation that exposed the limits of policy: new directives and orders from the Department of Defense that essentially contradicted this "principled" approach to operational regulation. The most notorious example of this impacted the status and treatment of individuals captured during this struggle. The operational assumption that all such individuals would be treated "as if" they were prisoners of war was quickly overridden by senior executive branch policymakers who imposed a new category of status and treatment: the unlawful enemy combatant.

As the full impact of this GWOT legal paradigm slowly emerged in the weeks and months following September 11th, it became increasingly clear that the United States was essentially exploiting the common article 2/3 law-triggering paradigm to expose a gap in LOAC application. This gap existed in the interstitial realm between inter-state conflict and "internationalized" conflict between a state and a nonstate entity, what we will refer to in the following chapters as "transnational" armed conflict. Relying on the inter-state/internal interpretation of the common article 2/3 law-triggering paradigm, high-level legal advisors in the Bush administration asserted (not illegitimately) that these treaties had never been intended to apply to extraterritorial armed conflict against a nonstate enemy. However, what these advisors failed to consider was the critical subsequent level of analysis for operational legal advisors: Does this interpretation of treaty-based obligations necessitate and justify the conclusion that no law applies to regulate this armed conflict?

How this issue was ultimately tackled will be addressed in subsequent chapters. These chapters will illustrate how military legal advisors realized from the very outset of this process that such a premise is ultimately incompatible with the historic purpose of the law of war: the balance of power and restraint. This realization, coupled with the reality that they could no longer avail themselves of the long-standing practice of policy-based LOAC compliance, forced them to finally address the question of whether the common article 2/3 law triggering paradigm was exclusive, or whether an underlying core of customary principles applies to any military operation characterized by the nation as armed conflict.

The United States Supreme Court mooted the need to analyze this question as it relates to the treatment of detainees when it ruled in *Hamdan v. Rumsfeld* that common article 3 applied in "contradistinction" to common article 2. While the treaty interpretation element of this ruling is certainly susceptible to criticism, it nonetheless constitutes a profound rejection of the "authority without obligation" theory that gripped the Bush administration. *Hamdan* is also an equally profound endorsement of the logic that drove Department of Defense policy for decades: that the invocation of LOAC authority requires acknowledgment of the balancing obligations derived from the same source of law.

How this core logic and spirit of the law of war have influenced operational decisions related to all aspects of the military response to the threat of transnational terror is ultimately the story that will play out in the following chapters. Each chapter will address a specific operational issue and illustrate how resolution of that issue will serve a commitment to preserving this balance between authority and obligation. Some chapters will go further, explaining why the legal principles alone are insufficient to address the challenges of this conflict, or how the law needs to be advanced to deal with continuing uncertainty. But all the book's chapters share a common thread: that legitimate, disciplined, and credible military operations cannot occur in the absence of an operational regulatory framework derived from the laws of war. This premise is not only central to the book itself, but is also the common perspective of each of the authors, all of whom share experience as both scholars and warriors.

A brief note on what this book is not about is in order. This book is not a critique of the theory that a nation can be engaged in an armed conflict with a transnational non-state enemy. All of the authors recognize the controversy associated with this proposition, and many scholars and legal experts reject the premise outright. However, because this book is focused on the operational resolution of issues related to the application of military power by the United States, it begins with the premise that because the United States has characterized the struggle against terror as an armed conflict—a characterization reflected in the decisions of all three branches of our government—there is no doubt that the United States has and will continue to invoke the law of war as a source of authority for military operations to destroy, disable, capture, and incapacitate terrorist enemies. As a result, the book's focus will be on how operational decisions ensure that the balance referred to above is preserved in this tremendously complex operational and legal environment.

Geoffrey S. Corn

1

Legal Basis for the Use of Armed Force

by Geoffrey S. Corn

NO EMPLOYMENT OF U.S. military power occurs without an assessment of domestic
and international legal authority. In U.S. practice, this assessment occurs at the strategic
level, normally involving interagency coordination. Although military lawyers are most
commonly associated with assessments of legal issues related to the execution of military
operations (the principal focus of this text), it would be error to suggest that they are neither concerned with nor involved in decisions as to the legal basis for these operations.
At the strategic level of command, military lawyers participate in the assessment of these
issues, offering their reasoned judgments on domestic and international legal authorities
applicable to proposed operational courses of action.

Unlike many other chapters in this text, this chapter will not focus on the process
for these assessments, or the "nuts and bolts" integration of military legal advisors in
this process. In this regard, it is sufficient to note that both the Secretary of Defense
and the Chairman of the Joint Chiefs of Staff—two essential players in the interagency
decision-making process related to military operations—receive advice from their
respective legal advisors. In the case of the Secretary of Defense, this advice is provided
by the General Counsel to the Department of Defense, the senior civilian attorney in
the Department.[2] In contrast, the Chairman is advised by the Legal Counsel to the
Chairman, a judge advocate in the rank of brigadier general or rear admiral (lower
half).[3] Each of these legal advisors is supported by a staff of military and civilian lawyers

---

[1] President Barack Obama, Remarks by the President at the Acceptance of the Nobel Peace Prize, 2009 DAILY
COMP. PRES. DOC. (Dec.10, 2009), *available at* http://www.gpo.gov/fdsys/pkg/DCPD-200900985/pdf/
DCPD-200900985.pdf.

[2] 10 U.S.C. § 140.

[3] *Id.* § 156.

of the highest level of expertise. Every military action planned and/or executed by the U.S. armed forces will therefore be subject to a formal legal opinion by each of these advisors indicating the legal basis for the operation.

Accordingly, this chapter will explain the U.S. interpretation of the international legal basis for the conduct of these operations (the *jus ad bellum*). This interpretation provides the critical foundation for projecting U.S. military power to reach identified terrorist targets. It also reflects an unquestioned international legal framework that defines when States may legitimately resort to force to achieve their national or multinational strategic objectives. While this framework may be unquestioned, its application in the context of counter-terror operations is anything but.

One need only consider the mission executed against Osama bin Laden to understand the complexity of the legal issues surrounding the use of military force as a counter-terrorism tool. Because of the transnational character of the terrorist threat, even prior to September 11, 2001, the United States considered it necessary to project military power into the sovereign territory of other States to target terrorist capabilities. This practice became significantly more common following the September 11th attacks, and triggered widespread controversy in the international legal and policy community. What right did the United States have to violate the sovereignty of other States in order to achieve its national counter-terrorism objectives? Was the United States obligated to rely on the efforts of these States to neutralize terrorist operatives identified within their borders? If not, did international law require the United States to obtain the consent of these States prior to launching a military attack against those terrorists? Was acting without such consent or cooperation illegal aggression against a fellow member of the international community?

These questions remain as complex today as they were on September 12, 2001. They can only be answered through the prism of international law, or more specifically the branch of international law that defines the authority and limitations on the use of military force by States—the *jus ad bellum*. Indeed, no treatment of the relationship between counter-terror military operations and international law is complete without considering the international legal basis to employ force at the outset. From an operational perspective, readers might be surprised to learn that every plan for the conduct of U.S. military action is subject to legal review. This review includes an assessment of both the international and domestic legal bases for the operation.

International law establishes State authority to use military force externally to achieve national security objectives. Known as the *jus ad bellum*,[4] loosely translated this term

---

[4] The term first appeared in legal writing in the 1920s. Carsten Stahn, "Jus ad bellum," "jus in bello"… "jus post bellum"?—*Rethinking the Conception of the Law of Armed Conflict*, 17 EURO. J. INT'L L. 921, 925 n.19 (2007) (citing Giuliano Enriques, *Considerazioni sulla teoria della guerra nel diritto internazionale* [Considerations on the Theory of War in International Law], 20 RIVISTA DI DIRITTO INTERNAZIONALE [JOURNAL OF INTERNATIONAL LAW] 172 (1928)).

refers to the legality of war. The contemporary legal framework establishing State authority to use of force was in large measure responsive to the carnage of World War I. Responding to the acknowledged failure of international law to prevent that war, the victorious Allies set about to remedy the deficiencies in the post–World War I effort to prohibit the use of force as a means of resolving international disputes. That effort was defined by a treaty prohibiting war as a means to resolving international disputes (the Kellogg-Briand Pact), and the creation of an international organization intended, inter alia, to provide a collective international security mechanism (the League of Nations). The post–World War II objective of improving upon these initial but failed efforts to limit resort to military force between States produced the use-of-force framework enshrined in the Charter of the United Nations, which has since evolved to become a universally accepted use-of-force standard.[5]

The foundation of the "U.N. Charter paradigm" is article 2(4) of the U.N. Charter, obligating all States to respect the territorial sovereignty of other States and prohibit the use of force or the threat of force among States.[6] Implicit in this prohibition is the absence of legal authority for any such use of force by one State against another, which results in such use qualifying as an act of unlawful aggression. The prohibition against the aggressive use of military force did not, however, originate with the Charter. The origins of this prohibition predated World War II when war was prohibited in the Pact of Paris (Kellogg-Briand Pact). Although obviously ineffective in preventing the greatest military conflict in human history, this international legal prohibition of war remains an important precursor to the contemporary legality equation. Building upon this prohibition, the U.N. Charter reflects the recognition that the efficacy of this prohibition would turn on both a meaningful international enforcement mechanism and the authority of States to come to the aid of other States subjected to acts of aggression.[7]

This understanding, and the two means of achieving an effective prohibition against aggression, came to define the U.N. Charter use-of-force paradigm. First, the prohibition against aggressive use of force was reaffirmed in article 2(4) of the Charter.[8] Second, the Charter vested the U.N. Security Council with the responsibility to respond to violations of article 2(4)—acts of aggression, breaches of the peace, and threats to international peace and security—by any necessary means to include authorizing use of military force by member States to restore international peace and security.[9] Such uses of force, because authorized by the community of nations through the Security Council, would be lawful

---

[5] *See generally* YORAM DINSTEIN, WAR, AGGRESSION, AND SELF-DEFENSE (3d ed. 2001) [hereinafter DINSTEIN 3D EDITION].

[6] U.N. Charter art. 2, para. 4.

[7] *Id.* arts. 42, 51 (stating that the use of force is authorized only for the purposes of collective or individual self-defense or pursuant to a resolution by the Security Council).

[8] *See id.* art. 2, para. 4.

[9] *Id.* art. 39.

precisely because they would be conducted for the purpose of restoring international peace and security. Finally, the Charter acknowledged the inherent right of States to use force for individual and collective self-defense in response to acts of aggression.[10] This right, enshrined in article 51 of the Charter, has been interpreted to apply not only to actual acts of aggression, but also to imminent threats of aggressive attack.[11]

Accordingly, the framework for assessing the international legality to use military force establishes a presumptive prohibition against such use. This presumption is rebutted by one of three conditions. First, the presumption can be rebutted if the use of force was requested by the State where the use occurred. Such consent-based military intervention in another State is consistent with article 2(4) because it is not directed against the sovereign interests of another State. Second, the use of force can be authorized by the Security Council exercising its power to authorize military action in response to a breach of international law, for the purpose of restoring international peace and security. Third, the use of force can be conducted in response to an act of aggression or an imminent threat of aggression pursuant to the inherent State authority to act in individual or collective self-defense.

With the exception of consent-based uses of force, determining what constitutes unlawful aggression or an imminent threat of unlawful aggression is obviously a critical aspect of assessing the legality of using military force. When a State is actually attacked by another State, such as when Iraq invaded Kuwait in 1989, aggression is relatively self-evident. However, identifying a threat to international peace and security triggering the individual and collective right of self-defense has always been complex.[12] In 1974, the United Nations General Assembly sought in General Assembly Resolution 3314,[13] defining aggression, to provide greater clarity of what triggers this. Although General Assembly Resolutions do not bind member States, this definition is regarded by distinguished *jus belli* scholars[14] as generally authoritative, and has been relied on by the International Court of Justice.[15] Resolution 3314 lists six situations that qualify as aggression:

(a) The invasion or attack by the armed forces of a State of the territory of another State, or any military occupation, however temporary, resulting from such invasion or attack, or any annexation by the use of force of the territory of another State or part thereof,

---

[10] *See id.* arts. 42, 51.

[11] U.N. Secretary-General, *In Larger Freedom: Towards Development, Security and Human Rights for All*, ¶ 124, U.N. Doc. A/59/2005 (May 21, 2005), *available at* http://www2.ohchr.org/english/bodies/hrcouncil/docs/gaA.59.2005_En.pdf.

[12] *See generally* YORAM DINSTEIN, WAR, AGGRESSION, AND SELF-DEFENSE (4th ed. 2005) [hereinafter DINSTEIN 4TH EDITION].

[13] G.A. Res. 3314 (XXIX), annex, U.N. Doc. A/9631 (Dec. 14, 1974).

[14] *See, e.g.*, DINSTEIN 4TH EDITION, *supra* note 12.

[15] *See* Military and Paramilitary Activities in and Against Nicaragua (Nicar. v. U.S.), 1986 I.C.J. 14, 103 (June 27) [hereinafter Nicaragua], *reprinted in* 25 I.L.M. 1023 (1986) (indicating that the definition of aggression annexed to the Resolution "may be taken to reflect customary international law.").

(b) Bombardment by the armed forces of a State against the territory of another State or the use of any weapons by a State against the territory of another State;

(c) The blockade of the ports or coasts of a State by the armed forces of another State;

(d) An attack by the armed forces of a State on the land, sea or air forces, or marine and air fleets of another State;

(e) The use of armed forces of one State which are within the territory of another State with the agreement of the receiving State, in contravention of the conditions provided for in the agreement or any extension of their presence in such territory beyond the termination of the agreement;

(f) The action of a State in allowing its territory, which it has placed at the disposal of another State, to be used by that other State for perpetrating an act of aggression against a third State;

(g) The sending by or on behalf of a State of armed bands, groups, irregulars or mercenaries, which carry out acts of armed force against another State of such gravity as to amount to the acts listed above, or its substantial involvement therein.[16]

How, if at all, this definition impacts the invocation of individual or collective self-defense in response to threats or acts of terrorism is an extremely complex question.[17] This

---

[16] G.A. Res. 3314 (XXIX), annex, U.N. Doc. A/9631 (1974).

[17] *See Resolution RC/Res.6, The Crime of Aggression, Adopted at the 13th plenary meeting, on 11 June 2010, by consensus in* Rev. Conf. of the Rome State of the Int'l Criminal Court: Official Records 17 (2010) [hereinafter *Crime of Aggression Amendment*], *available at* http://www.icc-cpi.int/iccdocs/asp_docs/ASP9/OR/RC-11-Part.II-ENG.pdf. The adoption of a definition of aggression by the Review Conference of the Rome Statute of the International Criminal Court (held in Kampala, Uganda, between May 31 and June 11, 2010) adds a potentially new dimension to this analysis. The amendment to article 8 of the Rome Statute of the International Criminal Court (ICC) defines aggression as follows:

1. For the purpose of this Statute, "crime of aggression" means the planning, preparation, initiation or execution, by a person in a position effectively to exercise control over or to direct the political or military action of a State, of an act of aggression which, by its character, gravity and scale, constitutes a manifest violation of the Charter of the United Nations.

2. For the purpose of paragraph 1, "act of aggression" means the use of armed force by a State against the sovereignty, territorial integrity or political independence of another State, or in any other manner inconsistent with the Charter of the United Nations. Any of the following acts, regardless of a declaration of war, shall, in accordance with United Nations General Assembly resolution 3314 (XXIX) of 14 December 1974.

The Resolution then incorporates the list of acts constituting aggression contained in General Assembly Resolution 3341. *Id.*

Assuming the amendment is ratified by the States Parties (13 States Parties had ratified the amendment as of December 20, 2013), a decision by States Parties must still be taken after January 1, 2017 to allow the International Criminal Court to exercise jurisdiction over the crime. Furthermore, the Security Council will play a significant role in any prosecutorial effort. First, the Security Council retains primacy in determining when a State has been the victim of aggression, and may (as in the case of any other crime defined by the Statute) refer the matter to the ICC. However, the ICC prosecutor is vested with authority to initiate an investigation into an allegation of aggression either on her own initiative of in response to a request by a State Party. In such situations, if the Security Council has not determined that the alleged

complexity is the result of several considerations. First, the primary focus of the General Assembly Resolution is State action, and not the actions of transnational nonstate terrorist groups. In fact, it is highly unlikely that the drafters of the Resolution (or more precisely the definition of aggression annexed to the Resolution) seriously contemplated individual or collective response to transnational terrorist threats (much less the other emerging nonstate threats to States, such as organized criminal syndicates, cyber threats, and widespread piracy). Second, the Resolution itself indicates that the list is non-exhaustive, and that the Security Council may determine that other acts constitute aggression. How this impacts the right of individual States to also make such determinations is unclear, although it does seem to indicate that such a right may exist. Third, the acts listed *presumptively* but not *conclusively* qualify as aggression. None of these acts fall into that definition when committed pursuant to the inherent right of individual or collective self-defense, or pursuant to Security Council authorization. Because the United States engages in such conduct only pursuant to an assertion of such lawful authority, the validity of these assertions is central to assessing whether military action producing effects referenced in the Resolution are legally justified or beyond the scope of international legal authority.

Adding to this complexity is the simple reality that the terrorist attacks of September 11, 2001, created an entirely new category of controversy surrounding the definition of aggression, the exercise of individual and collective self-defense, and the Security Council's power to authorize collective military action in response to the threat of transnational terrorism. How this controversy is impacted by the *jus ad bellum* is critical to the legitimacy and efficacy of the struggle against terrorism.

The U.N. Charter and the Right of Self Defense[18]

As noted above, the U.N. Charter established a per se prohibition against use of force as a means of achieving a national objective. Article 2(4) of the Charter of the United

---

incident qualifies as an act of aggression in a period of six months from the time of the request to initiate an investigation, the prosecutor must obtain authorization from the Court to proceed. The Security Council is authorized to block such an investigation, but doing so requires a Resolution (and therefore the agreement of all permanent members), which must be renewed annually. *Personam* jurisdiction extends only to nationals of a State Party that has not opted out of the aggression amendment. *See* Julia Martínez Vivancos, Questions & Answers on the Crime of Aggression Amendment Adopted at the ICC Review Conference in Kampala, Uganda, The American Non-Governmental Organizations Coalition for the International Criminal Court (July 22, 2010), *available at* http://www.amicc.org/docs/AggressionQA.pdf.

The potential impact of this amendment on U.S. officials responsible for ordering the execution of counter-terror military operations in the future seems too speculative to really assess at this point. Even assuming the United States accedes to the treaty and therefore becomes subject to the jurisdiction of the Court, how the Security Council and/or the ICC prosecutor would interpret such operations is impossible to predict. Nonetheless, the incorporation of the Resolution 3314 definition is an important endorsement of the significance of that definition.

[18] For an excellent summary of the U.N. Charter's use-of-force legal framework, *see* Int'l & Oper'l Law Dep't, The Judge Advocate Gen. Legal Ctr. & Sch., U.S. Army, JA 422, Operational Law

Nations provides that "[a]ll Members shall refrain in their international relations from the threat or use of force against the territorial integrity or political independence of any State, or in any other manner inconsistent with the purposes of the United Nations."[19] Uses of force are, however, lawful when they fall into any of three exceptions to this per se prohibition. The first exception is consent from the State in which the military action occurs. The second exception is a collective security action authorized by the Security Council pursuant to chapter VII of the Charter.[20] The third exception—recognized in article 51 of the Charter—is use of force as an act of individual or collective self-defense.[21]

Consent is a commonly utilized exception, and presents little definitional uncertainty. Since 1945, it has been common for States confronting internal and/or external threats to call upon other States to provide military support to their cause. Although less common, States have also consented to the armed intervention in their territory by a neighboring State responding to a nonstate threat emanating from the territory of the consenting State (for example, when the United States conducted a punitive raid into Mexico in 1916 with the consent of the Carranza government in response to cross-border attacks by Pancho Villa's insurgent forces). In either situation, State consent renders the intervention consistent with article 2(4) because it nullifies any assertion that the intervening State used military force "against" the intervened State's sovereignty.

Can consent be implied from lack of opposition to such an intervention? This issue was raised when Israel conducted a military intervention into Lebanon in 2006 for the purpose of degrading Hezbollah military capabilities. Neither Israel nor Lebanon characterized the intervention as an armed conflict between the two States, which created uncertainty as to whether the operation amounted to an act of aggression by Israel. From

---

HANDBOOK, 1–7 (2007), *available at* http://www.loc.gov/rr/frd/Military_Law/pdf/operational-law-handbook_2007.pdf. *See also* DINSTEIN 3D EDITION, *supra* note 5.

[19] *See* U.N Charter art. 2, para. 4.

[20] Article 42 provides:

Should the Security Council consider that measures provided for in Article 41 would be inadequate or have proved to be inadequate, it may take such action by air, sea, or land forces as may be necessary to maintain or restore international peace and security. Such action may include demonstrations, blockade, and other operations by air, sea, or land forces of Members of the United Nations.

Id. art. 42.

[21] Article 51 provides:

Nothing in the present Charter shall impair the inherent right of individual or collective self-defence if an armed attack occurs against a Member of the United Nations, until the Security Council has taken measures necessary to maintain international peace and security. Measures taken by Members in the exercise of this right of self-defence shall be immediately reported to the Security Council and shall not in any way affect the authority and responsibility of the Security Council under the present Charter to take at any time such action as it deems necessary in order to maintain or restore international peace and security.

Id. art. 51.

Israel's perspective, the failure of Lebanon to prevent attacks against Israel by Hezbollah justified a self-help military action pursuant to the inherent right of self-defense. However, it is easy to understand why other States might consider the intervention an impermissible act of aggression. In such a situation, how should the lack of opposition by the State in whose territory the intervention occurs factor into the analysis? Although it may be plausible to conclude that this is evidence of tacit recognition that the action is justified as an act of self-defense, it is difficult to reconcile a unilateral decision by one State to engage in combat operations in the territory of another State with valid implied consent. Nonetheless, the consequence of failing to object to such an action—either directly between the States or by seeking condemnation from the U.N. Security Council—may result in de facto, if not de jure consent.

Another complex issue related to a consent-based intervention is assessing the permissible scope of the intervening State's military action. In the domestic context, the scope of consent is either dictated by the consenting party or implied from the objective of the intrusion. Should an analogous approach be applied to consent-based interventions? It would seem that the ideal means of determining scope would take the form of an express agreement between the two States, with the consenting State defining the scope at the time of consent. However, this might not be a realistic expectation, especially because there may be significant political and diplomatic considerations that make the two States averse to any formal or explicit indication of consent. Ultimately, whether the actions of the intervening State are consistent with the consent granted by the territorial State will be a diplomatic matter between the two States.

Self-Defense and the Use of Force against Terrorist Threats

Inter-state relations—or perhaps more precisely stated as inter-state disputes—have been the historic focal point of law and practice related to State uses of force outside its own territory. The text and drafting history of the Charter reflect this focus. Accordingly, prior to September 11th, State-generated threats to international peace and security dominated use-of-force legality analysis. However, over time nonstate threats have become increasingly relevant to this analysis. Today, these nonstate threats are widely considered sufficient to justify invoking one of the Charter's two exceptions to the presumptive prohibition against the use of force. Mass exodus of refugees across borders, internal armed conflicts, internal acts of genocide, crimes against humanity, and even impunity for violations of international law have provided the basis for Security Council invocation of collective action. Of equal significance, States affected by the threat of transnational terrorism and other external nonstate threats have increasingly asserted the inherent right of self-defense as a legal justification for military action directed against these threats.

This trend reflects the responsiveness of *jus ad bellum* to the evolving perception of what constitutes a threat to international peace and stability. In the view of many experts, the right of self-defense and the authority for the Security Council to authorize collective security actions now extend to the threat to international peace and security resulting from transnational nonstate entities such as organized terrorist groups.[22] For the United States, this interpretation of the international legal authority to employ force in self-defense lies at the very foundation of the military component of our ongoing military operations directed against transnational terrorists. This theory is reflected not only in the statements of both President Bush and President Obama, but also in congressional action—notably, the Joint Resolution Authorizing the Use of Military Force enacted immediately after the terrorist attacks of September 11, 200l. In this Resolution, Congress noted:

> Whereas, on September 11, 2001, acts of treacherous violence were committed against the United States and its citizens; and
>
> Whereas, such acts render it both necessary and appropriate that the United States exercise its rights to self-defense and to protect United States citizens both at home and abroad; and
>
> Whereas, in light of the threat to the national security and foreign policy of the United States posed by these grave acts of violence; and
>
> Whereas, such acts continue to pose an unusual and extraordinary threat to the national security and foreign policy of the United States; and
>
> Whereas, the President has authority under the Constitution to take action to deter and prevent acts of international terrorism against the United States....[23]

Unaltered since the date of enactment, the continuing reliance on this authorization by President Obama, and by the courts reviewing the legality of the government's exercise of wartime powers, is a clear indication that self-defense remains at the core of the U.S. counter-terror policy. The Resolution, commonly referred to as the Authorization for Use of Military Force (AUMF), also provides the domestic legal basis for many of the U.S. counter-terror operations.

A more complex question is whether there is widespread international support for this interpretation, and especially whether that support has been manifested at the United Nations Security Council. As noted above, the authority to use military force in pursuit of collective security may only be invoked pursuant to chapter VII of the U.N. Charter. Article 41 of the Charter mandates as a predicate to such authorization a Security Council determination that there has been a breach of the peace, act of aggression, or threat to international peace and security.[24] Prior to the terror attacks

---

[22] *See* Jeremy M. Sharp, CONG. RESEARCH SERV., RS21324, CONGRESSIONAL ACTION ON IRAQ 1990–2002: A COMPILATION OF LEGISLATION (last updated Jan. 30, 2003), *available at* http://fpc.state.gov/documents/organization/17330.pdf.

[23] Authorization for the Use of Military Force, Pub. L. 107–40, 115 Stat. 224 (2001) [hereinafter AUMF].

[24] U.N. Charter art. 41.

of 9/11, the Security Council had expanded the range of international crises that fell within the scope of article 41 (for example humanitarian crises such as those that occurred in Kosovo and Somalia, or mass migrations such as were ongoing in Haiti in 1992). However, the threat of transnational terrorism had not up to that point been classified as a threat within the meaning of article 41. It was therefore unclear in the wake of those attacks whether the Security Council would endorse military action under the umbrella of collective security, thereby providing authority to use force against the transnational terrorist threat consistently with the Charter's presumptive prohibition.

Many experts believe this uncertainty was eliminated when, on September 12, 2001, the Security Council passed U.N. Security Council Resolution (UNSCR) 1368, which ostensibly reflected a Security Council determination that international terrorism qualified as a threat to international peace and security.[25] The Resolution emphasized member State determination "to combat by all means threats to international peace and security caused by terrorist acts."[26] It also recognized the right of individual and collective self-defense in response to acts of international terrorism, and expressed on behalf of the Security Council "its readiness to take all necessary steps to respond to the terrorist attacks of 11 September 2001, and to combat all forms of terrorism."[27]

UNSCR 1368 did not, however, include the language historically associated with authorizations to use military force in response to a threat to international peace and security—that member States are authorized to use "all necessary means" to restore international peace and security. As a result, it is uncertain whether Resolution 1368 is properly interpreted as authorizing a collective military response to international terrorism.[28] However, the United States clearly viewed the Resolution as an endorsement to its assertion that the terrorist groups responsible for the September 11th attacks presented an ongoing threat to international peace and security justifying a collective military response. Furthermore, even conceding some uncertainty as to the overall meaning of this Resolution, there is no uncertainty that it indicated the attacks triggered the inherent right of individual and collective self-defense.

This latter conclusion was manifested in a number of ways. First, the United States was obviously instrumental in bringing Resolution 1368 before the Security Council and in securing its adoption. More important, on October 7, 2001, Ambassador

---

[25] *See generally* S.C. Res. 1368, U.N. Doc. S/RES/1368 (Sept. 12, 2001) [hereinafter UNSCR 1368].

[26] *Id.*

[27] *Id.* at ¶ 5.

[28] *See* Geir Ulfstein, *Terrorism and the Use of Force*, 34 SECURITY DIALOGUE 153 (2003), *available at* http://www.sagepub.com/martin3study/articles/Ulfstein.pdf.; John H. Currie, *The Continuing Contributions of Ronald St. J. Macdonald to UN Charter and Peace and Security Issues*, 40 CAN. YEARBOOK INT'L L. 265, 274 (2002).

Negroponte, the U.S. Representative to the Security Council, submitted a letter to the Council President indicating that:[29]

> In accordance with Article 51 of the Charter of the United Nations, I wish, on behalf of my Government, to report that the United States of America, together with other States, has initiated actions in the exercise of its inherent right of individual and collective self-defense following armed attacks that were carried out against the United States on September 11, 2001.[30]

Negroponte also placed the Security Council on notice as to the use-of-force authority invoked by the United States derived from article 51's right of individual and collective self-defense:

> In response to these attacks, and in accordance with the inherent right of individual and collective self-defense, United States armed forces have initiated actions designed to prevent and deter further attacks on the United States. These actions include measures against Al-Qaeda terrorist training camps and military installations of the Taliban regime in Afghanistan.[31]

The United States provided this notice in accordance with article 51 of the Charter, which requires member States invoking the inherent right of self-defense to inform the Security Council of their action and the justification (ostensibly to enable Security Council action to effectively assume responsibility for the situation in an effort to restore international peace and security). This notice was a clear and unambiguous assertion by the United States of the legal basis for the forthcoming use of military force against the transnational terrorist threat.[32] Furthermore, no action to limit the U.S. exercise of self-defense or to have the Security Council assume responsibility for the military response followed this notification. Accordingly, not only does this letter clearly indicate the U.S. interpretation of its right to act in self-defense in response to the terror attacks of September 11th, it also suggests that other members of the Security Council accepted this interpretation (at least tacitly).

This is not to suggest that invoking the right of self-defense in response to international terrorism is without controversy. From the inception of the U.S. "War on Terror,"

---

[29] *See* John D. Negroponte, Representative of the United States of America to the United Nations. Letter to U.N. Security Council President (Oct. 7, 2001), *available at* http://www.bits.de/public/documents/US_Terrorist_Attacks/negroponte.htm. As will be discussed, the U.N. Charter requires such a report: "Measures taken by Members in the exercise of this right of self-defence shall be immediately reported to the Security Council...." U.N. Charter art. 51.

[30] *Id.*

[31] *Id.*

[32] *Id.*

many experts argued that the threat of international terrorism is insufficient to trigger a use of force pursuant to article 51;[33] or that if terrorism is a threat to international peace and security, only the Security Council is authorized to address the threat. These positions reflect the traditional focus of self-defense on threats to States by other States or by internal insurgencies and the traditional military threats associated with that focus. International terrorist groups rarely conduct the type of sustained combat operations normally associated with State armed forces or even organized insurgent groups.[34] According to many experts, this calls into question the validity of invoking military response authority normally justified only when confronting such a sustained military threat. Under this view, international terrorism has been and remains a form of international criminal activity to be addressed through cooperative law enforcement, and where necessary, military support to law enforcement.

Even assuming terrorism is a threat sufficient to justify resort to self-defense, another complicating factor related to the exercise of that right is assessing when a terrorist threat reaches a sufficient level of intensity. Article 51 does not define that trigger point with precision. However, because the article indicates that the right is triggered in response to an "armed attack," self-defense has always been understood to require a situation of absolute self-help necessity to resort to military force—the type of necessity resulting from an armed attack. Even that language, however, has never been understood to require a State to wait until it has become an actual victim of an attack in order to act in self-defense. If the State is attacked, the right to respond in self-defense to prevent continuing or potentially future attacks is relatively clear. What has always been more difficult is determining at what point a State may act to preempt an imminent attack before it occurs.

The controversy surrounding preemptive self-defense certainly predates the threat of international terrorism. As a general proposition, the existence of an imminent threat has always marked the outer limit of self-defense authority.[35] The imminence requirement has also been understood to limit the legitimate invocation of self-defense authority so that it is consistent with the U.N. Charter's presumptive prohibition against using force. Accordingly, although preemptive self-defense has and remains an accepted principle in the use of force equation, extending self-defense beyond preemption into the realm of prevention has always been perceived as overbroad and legally invalid because it decouples self-defense from an imminence trigger.

---

[33] Mary Ellen O'Connell, *The Myth of Pre-emptive Self-Defense*, AM. SOC. INT'L L. TASK FORCE ON TERRORISM (Aug. 2002) [hereinafter *The Myth of Pre-emptive Self-Defense*], *available at* http://cdm15029. contentdm.oclc.org/utils/getfile/collection/p266901coll4/id/2944/filename/2945.pdf.

[34] *Id.*

[35] *See generally* Mark L. Rockefeller, *The "Imminent Threat" Requirement for the Use of Preemptive Military Force: Is It Time for a Non-temporal Standard?*, 33 DENV. J. INT'L L. & POL'Y 131 (2004–2005); Anthony C. Arend, *International Law and the Preemptive Use of Military Force*, 26 WASH. Q., Spring 2003, at 89.

The concept of imminence as it relates to the contemporary debate over the legitimate scope of self-defense derives from a centuries-old incident involving a response by Canadian forces loyal to the Crown against dissident forces seeking to achieve independence.[36] In 1837, the dissident forces took refuge on a U.S. island in the Niagara River straddling the border between the United States and Canada. Canadian forces loyal to the Crown launched a raid against the dissident forces, captured a ship called the *Caroline* from them, and towed it back to a Canadian port where it was burned. The attack triggered a diplomatic dispute between United States and the United Kingdom over the legality of the action.

The diplomatic dispute was ultimately resolved peacefully. The significance of the *Caroline* incident lies in the correspondence that provided the foundation for the resolution. In that correspondence, U.S. Secretary of State Daniel Webster articulated a series of elements justifying resort to anticipatory self-defense, elements that evolved to define the concept of imminent threat.[37] According to Webster, employing force for the purpose of self-defense in anticipation of an act of aggression is justified only when the threat is considered "instant, overwhelming, and leaving no choice of means, and no moment for deliberation."[38] This imminence framework has been almost universally accepted as the appropriate criteria for determining when anticipatory self-defense is legally permissible.

It was this line between preemption and prevention that proved increasingly controversial in the wake of the September 11th terrorist attacks, and continues to generate controversy to this day. Responding to an asserted new type of threat to the nation, President Bush began to articulate what later came to be characterized as the Bush doctrine of preemption.[39] As articulated in the 2002 U.S. National Security Strategy, the combination of terrorist capability and access to weapons of mass destruction necessitated a much more expansive conception of individual and collective self-defense. The United States asserted that the imperative of eliminating such threats, even when they might be in their nascent stage, was justified as an act of self-defense precisely because the opportunity to eliminate the threat, when the threat becomes imminent, may be elusive or nonexistent.[40] Accordingly, the United States would invoke the inherent right of

---

[36] *See* Terence Taylor, *The End of Imminence?*, 27 WASH. Q., Autumn 2004, at 57.

[37] Christopher Greenwood, *International Law and the Pre-emptive Use of Force: Afghanistan, Al-Qaeda, and Iraq*, 4 SAN DIEGO INT'L L. J. 7, 12–13 (2003) (quoting letter from Daniel Webster to Henry S. Fox [British ambassador] of April 24, 1842).

[38] *Id.*

[39] President Bush spoke of "preemption" in a speech on combating terrorism he gave at West Point in May 2002. *See* Mike Allen & Karen DeYoung, *Bush: U.S. Will Strike First at Enemies; In West Point Speech, President Lays Out Broader U.S. Policy*, WASH. POST, June 2, 2002, at A01.

[40] *See* President George W. Bush, *The National Security Strategy of the United States* 6, 15 (Sept. 2002), *available at* http://www.state.gov/documents/organization/63562.pdf.

self-defense to justify resort to military force to disable terrorist capabilities even before those capabilities manifested themselves in the form of an imminent attack.[41]

It is clear that the response to the terror attacks of September 11th, and the Bush doctrine of preemption, went beyond the *Caroline* imminence principles and called into question the U.S. commitment to those principles. Many critics of the Bush doctrine argued that this was nothing more than a subterfuge to provide legal sanction for preventive military action, an exercise of authority unjustified by the inherent right of self-defense and inconsistent with the U.N. Charter.[42] Others, including the Bush administration, took the position that the nature of the threat of terrorism required a more expansive interpretation of the concept of imminence.

The administration of President Barack Obama appears to have adopted the view that the meaning of "imminence" must be contextually adjusted to deal with the threat of transnational terrorism. While there is no use of the term "prevention," it is clear that President Obama has not abandoned the use of military force to attack terrorist operatives outside of the theater of active combat operations in Afghanistan and Iraq. In fact, it is well documented that his administration has significantly increased the number of such attacks, relying on unmanned aerial vehicles (Predator drones) to execute these missions, and the inherent right of self-defense to legally justify them.[43] Whether characterized as preemption or prevention, the outcome seems consistent with the policies of President Bush: the United States will continue to invoke the right of self-defense to justify resort to military force to attack transnational terrorist targets.

President Obama's administration has, in fact, clarified the full scope of the authority asserted by the United States to use military force against the al-Qaeda threat. In a critically important speech on this subject, John O. Brennan, the Assistant to the President for Homeland Security and Counter Terrorism, explained that not only did the United States consider operations directed against al-Qaeda legally justified as acts of self-defense, but that these operations need not be confined to "hot" operational zones.

---

[41] *Id.* This apparent modification of the trigger for exercising self-defense was widely condemned as invalid. Critics asserted that expanding the scope of self-defense to include preemptive action would open the door to acts of aggression cloaked in a disingenuous legal characterization. *See generally, The Myth of Preemptive Self-Defense, supra* note 33; Committee on International Security Affairs of the Association of the Bar of the City of New York, *The Legality and Constitutionality of the President's Authority to Initiate an Invasion of Iraq, Report,* 41 COLUM. J. TRANSNAT'L L. 15 (2002). The degree of criticism generated by the Bush doctrine calls into question whether it significantly altered the traditional imminence requirement for resort to military force in self-defense or whether it will be treated as an aberration and not influence the evolution of this law.

[42] *See id.* at 21–22.

[43] *See* Kenneth Anderson, *Predators over Pakistan,* WEEKLY STANDARD, Mar. 8, 2010, *available at* http://www.weeklystandard.com/print/articles/predators-over-pakistan; *see also* Jane Mayer, *The Predator War,* NEW YORKER, Oct. 26, 2009, *available at* http://www.newyorker.com/reporting/2009/10/26/091026fa_fact_mayer.

Brennan began the speech by emphasizing the continuing justification for self-defense action:

> Obviously, the death of Usama Bin Laden marked a strategic milestone in our effort to defeat al-Qa'ida. Unfortunately, Bin Laden's death, and the death and capture of many other al-Qa'ida leaders and operatives, does not mark the end of that terrorist organization or its efforts to attack the United States and other countries. Indeed, al-Qa'ida, its affiliates and its adherents remain the preeminent security threat to our nation.[44]

Brennan then addressed the scope and duration of self-defense action:

> First, our definition of the conflict. As the President has said many times, we are at war with al-Qa'ida. In an indisputable act of aggression, al-Qa'ida attacked our nation and killed nearly 3,000 innocent people. And as we were reminded just last weekend, al-Qa'ida seeks to attack us again. Our ongoing armed conflict with al-Qa'ida stems from our right—recognized under international law—to self-defense.[45]
>
> An area in which there is some disagreement is the geographic scope of the conflict. The United States does not view our authority to use military force against al-Qa'ida as being restricted solely to "hot" battlefields like Afghanistan. Because we are engaged in an armed conflict with al-Qa'ida, the United States takes the legal position that—in accordance with international law—we have the authority to take action against al-Qa'ida and its associated forces without doing a separate self-defense analysis each time. And as President Obama has stated on numerous occasions, we reserve the right to take unilateral action if or when other governments are unwilling or unable to take the necessary actions themselves.

Finally, Brennan emphasized that although these operations may appear to be a continuing manifestation of what was characterized during the Bush era as preventive war, what they in fact indicate is an evolving and contextual definition of imminence:

> We are finding increasing recognition in the international community that a more flexible understanding of "imminence" may be appropriate when dealing with terrorist groups, in part because threats posed by non-state actors do not present

---

[44] John O. Brennan, Assistant to the President for Homeland Security and Counterterrorism, Strengthening Our Security by Adhering to Our Values and Laws, Remarks at Harvard Law School Program on Law and Security (Sept. 16, 2011) [hereinafter Brennan Remarks at Harvard], *available at* http://www. whitehouse.gov/the-press-office/2011/09/16/remarks-john-o-brennan-strengthening-our-security-adhe ring-our-values-an.

[45] *Id.*

themselves in the ways that evidenced imminence in more traditional conflicts. After all, al-Qa'ida does not follow a traditional command structure, wear uniforms, carry its arms openly, or mass its troops at the borders of the nations it attacks. Nonetheless, it possesses the demonstrated capability to strike with little notice and cause significant civilian or military casualties. Over time, an increasing number of our international counterterrorism partners have begun to recognize that the traditional conception of what constitutes an "imminent" attack should be broadened in light of the modern-day capabilities, techniques, and technological innovations of terrorist organizations.[46]

As Brennan noted, the United States is not alone in this view that terrorism is a threat of sufficient magnitude to trigger the right to self-defense, although as he acknowledged in his speech there is little consensus on the legitimate scope of self-defense authority:

Others in the international community—including some of our closest allies and partners—take a different view of the geographic scope of the conflict, limiting it only to the "hot" battlefields. As such, they argue that, outside of these two active theatres, the United States can only act in self-defense against al-Qa'ida when they are planning, engaging in, or threatening an armed attack against U.S. interests if it amounts to an "imminent" threat.[47]

Although Brennan is indeed correct that there remains significant division on the permissible scope of counter-terror military operations, it has become increasingly accepted that in at least some situations transnational terrorism does trigger the right of self-defense. Indeed, the first indication of broad consensus on this interpretation emerged immediately following the September 11th attacks. NATO's collective response to the attacks provides a particularly significant indication of this support. On September 12, 2001, the North Atlantic Council invoked (for the first time in its history) article 5 of the NATO treaty, authorizing member States to act in the collective self-defense of the United States.[48] There can be little doubt that this invocation was based on a consensus among the alliance members that the terror attacks qualified as an act of aggression, the sole trigger for invoking article 5:

Article 5
The Parties agree that an armed attack against one or more of them in Europe or North America shall be considered an attack against them all and consequently

---

[46] *Id.*

[47] *Id.*

[48] *See Collective Defence*, NORTH ATLANTIC TREATY ORG., http://www.nato.int/cps/en/SID-85648058-8934EDC9/natolive/topics_59378.htm (last visited, June 25, 2014).

they agree that, if such an armed attack occurs, each of them, in exercise of the right of individual or collective self-defence recognized by Article 51 of the Charter of the United Nations, will assist the Party or Parties so attacked by taking forthwith, individually and in concert with the other Parties, such action as it deems necessary, including the use of armed force, to restore and maintain the security of the North Atlantic area.

Any such armed attack and all measures taken as a result thereof shall immediately be reported to the Security Council. Such measures shall be terminated when the Security Council has taken the measures necessary to restore and maintain international peace and security.[49]

It is possible that at the time of this invocation the NATO member States assumed the attacks were executed by a State (i.e., Afghanistan), thereby diluting the significance of this action in terms of the relationship among terrorism, aggression, and self-defense. This, however, seems unlikely. Even on that early date, it was widely assumed the United States was the victim of terrorist attacks. Even conceding that such uncertainty existed on September 12th, the fact remains that NATO made no effort to repeal or modify its invocation as transnational terrorist responsibility for the attacks became clear in the days and weeks that followed. Accordingly, NATO's action stands as an important milestone not only in the history of the alliance, but also in the evolution of the *jus ad bellum*.

Nor have the two post–September 11th U.S. presidents been solely responsible for this invocation of the inherent right of self-defense. In the 2001 Authorization for the Use of Military Force, a Joint Resolution overwhelmingly passed by Congress and a law that remains in effect to this day, Congress noted that the terrorist attacks of September 11th "render it both necessary and appropriate that the United States exercise its rights to self-defense..."[50] The Resolution also provides:

That the President is authorized to use all necessary and appropriate force against those nations, organizations, or persons he determines planned, authorized, committed, or aided the terrorist attacks that occurred on September 11, 2001, or harbored such organizations or persons, in order to prevent any future acts of international terrorism against the United States by such nations, organizations or persons.[51]

This Resolution leaves absolutely no doubt about the interpretation of international law at the core of the U.S. struggle against transnational terrorism. Congress, the president who signed the Resolution into law, and his successor who continues to rely on it

---

[49] North Atlantic Treaty art. 5, Apr. 4, 1949, 63 Stat. 2241, 34 U.N.T.S. 243.
[50] AUMF, *supra* note 23.
[51] *Id.*

to justify targeting, detaining, and trying terrorist operatives, all believe transnational terrorism justifies a legal right to use military force in self-defense.

All of this indicates one indisputable fact: for U.S. armed forces, the inherent right of self-defense has been central to the ongoing use of combat power to disable or destroy al-Qaeda terrorist networks, whether in Afghanistan or other countries. Furthermore, the scope of these operations—which have been ongoing for more than a decade—demonstrate the theory articulated by Brennan: that the very nature of terrorism requires a contextual modification to the concept of imminence.[52] The long-term impact on international law of this U.S. interpretation of the right of self-defense (an interpretation reflected in the military operations of other States confronting the threat of transnational terrorism, such as Israel and Turkey) is unclear. It does seem clear, however, that as States continue to invoke self-defense in response to transnational terrorism, it will be increasingly difficult to condemn such actions as violations of international law.

The "Unable or Unwilling" Factor

Once the United States characterized the struggle against transnational terrorism as an armed conflict, it raised the prospect of identifying terrorist operatives in locations not engaged in ongoing ground combat operations (such as Afghanistan or Iraq). In the decade following September 11th, and especially since President Obama took office, this became an increasingly common occurrence.[53] Combined with the capability provided by remotely piloted aircraft (drones), this resulted in an increasingly common practice of attacking these operatives in the territory of States not engaged in armed conflict with the United States, even when there was no indication of consent for the attacks.

The Obama administration position is that these attacks are justified as an exercise of the inherent right of self-defense, a position not unlike that of the Bush administration. However, President Obama added another element to the legality analysis for these attacks: the "unable or unwilling" test: even absent consent, the United States may act in self-defense when a terrorist threat is identified in the territory of another State and that State is unable or unwilling to address the threat. This position was emphasized by Attorney General Holder in the same speech referenced above:

> International legal principles, including respect for another nation's sovereignty, constrain our ability to act unilaterally. But the use of force in foreign territory would be consistent with these international legal principles if conducted, for example, with the

---

[52] *See* Brennan Remarks at Harvard, *supra* note 44.

[53] Mark V. Vlasic, *Assassination & Targeted Killing—A Historical and Post-Bin Laden Legal Analysis*, 43 Geo. J. Int'l L. 259, 291 (2012).

consent of the nation involved—or after a determination that the nation is unable or unwilling to deal effectively with a threat to the United States.[54]

A number of international legal experts contest the validity of this theory of use-of-force legality, asserting that absent consent, actions such as the raid that killed bin Laden violate international law. There is now, however, clear evidence that the United States rejects such a reading of international law and has and will continue to assert the legal authority to act in self-defense against nonstate threats located in the territory of another sovereign. Harvard professor Jack Goldsmith, the former Director of the Office of Legal Counsel in the Department of Justice credited with reversing many of the overreaching legal opinions that first emerged from that office following September 11th, emphasized this point in 2012. According to his editorial on law and targeting terrorists, targeted killings:

> ...are consistent with the U.N. Charter's ban on using force "against the territorial integrity or political independence of any state" only if the targeted nation consents or the United States properly acts in self-defense. There are reports that Yemen consented to the strike on Awlaki. But even if it did not, the strike would still have been consistent with the Charter to the extent that Yemen was "unwilling or unable" to suppress the threat he posed. This standard is not settled in international law, but it is sufficiently grounded in law and practice that no American president charged with keeping the country safe could refuse to exercise international self-defense rights when presented with a concrete security threat in this situation. The "unwilling or unable" standard was almost certainly the one the United States relied on in the Osama bin Laden raid inside Pakistan.[55]

How the "unable or unwilling" assessment is made remains unclear.[56] The most that can be derived from the statements of the Obama administration is that this is an executive branch determination related to all uses of force in the territory of another sovereign.

---

[54] Attorney General Eric Holder, Remarks at Northwestern University School of Law (Mar. 5, 2012) [hereinafter General Holder Remarks at Northwestern Univ.], *available at* http://www.justice.gov/iso/opa/ag/speeches/2012/ag-speech-1203051.html.

[55] Jack Goldsmith, *Fire When Ready*, FOR. POL'Y, Mar. 19, 2012, http://www.foreignpolicy.com/articles/2012/03/19/fire_when_ready.

[56] Ashley S. Deeks, *"Unwilling or Unable": Toward a Normative Framework for Extraterritorial Self-Defense*, 52 VA. J. INT'L L. 483, 486–88 (2012). This theory of legal justification for using military force in the territory of another State was relied on in earlier contexts, such as the 1970 U.S. military incursion into Cambodia in response to North Vietnamese use of that nation's territory as a base of operations. In a 1989 speech at the U.S. Army Judge Advocate General's School, this theory was cited as a legal basis to conduct military operations in the territory of another nation in response to an imminent or ongoing threat of terrorist attacks. *See* Abraham Sofaer, *Terrorism, the Law and National Self-Defense*, 126 MIL. L. REV. 89, 106–09 (1989).

Objections to this theory of legality are understandable. Allowing one State to decide that another State is "unable" to prevent a threat from materializing from its territory is an exercise of self-help that seems inconsistent with the U.N. Charter principle that States "resolve disputes peacefully." If a State such as the United States believes another State is unable or unwilling to prevent its territory from being used as a staging base for terrorist attacks, one solution would be to bring the matter to the attention of the Security Council. Should the Council agree with such an assertion, it would certainly qualify as a threat to international peace and security triggering the Council's collective security powers. In the alternative, if the threatened State concludes the threat is imminent requiring immediate self-help action, it could attribute responsibility for the terrorist activity to the locus State.

Both of these approaches, however, present negative consequences. Referring a matter to the Security Council would indeed avert a unilateral exercise of self-help. In reality, such a referral might compromise the operational effectiveness of action against the terrorist target by either tipping off the target and/or providing time to react to the exposure to attack. For the United States, it appears the ability to exploit a window of opportunity is viewed as too valuable to forgo in the interest of collective security response. Attributing the terrorist threat to the locus State as an alternative is diplomatically charged. In some cases, this might be justified by the totality of the intelligence related to the threat. This was clearly the foundation for U.S. and Coalition action against the Taliban in 2001. However, in many other cases, the United States (or other States) will likely conclude that the terrorist group is exploiting the territory of another State without indication of State sponsorship. Attributing the terrorist presence to that State will therefore often be perceived as inconsistent with objective facts and with diplomatic interests.

What is a Proportional Response?

Once the right of self-defense is invoked, ensuring the military response to the threat is proportional is an important element of the legitimate exercise of that right.[57] States resorting to military force in response to an actual or imminent threat are obligated to use only the amount of force required to restore the status quo of peace and security.[58] The purpose of this proportionality requirement is clear: to prevent States from transforming a legitimate self-defense response into an act of aggression by exceeding the protective objective of the response.

---

[57] See DINSTEIN 3D EDITION, *supra* note 5, at 192–208.
[58] *Id.* at 208–12.

Like the imminence requirement, there has never been a clear consensus on how to define the proportionality element of a valid exercise of self-defense. The responding State or States are responsible for balancing their legitimate self-defense need with the limited lawful purpose of the action. If the use-of-force system operates ideally, the U.N. Security Council will intervene promptly to assume responsibility for restoring international peace and security. However, in practice this has rarely been the pattern of self-defense actions. Instead, States have been left to assess the permissible scope of military action and resolve disputes related to exceeding that scope diplomatically. Each exercise of self-defense since 1945 has accordingly contributed to a body of practice that adds substance to the parameters of the proportionality element.

The response to transnational terrorism adds a new layer of complexity to self-defense proportionality analysis. For example, some experts question the proportionality of the invasion of Afghanistan to oust the Taliban regime in response to the September 11th attacks. However, the fact that a substantial number of nations committed forces in support of this objective provides significant evidence in support of the conclusion that this military response was widely considered to be consistent with the proportionality requirement.[59] The use of military strikes against terrorist operatives outside of Afghanistan (especially drone attacks) raises a far more complicated issue of proportionality. However, the primary debate surrounding these attacks relates to the predicate issue of whether invocation of the right of self-defense can even extend to such operatives (as discussed above).

When Is the Right to Self-Defense Exhausted?

Another particularly difficult issue in relation to self-defense action is determining when that authority terminates. Article 51 of the U.N. Charter suggests that resort to self-defense, either individual or collective, should be understood as a temporary expedient pending intervention of the Security Council exercising its primary responsibility to maintain international peace and security.[60] Unfortunately, as noted above, practice is rarely consistent with this ideal distribution of authority over the use of military force. Instead, exercise of the right of self-defense has often been met by Security Council inaction, leaving the responding State or States to make their own determination of when the status quo ante has been restored and the authority of self-defense has terminated.

Determining the "expiration date" of a self-defense action has never been simple. However, determining the point at which an aggressive threat has been neutralized has always been easier when dealing with the conventional State threat than when dealing with unconventional nonstate threats. Characterizing transnational terror networks as

---

[59] *See* U.N Charter art. 51; *see also* DINSTEIN 3D EDITION, *supra* note 5, at 192–208.

[60] *See* U.N Charter art. 51.

armed groups triggering the inherent right of self-defense has made this determination even more complicated. The U.S. self-proclaimed "War on Terror" is now the longest war in the nation's history, with no clear end in sight. Indeed, the U.S. Supreme Court in its *Boumediene* decision suggested that individuals captured during the course of this conflict face a genuine prospect of detention for "the duration of hostilities that may last a generation or more."[61]

Identifying the point in time when the authority to take military action based on the inherent right of self-defense terminates is obviously critical in relation to the legal rights and obligations triggered by that authority. In the absence of Security Council action to assume responsibility for responding to the threat that triggered the individual or collective self-defense response, it seems difficult to avoid the reality that the responding State is ultimately entrusted with the responsibility to determine when that authority terminates. This in fact may be one of the reasons there is such widespread hostility to the notion of treating transnational terrorism as a threat justifying resort to self-defense; unlike more traditional military threats, the difficulty in determining when the threat has been neutralized produces an almost inevitable indefinite source of authority to use military force.

The right of self-defense is not, however, an indefinite source of authority. The underlying premise justifying resort to military force as a measure of self-defense is one based on pure necessity.[62] Doing so operates to restore an environment of international peace and security. Accordingly, the use of force employed pursuant to this authority is justified only so long as it is necessary to protect the State from the triggering threat; once that threat is neutralized, the State is obligated to cease military action.

Of course, this raises the difficult question of how a State is to judge when the threat of a highly dispersed transnational terrorist group has been degraded sufficiently to terminate the necessity for using military force. There is no clear answer to this question. To date, States such as the United States and Israel appear to be treating transnational terrorism as an ongoing threat, with no viable end-state or termination point. Indeed, the inability of the State to determine with any degree of precision when its actions have eliminated the threat of terrorism is a significant factor relied on by critics of characterizing terrorism as a trigger for the right of self-defense.[63] For these critics the very nature of terrorism falls outside this triggering category precisely because terrorism defies the traditional methods by which armed opponents are brought into submission. Nonetheless, so long as States continue to invoke the inherent right of self-defense in response to the threat of terrorism, the question of when action in self-defense is no longer justified by virtue of the disabling effect of their military response will remain critical.

---

[61] Boumediene v. Bush, 553 U.S. 723, 785 (2008).

[62] U.N. Charter art. 51.

[63] *See* O'Connell, *The Myth of Preemptive Self-Defense, supra* note 33.

Collective Security in Response to the Threat of Transnational Terrorism

Security Council authorization pursuant to chapter VII of the United Nations Charter could provide an alternate legal basis to use force against the threat of international terrorism.[64] Should the Security Council determine that a terrorist entity constituted a threat to international peace and security, and that peaceful measures would be ineffective in responding to such threat, the Council could authorize member States to employ military force for the purpose of defeating the threat, for the purpose of restoring international peace and security.[65] Although the collective security mechanism of the U.N. Charter was originally conceived to respond to threats to international peace and security resulting from the actions of States, it is today a reality that threats created by nonstate entities are considered sufficient to trigger this Security Council authority.

Although the Security Council routinely condemns international terrorism, and has authorized peaceful means (such as asset seizures) to combat terrorism, it has not to date authorized collective military action in response to international terrorism threats. The Security Council Resolution passed immediately following the terrorist attacks of September 11, 2001, while acknowledging the inherent right of self-defense in response to those attacks, did not authorize collective action against al-Qaeda or any other terrorist entity.[66] In fact, at least one distinguished scholar has challenged the interpretation that this Resolution authorized any type of military response to terrorism.[67] Indeed, it is difficult to conclude with certainty that even the acknowledgment of the article 51 right of self-defense contained within that Resolution permitted military action against transnational terrorist organizations. Instead, it is plausible that the reference to the inherent right of self-defense was focused not on such nonstate threats, but instead on the State (Afghanistan) that harbored and sponsored this terrorist threat.[68]

Confining either collective security efforts or the exercise of State self-defense to those States responsible for providing safe haven or sponsorship to transnational terrorist

---

[64] *See* U.N. Charter art. 39.

[65] *Id.* arts. 40–41.

[66] *See* UNSCR 1368, *supra* note 25.

[67] *See, e.g.,* W. Michael Reisman, *International Legal Responses to Terrorism*, 22 HOUSTON J. INT'L L. 3, 51–4 (1999).

[68] The following is the text of UNSCR 1368 in full:

The Security Council,

Reaffirming the principles and purposes of the Charter of the United Nations,

Determined to combat by all means threats to international peace and security caused by terrorist acts,

Recognizing the inherent right of individual or collective self-defence in accordance with the Charter,

    1. *Unequivocally condemns* in the strongest terms the horrifying terrorist attacks which took place on 11 September 2001 in New York, Washington, D.C. and Pennsylvania and *regards* such acts, like any act of international terrorism, as a threat to international peace and security;

organizations is certainly less controversial than applying both of those authorities to the terrorist organizations themselves. Consistent with well-established principles of State responsibility, terrorist attacks emanating from the State of sponsorship can appropriately be attributed to the sponsoring State for purposes of both collective security and inherent self-defense. The United States did not, however, view UNSCR 1368 in such limited terms. Nonetheless, even an expansive or liberal reading of that Resolution does not support the conclusion that it represented a chapter VII authorization for collective security action by the community of nations.

Although the Security Council has yet to invoke the collective security mechanism of the Charter to authorize military action in response to transnational terrorism, doing so might offer certain advantages over simply acknowledging the inherent right of self-defense. If the response authority were submitted to the judgment of the Security Council, the members of the Council would be in a position not only to determine when the terrorist threat justified resort to military action, but also the legitimate scope and duration of such action. This remains, however, an unlikely course of action, precisely because of the uncertainty created by the nature of the transnational terrorist threat and whether such a threat is properly considered the object of collective security military action.

Can the actions of transnational terrorist groups qualify as aggression within the meaning of international law? This is a vexing question and one on which there is no clear consensus. From the U.S. perspective, the answer is clearly yes, although this is not a view that garners widespread international support—at least not overt support. From an international legal perspective, two sources of authority are particularly relevant to such assessment: the decision by the International Court of Justice (ICJ) in the case of *Nicaragua v. United States*, and the U.N. General Assembly Resolution defining aggression. Although neither of these sources are binding on States or on the U.N. Security Council, the analytical methodology they reflect is widely regarded as authoritative on assessing aggression and the accordant legitimacy of self-defense response, and therefore they serve as important guideposts.

---

2. *Expresses* its deepest sympathy and condolences to the victims and their families and to the people and Government of the United States of America;

3. *Calls* on all States to work together urgently to bring to justice the perpetrators, organizers and sponsors of these terrorist attacks and *stresses* that those responsible for aiding, supporting or harbouring the perpetrators, organizers and sponsors of these acts will be held accountable;

4. *Calls also* on the international community to redouble their efforts to prevent and suppress terrorist acts including by increased cooperation and full implementation of the relevant international anti-terrorist conventions and Security Council resolutions, in particular resolution 1269 (1999) of 19 October 1999;

5. *Expresses* its readiness to take all necessary steps to respond to the terrorist attacks of 11 September 2001, and to combat all forms of terrorism, in accordance with its responsibilities under the Charter of the United Nations;

6. *Decides* to remain seized of the matter.

UNSCR 1368, *supra* note 25.

The ICJ's *Nicaragua* opinion arose out of Nicaragua's allegation that the United States had, inter alia, engaged in illegal aggression by mining Nicaraguan harbors; conducting sabotage missions against Nicaraguan ports, oil installations, and a naval base; and providing ongoing support to the Contras, an internal dissident group challenging the Sandanista government.[69] The United States challenged the jurisdiction of the Court to hear the case brought against it by Nicaragua. When the Court rejected this challenge, the United States terminated its participation in the proceedings. Prior to doing so, however, the United States asserted that its conduct in Nicaragua was legally justified as an act of collective self-defense in support of El Salvador.[70] This theory was premised on an assertion that Nicaragua's support for the leftist insurgents in El Salvador amounted to unlawful aggression against that neighboring State, and therefore pursuant to article 51 of the U.N. Charter, the United States acted legally when it engaged in conduct directed against Nicaragua for the purpose of assisting in the defense of El Salvador.[71]

After determining that the United States was in fact responsible for laying mines and the alleged acts of sabotage, the ICJ ruled that these actions did amount to "infringements of the prohibition of the use of force" in violation of customary international law.[72] However, what is more significant in relation to assessing the impact of nonstate terrorist actions directed against State interests was the Court's analysis of the relationship between State sponsorship of nonstate dissident forces (in this case the Contra insurgents sponsored by the United States) and the definition of aggression triggering the right of individual and collective self-defense. First, the Court concluded that:

> [I]t may be considered to be agreed that an armed attack must be understood as including not merely action by regular armed forces across an international border, but also "sending by or on behalf of a State of armed bands, groups, irregulars or mercenaries, which carry out acts of armed force against another State of such gravity as to amount to" (*inter alia*) an actual armed attack conducted by regular forces, "or substantial involvement therein."[73]

Accordingly, the decision supports the invocation of the inherent right of self-defense in response to an act of aggression by both regular armed forces of another State *and* paramilitary forces acting as an agent or on behalf of a State.[74] Extending this concept to the U.S. and Coalition attack against Afghanistan following the September 11th attacks therefore supports the conclusion that this action qualified as legitimate self-defense as

---

[69] Nicaragua, *supra* note 15, at 18–19.

[70] *Id.* at 27. *See also* Leslie Rose, *U.S. Bombing of Afghanistan Not Justified as Self-Defense under International Law*, 59 GUILD PRAC. 65, 66–67 (2002).

[71] *See* Nicaragua, *supra* note 15, at 22, 70–71.

[72] *Id.* at 118.

[73] *Id.* at 103.

[74] *Id.*

Afghanistan bore State responsibility for the conduct of the al-Qaeda. Furthermore, although the decision did not address the relationship between nonstate paramilitary activities and the inherent right of self-defense, the fact that the Court concluded military action by paramilitary forces can qualify as aggression bolsters the U.S. theory of self-defense in response to the attacks of September 11th.[75]

The Court also addressed the level of State sponsorship of paramilitary activities necessary for the attribution of those activities to the State. This issue was relevant to both the assertion that the United States had committed acts of aggression against Nicaragua (by supporting the Contras), and the assertion that armed activities against Nicaragua directed or supported by the United States were justified as collective self-defense in response to Nicaraguan aggression toward El Salvador (by supporting the FMLN leftist insurgents in El Salvador). The Court concluded that it

> ...does not believe that the concept of "armed attack" includes not only acts by armed bands where such acts occur on a significant scale but also assistance to rebels in the form of the provision of weapons or logistical or other support. Such assistance may be regarded as a threat or use of force, or amount to intervention in the internal or external affairs of other States.[76]

Thus, the Court drew a demarcation line between the use of paramilitary (or irregular) forces as a State proxy, with their hostilities effectively directed by the State, and the provision of logistical (including military logistics such as weapons and ammunition) to such forces. According to the Court, only the former category qualified as aggression triggering the inherent right of individual and collective self-defense.[77]

Based on this demarcation, the Court ruled that U.S. support for the Contras rose to the level of aggression, because this support included "organizing or encouraging the organization of irregular forces or armed bands...for incursion into the territory of another state."[78] In contrast, the Court rejected the assertion that Nicaraguan support for the FMLN in El Salvador qualified as an act of aggression.[79] Specifically, the Court found that:

> ...between July 1979 and the early months of 1981, an intermittent flow of arms was routed via the territory of Nicaragua to the armed opposition in that country. The Court was not however satisfied that assistance has reached the Salvadorian armed opposition, on a scale of any significance, since the early months of 1981, or

---

[75] *Id.* at 124.
[76] *Id.* at 104.
[77] *Id.* at 103–04.
[78] *Id.* at 118–19.
[79] *Id.*

that the Government of Nicaragua was responsible for any flow of arms at either period. Even assuming that the supply of arms to the opposition in El Salvador could be treated as imputable to the Government of Nicaragua, to justify invocation of the right of collective self-defence in customary international law, it would have to be equated with an armed attack by Nicaragua on El Salvador.[80]

The ICJ's analysis focused exclusively on State sponsorship of paramilitary or irregular forces and how that sponsorship triggers the right of self-defense. However, it must be considered instructive on the response to acts of violence by transnational terrorist groups. The Court's decision arguably establishes a criterion for determining what level of State sponsorship and support justifies attribution of terrorist violence to the State. If this is true, any State invoking the inherent right of self-defense to use force against another State based on a sponsorship theory—such as the international use of force against Afghanistan based on al-Qaeda sponsorship—must establish support more analogous to command and control than simply logistics. This is obviously a significant consideration for States such as Israel that face a continuing threat of terrorist violence facilitated by support from other States, such as Iran. What is less certain is how the nature of the support provided, and/or the organization supported, should impact this analysis. Specifically, would the provision of such support qualify as aggression if the weapons provided the capability to inflict mass destruction? Although the ICJ's opinion did not include any such qualifier, because those facts were not before the Court, such distinctions provide States facing such threats with a legitimate basis to distinguish State sponsorship of terrorism from other types of threats.

The *Nicaragua* decision also has potential significance in relation to the contemporary U.S. practice of drone attacks directed against suspected terrorist operatives outside of an area of traditional combat operations. The decision provides a useful template for assessing when terrorist actions are belligerent in nature, thereby providing a basis for asserting the right of self-defense to engage in such attacks.[81] The distinction between general logistical support and operational command and control of irregular forces arguably bolsters the U.S. view that attacking individuals in the operational chain of command is justified because they qualify as belligerent operatives. The significance of this command and control role in the legality analysis related to a decision to attack terrorist operatives with deadly force outside the area of traditional combat operations was emphasized by Attorney General Holder:

> Let me be clear: an operation using lethal force in a foreign country, targeted against a U.S. citizen who is a senior operational leader of al Qa'ida or associated forces, and who is actively engaged in planning to kill Americans, would be lawful

---

[80] *Id.*

[81] *Id.* at 103–04.

at least in the following circumstances: First, the U.S. government has determined, after a thorough and careful review, that the individual poses an imminent threat of violent attack against the United States; second, capture is not feasible; and third, the operation would be conducted in a manner consistent with applicable law of war principles.[82]

Although this analysis related specifically to an attack against a U.S. citizen, the emphasis on the operational command and control function seems consistent with the ICJ's view of conduct that qualifies as aggression. However, it also calls into serious question the legality of directing such attacks against individuals providing logistical support to terrorist operatives, such as financiers and terrorist recruiters. Although certainly not directly on point, the line between logistics and command and control—what Major General Charles Dunlap called "the kill chain"—seems an important factor for both assessing when activities of nonstate groups qualify as aggression and when individuals associated with such groups are lawfully subject to deliberate attack.[83]

Another aspect of the *Nicaragua* decision with potential significance for future U.S. counter-terror efforts was the Court's response to the U.S. invocation of the right of collective self-defense in support of El Salvador. While the Court acknowledged that customary international law recognizes the right of collective self-defense, it rejected the U.S. invocation of that right. This rejection was based not only on the determination that Nicaraguan support for the FMLN did not rise to the level of aggression, but also on its conclusion that El Salvador had never itself invoked the right of self-defense against Nicaragua.[84] In essence, the Court concluded that a State cannot assert collective self-defense unless and until the protected victim State invokes that right itself.

This limitation on invoking the right of collective self-defense could become significant if in the future the United States believes a terrorist group is threatening the stability of another State. In such a situation, it would be difficult to sustain a claim of collective self-defense to use force against that group unless the State being assisted requested that assistance. Of course, such a request would operate as consent for the military intervention, which would render irrelevant any concerns implicated by this aspect of the Nicaragua decision. However, it is also plausible that the United States will view the destabilizing terrorist activity as a threat not only to the State where the group is located, but also to the United States itself. In such a situation, the intersection of collective self-defense and U.S. national self-defense presents one of the most complex use-of-force legality dilemmas in contemporary practice.

---

[82] *See* General Holder Remarks at Northwestern Univ., *supra* note 54.

[83] Charles J. Dunlap, Jr., *The Role of the Lawyer in War: It Ain't No TV Show: JAGs and Modern Military Operations*, 4 Chi. J. Int'l. L. 479, 483 (2003).

[84] *See* Nicaragua, *supra* note 15, at 120.

The Wall and Uganda Decisions: The International Court of Justice's Rejection of Terrorism as a Self-Defense Trigger

Although it is clear that the United States, as well as a number of other States impacted by the threat of transnational terrorism, consider this threat sufficient to trigger the inherent right of self-defense, the ICJ seems to have rejected this interpretation of article 51.[85] In its decision on the legality of Israel's construction of a barrier wall between Israel and Palestinian-populated areas of the West Bank, the ICJ considered and rejected Israel's assertion that the wall was a justified measure of self-defense in response to widespread terrorist attacks launched from the occupied territories.[86] The Israeli High Court of Justice had already considered this same issue and concluded that the wall was in fact a legitimate exercise of the inherent right of self-defense, and a necessary and proportional response to the nonstate terrorist threat plaguing Israel.[87] The ICJ came to a radically different conclusion.

The ICJ never reached the issues of necessity or proportionality because it rejected the predicate invocation of the right of self-defense. According to the Court, a State could invoke this right only in response to an external threat—a threat emanating from another State.[88] Because the nonstate threat of terrorist activity asserted by Israel as the justification for its self-defense action emanated from within its occupied territories, the Court concluded Israel had no international legal right for this action.[89]

One dissenting judge criticized the Court's judgment because, inter alia, it failed to adequately consider that "the United Nations Charter, in affirming the inherent right of self-defence, does not make its exercise dependent upon an armed attack by another State."[90] According to this judge, the majority's opinion ignored other situations in which the Security Council recognized terrorist attacks as a threat to international

---

[85] Dr. Barry A. Feinstein & Justus Reid Weiner, *Israel's Security Barrier: An International Comparative Analysis and Legal Evaluation*, 37 GEO. WASH. INT'L L. REV. 309, 384–88 (2005) [hereinafter Feinstein & Weiner] (discussing the United States' perspective on Israel's security barrier and also discussing numerous examples of walls/barriers comparable to that of Israel and the lack of criticism received on those barriers); Legal Consequences of the Construction of a Wall in the Occupied Palestinian Territory, Advisory Opinion, 2004 I.C.J. 136 (July 9) [hereinafter ICJ Wall Advisory Opinion].

[86] *See* ICJ Wall Advisory Opinion at 194.

[87] H.C.J 2056/04 Beit Sourik Village Council v. The Government of Israel 58(5) PD 817 [2004] (Isr.), *available at* http://elyon1.court.gov.il/files_eng/04/560/020/a28/04020560.a28.pdf (The Israeli High Court of Justice was aware of the killing and destruction brought by the terror attacks against the State and its citizens, but held that Israel had a right to erect a "fence" for security reasons on territory it considers "disputed" and that the fence was a proportionate response to the terror attacks; however, the Court ordered a specific segment of the Wall moved to alleviate the hardship on Palestinian villagers).

[88] *See* ICJ Wall Advisory Opinion, *supra* note 86, at 194.

[89] *Id.*

[90] *Id.* at 240–45 (Judge Burgenthal dissenting).

peace and security, without limiting this recognition only to terrorist attacks sponsored by States, and noted that, in connection with such recognition, the Security Council reaffirmed "the inherent right of individual or collective self-defence as recognized by the Charter of the United Nations."[91]

The ICJ reached a similar, if not more expansive rejection of the right of self-defense in response to nonstate threats in its Uganda/DRC opinion.[92] In that case, Uganda claimed the right to invoke self-defense in response to nonstate rebel groups attacking its territory from the Democratic Republic of the Congo.[93] Although these attacks, unlike in the *Wall* case, did emanate from the territory of another State, the ICJ nonetheless rejected the invocation of the right of self-defense. This was because of the nonstate nature of the rebel groups. According to the decision:

> [...] It is further to be noted that, while Uganda claimed to have acted in self-defence, it did not ever claim that it had been subjected to an armed attack by the armed forces of the DRC. The "armed attacks" to which reference was made came rather from the ADF. The Court has found above (paragraphs 131–135) that there is no satisfactory proof of the involvement in these attacks, direct or indirect, of the Government of the DRC. The attacks did not emanate from armed bands or irregulars sent by the DRC or on behalf of the DRC, within the sense of Article 3 *(g)* of General Assembly resolution 3314 (XXIX) on the definition of aggression, adopted on 14 December 1974. The Court is of the view that, on the evidence before it, even if this series of deplorable attacks could be regarded as cumulative in character, they still remained non-attributable to the DRC.
>
> [...] For all these reasons, the Court finds that the legal and factual circumstances for the exercise of a right of self-defence by Uganda against the DRC were not present. Accordingly, the Court has no need to respond to the contentions of the Parties as to whether and under what conditions contemporary international law provides for a right of self-defence against large-scale attacks by irregular forces. Equally, since the preconditions for the exercise of self-defence do not exist in the circumstances of the present case, the Court has no need to enquire whether such an entitlement to self-defence was in fact exercised in circumstances of necessity and in a manner that was proportionate.[94]

---

[91] *Id.* at 242.

[92] Armed Activities on the Territory of the Congo (Democratic Republic of the Congo v. Uganda), Judgment, 2005 I.C.J. 168, 280–82 (Dec. 19) (finding that Uganda violated the principle of non-use of force in international relations and the principle of non-intervention, its obligations under international human rights law and international humanitarian law, and other obligations owed to the Democratic Republic of the Congo.

[93] *Id.* at 194–95.

[94] *Id.* at 222–23.

For the ICJ, the nature or gravity of the threat is obviously not the essential predicate for triggering the inherent right of self-defense. Instead, only a State-sponsored threat satisfies that triggering requirement.[95]

The combined impact of these two decisions on the use of military force against transnational terrorist threats is potentially profound. If this requirement for State action as a necessary element to trigger the inherent right of self-defense is an accurate interpretation of international law, it essentially undermines the entire U.S. military response to terrorism.[96] However, the impact of these decisions is difficult to assess. Unsurprisingly, proponents of a pragmatic interpretation of the inherent right of self-defense have been critical of the decisions, focusing on the same flaw as the dissenting justice.[97] Furthermore, it is clear that these decisions have had little impact on the continued assertion of this right by States such as the United States and Israel in response to the threat of transnational terrorism. Nonetheless, it is impossible to ignore the fact that the ICJ categorically rejected these assertions. Ultimately, how State practice continues to evolve on this issue should indicate whether these decisions will be viewed as aberrations, or will gain traction as an indication of a much more limited right than that asserted by the United States.

Conclusion

Characterizing terrorism as an armed attack has profound legal consequences. The first of these consequences is that the victim State may consider the act of terrorism a legitimate trigger for the inherent right of individual or collective self-defense. When a State conducts military action pursuant to this theory of legal authority, the action itself will trigger a law of armed conflict-based regulatory framework—a framework fundamentally distinct from that associated with a law enforcement response to terrorism. As a result, invoking the right of self-defense in response to a transnational terrorist threat

---

[95] *See id.* at 223.

[96] Feinstein & Weiner, *supra note* 85, at 522.

[97] Victor Kattan, *The Legality of the West Bank Wall: Israel's High Court of Justice v. the International Court of Justice*, 40 Vand. J. Transnat'l L. 1425, 1514–16 (2007) ("The ICJ could have addressed the question of self-defense and prolonged occupations in far more detail, as the law is not entirely clear in this area. Grappling with this issue, probably one of the most controversial areas in international law may have given the opinion more credibility. The ICJ could have also provided more of an analysis as to why the construction of the wall along its current route is unreasonable, justifying its decisions by legal argument"); Michael Reisman, *Holding the Center of the Law of Armed Conflict*, 100 Am. J. Int'l. L. 852, 856 (2006). *See also* Derek Jinks, *The Changing Laws of War: Do We Need a New Legal Regime after September 11?: Protective Parity and the Laws of War*, 79 Notre Dame L. Rev. 1493, 1497 (2004) ("the protection of noncombatants from attack is predicated on a clear distinction between combatants and noncombatants. If attacking forces cannot distinguish between enemy soldiers and civilians, this type of rule cannot work well....It is the goal of protecting innocent civilians that requires a sharp line between combatants and noncombatants").

will involve an exercise of State power that would normally be considered legally prohibited, potentially resulting in deprivations of life, liberty, and property inconsistent with peacetime legal authorities. The U.S. response to the terror attacks of September 11th provide the quintessential example of this effect for both the State actors engaged in response and the individuals they encounter during their counter-terror military operations. It is therefore unsurprising that such an approach to the threat of terrorism has and will continue to generate substantial criticism and legal opposition. Nonetheless, it seems impossible to ignore the reality that for at least some States and the international community invoking the right of self-defense in response to the threat of transnational terrorism will remain an important option for protecting national security.

2

Triggering the Law of Armed Conflict?

by Geoffrey S. Corn

Introduction

On September 11, 2001, the legal framework for the regulation of armed conflict, the framework that guides military lawyers and influences decisions made in reliance on their advice, was thrown into disarray.[1] Prior to that day of infamy, these lawyers applied an "either/or" law-triggering paradigm that dictated when the law of armed conflict (LOAC)[2]

---

[1] Adam Roberts, *Counter-terrorism, Armed Force and the Laws of War*, 44 SURVIVAL: GLOBAL POLITICS & STRATEGY 7 (2002) [hereinafter *Counter-Terrorism, Armed Force and the Laws of War*].

[2] The term "law of armed conflict," "laws of war," or "law of war" will be used throughout the book to refer to the law governing the conduct of belligerents engaged in armed conflict. This term, while certainly less in favor than "international humanitarian law," is the one used in official Department of Defense Doctrine. *See* U.S. DEP'T OF DEF., DIR. 2311.01E, DOD LAW OF WAR PROGRAM (9 May 2006); *see also* JOINT CHIEFS OF STAFF, INSTR. 5810.01B, IMPLEMENTATION OF THE DOD LAWS OF WAR PROGRAM (25 Mar. 2002). The following excerpt demonstrates the continuing significance of retaining this characterization in lieu of the more popular "international humanitarian" law:

> In this Article, I have used the term "laws of war" referring to those streams of international law, especially the various Hague and Geneva Conventions, intended to apply in armed conflicts. To some, the term "laws of war" is old-fashioned. However, its continued use has merits. It accurately reflects the well-established Latin phrase for the subject of this inquiry, jus in bello, and it is brief and easily understood. It has two modern equivalents, both of which are longer. One of these, the "law applicable in armed conflicts" is unexceptionable, but adds little. The other, "international humanitarian law" (IHL), often with the suffix "applicable in armed conflicts," has become the accepted term in most diplomatic and U.N. frameworks. *However, it has the defect that is seems to suggest that humanitarianism rather than professional standards is the main foundation on which the law is built, and thus invites a degree of criticism from academics, warriors and others who subscribe to a realist view of international relations.*

> Adam Roberts, *The Laws of War: Problems of Implementation in Contemporary Conflicts*, 6 DUKE J. COMP. & INT'L. L. 11, 14 (1995) (emphasis added).

applied to U.S. operations: either those operations involved hostilities against the armed forces of another State so as to qualify as international armed conflicts, or they involved hostilities against insurgent forces within a State on whose behalf the United States had intervened, thereby falling into the alternative category of internal armed conflict.[3] Derived from common articles 2 and 3 of the 1949 Geneva Conventions, this law-triggering paradigm was a genuine article of faith for U.S. military lawyers trained in the LOAC in their Services' respective introductory and advanced military law courses.

These lawyers and the forces they supported were well versed in military operations that fell outside these inter/intra state armed conflict paradigms. They had been taught that such operations were regulated by U.S. military policy that dictated compliance with LOAC principles even if those principles did not apply as a matter of law.[4] At a minimum, these principles included military necessity, distinction, proportionality, and humanity. From Panama in 1989 to Kosovo in 2000, this policy-based LOAC application proved remarkably effective. As a result, U.S. forces operated under the policy-driven assumption that they would follow these fundamental LOAC principles during all their operational missions regardless of technical legal characterization. Because of this, the operational impact of technical LOAC applicability was minimal because commanders at that level were expected to comply with the LOAC as the "default" standard.[5] Based on this methodology, when U.S. forces first "hit the ground" in Afghanistan, operational legal advisors, like their predecessors in Panama and Somalia, followed this

---

[3] *See* INT'L & OPERATIONAL LAW DEP'T, THE JUDGE ADVOCATE GENERAL'S SCHOOL, U.S. ARMY, THE LAW OF WAR DESKBOOK 30–31 (2000) (describing common article 3 conflicts as "internal armed conflict"), *available at* http://dspace.wrlc.org/doc/get/2041/63338/00099display.pdf [hereinafter 2000 LAW OF WAR DESKBOOK]. A 2004 fact sheet from the International Committee of the Red Cross (ICRC) clearly reflects the international/internal evolution of the triggering paradigm:

> International humanitarian law distinguishes between international and non-international armed conflict.
>
> **International armed conflicts** are those in which at least two States are involved. They are subject to a wide range of rules, including those set out in the four Geneva Conventions and Additional Protocol I.
>
> **Non-international armed conflicts** are those restricted to the territory of a single State, involving either regular armed forces fighting groups of armed dissidents, or armed groups fighting each other. A more limited range of rules apply to internal armed conflicts and are laid down in Article 3 common to the four Geneva Conventions as well as in Additional Protocol II.

Fact Sheet, Int'l Comm. of the Red Cross, Advisory Serv. on Int'l Humanitarian Law, *What Us International Humanitarian Law?* (July 2004), http://www.icrc.org/eng/assets/files/other/what_is_ihl. pdf [hereinafter ICRC Fact Sheet].

[4] *See* Geoffrey S. Corn, "*Snipers in the Minaret—What is the Rule*" *The Law of War and the Protection of Cultural Property: A Complex Equation*, ARMY LAW. 28 (July 2005) (discussing policy-based application of law-of-armed-conflict principles in accordance with DoD directives) [hereinafter *Snipers in the Minaret*].

[5] CHAIRMAN OF THE JOINT CHIEFS OF STAFF, INSTR. 3121.01B, STANDING RULES OF ENGAGEMENT/ STANDING RULES FOR THE USE OF FORCE FOR US FORCES, encl. A, para. 1d (13 Jun 2005); *see also Snipers in the Minaret, supra* note 4, at 34.

"default" approach and advised their commanders to comply with the LOAC as if they were involved in an international armed conflict.[6]

Unlike prior operations, however, the limits of this policy-based LOAC application were quickly exposed when U.S. forces began to capture and detain opposition fighters. Almost immediately, commanders were directed to halt the practice of treating captured personnel "as if" they were prisoners of war, because a new status had been adopted for these detainees: "unlawful enemy combatant."[7] This characterization was created to denote a detained enemy operative who did not qualify for status as a prisoner of war and who would therefore not be entitled to claim the benefit of LOAC protections. Relocation to a newly established high security detention facility in Guantanamo Bay, Cuba, thus became a permissible option that was highly controversial for the international community.[8]

In the months and years to follow its first utilization, this term became a lightning rod for U.S. policies related to the war on terror. However, for purposes of this chapter the significance of this new detainee characterization is the legal theory upon which it was founded. A new legal position began to emerge: the authority of the LOAC would be asserted to provide the legal basis for the execution of military operations against al-Qaeda—an entity considered to be engaged in an armed conflict with the United States. However, unlike their Taliban counterparts who could, at least in theory, claim the protections of the LOAC because they were captured in the context of what the United States ultimately conceded was an inter-state armed conflict, al-Qaeda captives were not afforded such a claim because the conflict they engaged in defied classification under either common article 2 or 3.[9]

The incongruity of this theory was readily apparent: the United States was engaged in an armed conflict that provided the authority to engage, destroy, capture, and detain the newly defined enemy. However, it was an armed conflict that did not fit into the traditional common article 2/3 "either/or" law-triggering paradigm, and as a result, the LOAC did not apply to constrain or regulate U.S. operations.[10] With regard to execution

---

[6] Center for Law and Military Operations, The Judge Advocate General's School, U.S. Army, Forged in the Fire 30–31 (2008). *See generally* Jennifer Elsea, Cong. Res. Serv., Terrorism and the Laws of War: Trying Terrorists as War Criminals before Military Commissions (Rpt. RL 31191) (Dec. 11, 2001) (analyzing whether the attacks of September 11, 2001, triggered the law of war), *available at* http://fpc.state.gov/documents/organization/7951.pdf [hereinafter *Trying Terrorists*].

[7] *See generally* Geoffrey S. Corn & Eric Talbot Jensen, *Untying the Gordian Knot: A Proposal for Determining Applicability of the Laws of War to the War on Terror,* 81 Temp. L. Rev. 787, 789 n.12 (2008) [hereinafter *Untying the Gordian Knot*].

[8] *See* Human Rights Watch, *United Nations Finds That U.S. Has Failed to Comply with International Obligations at Guantanamo Detention Center* (Feb. 16, 2006) (describing report criticizing the "lack of a legal basis for detentions" at Guantanamo), http://www.hrw.org/news/2006/02/15/united-nations-finds-us-has-failed-comply-international-obligations-guantanamo-deten.

[9] *Untying the Gordian Knot, supra* note 7, at 800.

[10] *See* Jay S. Bybee, Memorandum for Alberto Gonzales, Counsel to the President, and William J. Haynes II, General Counsel of the DoD, Re: Application of Treaties and Laws to al Qaeda and Taliban Detainees

of combat operations, this incongruity had little impact due to the military practice of following LOAC principles during all operations as a matter of policy. However, as the United States began to capture and detain alleged terrorist operatives, it became quickly apparent that the inapplicability of LOAC obligations would be a key component to the development of detainee treatment and interrogation policies.[11]

The Pre-9/11 Perception of the Military Component of Counter-Terror Operations

Prior to the terrorist attacks of September 11, 2001, response to international terrorism was viewed almost exclusively as an exercise of law enforcement authority. A number of terrorist attacks had been directed against U.S. military targets (for example, the U.S.S. *Cole* in Yemen), and the United States had employed military assets to strike at terrorist capabilities on at least one occasion (a missile attack against al-Qaeda base camps in Afghanistan and a suspected chemical weapons facility in Sudan, discussed below). Nonetheless, the use of military combat power to destroy or disable terrorist capabilities was an exceptional event as law enforcement efforts to apprehend and try alleged terrorists remained the primary tool in the U.S. counter-terrorism arsenal.[12]

This did not mean the military played no role in U.S. counter-terrorism efforts. The military took substantial steps to protect itself from the threat of terrorism—actions that fell collectively under the category of force protection.[13] But these actions did not involve offensive efforts to locate and destroy or disable terrorist capabilities. Instead, they were (and remain) better understood as defensive measures implemented to reduce the vulnerability of U.S. forces. The military also routinely conducted missions in support of law enforcement efforts. Such missions, characterized as military support to law enforcement, involve provision of logistics, intelligence, training, communication,

---

(Jan. 22, 2002), *available at* http://www.washingtonpost.com/wp-srv/nation/documents/012202bybee. pdf [hereinafter Bybee Memorandum].

[11] *See* Alberto R. Gonzales, Counsel to the President, Memorandum for the President, Subject: Decision re Application of the Geneva Convention on Prisoners of War to the Conflict with Al Qaeda and the Taliban (Jan. 25, 2002) (expressing the view that the war against terrorism is a new kind of war to which GPW does not apply), *available at* http://www.torturingdemocracy.org/documents/20020125.pdf [hereinafter Gonzales Memorandum].

[12] *See* RAPHAEL PERL, CONG. RES. SERV., TERRORISM AND NATIONAL SECURITY: ISSUES AND TRENDS (Rpt. IB10119) (2004), *available at* www.fas.org/irp/crs/IB10119.pdf.

[13] The Department of Defense Dictionary defines force protection as:

Preventive measures taken to mitigate hostile actions against Department of Defense personnel (to include family members), resources, facilities, and critical information.

JOINT CHIEFS OF STAFF, JOINT PUB. 1-02, DEPARTMENT OF DEFENSE DICTIONARY OF MILITARY AND ASSOCIATED TERMS 107 (8 November 2010) (amended through 15 Sept. 2013), *available at* http://www.dtic.mil/doctrine/new_pubs/jp1_02.pdf.

transport, and other support to civilian law enforcement agencies. Unlike traditional combat operations, these missions do not involve a lead role or responsibility for the military.

Although this support role generally defined the use of national military capabilities to respond to the threat of terrorism, there were exceptions involving direct military action against terrorist capabilities even before September 11th.[14] The U.S. response to the attacks on the U.S. embassies in Kenya and Tanzania is the most significant example that is publicly known. Based on a determination of al-Qaeda responsibility for these bombings, President Clinton ordered Operation Infinite Reach, a cruise missile attack against suspected training facilities in Afghanistan and a suspected chemical weapons plant in Sudan.[15] The United States invoked the inherent right of self-defense as a legal justification for this action, signaling a potential shift in paradigm from the traditional law enforcement approach to military-based counter-terror efforts.[16] However, there were no significant follow-on operations of a similar character that were made known to the public. Even assuming other covert military operations were directed against terrorist capabilities during this same time period, the use of the military in direct action as a primary response to terrorism certainly remained the exception and not the rule.

The Post-9/11 Response and the Invocation of the Law of Armed Conflict

In the days and weeks following September 11, 2001, the U.S. approach to the military's role in counter-terrorism changed substantially. The scale, intensity, and destructive effect of those attacks led the president,[17] followed soon thereafter by Congress,[18] to invoke the war powers of the nation as the primary modality for protecting it against future attacks. Almost immediately following the attacks, the Secretary of Defense began to articulate to the public the far more robust role that would be assumed by the armed forces in this effort. These statements, along with those of the president and

---

[14] *See, e.g.,* William S. Cohen, Statement of William S. Cohen to The National Commission on Terrorist Attacks upon the United States (Mar. 23, 2004), *available at* http://www.9-11commission.gov/hearings/hearing8/cohen_statement.pdf.

[15] Jan Kittrich, *Can Self-Defense Serve as an Appropriate Tool against International Terrorism?*, 61 ME. L. REV. 133, 162–63 (2009); *see also* NATIONAL COMMISSION ON TERRORIST ATTACKS UPON THE UNITED STATES, THE 9/11 COMMISSION REPORT: FINAL REPORT OF THE NATIONAL COMMISSION ON TERRORIST ATTACKS UPON THE UNITED STATES (2004), *available at* http://govinfo.library.unt.edu/911/report/index.htm.

[16] *See* William J. Clinton, U.S. President, Address to the Nation by the President (Aug. 20, 1998), *available at* http://clinton6.nara.gov/1998/08/1998-08-20-president-address-to-the-nation.html.

[17] *See* George W. Bush, U.S. President, *Transcript of President Bush's Address to a Joint Session of Congress on Thursday Night, September 20, 2001*, CNN.COM (Sept. 21, 2001) http://edition.cnn.com/2001/US/09/20/gen.bush.transcript/.

[18] *See* Authorization for Use of Military Force, Pub. L. No. 107–40, 115 Stat. 224 (2001) [hereinafter AUMF].

other high-level government officials, indicated that the military response would not be subordinate to a primary law enforcement effort. Nor would the military response be limited to striking al-Qaeda's State sponsor in Afghanistan. Instead, the United States would embark upon a military campaign of global reach, the scope of which was defined by the newly coined designation of a "global war on terrorism."[19] This new approach to protecting national security and disrupting and defeating the threat of transnational terrorism was articulated in the National Security Strategy of 2002:

> The struggle against global terrorism is different from any other war in our history. It will be fought on many fronts against a particularly elusive enemy over an extended period of time. Progress will come through the persistent accumulation of successes—some seen, some unseen.
>
> Today our enemies have seen the results of what civilized nations can, and will, do against regimes that harbor, support, and use terrorism to achieve their political goals. Afghanistan has been liberated; coalition forces continue to hunt down the Taliban and al-Qaida. But it is not only this battlefield on which we will engage terrorists. Thousands of trained terrorists remain at large with cells in North America, South America, Europe, Africa, the Middle East, and across Asia.
>
> *Our priority will be first to disrupt and destroy terrorist organizations of global reach* and attack their leadership; command, control, and communications; material support; and finances. This will have a disabling effect upon the terrorists' ability to plan and operate.[20]

Any doubt about the transformation in the U.S. approach to defending itself against transnational terrorism was eliminated when the president issued his order establishing military commissions. On November 13, 2001, President Bush issued Military Order No. 1, "Detention, Treatment and Trial of Certain Non-Citizens in the War against Terrorism." In that Order, the president determined that:

> International terrorists, including members of al Qaida, have carried out attacks on United States diplomatic and military personnel and facilities abroad and on citizens and property within the United States on a scale that has created a state of armed conflict that requires the use of the United States Armed Forces.[21]

---

[19] *See generally* THE NATIONAL SECURITY STRATEGY OF THE UNITED STATES OF AMERICA 27 (Sept. 2002), *available at* http://www.state.gov/documents/organization/63562.pdf [hereinafter 2002 National Security Strategy]; *see also* Exec. Order No. 13,289, 68 Fed. Reg. 512,567 (Mar. 14, 2003) (establishing "Global War on Terrorism" medals).

[20] 2002 National Security Strategy, *supra* note 19, at 5 (emphasis added).

[21] Military Order of November 13, 2002, *Detention, Treatment, and Trial of Certain Non-citizens in the War against Terrorism*, Sec. 1(a), 66 Fed. Reg. 57833 (Nov. 16, 2001).

With this determination, the president indicated that the United States would invoke the law of armed conflict as the source of authority to detain and punish (and by implication attack and kill) terrorist operatives and protect the nation from the continuing and global threat of international terrorism. By that time, the United States was engaged in a large-scale military campaign in Afghanistan directed against both al-Qaeda forces and the Taliban government that provided the safe haven and support for those forces. These operations reflected a fundamentally different role for the military than the support to law enforcement that defined its pre-September 11th participation in counter-terror efforts: terrorism was no longer to be regarded as a law enforcement challenge requiring periodic military support; instead, terrorism was an armed hostile threat to the nation requiring the employment of the full spectrum of combat capability.

The president's decision to characterize the struggle against terrorism as an armed conflict and invoke the war powers of the nation in response was endorsed by Congress. In fact, this endorsement occurred even before the president's explicit enunciation in Military Order #1 of the existence of an armed conflict. On September 18, 2001, Congress passed a Joint Resolution titled "Authorization for Use of Military Force" (AUMF) and authorized "the use of United States Armed Forces against those responsible for the recent attacks launched against the United States."[22] This Resolution explicitly authorized the president to

> …use all necessary and appropriate force against those nations, organizations, or persons he determines planned, authorized, committed, or aided the terrorist attacks that occurred on September 11, 2001, or harbored such organizations or persons, in order to prevent any future acts of international terrorism against the United States by such nations, organizations or persons.[23]

As this language indicates, the only limitation in scope of the authority granted to the president to respond to the threat of international terrorism with the full military force of the nation was that the response be limited to individuals, organizations, and States determined by the president to be responsible for the September 11th attacks.

The AUMF, which as of the date of publication of this text remains in force, serves as an explicit invocation of the war powers vested by the Constitution in the Congress. Although Article I, Section 8 of the Constitution vests Congress with the power to declare war and grant letters of marque and reprisal, joint resolutions authorizing the use of military forces have become the contemporary method used by Congress to exercise its war authorization power.[24] Since the end of the Second World War similar joint

---

[22] AUMF, *supra* note 18.

[23] *Id.* Sec. 2(a)

[24] *See* David Ackerman, Cong. Res. Serv., Response to Terrorism: Legal Aspects of the Use of Military Force (Rpt. RS 21009) 1 (Sept. 13, 2001), *available at* http://fpc.state.gov/documents/organization/6217.pdf.

resolutions have been used by Congress to provide express legislative support for the conflict in Vietnam, both conflicts in Iraq, and even contentious peacekeeping missions in Lebanon and Somalia. Furthermore, Congress is fully aware that these joint resolutions authorizing the use of military force are considered functional equivalents of declarations of war for purposes of determining the constitutional authority of the president to wage war. In fact, even the War Powers Act, a law passed at the height of congressional assertiveness of its war authorization role, explicitly provides in Section 1541(c)(2) that a statutory authorization (which will normally take the form of a joint resolution) fully satisfies the constitutional requirement of legislative authorization for the president to wage war.[25] This has also been an interpretation of the constitutional effect of statutory authorizations to wage war that has been consistently embraced by the judiciary.[26]

The AUMF reflects the congressional decision to invoke the broadest possible legal basis for military action directed against al-Qaeda and its State sponsors. Within the AUMF, Congress indicated that a military response to the terrorist attacks was justified both as an act of self-defense and pursuant to the authorization itself. This was somewhat confusing because, assuming a military response was a legitimate act of self-defense, no express statutory authorization would be necessary to conduct a response from a constitutional perspective. In the *Prize Cases*, the Supreme Court established what has become a well-accepted precedent that when war is thrust upon the nation the president is not only authorized but obligated to meet force with force.[27] In light of this, it is likely Congress sought to indicate in the strongest terms its express support for the continuing prosecution of a war initiated pursuant to the president's inherent authority to defend the United States with the full employment of military capability to achieve the national security objectives defined by the president.[28] Two things are certain: first, there can be no doubt that since the date the AUMF was enacted, both President Bush and President Obama have exercised war powers pursuant to the collective war-making authority vested in the two political branches of the national government. Second, this collective war-making effort was and remains in direct response to the perceived ongoing threat presented to the nation by transnational terrorism.

During the initial phases of the military operations launched against the terrorist threat in Afghanistan, there was some uncertainty as to whether the United States

---

[25] *See* War Powers Resolution, 50 U.S.C. §§ 1541–1548.

[26] *See* Orlando v. Laird, 443 F.2d 1039, 1042–43 (2d Cir. 1971); Holtzman v. Schlesinger, 484 F.2d 1307, 1313 (2d Cir. 1973).

[27] The Brig Amy Warwick (The Prize Cases), 67 U.S. (2 Black) 635, 668 (1862).

[28] Indicating that the military response was a justified act of self-defense seems to have also been intended by Congress to link this statutory authorization for the conduct of hostilities against al-Qaeda to the international legal framework for the use of force. By invoking the right of self-defense and referencing article 51 of the United Nations charter, Congress was signaling its belief that military action directed against transnational terrorism was a proper exercise of the inherent right of self-defense enshrined in the United Nations charter.

considered itself in an armed conflict with the terrorist entity al-Qaeda or, in the alternative, the State of Afghanistan with operations directed against al-Qaeda merely subsidiary to that conflict. In fact, since the inception of these military operations, many experts have taken the position that it is impossible for the United States to be engaged in armed conflict with a transnational nonstate entity, and that the struggle against al-Qaeda must be subordinated to the broader armed conflict in Afghanistan (initially between United States and the government of Afghanistan, and subsequently between U.S. forces operating in support of the legitimate Afghan government against a variety of dissident forces in that country).[29]

From an international law perspective, it was almost inevitable that the U.S. theory of a global armed conflict against terrorism would be rejected in light of the prevailing restrictive interpretation of the scope of the armed conflict. As will be explained in more detail below, international law—and specifically the law of armed conflict—had not contemplated the possibility of what the United States characterizes as a global war on terror or a noninternational armed conflict of global scope. Accordingly, in an effort to characterize the nature of the military operations launched by the United States in a manner that was consistent with the then existing understandings of international law related to the use of force, many experts rejected the suggestion that the United States was engaged in a distinct, global armed conflict with al-Qaeda, concluding that the use of LOAC authority against al-Qaeda must be confined to armed conflicts in Afghanistan and Iraq.[30]

It seems clear, however, that the United States viewed its post–September 11th military response to terrorism as involving two distinct armed conflicts: one against the Taliban regime of Afghanistan in response to its support for al-Qaeda, and the other against al-Qaeda itself. This bifurcated conflict policy was implicit in the global war terminology consistently invoked by the Bush administration.[31] While certainly authorizing military action against the Taliban regime, it was also implicit in the terms of the AUMF that authorized hostilities were not limited to those directed against the Taliban. This implicitly broader scope of authority has also been manifested in post–September 11th

---

[29] *See* Int'l Law Assoc., Use of Force Committee, Final Report on the Meaning of Armed Conflict in International Law 25–28 (2010), *available at* http://www.ila-hq.org/en/committees/index.cfm/cid/1022 [hereinafter ILA Report]. *See also* Mary Ellen O'Connell, *Defining Armed Conflict*, 13 J. Conflict & Sec. L. 393 (2008); Gabor Rona, *Interesting Times for International Humanitarian Law: Challenges from the "War on Terror,"* 27 Fletcher Forum of World Aff., Summer/Fall 2003, at 55, *available at* http://www.icrc.org/eng/assets/files/other/rona_terror.pdf.

[30] Presentation, Gabor Rona, Legal Adviser at the ICRC's Legal Division, *When Is a War Not a War?—The Proper Role of the Law of Armed Conflict in the "Global War on Terror,"* "International Action to Prevent and Combat Terrorism"—Workshop on the Protection of Human Rights while Countering Terrorism, Copenhagen (March 15–16, 2004) [hereinafter *When Is a War Not a War?*], *available at* http://www.icrc.org/eng/resources/documents/misc/5xcmnj.htm.

[31] *See* Geoffrey S. Corn, *Making the Case for Conflict Bifurcation in Afghanistan: Transnational Armed Conflict, Al Qaida, and the Limits of the Associated Militia Concept, in* U.S. Naval War College, Int'l Law Studies, The War in Afghanistan: A Legal Analysis (Michael N. Schmitt ed., 2009) (republished in the Israeli Yearbook of Human Rights).

U.S. counter-terror military operations, many of which have been conducted outside Afghanistan and directed against al-Qaeda and associated forces.

One such attack—a drone attack conducted against suspected al-Qaeda operatives in Yemen[32]—generated an exchange between the United Nations Human Rights Commission and the U.S. representative to the Commission that led to an explicit enunciation of the U.S. view of the struggle against al-Qaeda. In response to the drone attack, the Commission queried the United States on how the killing could be justified pursuant to international human rights law. In response, the U.S. representative indicated that the Commission lacked jurisdiction over the matter because the action fell under the regulatory framework of the law of armed conflict rather than human rights law. The response reiterated the position taken by President Bush in Military Order No. 1:

> International terrorists, including members of Al Qaida, have carried out attacks on United States diplomatic and military personnel and facilities abroad and on citizens and property within the United States on a scale that has created a state of armed conflict that requires the use of the United States Armed Forces.[33]

The notable absence of any linkage to the armed conflict with Afghanistan in this response was an early and explicit indication that the United States considered itself engaged in an armed conflict of potentially global scope with al-Qaeda.

Members of the Obama administration publicly addressed the specifics of these drone attacks, which they used as a platform to express the justification for the United States' borderless war against al-Qaeda. Attorney General Eric Holder was very direct in recognizing the United States' transnational armed conflict:

> Our legal authority is not limited to the battlefields in Afghanistan. Indeed, neither Congress nor our federal courts has limited the geographic scope of our ability to use force to the current conflict in Afghanistan. We are at war with a stateless enemy, prone to shifting operations from country to country. Over the last three years alone, al Qaeda and its associates have directed several attacks...against us from countries other than Afghanistan.[34]

As indicated in this excerpt, Holder drew attention to the fact that the other two branches of government have not attempted to prohibit or even curtail the executive

---

[32] *See* Dana Priest, *CIA Killed U.S. Citizen in Yemen Missile Strike: Action's Legality, Effectiveness Questioned*, WASH. POST, Nov. 8, 2002, *available at* http://www.commondreams.org/headlines02/1108-05.htm.

[33] *Civil and Political Rights, Including the Questions of: Disappearances and Summary Executions*, U.N. Econ. & Soc. Council, Comm'n on Human Rights, 59th Sess., at 3, U.N. Doc. E/CN.4/2003/G/80 (2003) (response of the United States quoting Military Order No. 1).

[34] Eric Holder, U.S. Att'y Gen., Address at Northwestern University School of Law, (Mar. 5, 2012), *available at* http://www.justice.gov/iso/opa/ag/speeches/2012/ag-speech-1203051.html.

branch's transnational operations against al-Qaeda, indicating at the very least a form of tacit approval.[35]

In a subsequent speech, John Brennan, Assistant to the President for Homeland Security, built upon Attorney General Holder's speech by specifying the different regions where al-Qaeda and its suspected affiliates operated—Somalia, Yemen, North/West Africa, and Nigeria—thus demonstrating how geographically expansive the terrorist network was and more importantly underscoring the United States' determination and intent to engage al-Qaeda wherever they may exist.[36] Notably, the operations targeting al-Qaeda leadership were paralleled with that of similar operations during World War II, hence equating and framing the United States' efforts in terms of an internationally recognized expansive armed conflict.[37] To fortify the United States' use of drones, the Obama administration spoke of the United States' adherence to the legal principles of war, the minimization of civilian casualties, and the advantages of a reduced intrusive military presence, but this also highlighted that the United States has no intention of limiting or stopping its ongoing conflict with al-Qaeda due to geographic constraints.[38]

Because other countries are on the verge of implementing similar technology, the administration also cautioned that the United States needed to be the standard-bearer in the international community as opposed to other less responsible nations.[39] If true and it came to fruition that other nations are poised to use this sort of technology for their own transnational conflicts, this could signal the beginning of a new phase in armed conflicts globally.

A more recent indication of this transnational armed conflict position is contained in the Obama administration's reply brief to the ongoing Guantanamo litigation it inherited from the Bush administration. In support of its position that preventive detention of terrorist operatives at Guantanamo remains justified pursuant to the law of armed conflict, the government noted:

> The laws of war have evolved primarily in the context of international armed conflicts between the armed forces of nation states. This body of law, however, is less well-codified with respect to our current, novel type of armed conflict against armed groups such as al Qaida and the Taliban.[40]

---

[35] *Id.*

[36] John O. Brennan, Ass't to the Pres. for Homeland Security and Counterterrorism, *The Ethics and Efficacy of the President's Counterterrorism Strategy* (Apr. 30, 2012), http://www.wilsoncenter.org/event/the-efficacy-and-ethics-us-counterterrorism-strategy.

[37] *Id.*

[38] *Id.*

[39] *Id.*

[40] Respondent's Memorandum Regarding the Government's Detention Authority Relative to Detainees Held at Guantanamo Bay, In re Guantanamo Bay Detainee Litigation, Misc. No. 08-442 (TFH) at 1 (D.D.C. Mar. 13, 2009), *available at* http://www.justice.gov/opa/documents/memo-re-det-auth.pdf.

It is therefore difficult to dispute the conclusion that both the president and Congress adopted a fundamentally different approach to the use of military power to defend the nation against transnational terrorism in the wake of the September 11th attacks. Subsequent decisions by the Supreme Court would complete the trilogy of tri-branch endorsement of an armed conflict characterization of this struggle.

Understanding the Triggering Mechanism for Application of the Law of Armed Conflict[41]

To understand why characterizing the struggle against al-Qaeda as an armed conflict sparked such controversy requires an understanding of the generally accepted Geneva Conventions–based law-triggering standard. This standard is based on common articles 2 and 3 of the four Geneva Conventions. Common article 2 defines the triggering event for application of the full corpus of the LOAC—international armed conflict.[42] Common article 3, in contrast, provides that the basic principle of humane treatment is applicable in noninternational armed conflicts occurring in the territory of a signatory State.[43] Although neither of these treaty provisions explicitly indicates that they serve as the exclusive trigger for LOAC applicability, they rapidly evolved to have such an effect.[44] As a result, these two treaty provisions have been long understood as establishing the definitive LOAC-triggering paradigm. In accordance with this paradigm,

---

[41] This section, with light edits, is based on Geoffrey S. Corn, Hamdan, *Lebanon, and the Regulation of Armed Conflict: The Need to Recognize a Hybrid Category of Armed Conflict*, 40 VAND. J. TRANSNAT'L L. 295 (2006).

[42] *See* GWS, art. 2; GWS-Sea, art. 2; GPW, art. 2; GCIV art. 2. Each of these Conventions includes the following identical common article 2:

> In addition to the provisions which shall be implemented in peacetime, the present Convention shall apply to all cases of declared war or of any other armed conflict which may arise between two or more of the High Contracting Parties, even if the state of war is not recognized by one of them. The Convention shall also apply to all cases of partial or total occupation of the territory of a High Contracting Party, even if the said occupation meets with no armed resistance.

[43] *See* GWS, art. 3; GWS-Sea, art. 3; GPW, art. 3; GCIV, art. 3. Each of these Conventions includes the following identical language in the following identical common article 3:

> In the case of armed conflict not of an international character occurring in the territory of one of the High Contracting Parties, each Party to the conflict shall be bound to apply, as a minimum, the following provisions:
> (1) Persons taking no active part in the hostilities, including members of armed forces who have laid down their arms and those placed "hors de combat" by sickness, wounds, detention, or any other cause, shall in all circumstances be treated humanely, without any adverse distinction founded on race, colour, religion or faith, sex, birth or wealth, or any other similar criteria.

[44] *See* 2000 LAW OF WAR DESKBOOK, *supra* note 3, 28–31 (2000); *see also* U.K. MINISTRY OF DEFENCE, MANUAL OF THE LAW OF ARMED CONFLICT (2004), at paras. 3.1–3.5 [hereinafter U.K. MANUAL]; ICRC Fact Sheet, *supra* note 3.

application of the LOAC has always been contingent on two fundamental factors: first, the existence of armed conflict, and second, the nature of the armed conflict.[45]

The first of these triggering requirements is the existence of an armed conflict. Although this is the most fundamental requirement for application of the LOAC, there is no definitive test for assessing when a situation amounts to an armed conflict (a term undefined by the express language of either common articles 2 or 3). However, the International Committee of the Red Cross (ICRC) Commentaries to these articles, widely considered as an authoritative interpretation of the Conventions, have traditionally been relied on to illuminate the meaning of armed conflict.[46] Widely regarded as the most authoritative and effective criteria for making such a determination, the Commentaries provide several factors for assessing the existence of armed conflict.[47]

When two or more States' armed forces engage in armed conflict, this use of force makes the determination fairly straightforward. Two principal concerns motivated the adoption of the armed conflict trigger vis-á-vis inter-state conflict. The two concerns indicated by the Commentaries were (1) that States would attempt to avoid the law by refusing to acknowledge a state of war, and (2) that parties would deny LOAC humanitarian protections due to the brevity/lack of intensity of such hostilities.[48] Both of these concerns grew out of the pre-1949 experience. With regard to the first concern, the very term "armed conflict" was adopted as a trigger for LOAC applicability for the specific purpose of emphasizing that such application must be triggered by de facto hostilities and not de jure war.[49] As for the second concern, the Commentaries emphasize that the existence of international armed conflict is in no way affected by the scope, duration, or intensity of hostilities. Instead, the term "armed conflict" was intended to apply to de facto hostilities no matter how brief or nondestructive they might be.[50] When such hostilities

---

[45] *See* INT'L & OPERATIONAL LAW DEP'T, THE JUDGE ADVOCATE GENERAL'S LEGAL CENTER & SCHOOL, LAW OF WAR DESKBOOK 23–28 (2011), *available at* http://www.fas.org/irp/doddir/army/deskbook.pdf [hereinafter 2011 LAW OF WAR DESKBOOK].

[46] *See* GWS COMMENTARY at 19–23. A Commentary was published by the ICRC for each of the four Geneva Conventions. However, because articles 2 and 3 are identical—or *common*—to each Convention, the explanation of these articles is substantively identical in each of the four Commentaries.

[47] *See* 2000 LAW OF WAR DESKBOOK, *supra* note 3, at 25–34. The International Criminal Tribunal for the Former Yugoslavia, while not explicitly relying on these criteria, nonetheless followed the general logic reflected therein when it determined in the first opinion addressing the jurisdiction of the Tribunal that "an armed conflict exists whenever there is a resort to armed force between States or protracted armed violence between governmental authorities and organized armed groups or between such groups within a State." *See also Prosecutor v. Tadic*, Case No. IT-94-1, Decision on the Defence Motion for Interlocutory Appeal on Jurisdiction (Appeals Chamber, Int'l Crim. Trib. for the Former Yugoslavia Oct. 2, 1995), *available at* http://www.icty.org/x/cases/tadic/acdec/en/51002.htm [hereinafter Tadic Jurisdiction Decision].

[48] *See, e.g.,* GWS COMMENTARY at 32 ("It makes no difference how long the conflict lasts, or how much slaughter takes place. The respect due to human personality is not measured by the number of victims.")

[49] *Id.*

[50] *Id.*

occurred between the regular armed forces of two States, the armed conflict prong of the triggering test for LOAC application would be satisfied.[51]

Determining the meaning of armed conflict in the noninternational context has been more difficult. The key concern addressed by the ICRC Commentaries in relation to this context was identifying the line between internal civil disturbances (situations subject to domestic legal regimes) and internal armed conflicts (situations triggering application of the humane treatment obligation of common article 3 to the four Geneva Conventions).[52] As the Commentaries emphasize, there is no single factor that establishes this demarcation line. Instead, a number of factors, when considered in any combination or even individually, were proposed to assess when a situation rises above the level of internal disturbance and moves into the realm of armed conflict.[53] Of the numerous factors offered by the Commentaries, perhaps the most instructive is the State response to the threat: when a State resorts to the use of regular (and by regular it is fair to presume that the Commentary refers to combat) armed forces, the situation has most likely crossed the threshold into the realm of armed conflict.[54]

Although applying this prong of the common article 2/3 conflict classification paradigm has not been without controversy, the ICRC Commentaries' criteria have proved remarkably effective in practice. For example, short duration/small scale hostilities between States have been treated as falling into the category of armed conflict, such as when U.S. Navy pilot Lieutenant Bobby Goodman was shot down by Syrian forces while flying a mission in relation to the U.S. peacekeeping presence in Lebanon in 1982.[55]

Even in the noninternational context, it is difficult for a State to credibly disavow the existence of armed conflict when it resorts to the use of regular armed forces for sustained operations against internal dissident groups that cannot be suppressed with only law enforcement capabilities.

---

[51] An example of this application concept was the capture of U.S. Army personnel by Serbia after they had strayed across the Macedonia/Serbia border while participating in a U.N.-authorized peacekeeping mission in Macedonia. Although neither the United States nor Serbia asserted a state of war existed, and although the confrontation between the U.S. forces and Serbian armed forces was brief and involved very little violence, the United States asserted the three soldiers were prisoners of war protected by the GPW because the confrontation in which they were captured qualified as an international armed conflict. *See* Geoffrey S. Corn, *To Be or Not to Be, That Is the Question: Contemporary Military Operations and the Status of Captured Personnel*, 1999 ARMY LAW. 1, 17 (1999) (cited in JENNIFER K. ELSEA, CONG. RES. SERV., TREATMENT OF "BATTLEFIELD DETAINEES" IN THE WAR ON TERRORISM (Rpt. RL31367) (2007), *available at* http://www.fas.org/sgp/crs/terror/RL31367.pdf).

[52] *See, e.g.,* GWS COMMENTARY at 49–50.

[53] *Id.*

[54] *Id.*

[55] Interview W. Hays Parks, a senior attorney for the Defense Department and recognized expert on the law of armed conflict. Mr. Parks was personally involved in developing the United States' position on the status of Lieutenant Goodman and indicated during the interview that the United States asserted prisoner-of-war status for Goodman as a matter of law due to the existence of an "armed conflict" between the United States and Syria within the meaning of common article 2.

This is not, however, the exclusive analytical aspect of the common article 2/3 law-triggering standard. It is the second consideration of this standard—the nature of the armed conflict—that links the extent of LOAC application to the character (international or noninternational) of a given armed conflict. As noted above, pursuant to the structure of the Geneva Conventions, international armed conflicts within the meaning of common article 2 trigger the full corpus of LOAC regulation.[56] In contrast, noninternational armed conflicts trigger a less comprehensive body of regulation: the humane treatment mandate of common article 3; in certain situations, the rules of Additional Protocol II to the Geneva Conventions; and customary LOAC norms applicable to all armed conflicts.[57]

Because there is no defined meaning of "international" or "noninternational" in articles 2 or 3, uncertainty continues in relation to application of this prong of the LOAC trigger.[58] As a result, reliance on the ICRC Commentaries is common when seeking to provide meaning to these terms. With regard to international armed conflict, the Commentary makes the existence of a dispute between States that leads to the intervention of armed forces the dispositive consideration.[59] Although this has been a generally effective de facto criterion, it has not eliminated all uncertainty related to when the use of armed force by one State in the territory of another State is the product of such a dispute (thereby triggering the law applicable to international armed conflicts). Such uncertainty emerges when the intervening State disavows the existence of a dispute between it and the other State as the predicate for the intervention.[60]

This "hostilities without dispute" theory was clearly manifest in the 2006 armed conflict in Lebanon, where neither Israel nor Lebanon took the position that the hostilities fell into the category of international armed conflict.[61] However, this was not the first example of use of such a theory. In fact, the U.S. intervention in Panama in 1989 represents perhaps the quintessential example of this theory of "applicability avoidance" due to the absence of the requisite dispute between nations. Executed to remove General

---

[56] *See, e.g.,* U.K. MANUAL, *supra* note 44, para. 2.1; *see also* 2000 LAW OF WAR DESKBOOK, *supra* note 3, at 25–34.

[57] *See* LESLIE C. GREEN, THE CONTEMPORARY LAW OF ARMED CONFLICT 59–61 (2d ed. 2000) [hereinafter GREEN]; *see also* 2011 LAW OF WAR DESKBOOK, *supra* note 45, at 19–28.

[58] Natasha Balendra, *Defining Armed Conflict*, 29 CARDOZO L. REV. 2461, 2463 (2008). *See generally Counter-Terrorism, Armed Force and the Laws of War, supra* note 1, at 44; *Trying Terrorists, supra* note 6 (analyzing whether the attacks of September 11, 2001, triggered the law of war).

[59] *See* GWS COMMENTARY.

[60] *See, e.g.,* United States v. Noriega, 808 F. Supp. 791, 794–95 (S.D. Fla. 1992) (addressing and rejecting the U.S. assertion that the intervention in Panama to topple General Noriega did not qualify as an international armed conflict).

[61] *See* Pierre Tristam, *The 2006 Lebanon War: Israel and Hezbollah Square Off,* ABOUT.COM, http://middleast.about.com/od/lebanon/a/me070918.htm, (last visited June 25, 2014); *see also* Press Release, Security Council, Security Council Calls for an End to Hostilities between Hizbollah, Israel, Unanimously Adopting Resolution 1701, U.N. Press Release SC/8808, (11 Aug 2006), http://www.un.org/News/Press/docs/2006/sc8808.doc.htm (indicating that Hezbollah and not Lebanon was responsible for the attacks).

Manuel Noriega from power in Panama and destroy the Panamanian Defense Force (the regular armed forces of Panama),[62] "Operation Just Cause" involved the use of more than 20,000 U.S. forces who engaged in intense combat with the Panamanian Defense Forces.[63] The United States asserted that the conflict did not qualify as an international armed conflict within the meaning of common article 2.[64] The basis for this assertion was that General Noriega was not the legitimate leader of Panama; therefore, the U.S. dispute with him did not qualify as a dispute with Panama. Although the U.S. federal district court that adjudicated Noriega's claim to prisoner-of-war status ultimately rejected this assertion,[65] it is not the only example of the emphasis on a lack of a dispute between States as a basis for denying the existence of a common article 2 conflict.[66]

Thus, despite the best efforts of the drafters of the Geneva Conventions by adopting a de facto standard for determining the existence of international armed conflicts so as to prevent law avoidance, uncertainty in coverage has remained problematic. However, this aspect of determining LOAC applicability has had virtually no impact on analysis of conflicts such as those between States and nonstate groups (such as terrorist organizations). This is because there is no plausible basis to conclude that such combat operations, although manifesting all the classic indicia of armed conflicts, involve disputes between States. Instead, it is the uncertainty related to whether the transnational geographic scope of operations excludes them from the definition of noninternational—with the accordant uncertainty as to what law such combat operations trigger—that has generated the greatest regulatory challenge in relation to combat operations against terrorist operatives.

The inclusion of common article 3 in the revision of the Geneva Conventions in 1949 represented the first interjection by treaty of international humanitarian regulation into the realm of noninternational armed conflicts.[67] This was without question a

---

[62] THOMAS DONNELLY, MARGARET ROTH & CALEB BAKER, OPERATION JUST CAUSE: THE STORMING OF PANAMA (1991).

[63] Id.

[64] See Noriega, 808 F. Supp. at 794–95.

[65] Id.

[66] A similar rationale was relied upon to conclude that combat operations conducted by U.S. forces in Somalia during Operation Provide Comfort did not result in an international armed conflict. See generally MAJ Timothy Bulman, A Dangerous Guessing Game Disguised as Enlightened Policy: United States Law of War Obligations during Military Operations Other than War, 159 MIL. L. REV. 152, 168–69 (1999).

[67] See GWS COMMENTARY at 38. According to the Commentary:

This Article is common to all four of the Geneva Conventions of 1949, and is one of their most important Articles. It marks a new step forward in the unceasing development of the idea on which the Red Cross is based, and in the embodiment of that idea in the form of international obligations. It is an almost unhoped for extension of Article 2 above.

Born on the battlefield, the Red Cross called into being the First Geneva Convention to protect wounded or sick military personnel. Extending its solicitude little by little to other categories of war victims, in logical application of its fundamental principle, it pointed the way, first to the revision of the original Convention, and then to the extension of legal protection in turn to prisoners of war and

landmark development in the regulation of hostilities. It is undeniable that the scope of the obligation imposed by common article 3 was minimal and in fact essentially redundant with peacetime human rights principles.[68] Nonetheless, because the conflicts subject to this provision of international law fell within what was at that time regarded as the exclusive realm of State sovereignty, the development was regarded as a major step forward in humanitarian regulation of conflict.[69]

The first step in understanding this component of the LOAC application equation is to understand the origins of common article 3. In response primarily to the brutal civil wars that ravaged Spain, Russia, and other States during the years between the two world wars, the trigger for application of this baseline humanitarian provision has historically been understood to include only one type of noninternational armed conflict: internal (or intra-state).[70] Accordingly, during the five-plus decades between 1949 and 2001, the term "noninternational" was accepted as synonymous with "internal." This most likely can be attributed to a combination of two factors: the original motivation leading to the development of common article 3 (the concern over civil wars) and the qualifying language indicating that common article 3 applies only to noninternational armed conflicts occurring within the territory of a High Contracting Party.[71] Although this "within the territory" qualifier became increasingly less meaningful as the Geneva Conventions progressed rapidly toward their current status of universal participation, it is difficult to ignore the logical impact of this term in the context of 1949—it limited the scope of application of this "mini convention" to true intra-state conflicts.[72] However, nowhere

---

civilians. The same logical process could not fail to lead to the idea of applying the principle to all cases of armed conflicts, including those of an internal character.

Id.

[68] *Id.* at 48.

[69] *See* AP COMMENTARY at 1324 (describing common article 3 as "the first major achievement with regard to this law [of noninternational armed conflict].").

[70] *See, e.g.,* U.K. MANUAL, *supra* note 44, para. 2.1; *see also* 2000 LAW OF WAR DESKBOOK, *supra* note 3, at 25–34.

[71] *See* U.K. MANUAL, *supra* note 44, para. 2.1.

[72] This point was relied upon by the Department of Justice's Office of Legal Counsel in the first law of war applicability analysis provided to the president after the attacks of September 11, 2001:

Common article 3 complements Common Article 2. Article 2 applies to cases of declared war or of any other armed conflict that may arise between two or more of the High Contracting Parties, even if the state of war is not recognized by one of them. Common article 3, however, covers "armed conflict not of an international character"—a war that does not involve cross-border attacks—that occurs within the territory of one of the High Contracting Parties.

Common article 3's text provides substantial reason to think that it refers specifically to a condition of civil war, or a large-scale armed conflict between a State and an armed movement within its own territory. First, the test of the provision refers specifically to an armed conflict that a) is not of an international character, and b) occurs in the territory of a state party to the Convention. It does not sweep in all armed conflicts, nor does it address a gap left by Common article 2 for international armed conflicts that involve non-state entities (such as an international terrorist organization) as parties to the conflict. Further, Common article 3 addresses only non-international armed conflicts that

does the article expressly use "internal" as the indicator of the type of armed conflict triggering its humanitarian mandate. Instead, common article 3 expressly indicates that its substantive protections are applicable to all conflicts "not of an international character."[73]

This original understanding of common article 3, coupled with the reality that the vast majority of noninternational armed conflicts between 1949 and 2001 were intra-state, resulted in an "either/or" LOAC-triggering paradigm. Armed conflicts falling under the definition of "international" within the meaning of common article 2 of the Geneva Conventions would trigger the entire corpus of the LOAC. In contrast, intra-state or internal armed conflicts—those between a State and internal dissident forces—would trigger a far more limited corpus of LOAC regulation, including common article 3.[74] This paradigm is reflected in the following excerpt from a presentation by the ICRC Legal Adviser:

> Humanitarian law recognizes two categories of armed conflict—international and non-international. Generally, when a State resorts to force against another State (for example, when the "war on terror" involves such use of force, as in the recent U.S. and allied invasion of Afghanistan), the international law of international armed conflict applies. When the "war on terror" amounts to the use of armed force within a State, between that State and a rebel group, or between rebel groups within the State, the situation may amount to non-international armed conflict....[75]

This excerpt illustrates the traditional interpretation of the situations that trigger LOAC application. According to this interpretation, there are only two possible characterizations for military activities conducted against transnational terrorist groups: international armed conflict (when the operations are conducted outside the territory of the State) or noninternational armed conflict (limited to operations conducted within the territory of the State).

Unfortunately, this "either/or" triggering paradigm failed to account for the possibility that an extraterritorial combat operation against a nonstate armed group launched by a State using regular armed forces could qualify as an armed conflict triggering LOAC regulation. Such an operation would fail to satisfy the requisite dispute between States

---

occur within the territory of a single state party, again, like a civil war. This provision would not reach an armed conflict in which one of the parties operated from multiple bases in several different states.

Bybee Memorandum, *supra* note 10, at 6.

[73] *See, e.g.*, GWS art. 3.

[74] *See, e.g.*, U.K. MANUAL, *supra* note 44, para. 2.1; *see also* 2000 LAW OF WAR DESKBOOK, *supra* note 3, at 25–34.

[75] *See When Is a War Not a War?, supra* note 30.

necessary to qualify as an international armed conflict within the meaning of common article 2. However, based on the traditional understanding of noninternational armed conflict—an understanding shared by virtually all scholars and practitioners prior to the U.S. military response to the terrorist attacks of September 11th—the possibility that an armed conflict falling somewhere between an internal armed conflict and an inter-state armed conflict could theoretically be subject to the LOAC was necessarily excluded. Accordingly, these "transnational" armed conflicts fell into a regulatory gap—a gap necessitating application of regulation by way of policy mandate.

Both the military component of the U.S. fight against al-Qaeda and the 2006 conflict between Israel and Hezbollah have strained the "either/or" LOAC application paradigm.[76] While this strain has produced international and national uncertainty as to the law that applies to such conflicts, it has also provided what may actually come to be appreciated as a beneficial reassessment of the trigger for application of the fundamental LOAC principles.[77] In the D.C. Circuit's judgment in *Hamdan v. Rumsfeld*,[78] Judge Williams, in his concurring opinion, articulated the logic motivating this reassessment. In that opinion, he responded to the majority conclusion that common article 3 did not apply to armed conflict with al-Qaeda because the president has determined that this conflict is one of international scope:

> Non-State actors cannot sign an international treaty. Nor is such an actor even a "Power" that would be eligible under Article 2 (¶ 3) to secure protection by complying with the Convention's requirements. Common Article 3 fills the gap, providing some minimal protection for such non-eligibles in an "armed conflict not of an international character occurring in the territory of one of the High Contracting Parties." The gap being filled is the non-eligible party's failure to be a nation. Thus the words "not of an international character" are sensibly understood to refer to a conflict between a signatory nation and a non-State actor. The most obvious form of such a conflict is a civil war. But given the Convention's structure, the logical

---

[76] *See* Kenneth Watkin, *Controlling the Use of Force: A Role for Human Rights Norms in Contemporary Armed Conflict*, 98 Am.J.Int'l. L. 1, 2–8 (2004) (discussing the complex challenge of conflict categorization in relation to military operations conducted against highly organized nonstate groups with transnational reach) [hereinafter *Controlling the Use of Force*]; *see also* Kirby Abbott, *"Terrorists: Criminals, Combatants or….?" The Question of Combatancy, in* The Measures of International Law: Effectiveness, Fairness and Validity (Proceedings of the Annual Conference of the Canadian Council on International Law) 366 (2004) [hereinafter *Terrorists: Criminals, Combatants*]; *Trying Terrorists, supra* note 6.

[77] Matthew Waxman, *The Structure of Terrorism Threats and the Laws of War*, 20 Duke J. Comp. & Int'l L. 429, 431 (2010); *see generally* Human Rights Council, *Report of the Commission of Inquiry on Lebanon*, U.N. Doc. A/HRC/3/2 (Nov. 23, 2006), *available at* http://www.refworld.org/docid/45c30b6e0.html; Memorandum from President George W. Bush for Vice President et al, Subject: Humane Treatment of al Qaeda and Taliban Detainees (Feb. 7, 2002), *available at* http://www.washingtonpost.com/wp-srv/nation/documents/020702bush.pdf [hereinafter President Bush Feb. 2002 Memorandum].

[78] Hamdan v. Rumsfeld, 415 F. 3d 33 (D.C. Cir. 2005), *rev'd,* 548 U.S. 557 (2006).

reading of "international character" is one that matches the basic derivation of the word "international," i.e., *between nations*. Thus, I think the context compels the view that a conflict between a signatory and a non-State actor is a conflict "not of an international character." In such a conflict, the signatory is bound to Common Article 3's modest requirements of "humane" treatment and "the judicial guarantees which are recognized as indispensable by civilized peoples."[79]

Although the logic expressed by Judge Williams seemed pragmatically compelling, the fact remains that he was unable to convince his peers to adopt this interpretation. This reflected the pervasive impact of common articles 2 and 3—and the legal paradigm they spawned—on conflict regulation analysis. But, as Judge Williams recognized, it is fundamentally inconsistent with the logic of the LOAC to detach the applicability of regulation from the necessity for regulation. What was needed was a pragmatic reconciliation of these two considerations.

Employing National Combat Power to Engage Transnational Nonstate Actors: Exposing the Limits of Policy-Based Regulation of Armed Conflict

Ironically, despite the effort to reject a hyper-technical LOAC application trigger,[80] the common article 2/3 LOAC-triggering paradigm (i.e., the "international/internal" focus) that evolved after 1949 did not eliminate this handicap. Nonetheless, prior to 9/11, few scholars or practitioners questioned this paradigm.[81] Instead, it was almost universally regarded as the definitive standard for determining LOAC applicability.[82] The large-scale combat operations the United States conducted with "global scope" to engage and destroy al-Qaeda military capabilities following September 11th stressed this paradigm as never before,[83] and it exposed that it was too restrictive to cover this new category of armed conflict between State armed forces and transnational nonstate military entities.[84]

---

[79] *Id.* at 44 (Williams, J. concurring).

[80] *See* GWS COMMENTARY at 32–33.

[81] *See generally Counter-terrorism, Armed Force and the Laws of War, supra* note 1.

[82] *See* 2000 LAW OF WAR DESKBOOK, *supra* note 3, at 25–34; *see* GREEN, *supra* note 57, *at* 54–61.

[83] *See Controlling the Use of Force, supra* note 76, at 3–4 (discussing the complex challenge of conflict categorization in relation to military operations conducted against highly organized nonstate groups with transnational reach); *see also Terrorists: Criminals, Combatants, supra* note 76, at 366; *Trying Terrorists, supra* note 6, at 10–14 (analyzing whether the attacks of September 11, 2001, triggered the law of war).

[84] *See* Rosa Brooks, *War Everywhere: Human Rights, National Security, and the Law of Armed Conflict in the Age of Terrorism*, 153 U. PA. L. REV. 675, 715–20 (2004–2005). Professor Brooks proposes an alternate response to this gap in legal regulation—reliance on international human rights law as a regulatory framework:

> As traditional categories lose their logical underpinnings, we are entering a new era: the era of War Everywhere. It is an era in which the legal rules that were designed to protect basic rights and vulnerable groups have lost their analytical force, and thus, too often, their practical force.

Like an operational commander exploiting a seam between the defensive positions of enemy units, during the five years following September 11th, the Bush administration persistently exploited what it identified as the seam in the LOAC triggering equation in order to justify the position that LOAC humanitarian protections applied *as a matter of law* to captured and detained al-Qaeda operatives.[85] While never abandoning the policy commitment to apply LOAC principles at the operational level of command,[86] deviation

---

...

In the long run, the old categories and rules need to be replaced by a radically different system that better reflects the changed nature of twenty-first century conflict and threat. What such a radically different system would look like is difficult to say, and the world community is unlikely to develop a consensus around such a new system anytime soon. This Article suggests, nonetheless, that international human rights law provides some benchmarks for evaluating U.S. government actions in the war on terror[...]

Unlike domestic U.S. law and the law of armed conflict, international human rights law applies to all people at all times, regardless of citizenship, location, and status. Although human rights law permits limited derogation in times of emergency, it also outlines core rights that cannot be eliminated regardless of the nature of the threat or the existence or non-existence of an armed conflict. Applying standards of international human rights law in both domestic and international contexts would not solve all the problems created by the increasing irrelevance of other legal frameworks, but it would provide at least a basic floor, a minimum set of standards by which international and domestic governmental actions could be evaluated.

Id. at 681–82, 684–85.

Although such a concept of conflict regulation might indeed be effective to achieve the concurrent humanitarian objectives of both the law of armed conflict and human rights law, in the opinion of the authors the traditional culture among professional armed forces linking regulation to the laws of war makes this a less feasible response than expanding the triggering criteria for principles of the laws of war. Indeed, the reliance by many armed forces over the past two decades on a policy-based application of these principles instead of reliance on human rights norms as a source of operational regulation in situations of legal uncertainty corroborates the significance of this cultural dynamic, a consideration that seems to be ignored by proponents of a human rights military regulatory framework. Nonetheless, the mere fact that such an alternate regulatory approach is offered supports both the conclusion that the traditional regulatory paradigm is insufficient to meet the requirements of the contemporary battlefield and that some legally based regulatory framework is essential on that battlefield.

[85] *See generally* Bybee Memorandum, *supra* note 10; see also Gonzales Memorandum, *supra* note 11; Donald Rumsfeld, Memorandum for the Chairman of the Joint Chiefs of Staff, Subject: Status of the Taliban and Al Qaida, (Jan. 19, 2002), *available at* http://news.findlaw.com/hdocs/docs/dod/11902mem.pdf. In a message dated January 21, 2002, the Chairman of the Joint Chiefs of Staff notified combatant commanders of the Secretary of Defense's determination. Message from the Chairman of the Joint Chiefs of Staff, Subject: Status of Taliban and Al Qaida (Jan. 21, 2002), *available at*: http://news.findlaw.com/hdocs/docs/dod/12202mem.pdf.; *see also* President Bush Feb. 2002 Memorandum, *supra* note 77 (announcing the president's determination that although the conflict against Afghanistan triggered the Geneva Conventions, captured Taliban forces were not entitled to prisoner-of-war status because they failed to meet the implied requirements imposed by the Convention on members of the regular armed forces).

President Bush's February 2002 determination endorsed the analysis provided by the Office of Legal Counsel of the Department of Justice to the General Counsel of the Department of Defense that reflected a restrictive interpretation of legal applicability of the laws of war. *See* Bybee Memorandum, *supra* note 10.

[86] *See* President Bush Feb. 2002 Memorandum, *supra* note 77. According to this memorandum:

Of course, our values as a nation, values that we share with many nations in the world, call for us to treat detainees humanely, including those who are not legally entitled to such treatment. Our nation

from these principles in relation to al-Qaeda detainees became a focal point for criticism of U.S. policy.[87] This theory that a seam existed in the applicability of LOAC principles in the extraterritorial nonstate context exposed the limits of the common article 2/3 "either/ or" paradigm. The Bush administration's LOAC interpretation that generated this critical reaction focused on two principal factors: the nonstate nature of al-Qaeda and the global nature of the conflict.[88] Al-Qaeda's nonstate character resulted in the legitimate conclusion that the Global War on Terror could not properly be classified as a common article 2 conflict.[89] The second factor led to the more controversial conclusion that the global scope of the conflict excluded it from classification as a common article 3 noninternational armed conflict. According to President Bush:

[C]ommon Article 3 of Geneva does not apply to either al Qaeda or Taliban detainees, because, among other reasons, the relevant conflicts are international in scope and Common Article 3 applies only to "armed conflict not of an international character."[90]

This interpretation is also reflected in the following language from the Department of Justice analysis of LOAC applicability to al-Qaeda and Taliban detainees:

Analysis of the background to the adoption of the Geneva Conventions in 1949 confirms our understanding of Common Article 3. It appears that the drafters of the Conventions had in mind only the two forms of armed conflict that were regarded as a matter of general *international* concern at the time: armed conflict between nation-States (subject to article 2), and large-scale civil war within a nation-State (subject to article 3).

...

If the state parties had intended the Conventions to apply to *all* forms of armed conflict, they could have used broader, clearer language. To interpret Common

---

has been and will continue to be a strong supporter of Geneva and its principles. As a matter of policy, the United States Armed Forces shall continue to treat detainees humanely and, to the extent appropriate and consistent with military necessity, in a manner consistent with the principles of Geneva.

Id. para. 3.

[87] *See, e.g., Trying Terrorists, supra* note 6 (analyzing whether the attacks of September 11, 2001, triggered the law of war). *See also* Human Rights Watch, *U.S. Officials Misstate Geneva Convention Requirements* (Jan. 29, 2002), http://www.hrw.org/en/news/2002/01/28/us-officials-misstate-geneva-convention-requirements; Human Rights Watch, *United Nations Finds That U.S. Has Failed to Comply with International Obligations at Guantanamo Detention Center* (Feb. 16, 2006), http://hrw.org/english/docs/2006/02/16/usdom12833.

[88] Gonzales Memorandum, *supra* note 11 (articulating the basis for the conclusion that al-Qaeda detainees did not fall under either the law triggered by common article 2 or the humane treatment obligation of common article 3).

[89] *Id.*

[90] *See* President Bush Feb. 2002 Memorandum, *supra* note 77.

Article 3 by expanding its scope well beyond the meaning borne by its text is effectively to amend the Geneva Conventions without the approval of the State parties to the treaties.... [G]iving due weight to the state practice and doctrinal understanding of the time, the idea of an armed conflict between a nation-State and a transnational terrorist organization...could not have been within the contemplation of the drafters of Common Article 3.[91]

The accordant denial of the substantive humanitarian protections of common article 3 to detainees subject to trial by military commission led ultimately to the Supreme Court's decision in *Hamdan v. Rumsfeld*.[92] Because Hamdan asserted that the procedures for the military commission established by order of President Bush violated the humane treatment mandate of common article 3, it was necessary for the Court to determine whether armed conflict between the United States and al-Qaeda fell within the scope of noninternational armed conflict within the meaning of that article.[93]

The Supreme Court rejected the Bush administration's interpretation of noninternational armed conflict and held that the substantive protections of common article 3 applied to individuals detained during the course of the noninternational armed conflict in which Hamdan participated.[94] The Court interpreted common article 3 as occupying the field of conflict regulation for any armed conflict not qualifying as an international armed conflict in accordance with common article 2. Thus, the Court endorsed the exact "residual conflict" concept explicitly rejected in the Department of Justice analysis of this treaty provision.[95] According to Justice Stevens's majority opinion:

The Court of Appeals thought, and the Government asserts, that Common Article 3 does not apply to Hamdan because the conflict with al Qaeda, being "international in scope" does not qualify as a "conflict not of an international character."... That reasoning is erroneous. The term "conflict not of an international character" is used here in contradistinction to a conflict between nations. [96]

---

[91] *See* Bybee Memorandum, *supra* note 10.

[92] Hamdan v. Rumsfeld, 548 U.S. 557 (2006).

[93] *Id.* at 628–31.

[94] *Id.* It is likely the Court understood this armed conflict to be one between the United States and al-Qaeda. However, the Court never explicitly endorsed the theory that Hamdan had been captured in the context of a distinct armed conflict between the United States and al-Qaeda. This has led some scholars to assert that the decision merely recognized that a noninternational armed conflict occurred in Afghanistan after the fall of the Taliban regime and that Hamdan had been captured in the context of that armed conflict. However, considering the Court's reliance on the AUMF, a statute that authorized the use of all necessary force against, inter alia, al-Qaeda, coupled with the fact that the U.S. government argued that common article 3 was inapplicable to Hamdan because of his involvement in a distinct armed conflict between the United States and al-Qaeda, it is more likely the Court effectively acknowledged the existence of that distinct armed conflict.

[95] *See* Bybee Memorandum, *supra* note 10.

[96] *Hamdan*, 548 U.S. at 630 (citations omitted).

Ironically, this analysis mirrors the logic that animated Department of Defense policy for decades. However, this was no statement of policy, but instead an enunciation of a legal obligation derived from the Supreme Court's controlling interpretation of a binding treaty.[97] Hailed as "landmark" by some and criticized as invalid by others, the decision resulted in an immediate "about face" by the Department of Defense.[98] On the day of the decision, Under Secretary of Defense Gordon England issued a directive to all branches of the armed forces requiring the humane treatment of all detainees as a matter of legal obligation pursuant to common article 3.[99]

Almost immediately following this decision, the world witnessed five weeks of intense combat operations between the Israeli Defense Forces and the armed component of Hezbollah.[100] The intensity of this conflict, especially the resulting collateral damage inflicted on civilians and civilian property, immediately shifted the international focus of LOAC applicability from the humane treatment principle implicated in the *Hamdan* decision to other core LOAC principles, including distinction, proportionality, and necessity.[101] This conflict and the international response it evoked indicate an obvious reality: the international community expects compliance with these principles during all armed conflicts not merely as a matter of policy but as a matter of legal obligation. In essence, the international reaction to this conflict implicated the same rationale relied on by the Supreme Court in *Hamdan*—all armed conflicts are subject to legal regulation and therefore any conflict not qualified as an international armed conflict is ipso facto a noninternational armed conflict. However, the issues of concern related to the conflict between Israel and Hezbollah indicate that *all* armed conflicts not falling within the scope of common article 2 must trigger not only the humane treatment obligation in common article 3 but *all* foundational LOAC principles.

---

[97] *See* Sanches-Llamas v. Oregon, 548 U.S. 331 (2006). According to Chief Justice Roberts:

> If treaties are to be given effect as federal law, determining their meaning as a matter of federal law "is emphatically the province and duty of the judicial department," headed by the "one supreme Court...."

Id. at 354 (citations omitted).

[98] *See* Marc Goldman, *What the* Hamdan *Ruling Really Meant*, WASH. POST, July 26, 2006, at A16; *see also* Jess Bravin, *Trial and Error: Justices Bar Guantanamo Tribunals—High Court Says President Exceeded War Powers; He May Turn to Congress—Ruling Won't Free Prisoners*, WALL ST. J., June 30, 2006, at A1.

[99] Donna Miles, *England Memo Underscores Policy on Humane Treatment of Detainees*, GLOBALSECURITY. ORG (July 11, 2006), http://www.globalsecurity.org/security/library/news/2006/07/sec-060711-afps01. htm [hereinafter *England Memo Underscores Policy*].

[100] *See* John Ward Anderson & Edward Cody, *Israel Fights to Secure Key Region in Lebanon*, WASH. POST, July 23, 2006, at A01.

[101] *See* Richard Cohen, *No, It's Survival*, WASH. POST, July 25, 2006, at A15. For a discussion of core LOAC principles, *see* A.P.V. ROGERS, LAW ON THE BATTLEFIELD 1–29 (2d ed. 2004).

The combination of these two events—the *Hamdan* decision and the armed conflict in Lebanon—initiated an important evolution—or perhaps re-evaluation—of the legal triggers for application of the LOAC to a noninternational armed conflict. This evolution may indicate an emerging legalization of the policy approach adopted by U.S. armed forces more than two decades ago and relied upon since then to provide a pragmatic response to the problems with the legal paradigms that grew out of the Geneva Conventions. Like the common article 2/3 triggers, the key factor related to the LOAC applicability concept reflected in both the *Hamdan* decision and the reaction to the armed conflict in Lebanon is the de facto existence of armed hostilities. Unlike the common article 2/3 trigger, this new approach is not limited by either the nonstate status of a party to the conflict or the geographic scope of the conflict. Instead, it represents an ipso facto application of humanitarian obligations and core LOAC principles to any situation involving de facto hostilities where at least one of the parties to the conflict is a State.[102]

Although it is reasonable to assert that common article 3's plain meaning indicates it has always served as a trigger for such an expansive scope of LOAC application, as noted above, the "international/internal" armed conflict paradigm that evolved after 1949 became the definitive standard for determining such applicability. This paradigm did not contemplate the modern problem of transnational armed conflicts and it created the perceived necessity of establishing national policies to extend application of core LOAC principles to "all" military operations, no matter how characterized. Because this paradigm made conflict characterization the sine qua non of LOAC applicability, only such a policy extension could satisfy the military need to ensure all operations were subject to this regulatory framework. Absent such a policy, uncertainty as to the nature of a conflict operation would produce uncertainty as to "what rules should apply"—an uncertainty unacceptable from a military efficiency and discipline perspective. Thus, the policy extension is a powerful indication that ipso facto application of these principles to any armed conflict is in fact consistent with the purposes of the LOAC,[103] the needs of military discipline and efficiency, the humanitarian objective of the LOAC treaties

---

[102] *See* Geoffrey S. Corn & Eric Talbot Jensen, *Transnational Armed Conflict: A "Principled" Approach to the Regulation of Counter-Terror Combat Operations*, 42 ISRAEL L. REV. 45, 53–54 (2009).

[103] *See* FM 27-10, para. 3. According to this authoritative Department of the Army statement:

> The conduct of armed hostilities on land is regulated by the law of land warfare which is both written and unwritten. It is inspired by the desire to diminish the evils of war by:
> *a.* Protecting both combatants and noncombatants from unnecessary suffering;
> *b.* Safeguarding certain fundamental human rights of persons who fall into the hands of the enemy, particularly prisoners of war, the wounded and sick, and civilians; and
> *c.* Facilitating the restoration of peace.

Id. para 2.

(which emphasize the significance of underlying principles),[104] and the historical internal disciplinary codes of regular armed forces.[105]

---

[104] GWS COMMENTARY at 19–23. According to this Commentary:

> However carefully the texts were drawn up, and however clearly they were worded, it would not have been possible to expect every soldier and every civilian to know the details of the odd four hundred Articles of the Conventions, and to be able to understand and apply them. Such knowledge as that can be expected only of jurists and military and civilian authorities with special qualifications. But anyone of good faith is capable of applying with approximate accuracy what he is called upon to apply under one or other of the Conventions, provided he is acquainted with the basic principle involved.

Id. at 21.

[105] *See* GREEN, *supra* note 57, at 20–33; *see also* Leslie Green, *What Is—Why Is There—the Law of War, in* THE LAW OF ARMED CONFLICT: INTO THE NEXT MILLENNIUM, 71 U.S. NAVAL WAR COLL. INT'L STUD. 141 (1998), *available at* http://www.usnwc.edu/Research—Gaming/International-Law/Studies-Series/documents/Naval-War-College-vol-71.aspx. [hereinafter *What Is—Why Is There—the Law of War*].

This conclusion is not just reflected in the extension of this regulatory framework by military policy. It is also reflected in the history from which these principles evolved. Throughout the post-Westphalian history of warfare, armed forces complied with such codes. *See* GREEN, *supra* note 57, at 20–33. Because such codes took the form of internal disciplinary mandates, little attention was given to the question of whether they were derived from legal obligation. However, the content of these internal military codes of conduct provided the seeds from which grew the contemporary international legal principles regulating armed conflicts. *See generally What Is—Why Is There—the Law of War*, *supra* note 105; *see also* Thomas C. Wingfield, *Chivalry in the Use of Force*, 32 U. TOL. L. REV. 111, 114 (2001). Thus, although treating application of these principles to any armed conflict as a matter of legal obligation is a significant shift from the pre-2001 legal paradigm, the substantive impact of such application is not only consistent with the practices of many professional armed forces, but also with the historic understanding by armed forces that a battlefield without rules was an anathema to a disciplined force.

Several prominent law-of-war scholars who have written on this subject begin with a discussion of these historical roots to the contemporary legal regime for the regulation of armed conflict. For example, A.P.V. Rogers begins the 1996 edition of his book, LAW ON THE BATTLEFIELD, with the following introduction:

> Writers delve back through the history of centuries to the ancient civilizations of India and Egypt to find in their writings evidence of the practices intended to alleviate the sufferings of war. This evidence is to be found in agreements and treaties, in the works of religious leaders and philosophers, in regulations and articles of war issued by military leaders, and in the rules of chivalry. It is said that the first systematic code of war was that of the Saracens and was based on the Koran. The writers of the Age of Enlightenment, notably Grotius and Vattel, were especially influential. It has been suggested that more humane rules were able to flourish in the period of limited wars from 1648 to 1792 but that they then came under pressure in the drift towards continental warfare, the concept of the nation in arms and the increasing destructiveness of weapons from 1792 to 1914. *So efforts had to be made in the middle of the last century to reimpose on war limits which up to that time had been based on custom and usage.*

A.P.V. ROGERS, LAW ON THE BATTLEFIELD 1 (1996) (emphasis added) (internal citations omitted).

Professor Leslie Green has also written extensively on the historical underpinnings of the laws of war, highlighting the fact that throughout history, military leaders from a wide array of cultures have always imposed limits on the conduct of hostilities by their own forces. *See* GREEN, *supra* note 57, at 20–33; *see also What Is—Why Is There—the Law of War*, *supra* note 105.

Professors Rogers and Green remind readers not only that the regulation of warfare is as ancient as organized warfare itself, but that the logic of such regulation transcends hyper-technical legal paradigms defining what is "war" and when such rules should apply.

The "either/or" law-triggering paradigm may have proved generally sufficient to address the types of armed conflicts occurring up until 9/11. However, this fact no longer justifies the conclusion that no other triggering standard should be recognized. Instead, as the events since 9/11 have illustrated so convincingly, such recognition is essential in order to keep pace with the evolving nature of armed conflicts themselves. The prospect of an unregulated battlefield is simply unacceptable in the international community, a fact demonstrated by the response to the conflict in Lebanon.[106]

The Supreme Court Endorses Armed Conflict against Terrorism?

The Supreme Court decision in *Hamdan v. Rumsfeld* was not the only indication that the Court recognizes the existence of an armed conflict between the United States and al-Qaeda. Both LOAC-based preventive detention and trial by military commission of captured terrorist operatives generated several critical Supreme Court decisions between 2005 and 2009. Subsequent chapters of this text will address in more detail the impact of these decisions on the authority of the government to engage in such practices. What is significant in relation to the foregoing discussion is how these decisions effectively endorsed the armed conflict characterization of the government's counter-terrorism efforts.

The first decision to scrutinize the invocation of wartime authority in relation to the use of military force against al-Qaeda and Taliban enemies was *Hamdi v. Rumsfeld*[107]. Hamdi, a U.S. citizen, had been captured in Afghanistan by the Northern Alliance (the anti-Taliban Afghan forces supported by the United States and other Coalition forces) and turned over to U.S. forces. Based on a determination by the U.S. military that he had been a member of Taliban and/or al-Qaeda forces fighting against Coalition forces, Hamdi was detained and transferred to the recently established detention facility at the U.S. Naval Station in Guantanamo Bay, Cuba. When it was subsequently determined that Hamdi had been born in the United States and was a U.S. citizen and therefore not subject to the Military Order issued by the president authorizing detention of alien enemy combatants at Guantanamo, he was transferred to the U.S. Naval Brig in Charleston, South Carolina. However, the government continued to treat him as an enemy combatant subject to military detention for the duration of hostilities.[108]

---

[106] *See* HUMAN RIGHTS WATCH, *Lebanon/Israel: U.N. Rights Body Squanders Chance to Help Civilians* (Aug. 11, 2006), http://hrw.org/english/docs/2006/08/11/lebano13969_txt.htm (summarizing statements by Louise Arbour, U.N. High Commissioner for Human Rights; *see also* Human Rights Watch, *U.N.: Open Independent Inquiry into Civilian Deaths* (Aug. 7, 2006), http://hrw.org/english/docs/2006/08/08/lebano13939.htm (statements by Kofi Annan).

[107] 542 U.S. 507 (2004).

[108] *Id.* at 510–11.

The legality of Hamdi's detention reached the Supreme Court on a writ of habeas corpus filed by his father on his behalf.[109] The Court concluded that once Hamdi was properly determined to be an enemy belligerent who had engaged in hostilities against U.S. forces in an area of active combat operations, his detention by the military was permitted pursuant to the laws and customs of war.[110] According to the Court, the AUMF enacted by Congress implicitly authorized preventive detention of such enemy belligerents as a necessary incident of successfully waging war.[111] Although the Court did not explicitly invoke the LOAC principle of military necessity, the link between the customary necessities of war and the AUMF indicate that it was the LOAC that led the Court to conclude Hamdi's detention was lawful.[112] Furthermore, although Hamdi had been a member of the Taliban, that fact did not seem particularly significant to the Court. Instead, it was his participation in belligerent conduct against U.S. and Coalition forces that justified his detention pursuant to the LOAC.[113]

The impact of this decision on the development of procedures for determining enemy belligerent status will be addressed in more detail in a subsequent chapter. What is important here is that the Court's opinion was implicitly predicated upon the conclusion that military operations conducted against the individuals, organizations, and States included within the AUMF triggered LOAC rights and obligations. Even Justice Scalia, whose dissenting opinion asserted that as a citizen, Hamdi could not be preventively detained as an enemy belligerent but was instead entitled to criminal process, did not question the validity of invoking an armed conflict paradigm in the struggle against transnational terrorism. Instead, he took the position that U.S. citizens associated with enemy forces during periods of armed conflict could not be held indefinitely and instead should be tried for treason or some other offense of disloyalty.[114] However, although the Court did not challenge the invocation of wartime legal authority vis-á-vis Hamdi, the opinion cannot be read as a broad endorsement of a "global" war on terror. Unfortunately, the Court left to the lower courts the task of defining the permissible scope of application of LOAC-based preventive detention authority in the context of the "global" war. Nonetheless, *Hamdi* served as an important first salvo in a line of decisions that would implicitly endorse the LOAC as a source of legal authority to prosecute the struggle against terrorism.

---

[109] *Id.* at 511.

[110] *Id.* at 521.

[111] *Id.* at 518.

[112] *Id.* The court did conclude, however, that the summary nature of Hamdi's designation as a detainable enemy combatant was insufficient to satisfy his due process liberty interest, and therefore absent a more effective status determination process, Hamdi was entitled to pursue a writ of habeas corpus in federal court to challenge the U.S. government's conclusion that he fit the criteria for detention. *Id.* at 532–33.

[113] *Id.* at 518.

[114] *Id.* at 554–79 (Scalia, J., dissenting).

Rasul v. Bush,[115] decided the same day as *Hamdi,* bolstered the endorsement of the government's invocation of wartime authority in relation to counter-terror operations. Like Hamdi, the petitioners in *Rasul* (two Australian citizens and 12 Kuwait citizens) had been captured in Afghanistan, detained by the U.S. military, and transported to Guantanamo.[116] Unlike Hamdi, the *Rasul* petitioners were not U.S. citizens and were therefore retained in Guantanamo. The *Rasul* petitioners filed a writ of habeas corpus challenging the legal authority for this preventive detention, which ultimately reached the Supreme Court on the question of whether the federal habeas corpus statute applied to the Naval Base at Guantanamo.[117]

The Supreme Court rejected the lower court's determination that the habeas statute did not run to Guantanamo.[118] In doing so, it also rejected the government's invocation of the holding in *Johnson v. Eisentrager,* a World War II–era opinion that denied the writ of habeas corpus to enemy nationals tried by a military tribunal within the context of a declared war.[119] While the opinion dealt primarily with interpretation of the federal habeas statue, the centrality of *Eisentrager* to the opinion indicates that like *Hamdi, Rasul* reflected the Court's acknowledgment that it was addressing a wartime invocation of executive authority.

The Court's next foray into the war-on-terror issue was its decision in *Hamdan v. Rumsfeld.*[120] As noted above, that case involved a challenge by Osama bin Laden's driver to the legality of trial by the military commission pursuant to the military order issued by President Bush in November 2001 directing the Secretary of Defense to try captured unlawful alien enemy combatants for violations of the laws and customs of war. Although the Supreme Court invalidated the commission established pursuant to that order by the Secretary of Defense, the opinion in no way questioned the validity of invoking the LOAC as a source of authority to deal with captured al-Qaeda operatives. On the contrary, by relying on the LOAC—or more specifically concluding that common article 3 applied to the armed conflict in which Hamdan was captured—as a basis to conclude the commission was invalid, the Court implicitly endorsed LOAC applicability to the military operations directed against transnational terrorism by treating that struggle as a noninternational armed conflict.

Two aspects of the *Hamdan* decision are particularly significant in relation to this endorsement. First, unlike Hamdi, Hamdan was unquestionably a member of al-Qaeda, not the Taliban. As a result of the fact that Hamdan's detention and trial resulted from his association with al-Qaeda, the decision directly implicated the characterization of the

---

[115] 542 U.S. 466 (2004).

[116] *Id.* at 470–71.

[117] *Id.* at 472.

[118] *Id.* at 479.

[119] *Id.* at 475–79. The *Eisentrager* decision is discussed in greater detail in Chapter 5 of this book.

[120] Hamdan v. Rumsfeld, 548 U.S. 557 (2006).

struggle against that transnational terrorist group as an armed conflict. Second, accepting the premise that the struggle against al-Qaeda qualified as an armed conflict was the critical predicate to the Court's invocation of the LOAC as a source of legal obligations on the United States vis-á-vis its treatment of Hamdan. This may have resulted from the failure of the petitioner to challenge the armed conflict characterization in his appeal. Nonetheless, *Hamdan* must be understood as having that validating effect, an understanding bolstered by the subsequent response by both the president and Congress.[121]

Another intriguing indication that the *Hamdan* Court understood it was addressing LOAC applicability to the distinct transnational armed conflict between the United States and al-Qaeda came in the context of the then recent efforts by General Manuel Noriega to resist his extradition to France. After being captured by the United States during Operation Just Cause in 1989, the U.S. invasion of Panama to oust Noriega and install the democratically elected government, Noriega was transported to the United States to stand trial in federal court for pre-conflict narcotics offenses. Noriega claimed prisoner-of-war status because he was a member of the Panamanian armed forces captured in the context of an international armed conflict. The United States contested his entitlement to that status, arguing that the intervention had been in response to a request from the democratically elected president of Panama, Guillermo Endara. Relying heavily on the ICRC Commentary to common article 2, the trial court concluded that the armed conflict in Panama had been international and accordingly granted Noriega's request to be designated a prisoner of war (POW).[122]

Unfortunately for Noriega, this in no way undermined the government's ability to prosecute him for his pre-capture criminal activities. Noriega was ultimately convicted and sentenced to a long-term incarceration in federal prison. However, as the result of his POW status, he was afforded certain treaty-mandated privileges such as the right to wear his uniform, annual visits from the ICRC, access to care packages, and segregation from the general population.[123]

As Noriega's term of incarceration approached, France requested that he be extradited to stand trial for money laundering offenses he had been convicted of in absentia (France would set aside that conviction and retry Noriega). Noriega challenged the extradition by invoking his status as a POW.[124] Noriega asserted that because France had not indicated a commitment to acknowledge his POW status and comply with GPW (the Geneva Convention Relative to the Treatment of Prisoners of War), his transfer to France would violate article 12 of GPW, which indicates that "[p]risoners of war may only be transferred by the Detaining Power to a Power which is a party to the Convention and after

---

[121] *See England Memo Underscores Policy, supra* note 99.

[122] *See* United States v. Noriega, 808 F. Supp. 791, 793–96 (S.D. Fla. 1992).

[123] *See id.* at 796.

[124] *See U.S. Judge OKs Noriega Extradition to France,* CNN.COM, Aug. 28, 2007, http://www.cnn.com/2007/US/law/08/28/noriega/.

the retaining Power has satisfied itself of the willingness and ability of such transferee Power to apply the Convention."[125]

The U.S. government challenged Noriega's ability to invoke article 12 of GPW to resist extradition. Ironically, it was the Military Commissions Act of 2006 (2006 MCA) that provided the basis for this challenge, specifically section 5(a), which provides that:

> No person may invoke the Geneva Conventions or any protocols thereto in any habeas corpus or other civil action or proceeding to which the United States, or a current or former officer, employee, member of the Armed Forces, or other agent of the United States is a party as a source of rights in any court of the United States or its States or territories.[126]

It is unlikely Congress contemplated that this provision, included in the 2006 MCA in an effort to limit the judiciary to domestic law when addressing issues of terrorist detainee treatment, would provide the basis to contest Noriega's challenge to extradition. Nonetheless, the challenge placed before the courts the ability of Congress to place such limits on judicial review.

Both the trial court and the 11th Circuit Court of Appeals ruled in favor of the government and rejected Noriega's effort to block extradition.[127] Both courts relied on the MCA to conclude that Noriega could not invoke GPW in support of his challenge. Noriega then petitioned the Supreme Court on a writ of certiorari. Although the petition was denied, the following excerpt from Justice Thomas's dissenting opinion indicates quite clearly that the Court considers the armed conflict with al-Qaeda to be a distinct noninternational armed conflict and not one subordinated to the ongoing armed conflict with the Taliban:

> As the Eleventh Circuit's opinion makes clear, the threshold question in this case is whether MCA §5(a) is valid. Answering that question this Term would provide courts and the political branches with much needed guidance on issues we left open in *Boumediene*. See *Boumediene*, 553 U. S, at ___, ___ (slip op. at 64–66, 68–70). Providing that guidance in this case would allow us to say what the law is without the unnecessary delay and other complications that could burden a decision on these questions in Guantanamo or other detainee litigation *arising out of the conflict with Al Qaeda*.[128]

---

[125] GPW art. 12.

[126] Military Commissions Act of 2006, Pub. L. No. 109-366, 120 Stat. 2600 (2006). The 2006 MCA was substantially amended in 2009, as discussed, *infra*, in Chapter 6, but section 5(a) of the 2006 MCA was not modified in the 2009 amendments.

[127] *See generally Noriega*, 808 F. Supp. 791.

[128] Noriega v. Pastrana, 130 S. Ct. 1002, 1006 (2010) (Thomas, J. dissenting to denial of certiorari) (emphasis added).

To further confirm this notion, in recent lower court opinions concerning al-Qaeda–related military commissions (*Hamdan* and *Al Bahlul*[129]), the existence and nature of the conflict no longer seemed to be of central importance; instead, it seemed to be an accepted matter altogether ("[t]he Government has broad powers to safeguard the United States under the Constitution in *time of war*"[130]), and the courts further reinforced the United States' right "to *wage war* successfully ... [s]ince the Constitution commits to the Executive and to Congress the exercise of the *war power* in all the vicissitudes and conditions of *warfare.*"[131] Rather, the legal battles have centered on whether the individual defendants can be tied to the armed conflict with al-Qaeda in one form or another sufficiently to justify their trial by military commission.[132] Arguments have focused on the legal legitimacy of a U.S. common law of war, the military commission's jurisdiction to try the defendants, and the question whether prosecution for conduct as war crimes (e.g., material support to terrorists) are violations of the Constitution's Ex Post Facto clause.[133]

The seminal Supreme Court opinions discussed above, including *Hamdi, Rasul,* and *Hamdan,* collectively indicate that the decision by the two political branches of government to redefine the nature of the struggle against transnational terrorism following the September 11th attacks has enjoyed the implicit if not explicit support of the Supreme Court. The interesting illumination provided by the *Noriega* litigation and the consistent lower court opinions in *Hamdan* and *Al Bahlul* only serve to confirm that these decisions should not be read narrowly as recognizing only an armed conflict in Afghanistan. Instead, they reflect a recognition that at least certain aspects of the struggle against al-Qaeda qualify as an armed conflict triggering LOAC rights and obligations. Accordingly, there is little doubt related to the legitimacy of this redefinition—at least from the perspective of the United States. This does not, however, reflect a broader international consensus on the legitimacy of characterizing counter-terror efforts as an armed conflict and invoking the LOAC authorities as a legal framework to support the prosecution of that struggle. On the contrary, the U.S. position on this issue remains the subject of substantial criticism in the international legal community.

---

[129] United States v. Hamdan, 801 F. Supp. 2d 1247 (U.S. Ct. Mil. Comm'n Rev. 2011), *rev'd,* Hamdan v. United States, 676 F.3d 1238 (D.C. Cir. 2012) [hereinafter Hamdan CMCR Decision]; *see also* United States v. Al Bahlul, 820 F. Supp. 2d 1141 (U.S. Ct. Mil. Comm'n Rev. 2011). As of the time of this writing, the *Al Bahlul* decision is being reviewed *en banc* by the U.S. Circuit Court of Appeals for the D.C. Circuit.

[130] Hamdan CMCR Decision, *supra* note 129, at 1264.

[131] *Id.* at 1264–65 (quoting Lichter v. United States, 334 U.S. 742, 767 n.9 (1948)).

[132] *Id.* at 1278.

[133] *Id.* at 1310.

An Alternative View: Rejecting the Designation of Counter-Terror Operations as Armed Conflict

As noted previously, prior to 1949 there were no defined criteria to determine when the LOAC (at that time called the law of war) came into force. As a general proposition, it was understood that it would apply to any war. However, uncertainty as to the international legal definition of war resulted in the existence of hostilities with an accordant disavowal by States that they were bound by the law of war.[134] Providing the law applicability trigger in terms other than "war" was a deliberate effort to maximize the humanitarian protections imposed by these treaties and to minimize the opportunity for the type of definitional law avoidance that defined the era between 1918 and 1945. The term "armed conflict" was intended to link applicability of the law with the pragmatic realities of military operations and not with a complex legal term.[135]

Events following September 11th fundamentally transformed the focus of the LOAC applicability debate. Suddenly, international law experts were presented with the invocation of LOAC-based authority to attack, detain, and try transnational terrorist operatives. Lodging these operations under the broader umbrella of the conflict against the Taliban in Afghanistan presented little analytical difficulty: the conflict was international within the meaning of the LOAC, and al-Qaeda operatives were part of volunteer forces operating on behalf of the Taliban.[136] However, as noted above, the United States adopted a different interpretation of its conflict with al-Qaeda. It viewed operations in Afghanistan as two distinct armed conflicts—one against the Taliban and one against al-Qaeda. The latter conflict extended well beyond Afghanistan to any location where al-Qaeda planned or executed its operations, hence the term "Global War on Terror."[137]

International law experts, even including many U.S. allies, challenged the validity of this theory of LOAC applicability.[138] Opponents of the interpretation emphasized the LOAC-triggering paradigm that evolved prior to September 11th. For them, the notion that an armed conflict can exist between a State and a loosely organized nonstate entity that operates transnationally is a legal fiction.[139] Instead, only two types of situations may properly trigger LOAC applicability: (1) an armed conflict between two States—known in international law as an international armed conflict, and (2) an armed conflict between a State and an armed and organized nonstate group or between two or more such groups of significant intensity and duration—known in international law as

---

[134] *See* GWS COMMENTARY at 28.

[135] *Id.* at 32.

[136] *See* ILA Report, *supra* note 29, at 3.

[137] *See* 2002 National Security Strategy, *supra* note 19, at 5.

[138] *See, e.g.,* Mary Ellen O'Connell, *Defining Armed Conflict* 13 J. CONFLICT & SEC. L., Winter 2008, at 393.

[139] ILA Report, *supra* note 29, at 10–18.

a noninternational armed conflict.[140] Because al-Qaeda (like virtually all international terrorist organizations) lacks the requisite level of organization and its operations lack the requisite intensity and duration necessary to satisfy the definition of noninternational armed conflict, such operations simply remain in the realm of law enforcement.[141]

This LOAC interpretation is based on two primary sources of expert authority: (1) the Geneva Conventions and their associated ICRC Commentaries, and (2) the jurisprudence of the International Criminal Tribunal for the Former Yugoslavia (ICTY) analyzing the meaning of noninternational armed conflict. It is the definition of this latter category of armed conflict where a significant divide has developed between the United States and these experts, a divide attributable primarily to the diverging assessment of the authority of the ICTY's jurisprudence.[142]

A recent report by a committee established by the International Law Association (ILA) to analyze the meaning of the term "armed conflict" provides perhaps the clearest manifestation of this alternate LOAC interpretation.[143] That report, issued in August 2010, rejects the validity of a "Global War on Terror" as an armed conflict. Accordingly, it concludes that the LOAC cannot be invoked as a source of either authority or obligation in the context of counter-terror operations defined by U.S. operations directed against al-Qaeda unless those operations are subordinate to a broader armed conflict involving another State or an armed and organized dissident group within a State.[144] According to the report:

> In May 2005, the Executive Committee of the International Law Association (ILA) approved a mandate for the Use of Force Committee to produce a report on the meaning of war or armed conflict in international law. The report was motivated by the United States' position following the attacks of 11 September 2001 that it was involved in a "Global War on Terror." In other words, the U.S. has claimed the right to exercise belligerent privileges applicable only during armed conflict anywhere in the world where members of terrorist groups are found. The U.S. position was contrary to a trend by states attempting to avoid acknowledging involvement in wars or armed conflicts.
>
> ...
>
> Plainly, the existence of armed conflict is a significant fact in the international legal system, and, yet, the Committee found no widely accepted definition of armed conflict in any treaty. It did, however, discover significant evidence in the sources of international law that the international community embraces a common understanding of armed conflict. All armed conflict has certain minimal,

---

[140] *Id.*

[141] *Id.* at 26, 209.

[142] *See* Tadic Jurisdiction Decision, *supra* note 47, para. 70.

[143] *See generally* ILA Report, *supra* note 29, at 10.

[144] *Id.*

defining characteristics that distinguish it from situations of non-armed conflict or peace. In the absence of these characteristics, states may not, consistently with international law, simply declare that a situation is or is not armed conflict based on policy preferences. The Committee confirmed that at least two characteristics are found with respect to all armed conflict:

1.) The existence of organized armed groups
2.) Engaged in fighting of some intensity

In addition to these minimum criteria respecting all armed conflict, IHL includes additional criteria so as to classify conflicts as either international or non-international in nature.

...

The Committee, however, found little evidence to support the view that the Conventions apply in the absence of fighting of some intensity. For non-state actors to move from chaotic violence to being able to challenge the armed forces of a state requires organization, meaning a command structure, training, recruiting ability, communications, and logistical capacity. Such organized forces are only recognized as engaged in armed conflict when fighting between them is more than a minimal engagement or incident.[145]

The report indicates substantial reliance on the seminal decision by the ICTY in the case of *Prosecutor v. Tadic*.[146] That case involved the first war crimes trial at the ICTY related to the conflict in the former Yugoslavia. In order to respond to the defendant's jurisdictional challenge, the Tribunal was required to determine whether and what type of armed conflict existed in Bosnia at the time of the alleged war crimes. The Tribunal concluded that the conflict was noninternational within the meaning of the Geneva Conventions, thereby falling within its jurisdiction. In reaching this conclusion, the Tribunal identified what might best be characterized as the "Tadic factors" or the "organizational test" to determine when a situation evolves from a response to internal civil unrest involving the exercise of peacetime law enforcement to that of armed conflict triggering LOAC authority.[147] According to the Tribunal, in order for an armed conflict to exist outside the context of interstate hostilities, the dissident forces engaged in the struggle must operate pursuant to military organization, must conduct sustained operations, and must operate with military capability.[148] The International Law Association

---

[145] ILA Report, *supra* note 29.
[146] *Prosecutor v. Tadic*, Case No. IT-94–1, Judgment (Appeals Chamber, Int'l Crim. Trib. for the Former Yugoslavia July 15, 1999), *available at* http://www.icty.org/x/cases/tadic/acjug/en/tad-aj990715e.pdf.
[147] *Id.*
[148] *Id.*

committee relied on these factors to conclude that transnational terrorist groups do not qualify as the type of dissident group required to trigger the LOAC in relation to a State response to that threat.[149] Accordingly, such operations are not armed conflicts. This interpretation of the LOAC-triggering requirements is generally representative of a majority of States, international law experts, and international nongovernment organizations with competence in humanitarian law.[150]

The ICRC holds a similar position on the matter.[151] According to the ICRC, because al-Qaeda is a "loosely connected, clandestine network of cells... [t]hese cells do not meet the organization criterion for... a non-international armed conflict."[152] Questions of how to designate such a "network" and how such a designation would relate to other transnational criminal groups have been brought up to demonstrate the potential black holes in the United States' position.[153] The ICRC holds that no gap exists requiring a new type of armed conflict designation and that the legal framework when confronting terrorism already exists:

> Non-international armed conflict rules are, in fact, well suited to governing this type of conflict because they are not based upon a concept of "combatant" status and of the legal consequences that arise from it in international armed conflicts. Captured "terrorists" would thus not enjoy immunity from criminal prosecution for participation in the armed conflict or other lawful acts of war and would not have to be released at the end of the armed conflict. Both "sides" would, however, have to abide by the rules on the conduct of hostilities aimed primarily at sparing civilians and civilian objects.[154]
>
> ...
>
> Terrorist acts must be dealt with using the specific tools designed for addressing criminal activity, which are domestic and international law enforcement. In practice, affected states have used precisely such measures to prevent acts of terrorism, or to arrest and bring the perpetrators to justice when they have been able to do so.[155]
>
> ...
>
> The counter-terrorist effort is being carried out by a variety of means, including law enforcement, intelligence gathering, police and judicial cooperation,

---

[149] See ILA Report, *supra* note 29, at 14–15.

[150] See generally id.

[151] Sylvain Vite, *Typology of Armed Conflicts in International Humanitarian Law: Legal Concepts and Actual Situations*, 91 INT'L REV. RED CROSS, 69, 82 (2009).

[152] *Id.* at 93

[153] *Id.*

[154] Jelena Pejic, *Terrorist Acts and Groups: A Role for International Law?* 75(1) BRIT. YEARBOOK INT'L L. 71, 85 (2004).

[155] *Id.* at 87.

extradition, financial investigations, the freezing of assets, diplomatic demarches and criminal sanctions. "Terrorism" is a phenomenon. Both practically and as a matter of law, war cannot be waged against a phenomenon.[156]

Some, including members of the ICRC Legal Advisers, question the linkages made between all of the post-September 11th terrorist attacks and al-Qaeda: "very little about the exact nature of such a 'link' [to al Qaeda] is ever provided...."[157] Some of the criminal acts may have nothing to do with al-Qaeda altogether but may be a result of a common ideological goal of autonomy or independence for those in a certain region, as is the case with the Chechen-related terrorist attacks in Moscow and Beslan.[158] Therefore, if the acts are in fact a series of disparate and disconnected terrorist attacks by disparate and disconnected groups, they would not qualify as a transglobal conflict.[159]

At the present time, there is no indication the United States will modify in response to the ILA report or any other external criticism its position that the struggle against al-Qaeda qualifies as an armed conflict. President Obama has continued to assert authorities implicitly derived from the LOAC to justify his administration's efforts to destroy, disable, and degrade the threat of transnational terrorism. In his Nobel Prize acceptance speech, the new president specifically characterized the struggle against transnational terrorism as a war:

> But perhaps the most profound issue surrounding my receipt of this prize is the fact that I am the Commander-in-Chief of the military of a nation in the midst of two wars. One of these wars is winding down. The other is a conflict that America did not seek; one in which we are joined by forty two other countries—including Norway—in an effort to defend ourselves and all nations from further attacks.
>
> Still, we are at war, and I am responsible for the deployment of thousands of young Americans to battle in a distant land. Some will kill, and some will be killed. And so I come here with an acute sense of the cost of armed conflict—filled with difficult questions about the relationship between war and peace, and our effort to replace one with the other.
>
> ...
>
> A decade into a new century, this old architecture is buckling under the weight of new threats. The world may no longer shudder at the prospect of war between two nuclear superpowers, but proliferation may increase the risk of catastrophe.

---

[156] *Id.* at 87–88.

[157] *Id.* at 87 n.78.

[158] *Id.* at 87 n.77.

[159] *Id.* at 87–88.

Terrorism has long been a tactic, but modern technology allows a few small men with outsized rage to murder innocents on a horrific scale.[160]

There is, however, one important difference between President Obama's LOAC interpretation in relation to this armed conflict and that of his predecessor—unlike President Bush, President Obama has not only invoked LOAC authority, but has emphasized the U.S. commitment to comply with the humanitarian constraints of the law:

> Let me make one final point about the use of force. Even as we make difficult decisions about going to war, we must also think clearly about how we fight it. The Nobel Committee recognized this truth in awarding its first prize for peace to Henry Dunant—the founder of the Red Cross, and a driving force behind the Geneva Conventions.
>
> Where force is necessary, we have a moral and strategic interest in binding ourselves to certain rules of conduct. And even as we confront a vicious adversary that abides by no rules, I believe that the United States of America must remain a standard bearer in the conduct of war. That is what makes us different from those whom we fight. That is a source of our strength. That is why I prohibited torture. That is why I ordered the prison at Guantanamo Bay closed. And that is why I have reaffirmed America's commitment to abide by the Geneva Conventions. We lose ourselves when we compromise the very ideals that we fight to defend. And we honor those ideals by upholding them not just when it is easy, but when it is hard.[161]

This is indeed an important step forward in the regulation of hostilities between the United States and al-Qaeda. Nonetheless, characterizing this struggle as an armed conflict remains highly controversial and invalid in the view of many international legal experts. It is therefore essential that any scholar engaged in the study of this issue recognize the controversy related to this interpretation of the law and the source of that controversy. How these competing views will evolve over time and whether the U.S. interpretation will influence a more widespread evolution of LOAC understanding remains to be seen.

---

[160] President Barack Obama, Remarks by the President at the Acceptance of the Nobel Peace Prize, 2009 Daily Comp. Pres. Doc. (Dec.10, 2009), http://www.gpo.gov/fdsys/pkg/DCPD-200900985/pdf/DCPD-200900985.pdf.

[161] *Id.*

3

Targeting of Persons and Property

by Eric Talbot Jensen

IT IS A simple reality of warfare that in order to defeat an enemy it is necessary to attack and destroy the enemy's combat capability. Employment of combat power for this purpose is referred to in the lexicon of military operations as targeting. The targeting process involves identifying a potential target or desired effect and determining if it is a military objective; selecting the most appropriate capability, whether kinetic or non-kinetic, to achieve the desired operational effect; executing military operations to employ the combat capability; and assessing the effects achieved. Once the effects are assessed, that information is fed back into the targeting process, and the cycle continuously repeats itself.[1]

Executing such operations within the bounds of the law of armed conflict is undoubtedly challenging in any operational context. However, in the context of transnational armed conflict (TAC) against terrorists, this challenge is exacerbated by the uncertainty regarding the boundaries of what constitutes a military objective in such a conflict and the unconventional nature of the nonstate enemy. Questions concerning the identity of terrorists, including their location and citizenship and their mixing within the civilian populace; the desire to interdict those who support them in their terrorist acts; and the length of time those conducting and supporting terrorist acts can be targeted are all ones that highlight the increased difficulty in applying the core principles of targeting to a conflict against terrorists. It is therefore critical to identify and embrace a meaningful and effective regulatory framework for targeting operations in this context: one that does not disregard the fundamental principles of wartime targeting upon which

---

[1] U.S. Dep't of the Army, Field Manual 6-20-10, Tactics, Techniques and Procedures for the Targeting Process, ch. 2 (8 May 1996).

militaries have consistently trained, but does account for the unique difficulties of targeting in this complex TAC environment.

Although a characteristic of the TAC against terrorists is often its proximity to the civilian population, warfare has always affected the local population and seldom ever occurred on a contained, sterile battlefield where two combatant groups who were easily recognizable to each other fought under the same rules, with the victor conquering the vanquished and leaving hostilities on the battlefield while moving through the conquered territory without substantial contact with the civilian population. More often, the fighting forces have moved freely in and out of the population not only during, but also before and after the major battles. Given this historical reality, the percentage of civilian casualties injured during armed conflict has risen steadily in the twentieth century, from 19 percent in World War I to 48 percent in World War II (WWII) and to more than 80 percent in the armed conflicts of the 1990s.[2]

Though there are undoubtedly numerous reasons for these statistics, it is interesting to note that concurrent with this increase in risk to those not directly involved in combat has been a dramatic increase in the technological advancement of weaponry and the codification of rules on how to employ those weapons. Ironically, an inherent purpose of developing weapons that can more accurately strike legitimate military objectives and a primary purpose of the law that regulates targeting is the mitigation of the risk of harming innocent civilians and their property. It is a matter of debate as to whether these technological and legal innovations have had their desired effect.

This disparity between intent and execution is nowhere more apparent than in the "Global War on Terror," including the recent conflicts in Iraq and Afghanistan where terrorists have not only fueled insurgencies but taken an active part in both military and support operations. Coalition armed forces in both conflict areas have been confounded in their attempts to spare the civilian population from the effects of proper targeting of military objectives in areas where terrorist fighters, financiers, suppliers, and trainers intentionally integrate themselves into the civilian populace to accrue undeserved protections.[3] These State militaries are committed to applying the core principles of the law of war by refraining from attacking the civilian population. However, they also

---

[2] Ronald R. Lett, Olive Chifefe Kobusingye & Paul Ekwaru, *Burden of Injury during the Complex Political Emergency in Northern Uganda*, 49 CAN. J. SURGERY 51, 53 (Feb. 2006), *available at* http://www.cma.ca/multimedia/staticContent/HTML/N0/l2/cjs/vol-49/issue-1/pdf/pg51.pdf.

[3] *See* Kelly McCann, *CNN Live Sunday: U.S. Helicopter Shot Down in Iraq, Both Pilots Killed; 7 Chinese Citizens Taken Hostage in Iraq* (CNN television broadcast, Apr. 11, 2004) (041104CN.V36) LEXIS, News File where the author quotes a military spokesperson as saying:

> We are working at a disadvantage.... The lack of uniforms, so that you can't define the enemy very well. And the intertwining of the enemy with combatants is very, very difficult. So you've got combatants and non-combatants mixed together intentionally.

Id.

recognize that they still have to be able to conduct military operations in an effective manner.

This chapter will analyze the targeting of persons and property in the war on terror. This analysis will begin by exploring the legal principles related to targeting that apply in combat operations generally, including the origins of these principles and how they form the foundation of the hostility regulation prong of the law of war. The chapter will then address how these principles apply in operations directed against transnational terrorist enemies, with particular attention to the challenging aspects of the application of these principles, such as dealing with enemy forces co-mingled with the civilian population and limiting collateral damage in densely populated areas. This will include an analysis of the increasing use of drones, both on hot battlefields and in areas where there is no ongoing armed conflict. The chapter will then address targeting U.S. persons abroad who may be participating in terrorist activities. Additionally, the targeting of both U.S. and non-U.S. persons within the United States will be discussed. The chapter will conclude with the assertion that though the law of armed conflict is highly developed, nations are now imposing policy limitations on their militaries that are far more restrictive than the law would require, making the targeting process in transnational armed conflicts, such as the war on terror, even more complex.

The Law of Targeting

I. ORIGINS OF THE LAW

Laws of war are not a modern conception. Many ancient cultures have had rules concerning the conduct of hostilities, including the Chinese, Babylonians, Hittites, Persians, Greeks, and others.[4] These rules addressed a broad range of issues, from what weapons could be used in combat, to the proper treatment of captives. While the rules often differed from civilization to civilization and from era to era, almost every armed force was guided by some rules that limited its actions.

---

[4] For information on the historical development of the laws of war, *see* William Bradford, *Barbarians at the Gates: A Post-September 11th Proposal to Rationalize the Laws of War*, 73 Miss. L. J. 639 (2004); Chris af Jochnick & Roger Normand, *The Legitimation of Violence: A Critical History of the Laws of War*, 35 Harv. Int'l Law J. 35 Harv. Int'l L.J. 49 (1994); Gregory P. Noone, *The History and Evolution of the Law of War prior to WWII*, 47 Naval L. Rev 176 (2000); Thomas C. Wingfield, *Chivalry in the Use of Force*, 32 U. Tol. L. Rev. 111 (2001); Scott R. Morris, *The Laws of War: Rules by Warriors for Warriors*, 1997 Army Law. 4 (Dec. 1997); Nathan A. Canestaro, *"Small Wars" and the Law: Options for Prosecuting the Insurgents in Iraq*, 43 Colum. J. Transnat'l L. 73 (2004); Eric Krauss & Michael Lacey, *Utilitarian vs. Humanitarian: The Battle over the Law of War*, Parameters, Summer 2002, at 73, 74–76; Eric Talbot Jensen, *Combatant Status: It Is Time for Intermediate Levels of Recognition for Partial Compliance*, 46 Va. J. Int'l L. 214 (2005); Rosa Ehrenreich Brooks, *War Everywhere: Rights, National Security Law, and the Law of Armed Conflict in the Age of Terror*, 153 U. Pa. L. Rev. 675, 706 (2004).

In the nineteenth century, nations began to codify the rules governing warfare that had developed over time. These rules proceeded down two general paths, one addressing methods and tactics of targeting and the other placing limitations on specific weapons systems, or means of targeting. Examples of these limitations include the 1863 Lieber Code, which established rules for the conduct of hostilities by Union forces in the American Civil War, and the Hague Conventions of 1899 and 1907, which included regulations that codified the customs of war that were accepted by the major European nations.[5] These codes and conventions and others like them came to be known as the "Hague tradition." The Hague tradition, typified by the 1907 Hague regulations, became one of the foundations upon which all modern laws of armed conflict are built and embody concepts still valid today.

Though not extensive, the regulations annexed to the 1907 Hague Convention (IV) Respecting the Laws and Customs of War on Land[6] contain several articles that concern the targeting of persons and property during armed conflict. Article 22 states that "[t]he right of belligerents to adopt means of injuring the enemy is not unlimited." Articles 23 through 27 then list some specific prohibitions on actions in war.[7]

Although these provisions will seem antiquated and incomplete to the modern soldier, they are the foundation upon which current law is constructed. The Hague tradition includes other agreements that contain specific prohibitions, such as the 1868 Declaration of St. Petersburg that prohibited explosive projectiles under 400 grams, and the 1925 Geneva Protocol that prohibited biological and chemical weapons in warfare.

As previously suggested, WWII exhibited an exponential rise in wartime costs in human lives. There was a similar cost in the destruction of property. In the years immediately following WWII the world community turned its focus to regulating warfare and its impact. Codification began with the 1949 Geneva Conventions, which dealt with the wounded and sick in the armed forces in the field; wounded, sick, and shipwrecked in the armed forces at sea; prisoners of war (hereinafter GPW), and civilians during times of armed conflict (hereinafter GCIV).[8] While the first three Geneva Conventions built upon preexisting established principles that survived WWII and primarily were aimed at members of the military, the GCIV extended certain protections to civilians based on the fact that they are not covered by provisions of the other three Conventions. Very

---

[5] *See generally* DIETRICH SCHINDLER & JIRI TOMAN, THE LAWS OF ARMED CONFLICTS: A COLLECTION OF CONVENTIONS, RESOLUTIONS & OTHER DOCUMENTS (4th ed. 2004).

[6] Hague IV.

[7] These include prohibitions on employing poisoned weapons, killing or wounding treacherously, and improperly using a flag of truce (art. 23); attack or bombardment of undefended places (art. 25); and attacking buildings dedicated to religion, art, science, or charitable purposes, historic monuments, hospitals, and places where the sick and wounded are collected, provided they are not being used at the time for military purposes (art. 27).

[8] *See* GWS art. 2, GWS-Sea art. 2, GPW art. 2, and GCIV art. 2.

few of those provisions dealt specifically with the targeting of civilians and nonmilitary property, but they affected the methods by which targeting should be accomplished by codifying the idea that civilians were victims of armed conflict, not participants, and deserved certain protections from hostilities.

The next major LOAC codification came about in response to the Vietnam War and other similar conflicts across the globe in which there were widely publicized violations of the law of war.[9] Partially in response to these violations and in an attempt to update the 1949 Geneva Conventions, and also as part of efforts, begun in the 1950s and continuing into the early 1970s, by the International Committee of the Red Cross (ICRC) to supplement the existing law of armed conflict, a diplomatic conference was convened by the Swiss government from 1974 to 1977 that resulted in two 1977 Additional Protocols to the Geneva Conventions (hereinafter AP I and AP II). These Protocols revisited the rules of warfare and produced the most complete codification of those rules to that time. AP I and AP II were focused largely on rules for the conduct of warfare and were meant as supplements to the existing Geneva Conventions and Hague tradition. As supplements, they added substantive rules in many areas of the law of armed conflict, including key provisions on the regulation of targeting of persons and property. Though not ratified by the United States, AP I and AP II have been ratified by most of the nations of the world and are considered by many to be customary international law, and therefore binding on all nations.[10]

As well as more general rules limiting methods of targeting, regulation of specific weapons systems and tactics that affect targeting has also continued in the post-WWII era. The 1980 Convention on Prohibitions or Restrictions on the Use of Certain Conventional Weapons which may be Deemed to be Excessively Injurious or to Have Indiscriminate Effects (CCW) with its Protocols,[11] the 1993 Convention on the Prohibition of the Development, Production, Stockpiling, and Use of Chemical

---

[9] *See* Cara Levy Rodriguez, *Slaying the Monster: Why the United States Should Not Support the Rome Treaty*, 14 AM. U. INT'L L. REV. 805, 827 n.130 (1999) (referencing the alleged American violations of the Law of War); Major Jeffrey F. Addicott & Major William A. Hudson, Jr., *The Twenty-Fifth Anniversary of My Lai: A Time to Inculcate the Lessons*, 139 MIL. L. REV. 153, 174–75 (1993) (referencing the alleged North Vietnamese violations of the Law of War). *Cf.* Adam Roberts, *The Laws of War: Problems of Implementation in Contemporary Conflicts*, 6 DUKE J. COMP. & INT'L L. 11, 43 (1995) (where the author states that law-of-war violations were not prosecuted during this time period because of the superpower deadlock between the United States and the Soviet Union); Earl H. Lubensky, *Internal Security & Human Rights: Militarism and Diplomacy*, AMERICAN DIPLOMACY (website), Feb. 2002, http://www.unc.edu/depts/diplomat/archives_roll/2002_01-03/lubensky_internal/lubensky_internal.html.

[10] *See* Michael J. Matheson, *The United States Position on the Relation of Customary Law to the 1977 Protocols Additional to the 1949 Geneva Conventions*, 2 AM. U. J. INT'L L. & POL'Y 419 (1987) (discussing which articles of AP I the United States believes reflect customary international law and which the United States objects to).

[11] For citations to this treaty and others used in this chapter, *see* the "List of Treaties and Sources Frequently Cited in this Book" at the beginning of the book.

Weapons and on their Destruction (CWC),[12] and the 1997 Convention on the Prohibition of the Use, Stockpiling, Production and Transfer of Anti-Personnel Mines and on their Destruction[13] are examples of this. In each case, State parties have agreed to limit their warfighting capabilities or methods, often despite the objection of their militaries.[14]

The regulation of targeting of persons and property has an ongoing history as illustrated by the recent initiative to prohibit cluster munitions.[15] The means and methods of warfare will always be a topic of discussion, not only among militaries and governments, but also among nongovernmental organizations and other like-minded groups who are concerned about the effects of war, both on participants and nonparticipants alike. It is appropriate next, therefore, to look at where this history has left the current law on targeting of persons and property.

2. THE CURRENT LAW OF TARGETING PERSONS AND PROPERTY

As addressed previously in this book, there are generally two types of armed conflict, as defined by articles 2 and 3 of the Geneva Conventions. Article 2 defines international armed conflict as "armed conflict which may arise between two or more of the High Contracting Parties."[16] Such conflicts explicitly invoke the full body of the law of war, including the Geneva Conventions and the Hague tradition, as well as other conventional and customary international law. For those who have ratified it, AP I also applies to international armed conflict and contains many provisions that apply to the law of targeting.

In contrast, article 3 conflicts are conflicts "not of an international character,"[17] and the provisions concerning this type of armed conflict are much less extensive. This is particularly true in the area of targeting, where article 3 is completely silent. However, for those who have ratified AP II, several provisions apply fundamental principles of the law of targeting to noninternational armed conflicts. Despite the clear bifurcation in the application of the law to armed conflict, decisions of international tribunals, State

---

[12] Convention on the Prohibition of the Development, Production, Stockpiling and Use of Chemical Weapons and on Their Destruction, Jan. 13, 1993, S. TREATY DOC. No. 103-21, 1974 U.N.T.S. 3 [hereinafter CWC], *available at* http://www.opcw.org/.

[13] *Available at* http://www.icrc.org/IHL.nsf/52d68d14de6160e0c12563da005fdb1b/d111fff4b9c85b0f412565 85003caec3?OpenDocument (last visited July 2, 2014).

[14] *See* Major Christopher W. Jacobs, *Taking the Next Step: An Analysis of the Effects the Ottawa Convention May Have on the Interoperability of United States Forces with the Armed Forces of Australia, Great Britain, and Canada*, 180 MIL. L. REV. 49 (2004).

[15] Convention on Cluster Munitions, Dec. 3, 2008, 48 I.L.M. 357, *available at* http://www.clustermunition-sdublin.ie/pdf/ENGLISHfinaltext.pdf.

[16] GPW art.2.

[17] *Id.* art. 3.

practice, and scholarly writings indicate that the principles of targeting now apply to armed conflict generally, regardless of how the conflict is characterized.[18] Therefore, the rules are generally the same in international and noninternational armed conflict for the purposes of targeting.

Distinction is a principle of warfare that has existed as long as organized conflict itself.[19] The codified statement of distinction comes from AP I and requires militaries to "distinguish between the civilian population and combatants and between civilian objects and military objectives and accordingly [to] direct their operations only against military objectives."[20] To support this principle, the law of armed conflict evolved to establish three general categories of individuals on the battlefield: combatants, non-combatants, and civilians. Under AP I, combatants are those persons who meet the criteria of GPW article 4a(1), (2), (3), or (6).[21] Non-combatants include medical personnel and chaplains who are part of the armed forces and authorized to be on the battlefield but may not be directly targeted. They are not authorized to directly participate in hostilities, but

---

[18] INTERNATIONAL INSTITUTE OF HUMANITARIAN LAW, THE MANUAL ON THE LAW OF NON-INTERNATIONAL ARMED CONFLICT WITH COMMENTARY, paras. 2.1.1 & 2.1.2 (2006), *available at* http://www.iihl.org/iihl/Documents/The%20Manual%20on%20the%20Law%20of%20NIAC.pdf [hereinafter NIAC MANUAL]; AP COMMENTARY, para. 4761; International Criminal Tribunal for Yugoslavia, Prosecutor v. Tadic, Decision on The Defence Motion For Interlocutory Appeal on Jurisdiction, Appeals Chamber, Case No. IT-94-1-I, Decision on Defence Motion for Interlocutory Appeal on Jurisdiction, paras. 96–127 (Int'l Crim. Trib. for the Former Yugoslavia Oct. 2, 1995).

[19] NIAC MANUAL, *supra* note 18, para. 1.2.2 (quoting AP commentary); ROGERS, *infra* note 34, at 3 ("The great principles of customary law, from which all else stems, are those of military necessity, humanity, distinction and proportionality.").

[20] AP I art. 48.

[21] *See* GPW art. 4, which requires:

A. Prisoners of War, in the sense of the present Convention, are persons belonging to one of the following categories, who have fallen into the power of the enemy:

   (1) Members of the armed forces of a Party to the conflict as well as members of militias or volunteer corps forming part of such armed forces.

   (2) Members of other militias and members of other volunteer corps, including those of organized resistance movements, belonging to a Party to the conflict and operating in or outside their own territory, even if this territory is occupied, provided that such militias or volunteer corps, including such organized resistance movements, fulfill the following conditions:

      (a) that of being commanded by a person responsible for his subordinates;

      (b) that of having a fixed distinctive sign recognizable at a distance;

      (c) that of carrying arms openly;

      (d) that of conducting their operations in accordance with the laws and customs of war.

   (3) Members of regular armed forces who profess allegiance to a government or an authority not recognized by the Detaining Power.

   …

   (6) Inhabitants of a non-occupied territory, who on the approach of the enemy spontaneously take up arms to resist the invading forces, without having had time to form themselves into regular armed units, provided they carry arms openly and respect the laws and customs of war.

can lose their protections if they engage in hostilities.[22] All other persons are classified as civilians[23] and benefit from presumptive immunity against being made the object of attack. Both the International Criminal Tribunal for the former Yugoslavia (ICTY) in the *Tadic* decision[24] and the International Institute of Humanitarian Law's Manual on the Law of Non-International Armed Conflict (hereinafter NIAC Manual) embrace this interpretation. The NIAC Manual states that it is "indisputable that the principle of distinction is customary international law for both international and non-international armed conflict."[25]

Distinction is really about target selection. When a targeter analyzes whom he may target, he is really applying the concept of distinction. Because modern conflicts seem to increasingly occur in close proximity to civilian population centers and opposing forces co-mingle with civilians, the principle of distinction is increasingly central to the effective regulation of all armed conflicts. Modern conflicts also increasingly involve fights between the armed forces of one State and civilians who organize themselves as fighters, but are not the recognized armed forces of a State. This phenomenon forces a closer look at civilian immunity from attack.

a. Targeting Persons

The law makes it clear that civilians are not targetable. The clearest statement of this standard is found in AP I article 51, which states:

Art 51. Protection of the civilian population
1. The civilian population and individual civilians shall enjoy general protection against dangers arising from military operations. To give effect to this protection, the following rules, which are additional to other applicable rules of international law, shall be observed in all circumstances.
2. The civilian population as such, as well as individual civilians, shall not be the object of attack. Acts or threats of violence the primary purpose of which is to spread terror among the civilian population are prohibited.
3. Civilians shall enjoy the protection afforded by this section, unless and for such time as they take a direct part in hostilities.[26]

Paragraphs 1 and 2 state the civilian population's immunity from attack. The international community was anxious to restate and codify the desire to preserve the civilian

---

[22] AP I arts. 13, 43.2.

[23] *Id.* art. 50.

[24] Prosecutor v. Tadic, *supra* note 18, at ¶¶ 102–104, where the appellate chamber opined that the principle of distinction was so fundamental to the conduct of hostilities that it applied equally to all armed conflicts.

[25] NIAC MANUAL, *supra* note 18, at ¶ 1.2.2.3.

[26] AP I art. 51.

population from the effects of conflict. However, this immunity is not absolute for all civilians, as paragraph 3 makes clear.

The immunity granted to civilians is subject to divestment, but only "unless and for such time as they take a direct part in hostilities." There has been a great deal of discussion and disagreement on what that provision actually means. This is a discussion of no small import. In recent conflicts, there has been a tendency for at least one side in the conflict to intermingle itself with the local population, making it extremely difficult for nations that wish to comply with the distinction rule. Therefore, understanding article 51 is key to the correct application of targeting.

Even though most civilians never take part in hostilities and therefore never forfeit their immunity from attack, there are civilians who, to varying levels, do participate in hostilities, and the law must account for these civilians also. The first and most involved group includes those civilians who are not members of a State's armed forces or other associated forces, but organize themselves into armed groups who then take an active role in the conflict. Though they are technically still civilians, they are acting in the same way as armed forces. The second group includes those civilians who are not members of armed groups, but still participate in hostilities, either continuously or on an infrequent or one-time basis. The ongoing conflict with terrorist groups has served to highlight the difficulty these two groups present. Recently, States and international organizations, such as the ICRC, have sought greater clarity on the targeting of both of these groups of civilians.

In relation to organized armed groups, both States and the ICRC have recognized that civilians who become fighting members of these types of groups have forfeited their civilian protections. The United States takes an aggressive approach, arguing that any member of this type of group, simply by virtue of membership in that group, is targetable at any time. In contrast, the ICRC argues that only members who serve a "continuous combat function" within these groups should be targetable constantly.[27] For example, the ICRC would agree that a foot soldier of an organized armed group was targetable generally but would argue that a cook or a maintenance person was not targetable unless that person took some specific action that qualified as individual direct participation.

This situation is exemplified by a non-fighting member of al-Qaeda in Afghanistan. The United States would argue that by his membership in al-Qaeda, an organized armed group with which the United States is in armed conflict, the non-fighter becomes targetable. The ICRC, and the States that adopt its view, would argue that if he is a non-fighting member who does not have a continuous combat function, he can only be targeted if he directly participates in hostilities. The United States believes

---

[27] *See* Nils Melzer, Interpretive Guidance on the Notion of Direct Participation in Hostilities under International Humanitarian Law 27 (2009), *available at* http://www.icrc.org/eng/assets/files/other/icrc-002-0990.pdf.

that the ICRC's interpretive guidance creates an illogical asymmetry between armed forces and organized armed groups that rewards civilians for supporting the operation of nonstate armed groups by rendering them immune from direct attack (absent direct participation in hostilities), while cooks and logisticians who are members of the armed forces of a State remain targetable based on their status as members of the armed forces. However, many States have adopted the ICRC view, leaving this issue unresolved at this time.

Other civilians, though not members of organized armed groups, may take a direct part in hostilities. They will generally fall into one of two categories—those who are not members of an organized armed group but are continuously engaged in hostilities—what some call the "revolving door" participant—and others who might take up a weapon against the armed forces of a State on a single or infrequent basis. Individuals in both categories would not be targetable based on membership, but would instead only be targetable "for such time" as they directly participate.

In the case of the civilian who is participating on a revolving door basis, that is, he acts as a farmer each day, but every night he engages in hostile acts toward the opposing armed forces, the United States generally takes the view that this individual, so long as he demonstrates the intent and capability to continue to participate in such activities, is targetable at any time. In contrast, the ICRC argues that the "unless and for such time" rule in article 51 of AP I would limit his targetability to the times when he is directly participating. In other words, while the United States might target that individual while he was working his farm by day, the ICRC would require the United States to wait to target him until the evening when the farmer was either committing hostile acts or preparing to commit such acts by moving to and from the place where the acts will occur.

Even the targetability of the category of civilians who only infrequently or on a one-time basis participate in hostilities is not without controversy. Here, the basis of debate is not the timing of the individual's participation, but the substance—in other words, what is participation? Do financiers, or those who make munitions or explosives, or those who store ammunition or weapons, directly participate and thus become targetable? As before, the United States takes a more aggressive approach to this question than does the ICRC. The ICRC argues that an individual's direct participation must meet three cumulative criteria. The first criterion is the threshold of harm: the act in question must be likely to adversely affect the military operations or military capacity of a party to the conflict, or, to inflict death, injury, or destruction on persons or objects protected against direct attack. To meet this criterion, the action must create harm of a sufficient degree to the enemy or to civilians.

If the first criterion is met, the second criterion is to establish a direct link between the action and the harm. This second criterion is direct causation and requires that there must be a direct causal link (i.e., "one step" causation) between the act in question and the harm likely to result from that act, or from a concrete and coordinated military operation of which that act constitutes an integral part. This does not include an indirect link (which would amount to indirect participation), such as working in a munitions factory or an oil refinery that supplies the enemy's military with war-sustaining capability. Rather, the action must be an integral part of a concrete military action.

Finally, the third criterion requires a belligerent nexus, or that the act must be designed to directly cause the required threshold of harm in support of a party to the conflict and to the detriment of another party to the conflict. If all three criteria are met, the individual can be targeted, but only for such time as he is taking direct part in hostilities.

b. Targeting Property

In addition to the targeting of persons, there are also specific provisions concerning the law of targeting military objectives. The current statement on this portion of the law of targeting is found in article 52 of AP I. The article states:

> Art 52. General Protection of civilian objects
> 1. Civilian objects shall not be the object of attack or of reprisals. Civilian objects are all objects which are not military objectives as defined in paragraph 2.
> 2. Attacks shall be limited strictly to military objectives. In so far as objects are concerned, military objectives are limited to those objects which by their nature, location, purpose or use make an effective contribution to military action and whose total or partial destruction, capture or neutralization, in the circumstances ruling at the time, offers a definite military advantage.
> 3. In case of doubt whether an object which is normally dedicated to civilian purposes, such as a place of worship, a house or other dwelling or a school, is being used to make an effective contribution to military action, it shall be presumed not to be so used.[28]

The first paragraph of this article grants the same immunity to civilian objects as is granted in the prior article of AP I to the civilian populace and individual civilians— immunity from attack. As in the case of civilians, this immunity can be forfeited.

Paragraph 2 of article 52 requires the commander to analyze an object's nature, location, purpose, or use to determine if it is a valid military objective. Some objects are military by their nature, such as tanks, artillery, and military aircraft. Objects that are not targetable due to their nature may become military objects, based on their location, purpose, or use. For example, a building that normally houses a civilian business would normally be a civilian object and protected from direct attack. However, if a portion of the building were used to house a military command post, its use would transform the

---

[28] *See* AP I art. 52.

normally civilian object into a targetable military objective. This would be true even if the rest of the building were still being used by civilians for nonmilitary purposes.[29] Objects that are concurrently both military and civilian are known as dual-use objects and can be targeted.

Paragraph 2 of article 52 contains two further qualifiers on the commander's ability to target property. Under paragraph 2, even if the commander has determined that the piece of property is a military object by its nature, location, purpose, or use, he must also determine (1) that the property makes an effective contribution to the military action, and (2) that the "total or partial destruction, capture or neutralization, in the circumstances ruling at the time, offers a definite military advantage." The first of these (item (1)) is a relatively low standard. One might argue that a piece of military equipment such as a tank that is in disrepair and nonfunctional may not be making an effective contribution to the military effort. However, the commander may determine that it could be used for spare parts or in a ruse or for some other military purpose and legitimately determine to target it.

The concluding portion of paragraph 2 (item (ii)) of article 52 of AP I requires a similar analysis but with a slightly higher standard. Once the commander has determined that the object's nature, location, purpose, or use provides the enemy with a military benefit, he must determine that the destruction of the object will provide his forces a

---

[29] AP COMMENTARY, paras. 2020–23, defines the terms "nature," "location," "purpose," and "use":

2020 A closer look at the various criteria used reveals that the first refers to objects which, by their "nature", make an effective contribution to military action. This category comprises all objects directly used by the armed forces: weapons, equipment, transports, fortifications, depots, buildings occupied by armed forces, staff headquarters, communications centres etc.

2021 The second criterion is concerned with the "location" of objects. Clearly, there are objects which by their nature have no military function but which, by virtue of their location, make an effective contribution to military action. This may be, for example, a bridge or other construction, or it could also be, as mentioned above, (13) a site which is of special importance for military operations in view of its location, either because it is a site that must be seized or because it is important to prevent the enemy from seizing it, or otherwise because it is a matter of forcing the enemy to retreat from it. It should be noted that the Working Group of Committee III introduced the location criterion without giving reasons.

2022 The criterion of "purpose" is concerned with the intended future use of an object, while that of "use" is concerned with its present function. Most civilian objects can become useful objects to the armed forces. Thus, for example, a school or a hotel is a civilian object, but if they are used to accommodate troops or headquarters staff, they become military objectives. It is clear from paragraph 3 that in case of doubt, such places must be presumed to serve civilian purposes.

2023 Other establishments or buildings which are dedicated to the production of civilian goods may also be used for the benefit of the army. In this case the object has a dual function and is of value for the civilian population, but also for the military. In such situations the time and place of the attack should be taken into consideration, together with, on the one hand, the military advantage anticipated, and on the other hand, the loss of human life which must be expected among the civilian population and the damage which would be caused to civilian objects.

"definite military advantage." Although these words are not clearly defined in the text, the AP Commentary states:

> …it is not legitimate to launch an attack which only offers potential or indeterminate advantages. Those ordering or executing the attack must have sufficient information available to take this requirement into account; in case of doubt, the safety of the civilian population, which is the aim of the Protocol, must be taken into consideration.[30]

Unless the target meets all three tests—the nature, location, purpose, or use test; the effective contribution test; *and* the "definite military advantage" test, the commander is precluded from attacking an object.

c. Weaponeering

Once it has been determined that the individual or object is a legitimate target, the person doing the targeting must then consider the means used to target and the method of munitions employment—both of which are an integral part of targeting, and both of which present legal proscriptions within the law of targeting. The means of targeting generally refers to the weapon used to engage the person, whether that be an infantryman's rifle, an explosive round fired from an artillery tube, or a bomb dropped from an aircraft. Every weapon used by the U.S military must pass a legal review to ensure that it complies with international law[31] and is not specifically prohibited.[32] As long as the weapon is not prohibited and has been appropriately reviewed, it is a valid means of targeting. However, it must also not be employed in a method that is a violation of the law of armed conflict.

The method of targeting is most often a matter of tactics where the commander decides how and when to employ a weapon system. However, it also has legal implications, particularly in light of the principle of proportionality.[33] The rule of proportionality is "an attempt to balance the conflicting military and humanitarian interests (or to balance military necessity and humanity) and is most evident in connection with the reduction of incidental damage caused by military operations."[34] As mentioned in the AP Commentary, proportionality, like distinction, is among the "general principles

---

[30] *Id.* para. 2024.

[31] *See* U.S. Dep't of the Army, Army Regulation 27-53, Review of Legality of Weapons under International Law (1 January 1979).

[32] For example, the CWC, *supra* note 12 and accompanying text, made the use of chemical weapons illegal as a method of warfare.

[33] *See generally* Jensen, *supra* note 4, at 1170–73.

[34] *See* A.P.V. Rogers, Law on the Battlefield 14 (1996).

relating to the protection of the civilian population which apply irrespective of whether the conflict is an international or an internal one."[35]

The authoritative statement on proportionality is found in AP I, articles 51.5(b) and 57.2(iii), which compel a member of the military to "refrain from deciding to launch any attack which may be expected to cause incidental loss of civilian life, injury to civilians, damage to civilian objects, or a combination thereof, which would be excessive in relation to the concrete and direct military advantage anticipated."[36]

The NIAC Manual provides an excellent explanation of the terms and meaning of proportionality[37] that need not be repeated here. The rule of proportionality applies only to civilians and civilian property.[38] There is no requirement that a combatant limit the quantum of his force when engaging another combatant or civilians who take a direct part in hostilities, unless there is potential risk to nonparticipating civilians. The rule of proportionality affects the method of targeting only if the commander anticipates that it may be expected to cause incidental injury to civilians or damage civilian property, otherwise known as collateral damage. There are several key words in this definition, including "may be expected," "concrete and direct," and "anticipated."

For the commander to be required to refrain from an attack, there must be some expectation of collateral damage. Therefore, if after reviewing the target, the commander determines that, given the information he has, there are no civilians in the area or civilian objects, he need not expect collateral damage. If that expectation, based on faulty information, proves to be wrong after the attack, there is no violation. This determination prior to the attack is made based on the best information available to him at the time the decision must be made.[39] It is the targeter's reasonable expectation that is the standard. If the targeter is relying on information from a source that has been faulty in the recent past, he may need to take additional steps to confirm the information before launching the attack. However, if the information comes from a trusted source, the commander can place full reliance on that information.

Once the targeter has ascertained the expected collateral damage, he must balance the damage against the anticipated concrete and direct military advantage to determine

---

[35] *See* AP COMMENTARY, para. 1449.

[36] AP I art. 57.2(iii).

[37] NIAC Manual, *supra* note 18, ¶ 2.1.1.4.

[38] *See* Michael N. Schmitt, *Ethics and Military Force: The Jus in Bello*, Address at the Carnegie Council for Ethics in International Affairs workshop on European and North American perspectives on ethics and the use of force, at 9 (Jan. 2002), *available at* http://www.carnegiecouncil.org/test/about/transcript_schmitt. html http://www.carnegiecouncil.org/studio/multimedia/20020107/index.html (last visited July 2, 2014).

[39] *See* Matthew Lippman, *Conundrums of Armed Conflict: Criminal Defenses to Violations of the Humanitarian Law of War*, 15 DICK. J. INT'L L. 1, 63 (1996) (discussing the *Rendulic* case where German general Rendulic was acquitted of charges of unnecessarily destroying civilian property, based on the ground that "the conditions, as they appeared to the defendant at the time, were sufficient upon which he could honestly conclude that urgent military necessity warrant the decision made.").

if the collateral damage will be excessive as compared to the military advantage to be gained from the attack. Concrete and direct military advantage is discussed in the AP Commentary. The Commentary states: "A military advantage can only consist in ground gained and in annihilating or weakening the enemy armed forces. In addition, it should be noted that the words 'concrete and direct' impose stricter conditions on the attacker than those implied by the criteria defining military objectives in Article 52."[40]

Although concrete and direct is a fairly high standard, it is based on the advantage anticipated by the targeter. In other words, if the attack is carried out and there is little military advantage gained, that is not relevant in the consideration of whether the commander appropriately applied the standard. The standard is completely forward looking, not retrospective. Of course, as with the expectation of collateral damage, the anticipation must be reasonable, but it need not be perfect.[41]

Even if these conditions are not met, that does not necessarily preclude the overall attack. Instead, the commander may reconsider his means or methods of attack in order to produce different results. The U.S. military has developed an intricate modeling process for estimating collateral damage that is not available outside of military channels but provides the commander with an accurate picture of the damage a munition will do in a particular scenario.[42]

In summary, when engaging a target, a targeter must first determine that the target is a combatant or a civilian who is taking direct part in hostilities by committing or having committed an act that is designed to directly harm the enemy. That civilian can be targeted "for such time" as he is participating directly. When targeting, the targeter must apply a reviewed and approved weapon system in a method that is not expected to cause collateral damage that would be excessive in relation to the concrete and direct military advantage anticipated from the attack.

Targeting in Transnational Armed Conflict against Terrorists

As demonstrated above, there is virtually no dispute within the international community or within the armed forces of the United States and its allies that civilians are and must remain immune from attack. Nor is there much dispute that, at times, the legitimate needs of an armed force justify divesting civilians and their property of this immunity when, as the result of their conduct, they participate directly in hostilities or become members of armed groups. As discussed above, the proverbial devil is in the details. Nowhere is this truer than in a TAC against terrorists.

---

[40] *See* AP COMMENTARY, para. 2218.

[41] *Prosecutor v. Ante Gotovina and Mladen Markac*, IT-06-90-A, Judgement (Int'l Crim. Trib. for the Former Yugoslavia), Nov. 16, 2012, *available at* http://www.unhcr.org/refworld/docid/50acffdd2.html.

[42] *See generally* Gregory S. McNeal, *Targeted Killing and Accountability*, 102 GEO. L.J. 681 (2014) [hereinafter McNeal].

I. TARGETING IN TAC

The complexity of complying with the distinction obligation is exponentially increased in the context of any TAC. This is because such conflicts are not, by definition, armed conflicts between the armed forces of warring States. Instead, at least one party to the conflict will be composed of nonstate fighters. Much like the typical noninternational or internal armed conflict, these fighters will normally appear to be civilians and utilize objects that would otherwise be civilian in nature and protected from attack. However, in addition to the traditional difficulties of internal armed conflict, TAC produces further complicating factors—decentralized organizational command and control and the dispersion of fighters.

Unlike traditional "internal" armed conflicts, where the control of the opposition forces is often centralized and the fighters are geographically bounded, TAC is characterized by the lack of geographic proximity between the fighting forces and the nonstate organization's leadership. Instead, the head of the nonstate organization may stay far away from the actual battle and exercise almost no control of the day-to-day actions of his fighters. Rather, he sends intermittent messages through various media, mostly carried over the Internet with general instructions, and then relies on his fighters to implement those instructions as they are able. Further, his fighters are not in communication with each other and may not even recognize each other as members of the same organization. They congregate in very small cells that are purposefully dispersed throughout the world and remain insular, acting with relative freedom on the general guidance that comes from the organization's leadership. As a result, using the traditional armed conflict methodology to discern which members of these organizations may be lawfully targeted is particularly challenging.

Therefore, it is vital to determine which rules apply to regulate the targeting of nonstate actors and assets to mitigate as much as possible the potentially devastating devaluation of the civilian protections through the effects of armed conflict. At the same time, it seems utterly illogical to suggest that outside the context of international armed conflict, there is no such thing as an "enemy" for purposes of targeting, but only civilians who temporarily lose their immunity by virtue of taking a direct part in hostilities which result in some "actual harm." Such a conception is fundamentally inconsistent with the history of noninternational armed conflicts during which government forces routinely treated organized opposition armed groups in the same way as they would treat the armed forces of opposing States during international armed conflicts. That conception also ignores the realities of armed transnational terrorist groups who often control State-like means of violence. Governments deserve the same authority to respond to organized terrorist "cells" whose intent and capabilities may be as dangerous and destructive as a State "enemy."

Application of targeting principles to TAC therefore warrants a broader scope of targeting authority than merely responding to civilians who take a direct part in hostilities.

It requires some methodology to distinguish individuals who remain immune from attack by virtue of their abstention from any participation in hostilities from those individuals who, by virtue of their connection with and conduct in support of, an armed hostile group, are justifiably characterized as lawful objects of attack. This methodology must be consistent with the underlying purposes of the LOAC.

Returning to the fundamental LOAC principle that everyone on the battlefield may be divided into three categories: combatants, noncombatants, and civilians, targeting of terrorists in TAC must remain true to the principle of distinction that underlies this division. Transnational armed terrorists are seldom, if ever, going to qualify as lawful combatants under LOAC principles because they do not meet the requirements of GPW, article 4.[43] They are also clearly not noncombatants. Therefore, they are civilians. However, as stated above, designating individuals devoted to committing hostile acts that will kill or injure large numbers of innocent civilians, or inflict death, injury, or damage to State armed forces, as persons protected by civilian immunity from direct attack, is inconsistent with the principles of the law of war. The United States has resolved this dilemma by designating such persons as "unprivileged enemy belligerents," a term that has its pedigree in the law of war. While this term is also much maligned as a method for determining treatment or legal status, as a tool of targeting it remains consistent with LOAC principles and provides a reasonable methodology for targeting in TAC.

In the 2009 Military Commissions Act, an Act dealing with the use of military commissions to try alien unprivileged enemy belligerents by military commission, not targeting, "unprivileged enemy belligerent" is defined as:

UNPRIVILEGED ENEMY BELLIGERENT.—The term "unprivileged enemy belligerent" means an individual (other than a privileged belligerent) who—

(A) has engaged in hostilities against the United States or its coalition partners;
(B) has purposefully and materially supported hostilities against the United States or its coalition partners; or
(C) was a part of al Qaeda at the time of the alleged offense under this chapter.[44]

It is clear that this detention standard was not intended to be a targeting standard; an individual who can be lawfully targeted can also be lawfully detained, but the reverse

---

[43] Memorandum from Office of the Assistant Att'y Gen. to Alberto R. Gonzales, Counsel to the President, at 6 (Aug. 1, 2002), *available at* http://www.justice.gov/olc/docs/memo-gonzales-aug1.pdf.

[44] 10 U.S.C. § 948a(7) (2009). As discussed *infra* in Chapter 5, while the definition was adopted to identify the category of individuals subject to trial by military commission, the definition mirrors the standard for detention of unprivileged belligerents applied by all three branches of the U.S. government, and therefore may properly be seen as the U.S. view on who is detainable under the LOAC in the war on terror.

is not necessarily true. However, in this case, these three categories also neatly supply a basis for analyzing targeting criteria in the war on terror, because the statutory provision has effectively embraced the targeting options outlined above. The first two, (A) and (B), are based on the actions of civilians that demonstrate that they have forfeited their civilian protections. The last paragraph, (C), accepts the membership theory, which allows the targeting of individuals based solely on their membership.

Beginning with paragraph (A), this standard reflects the application of the "direct participation in hostilities" test to targeting terrorists who continuously participate or do so on an infrequent or one-time basis. Once a terrorist has engaged in hostilities with U.S. forces, he may be attacked for such time as he is directly participating. For the "revolving door" terrorist, that means he can be targeted until he openly ceases to participate and withdraws himself from the fight. For the intermittent or one-time attacker, he can be targeted while preparing for, conducting, and returning from the attack.

In paragraph (B), the key phrase is "purposefully and materially supported hostilities." This is a very general definition and can be read very broadly to include persons who merely supply financial support to an organization involved in hostilities against the United States, though in State practice the definition has not been used to treat such persons as lawful targets.

As noted above, the statute is designed for purposes other than targeting, but it also provides insight into the targeting analysis. For targeting purposes, the statute's broad definition gives the commander great discretion while providing a discernible standard upon which to base his judgment. If the commander discovers a person who is purposefully or materially supporting hostilities, he can take action to target that individual, including the use of deadly force, if the support reaches the level of direct participation. It is here that the ICRC interpretive guidance is especially helpful.

For example, this standard would overcome the problem presented by the individual who constructs improvised explosive devices to be used on the streets of Baghdad but is not the person who actually places or triggers the device. On a strict reading of "actual harm," the individual who merely builds the device is not causing actual harm. However, it is clear that that individual is participating in terrorist activities. Similarly, the individual who is recruiting and paying individuals to act as suicide bombers is certainly participating in the hostilities but would not be targetable under a strict requirement of causing actual harm.

This methodology also supports the underlying principles of the LOAC, particularly the principle of distinction, because it removes from these fighters their civilian protections, thus emphasizing the immunity from targeting that civilians inherently possess.

This analysis has its analogy in a State's armed forces. Each military throughout the world has persons who do not normally serve a combat role, such as cooks, paymasters, clerks, and legal personnel. However, each of these persons who are members of the military are equally targetable with infantrymen, artilleryman, and aircraft pilots. Because they have joined the military, the equivalent to the armed wing of a nonstate organization, they have surrendered their civilian status as part of the organization they have embraced. Under a membership theory of direct participation in hostilities, it would be a similar argument for terrorists. For example, once a civilian joins the armed wing of a nonstate organization, as opposed to the political wing, he becomes targetable by opposing forces based on his membership, regardless of whether he is functioning as a cook, a paymaster, a clerk, or a legal specialist. Until he affirmatively renounces that membership and restricts his participation in that organization to political activities, he remains targetable.

This analysis is also consistent with the LOAC principle of proportionality. Because of the nature of the fighters and the fact that they are civilians who are either members of armed groups or persons who are taking part in hostilities, the proportionality analysis must reflect the reality of the situation. By participating in hostilities, these civilians have surrendered the protections they would otherwise be granted. Therefore, when a commander conducts his proportionality analysis, he need not account for the civilians who are fighters but instead must only apply the principle as he would under the Protocol to any other (non-targetable) civilians and civilian property that will be affected by his attack. In applying this proportionality analysis, the commander must still determine that danger of death or injury to non-targetable civilians is not excessive in relation to the concrete and direct military advantage anticipated from the attack. However, in doing so, he must balance that against the military advantage gained from the death of the targetable terrorists.

2. DRONES

One of the most used targeting methods by both President Bush and President Obama is unmanned aerial vehicles, or drones.[45] This has become very controversial for a number of reasons, surprisingly few of which have anything to do with targeting. The U.S. government has defended its position on a number of occasions and through various spokesmen. Attorney General Eric Holder stated: "In response to the attacks perpetrated—and the continuing threat posed—by al Qaeda, the Taliban and associated forces, Congress has authorized the President to use all necessary and appropriate force against these groups. Because the United States is in an armed conflict, we are authorized to take action against enemy belligerents under international law. The Constitution empowers the President to protect the nation from any imminent threat of violent attack. And

---

[45] *See* Uri Friedman, *Anthropology of an Idea: Targeted Killing*, FOREIGN POL'Y (Sept./Oct. 2012), *available at* http://www.foreignpolicy.com/articles/2012/08/13/targeted_killings; Lena Groeger & Cora Currier, *Stacking Up the Administration's Drone Claims*, PROPUBLICA (Sept. 13, 2012, 1:15 p.m.), http://projects. propublica.org/graphics/cia-drones-strikes.

international law recognizes the inherent right of national self-defense. None of this has changed by the fact that we are not in a conventional war."[46]

Additionally, the technologically advanced nature of a drone is immaterial to its lawful use in armed conflict. As Attorney General Holder has stated:

> These [LOAC] principles do not forbid the use of stealth or technologically advanced weapons. In fact the use of advanced weapons may help to ensure that the best intelligence is available for planning and carrying out operations, and that the risk of civilian casualties can be minimized or avoided all together.[47]

The legality under international law of using drones to make these strikes is seldom questioned. In recent presentations, members of both the ICRC and Human Rights First have agreed that if the targeting principles outlined above are followed, drones present no unique issues.[48]

Rather, most of the concern over the use of drones has focused on two issues: (1) the lack of transparency of the analysis conducted when commanders make the LOAC decisions concerning the designation of individuals as targetable, and then the subsequent proportionality analysis in connection with attacks against such individuals; and (2) the use of drones to target individuals who are not geographically in an area of active armed conflict.

On the issue of transparency, different groups have produced widely divergent estimates of the numbers of civilians killed or injured by armed drone attacks. The United States has been hesitant to discuss with too much openness its classified process for making targeting decisions. Critics have argued that increased transparency on the part of the United States will not only allow critical review (and potential justification) for designating individuals as targetable under the law of targeting, but will also allow review of the proportionality decisions made in each attack.

Opponents of the current U.S. process also argue that such transparency would play a key role in establishing State practice going forward. It is clear that drones will continue to play an increasing role in armed conflict. The norms and best practices established now by the United States will serve as the basis for continuing use by other nations in other conflicts. To the degree that increased transparency will not only increase the (perceived) lawfulness of this targeting methodology but also legitimate its proper use, it is in the best interest of the United States and the international community at large.

---

[46] *Contemporary Practice of the United States Relating to International Law, Use of Force and Arms Control: Attorney General Discusses Targeting of U.S. Persons*, 106 AM. J. INT'L L 673, 674 (2012) [hereinafter *Attorney General Discusses Targeting*].

[47] *Id.* at 675.

[48] Panel Discussion, *Drone Wars*, Nov. 28, 2012, Brigham Young University (discussion of the legal, ethical, and strategic issues relating to the use of drones, with Eric Jensen, moderator, and panelists Christopher M. Jenks, Gary Brown, and Gabor Rona.) Video *available at* http://kennedy.byu.edu/archive/lecture.php?id=2615.

Then Assistant to the President for Homeland Security and Counterterrorism, John O. Brennan, acknowledged this in April 2012 when he said:

> If we want other nations to use [drones] responsibly, we must use them responsibly. If we want other nations to adhere to high and rigorous standards for their use, then we must do so as well. We cannot expect of others what we will not do ourselves. President Obama has therefore demanded that we hold ourselves to the highest possible standards, that, at every step, we be as thorough and deliberate as possible.[49]

A second source of criticism of the use of drones by U.S. forces is that it is taking place away from areas of current conflict, or so-called "hot battlefields." The argument against such targeting methods is that if the attack occurs outside the current battlefield, the LOAC does not apply, but rather human rights law, which might result in very different targeting decision outcomes. In response to this criticism, the U.S. Attorney General has stated:

> Our legal authority is not limited to the battlefields in Afghanistan. Indeed, neither Congress nor our federal courts have limited the geographic scope of our ability to use force to the current conflict in Afghanistan. We are at war with a stateless enemy, prone to shifting operations from country to country.... This does not mean that we can use force whenever or wherever we want. International legal principles, including respect for another nation's sovereignty, constrain our ability to act unilaterally. But the use of force in foreign territory would be consistent with these international legal principles if conducted, for example, with the consent of the nation involved—or a determination that the nation is unable or unwilling to deal effectively with a threat to the United States.[50]

Until this approach changes, it appears that the United States does not believe it is limited to "hot" battlefields when engaging terrorists, as a matter of law. On the other hand, the United States has taken a restrained policy approach to attacking terrorists outside of active battlefields. In President Obama's May 2013 speech at the National Defense University, he stated:

> Beyond the Afghan theater, we only target al Qaeda and its associated forces. And even then, the use of drones is heavily constrained. America does not take strikes

---

[49] *Contemporary Practice of the United States Relating to International Law, Use of Force and Arms Control: Senior White House Official Confirms Drone Strikes, Discusses U.S. Targeting Principles and Practices*, 106 AM. J. INT'L L. 670, 672 (2012).

[50] *Attorney General Discusses Targeting, supra* note 46, at 674.

when we have the ability to capture individual terrorists; our preference is always to detain, interrogate, and prosecute. America cannot take strikes wherever we choose; our actions are bound by consultations with partners, and respect for state sovereignty. America does not take strikes to punish individuals; we act against terrorists who pose a continuing and imminent threat to the American people, and when there are no other governments capable of effectively addressing the threat. And before any strike is taken, there must be near-certainty that no civilians will be killed or injured—the highest standard we can set.[51]

There is no doubt that TAC creates difficulties in the targeting of persons and property. The complexity of the situations that commanders face is dramatically increased in TAC. A restrictive view of targeting of terrorists, whether as a matter of law or of policy, will act as an incentive for terrorists to continue to move and work among the civilian population, thus increasing the danger to civilians. A less restrictive view may not only increase a State's ability to respond to terrorists, but may also reinforce the fundamental principles of the LOAC that are designed to protect civilians from the effects of hostilities.

Targeting U.S. Persons Abroad and Targeting within the United States

In September 2011, Anwar Al-Aulaqi was killed by a drone strike in Yemen. This strike was different than others before it because Al-Aulaqi was a U.S. citizen and had already been the subject of some litigation attempting to preserve him from being targeted. That litigation was unsuccessful,[52] but the courts never resolved the ultimate question, and his death created a great deal of controversy as to the legal justification for using force against a U.S. citizen abroad. In response to the controversy, U.S. Attorney General Eric Holder spoke at Northwestern University School of Law in March 2012. In his speech, he presented the view of the Obama administration on the targeting of U.S. persons abroad. He said:

Now, it is an unfortunate but undeniable fact that some of the threats we face come from a small number of United States citizens who have decided to commit violent attacks against their own country from abroad. Based on generations-old legal principles and Supreme Court decisions handed down during World War II,

---

[51]   Remarks at National Defense University, 2013 DAILY COMP. PRES. DOC. (May 23, 2013) [hereinafter May 2013 NDU Speech], *available at* http://www.gpo.gov/fdsys/pkg/FR-2009-01-27/pdf/E9-1885.pdf.

[52]   Al-Aulaqi v. Obama, 727 F. Supp. 2d 1 (D.D.C. 2010) (granting motion to dismiss). A subsequent case, Al-Aulaqi v. Panetta, No. 1:12-cv-01192, 2012 WL 3024212 (D.D.C. July 18, 2012), concerns the now-deceased Al-Aulaqi and two additional deceased individuals (including Al-Aulaqi's son) and alleges, inter alia, deprivation of life without due process of law.

as well as during this current conflict, it's clear that United States citizenship alone does not make such individuals immune from being targeted. But it does mean that the government must take into account all relevant constitutional considerations with respect to United States citizens—even those who are leading efforts to kill innocent Americans. Of course, the most relevant is the Fifth Amendment's Due Process Clause, which says that the government may not deprive a citizen of his or her life without due process.

The Supreme Court has made clear that the Due Process Clause does not impose one-size-fits-all requirements, but instead mandates procedural safeguards that depend on specific circumstances. In cases arising under the Due Process Clause—including a case involving a U.S. citizen captured in the conflict against al Qaeda—the Court has applied a balancing approach weighing the private interest that will be affected against the interest the government is trying to protect, and the burdens the government would face in providing additional process. Where national security operations are at stake, due process takes into account the realities of combat.

. . .

Let me be clear: an operation using lethal force in a foreign country, targeted against a U.S. citizen who is a senior operational leader of al Qaeda or associated forces, and who is actively engaged in planning to kill Americans, would be lawful in at least the following circumstances: First, the U.S. government has determined, after a thorough and careful review, that the individual poses an imminent threat of violent attack against the United States; second, capture is not feasible; and third, the operation would be conducted in a manner consistent with applicable law of war principles.

. . .

Some have argued that the President is required to get permission from a federal court before taking action against a U.S. citizen who is a senior operational leader of al Qaeda or associated forces. This is simply not accurate. "Due Process" and "judicial process" are not the same, particularly when it comes to national security. The Constitution guarantees due process, not judicial process.[53]

This speech by Attorney General Holder is a very clear statement of how the Obama administration views targeting U.S. persons engaged in the war against terrorism. It

---

[53] *Attorney General Discusses Targeting, supra* note 46, *at* 674–76. The Congressional Research Service has also produced a memorandum analyzing the targeting of U.S. persons by drones, JENNIFER K. ELSEA, CONG. RESEARCH SERV., MEMORANDUM: LEGAL ISSUES RELATED TO THE LETHAL TARGETING OF U.S. CITIZENS SUSPECTED OF TERRORIST ACTIVITIES (May 4, 2012), *available at* http://www.fas.org/sgp/crs/natsec/target.pdf.

was followed by President Obama's May 2013 speech at the National Defense University where he said:

> For the record, I do not believe it would be constitutional for the government to target and kill any U.S. citizen—with a drone or with a shotgun—without due process. Nor should any president deploy armed drones over U.S. soil.
>
> But when a U.S. citizen goes abroad to wage war against America and is actively plotting to kill U.S. citizens, and when neither the United States nor our partners are in a position to capture him before he carries out a plot, his citizenship should no more serve as a shield than a sniper shooting down on an innocent crowd should be protected from a swat team.[54]

President Obama provided no greater clarity on what "due process" means in the context of targeting United States' persons overseas, so it appears that Attorney General Holder's explanation is still current U.S. policy.

Ongoing litigation, congressional action, and public opinion may bring about changes to this current position, but for now, the Obama administration argues that there are no legal impediments to targeting U.S. persons abroad, provided the outlined processes are taken.

The issue of targeting U.S. persons engaged in terrorist activities within the United States has also been raised, but the Obama administration has produced no similar statement. However, it seems like the same legal arguments for targeting U.S. persons abroad would also allow such targeting in the United States.[55]

Modern Policy in the Law of Targeting

While a review of the law is a vitally important discussion for the continued viability of the LOAC, current U.S. military practice makes much of the discussion unnecessary, at least with regard to the proportionality analysis. Current military targeting procedures have placed such restrictions on a commander's ability to engage targets where collateral damage is anticipated that the targeting commander never gets to the point of applying the LOAC standard.

With the ubiquitous nature of media coverage in modern warfare, few military operations happen without immediately being broadcast throughout the world over television, radio, and the Internet. The arrival of the U.S. Marines on the beaches of

---

[54] May 2013 NDU Speech, *supra* note 51.

[55] Marshall Thompson, *The Legality of Armed Drone Strikes against U.S. Citizens within the United States*, 2013 BYU L. REV. 153, *available at* http://digitalcommons.law.byu.edu/cgi/viewcontent.cgi?article=2704 &context=lawreview.

Somalia to awaiting news crews was but the precursor to the in-depth media coverage and scrutiny in today's armed conflicts. In recognition of the role of media, the U.S. Department of Defense solicited media outlets to provide reporters who could be embedded within military units throughout its recent operations in Iraq. Although the value and benefits of such a plan may be open to discussion, the recognition of the effect of media on armed conflict is virtually uncontested.

One of the areas where the media's effect has been the most pronounced is in the area of targeting. The real-time broadcast of military operations and their effects have brought each collateral damage assessment made by a commander into sharp focus for hundreds of millions of people who read or listen to the media reports of the attack. After each engagement, the media lists in great detail the number of civilians killed or injured and the civilian property damaged by the attack, with special emphasis if any of the casualties were children. The general outrage at each civilian death, whether considered necessary by the attacking commander or not, has created immense pressure on governments, particularly those in Europe and North America, to alter their military procedures and operations to account for the negative effects of any collateral damage. They have done this in two ways: the establishment of procedures and approval levels for an attack where collateral damage is anticipated that completely overlay the LOAC targeting standard, and the increased focus on information warfare and non-kinetic targeting to both prevent the need for kinetic targeting and to counter the effects of kinetic targeting when it occurs.

As noted above, the law-of-armed-conflict standard clearly is based on the "anticipated" advantage of the attack by the commander conducting it. The commander is not required to be able to predict the future. Nor is he required to search out every possible misapplication of force that could occur from his targeting strategy—only those that may be expected. The standard is the reasonableness of the commander's decision, and the reasonableness of the commander's decision is determined in light of the anticipated results, not the actual results. Despite this clear standard, many governments have placed additional restrictions on the military commander's ability to target that are not required by the LOAC. Two examples are illustrative.

In a recent case brought before the Israeli Supreme Court,[56] petitioners argued that the Israeli military practice of "targeted killings" violated both human rights and the law of war. The Court limited its consideration of the principle of proportionality in

---

[56] The Public Committee Against Torture in Israel, et al. v. The Government of Israel, et al. HCJ 769/02, [2006] (vol. 2) ISR. L. REP. 459 (December 14, 2006) (opinion of A. Barak) [hereinafter Public Committee]. Note that the use of the word "proportionate" by the Israeli court to describe the test for proportionality is not the normal annunciation of the rule. As stated above, the rule of proportionality requires a commander to "refrain from deciding to launch any attack which may be expected to cause incidental loss of civilian life, injury to civilians, damage to civilian objects, or a combination thereof, which would be excessive in relation to the concrete and direct military advantage anticipated." AP I art. 57.2(iii). The LOAC standard is that the damage cannot be "excessive" rather than that it must be proportionate.

this case to its application in the law of armed conflict, and then restated the principle as thus:

> The proportionality test determines that attack upon innocent civilians is not permitted if the collateral damage caused to them is not proportionate to the military advantage (in protecting combatants and civilians). In other words, attack is proportionate if the benefit stemming from the attainment of the proper military objective is proportionate to the damage caused to innocent civilians harmed by it.[57]

The Court then went on to state "the law dealing with preventative acts on the part of the army which cause the deaths of terrorists and of innocent by-standers requires *ex post* examination of the conduct of the army. That examination must—thus determines customary international law—be of an objective character."[58] It is unclear where in customary international law the Court found this requirement. It is certainly not contained within the LOAC.

The Court continued by stating that when doing a post-operation review "[t]he question is whether the decision of the military commander falls within the zone of reasonable activity on the part of the military commander. If the answer is yes, the Court will not exchange the military commander's security discretion with the security discretion of the Court."[59] The Court further stated: "[t]he decision of the question whether the benefit stemming from the preventative strike is proportionate to the collateral damage caused to innocent civilians harmed by it is a legal question, the expertise about which is in the hands of the judicial branch."[60] By turning the collateral damage analysis into a judicial question, the Court has removed what has traditionally been a commander's decision from the military and placed it in the judicial branch. This is, again, not part of the LOAC, but a domestic attempt to provide greater overview of military operations that may cause collateral damage.

In the end, the Israeli Supreme Court refused to grant the petitioners' request to strike down the government's policy of targeted killings, but it did remove the ultimate discretion of the commander because he could now assume that, on a case-by-case basis, the Court would review his decision and determine the legality of the attack. There is no doubt that this will cause increased hesitation on the part of the commander when making a targeting decision. Although there is a normative aspect to this development, the important point for this chapter is that modern policy and procedure are injecting different and more constraining requirements on the LOAC principles applicable to targeting that make the targeting of terrorists in TAC much more difficult than the LOAC standard would require.

---

[57] Public Committee, *supra* note 56, para. 45.
[58] *Id.* para. 54.
[59] *Id.* para. 57.
[60] *Id.* para. 58.

Another example of this phenomenon is the escalation of approval authority for launching an attack where collateral damage is anticipated. As explained above, under the LOAC, the decision to launch an attack lies with the commander who is ordering the attack. While the Israeli court has added a post-hoc review, the United States has elevated the initial decision approval authority to levels well above the commander at the scene of the attack. Rather than the attacking commander making that determination, the request must be sent to higher authorities and acted upon at levels far from the battlefield.

A recent paper by Professor Gregory S. McNeal of Pepperdine University provides important details on the U.S. process of targeting and the application of policy limitations on battlefield targeting.[61] Most of these steps are not required by the LOAC and actually make the LOAC principles virtually less meaningful through requiring standards far more restrictive than the law requires. As responsive as the military systems are, there is no doubt that seeking approval authority from commanders or civilians away from the battlefield must increase the time necessary to launch the attack. In a world where terrorists are fleeting targets, any delay may mean an opportunity is missed.

Additionally, if the anticipated death of a certain number of civilians as collateral damage in an attack would disqualify that attack, this serves the perverse purpose of incentivizing terrorists to continue to operate among innocent civilians. The more civilians the terrorists can surround themselves with, the less responsive the targeting decision will be, and the less likely it will be that the attack is even launched. Thus, modern law and policy in TAC against terrorists is not only detached from the LOAC principles applicable to targeting but ironically may be encouraging the most undesirable outcome: for terrorists to operate among civilians to the maximum extent possible.

In addition to the increased approval levels and post-decision review of targeting, modern militaries have also turned their targeting against terrorists in TAC to non-kinetic methods in an effort to increase effectiveness and to decrease public outcry over the death of innocent civilians. Over the past decade, the military discipline of information operations has moved farther to the forefront of planning both at the tactical and strategic levels. Military manuals have been written and doctrine promulgated to raise the level of focus on these non-kinetic tools at the commander's disposal. Much of this has been in response to increased capability through advancing technology, but it has also been viewed as an effective non-kinetic method of target engagement that removes the risk of collateral damage and its resulting popular outcry. Two of the most prominent aspects of information operations include psychological operations and computer network operations (CNO).

Psychological operations, or military information support operations as they are now known, have been defined as "planned operations to convey selected information and indicators to foreign audiences to influence their emotions, motives, objective

---

[61] *See* McNeal, *supra* note 42.

reasoning, and ultimately the behavior of foreign governments, organizations, groups, and individuals."[62] It is not a new capability in the military arsenal, but increased focus has been put on its effectiveness in TAC. The idea behind psychological operations is to use information as a weapon. In practice, the information is most often true, but the method of using the information becomes an effective tool to target specific audiences.

Unfortunately it is not only Western militaries that are making effective use of psychological operations. One of the best examples of the effective use of psychological operations is that used against coalition forces in both Afghanistan and Iraq. Knowing that the civilian populace and governments of the coalition partners have little patience for civilian casualties, terrorists have purposely conducted their attacks in ways that will put the local civilian populace at risk to any military response. As the military responds, it is inevitable that some civilian casualties result. The terrorists have become experts at then publicizing these civilian casualties and emphasizing the fact that the deaths and injuries were caused by military action, but downplaying their own role in creating the target among the civilian populace. While this is a clear violation of article 58, AP I,[63] the terrorists are able to present the facts through various cooperative media outlets in a very effective manner that focuses the attention on the military response, as opposed to the terrorist actions.

Of course, those fighting TAC are also engaged in psychological operations on a grand scale, targeting both the local populaces and the terrorists themselves. This war of words and ideas is an essential, and mostly bloodless, part of the conflict. Sometimes, the only way to victory is to somehow exchange one set of ideas in the minds of an enemy with another set of ideas.

Cyberspace provides another non-kinetic means of targeting that is dramatically increasing in importance. The recent creation of Cyber Command by the U.S. government, as well as the fact that over 140 nations are reported to have or be developing cyber weapons,[64] and that over 30 countries are creating cyber units in their

---

[62] Joint Chiefs of Staff, Joint Pub 3–13, Information Operations II-9–II-10 (Nov. 17, 2012).

[63] Article 58 states:

Article 58—Precautions against the effects of attacks
The Parties to the conflict shall, to the maximum extent feasible:
  (a) without prejudice to Article 49 of the Fourth Convention, endeavour to remove the civilian population, individual civilians and civilian objects under their control from the vicinity of military objectives;
  (b) avoid locating military objectives within or near densely populated areas;
  (c) take the other necessary precautions to protect the civilian population, individual civilians and civilian objects under their control against the dangers resulting from military operations.

AP I art. 58.

[64] Susan W. Brenner & Leo L. Clarke, *Civilians in Cyberwarfare: Casualties*, 13 SMU Sci. & Tech. L. Rev. 249, 249 (2009–2010).

militaries,[65] reflects the importance of this new means of targeting. Cyberspace will play an increasing role in the fight against terrorism as terrorists continue to use the Internet to both coordinate their efforts and conduct their operations.

In a celebrated case, intelligence operatives from the United Kingdom conducted cyber operations on a terrorist website and substituted a recipe for making cupcakes for information on the website for making explosive devices.[66] While this is only one example of the use of CNO in the fight against terrorists, it highlights the potential for such capabilities in this fight.

These methods of targeting have the potential to be extremely effective in TAC against terrorists. Because of the nature of the dispersion of terrorist organizations, much of their communication travels over the Internet. Attacking that method of communication, or even exploiting it for one's own purposes, could potentially yield significant benefits in combating transnational terrorists. If it were possible to gain access over the Internet to information that was being sent from one terrorist operative to another, it would be a great intelligence-gathering technique. Perhaps even more beneficial would be gaining access to a terrorist leader's e-mail or messaging system and sending out false or inaccurate communications that would potentially foil future plots or lead to the capture or death of terrorist operatives.

There is no doubt that as this TAC against terrorists continues, both psychological and cyberspace operations can be very effective non-kinetic means of targeting terrorists, not only for information, but also to disrupt activities and potentially lead to the capture or death of terrorists. Further, because of the strain on governments caused by traditional targeting methods and the resulting collateral damage as amplified by ubiquitous media coverage, modern policy will drive governments to more comprehensive reliance on these non-kinetic tools. The current constraints on targeting procedures, such as heightened approval levels, demonstrate the governments' desire to avoid the media scrutiny collateral damage brings. Non-kinetic alternatives may reduce this public outcry and become an effective tool in this fight. However, it is important to note that some CNO may have adverse effects on civilians and civilian property and would be required to comply with traditional law-of-war principles regarding protection of civilians and civilian property, particularly in those instances where those effects may be equivalent to the effects of a kinetic attack.[67]

---

[65] William J. Lynn, III, *The Pentagon's Cyberstrategy, One Year Later: Defending Against the Next Cyberattack*, FOREIGN AFFAIRS (website), Sept. 28, 2011, http://www.foreignaffairs.com/articles/68305/william-j-lynn-iii/the-pentagons-cyberstrategy-one-year-later.

[66] *See* Duncan Gardham, *MI6 Attacks al-Qaeda in "Operation Cupcake,"* TELEGRAPH, June 2, 2011, http://www.telegraph.co.uk/news/uknews/terrorism-in-the-uk/8553366/MI6-attacks-al-Qaeda-in-Operation-Cupcake.html.

[67] *See generally* Jensen, *supra* note 4, at 1170–73 (discussing key law of principles and their application to computer network attacks).

Conclusion

Though the transnational armed conflict against terrorists is neither a traditional international armed conflict nor a traditional noninternational armed conflict, the LOAC still applies to all military operations supporting this fight. Questions such as the identity of terrorists and the ability to target them while intermixed within the civilian populace can be answered by the application of traditional LOAC principles, even when using advanced technological means or targeting. Further, the desire to interdict those who support them in their terrorist acts, and the length of time those conducting and supporting terrorist acts can be targeted, are all questions that can be answered based on the core principles of targeting.

Some adaptation will be necessary to allow a commander to target terrorists, whether considered unprivileged enemy belligerents, members of organized armed groups, or civilians participating directly in hostilities, over an extended period of time. Otherwise, the fundamental principles of LOAC, such as distinction and proportionality, will eventually be eroded because of the realities of fighting transnational armed conflicts.

4

Interrogation and Treatment of Detainees in the Global War on Terror

by Richard B. "Dick" Jackson

Introduction

Interrogation is at the core of the legal debates regarding the al-Qaeda and Taliban members detained by the U.S. government after the inception of the Global War on Terror (GWOT) in October 2001. The desire to obtain timely and accurate intelligence from captured terrorists drove the discussion, from the fall of 2001 to late 2008, when Supreme Court cases, legislation, and policy developments restored specific law-of-war standards to the U.S. military's treatment and interrogation of detainees.[1] In the interim, the military (with substantial policy direction from the leadership of the U.S. Department of Defense [DoD], the U.S. Department of Justice's Office of Legal Counsel [OLC], and the White House) essentially abandoned its long-standing reliance on law-of-war treaties and principles applicable to international armed conflict as the baseline for the treatment of detained terrorists, in favor of a narrowly drawn legal position that allowed the U.S. government to selectively use aggressive interrogation and treatment techniques that did not comport with the time-tested law-of-war standards traditionally applied by the military to all of its detainees. Although the change in approach to the application of the law of war was resisted at every level by the military legal community, some of the aggressive interrogation and treatment techniques

---

[1] President Obama's January 22, 2009, Executive Order applied the Army Field Manual standard, discussed *infra* at notes 135–140 and accompanying text, which is based on an international law standard, to the Central Intelligence Agency's (CIA) interrogation action, withdrawing President Bush's Executive Order 13440. The CIA standard for interrogation is not the subject of this chapter.

adopted for these terrorists were able to migrate to the field and resulted in mistreatment of detainees in several instances despite the efforts of many Judge Advocates in the chain of command. Those standards of treatment were restored between 2005 and 2009 and they were reinforced for military personnel engaged in GWOT.

The Historical Application of Geneva Convention Standards

The U.S. military has been at the forefront of training and applying the law of war to detention in military operations since well before the 1907 Hague Regulations or the 1949 Geneva Conventions. The Lieber Code, developed at the request of the Chief of Staff of the Army, General Halleck, by a Napoleonic War veteran, Francis Lieber, set the standard for treatment of a captured enemy in the American Civil War.[2] Despite the potential for applying a brutal internal armed conflict standard to "rebels" who had seceded from the Union, the "Lieber Code" required Union soldiers to treat a captured enemy with respect and humanity, in accordance with standards for international armed conflict:

Art. 49. A prisoner of war is a public enemy armed or attached to the hostile army for active aid, who has fallen into the hands of the captor, either fighting or wounded, on the field or in the hospital, by individual surrender or by capitulation.

All soldiers, of whatever species of arms; all men who belong to the rising en masse of the hostile country; all those who are attached to the army for its efficiency and promote directly the object of the war, except such as are hereinafter provided for; all disabled men or officers on the field or elsewhere, if captured; all enemies who have thrown away their arms and ask for quarter, are prisoners of war, and as such exposed to the inconveniences as well as entitled to the privileges of a prisoner of war....

Art. 56. A prisoner of war is subject to no punishment for being a public enemy, nor is any revenge wreaked upon him by the intentional infliction of any suffering, or disgrace, by cruel imprisonment, want of food, by mutilation, death, or any other barbarity.

Neither did the Code condone cruelty or torture. Instead, Lieber advised:

Art. 16. Military necessity does not admit of cruelty—that is, the infliction of suffering for the sake of suffering or for revenge, nor of maiming or wounding except in fight, nor of torture to extort confessions.

---

[2] Francis Lieber, Instructions for the Government of Armies of the United States in the Field (The Lieber Code), U.S. War Dep't General Orders No. 100 (Apr. 24, 1863), *reprinted in* Laws of Armed Conflicts: A Collection of Conventions, Resolutions & Other Documents (Dietrich Schindler & Jiri Toman eds., 4th ed. 2004) [hereinafter Lieber Code]. The Lieber Code is the first codification of the Law of War, prepared by a former soldier, for soldiers, to regulate armed conflict.

By promulgating this Code as General Order 100 to the Union Armies, President Lincoln endorsed one of the basic premises of the law of war: "Men who take up arms against one another in public war do not cease on this account to be moral beings, responsible to one another and to God."[3]

The United States participated fully in the negotiation and ratification of the principal law of war treaties of the twentieth century, the Hague Regulations of 1907,[4] and the Geneva Conventions of 1929 and 1949,[5] which regulated the treatment of a captured enemy and applied these same standards to their capture and treatment. The 1929 Geneva Convention for the Treatment of Prisoners of War (1929 Geneva Convention),[6] which applied to many countries during World War II, mandated treatment standards for captured personnel, similar to those of the Lieber Code:

> Art. 2 ... [Prisoners of war] shall at all times be humanely treated and protected, particularly against acts of violence, from insults and from public curiosity....
>
> Art. 3 Prisoners of war are entitled to respect for their persons and honour....
>
> Art. 5 ... No pressure shall be exercised on prisoners to obtain information regarding the situation in their armed forces or their country. Prisoners who refuse to reply may not be threatened, insulted, or exposed to unpleasantness or disadvantages of any kind whatsoever.

The U.S. Army field manuals promulgated for use during World War II and afterward maintained the high standards of treatment prescribed by the 1929 Geneva Convention. The interrogation field manuals published in 1940 and 1945 prohibited coercion, consistent with the requirements of article 5 of the 1929 Geneva Convention.[7] The 1940 version commented on the inefficacy of coercion, recommending "recognized law enforcement" methods instead, adding, "Resort to third degree or torture generally indicates that the examiner lacks aptitude or training or is too indifferent and lazy to apply sound methods of interrogation."[8] The U.S. Army's Prisoner of War Technical Manual from 1944 applied the "spirit as well as the letter" of the 1929 Geneva Convention, quoting

---

[3] *Id.* art. 15.

[4] Article 1 of Hague IV adopted a four-part standard for defining members of the armed forces, militia, and volunteer corps entitled to be treated as prisoners of war upon capture, Hague IV art. 4 mandated that prisoners of war be "humanely treated."

[5] The Hague IV definition is also found in GPW art. 4, and the GPW also mandated humane treatment of those who fit the definition.

[6] Convention Relative to the Treatment of Prisoners of War, July 27, 1929, 47 Stat. 2021, 118 L.N.T.S. 343.

[7] U.S. War Dep't, Field Manual 30-15, Military Intelligence: Examination of Enemy Personnel, Repatriates, Documents, and Materiel, para. 9a. (22 July 1940) [hereinafter 1940 Field Manual 30-15]; U.S. War Dep't, Field Manual 30-15, Military Intelligence: Examination of Enemy Personnel, Repatriates, Documents, and Materiel, para. 45 (June 1945).

[8] 1940 Field Manual 30-15, *supra* note 7, para. 9c.

directly the "humane treatment" provisions of articles 2 and 3, while the "Enforcement of Discipline" section prohibited "cruel and inhuman" treatment.[9]

After the adoption of the Geneva Conventions of 1949, which incorporated provisions to protect partisan groups and civilians on the battlefield,[10] as well as minimum standards of humane treatment for "non-international armed conflict" in common article 3 to all four Geneva Conventions (GC or "the Geneva Conventions"), the U.S. military adopted the Prisoner of War (PW) treatment standard from GPW for treatment and interrogation of detainees. Civilians who were interned for reasons of security or their own safety in occupied territory were to be treated in accordance with GCIV.[11] In a seminal 1951 academic article on the subject of "unprivileged belligerents," Major Richard Baxter (who worked for the Office of the Judge Advocate General, International Law Division, at the time) indicated that the GC left a gap between GPW and GCIV, particularly for civilians who were found to be committing belligerent acts in a zone of conflict, but were not part of a "levée en mass" (a spontaneous uprising of the populace against the invaders).[12] Several years later, however, in preparing a field manual to guide U.S. soldiers in the field in implementing the GC (which were ratified by the United States in 1955), Major Baxter penned the following admonition: "those protected by GC[IV] also include all persons who have engaged in hostile or belligerent conduct but who are not entitled to treatment as prisoners of war."[13] The U.S. Army's 1951 Interrogation Field Manual adopted the GPW or GCIV treatment standards for all those subject to interrogation, particularly with

---

[9] U.S. War Dep't, Technical Manual 19-500, Prisoner of War Administration para. 2. and 57c., respectively (5 October 1944).

[10] GPW Commentary. According to the Commentary:

> During the preparatory work for the Conference, and even during the Conference itself, two schools of thought were observed. Some delegates considered that partisans should have to fulfill conditions even stricter than those laid down by the Hague Regulations in order to benefit by the provisions of the Convention. On the other hand, other experts or delegates held the view that resistance movements should be given more latitude. The problem was finally solved by the assimilation of resistance movements to militias and corps of volunteers "not forming part of the armed forces" of a Party to the conflict.

Id. at 49–50. *See generally* IIA Final Record of the Diplomatic Conference of Geneva of 1949, at 241–43 (1949). The partisan debate was informed by the delegates' recent experience in World War II, where partisans in Russia were mistreated with impunity by the German military. *See* U.S. v. von Leeb et al. (The German High Command Trial), XII Law Reports of Trials of War Criminals 40 (U.N. War Crimes Commission 1949) (noting evidence that German policy was to summarily execute suspected partisans). The recent experience of the Spanish Civil War prompted the delegates to address the protection of civilians and others not actively participating in hostilities in civil war. *See* Denise Plattner, *Assistance to the Civilian Population: The Development and Present State of International Humanitarian Law*, 288 Int'l Rev. Red Cross 249 (1992).

[11] GCIV art. 78.

[12] Major Richard R. Baxter, *"So-Called 'Unprivileged Belligerency': Spies, Guerillas and Saboteurs,"* 28 Brit. Y.B. Int'l L. 323, 327–28 (1951). The majority of the article, however, deals with the lack of "combatant immunity" for civilians participating in hostilities, exposing them to prosecution under the domestic law of the capturing state for their belligerent acts.

[13] U.S. Dep't of Army, Field Manual 27-10, Law of Land Warfare para. 247 (July 1956).

regard to coercion and "threats, insults, or unpleasant or disadvantageous treatment."[14] Thus, military doctrine contained no gap in treatment standards for detainees of any kind; all detainees were to be treated in accordance with the provisions of GPW (if they were entitled to be treated as PWs) or GCIV (in all other cases). There was no gap.

Throughout the Cold War, even during insurgencies (internal or noninternational armed conflict) with communist guerrilla groups, U.S. doctrine maintained this paradigm—treatment of captured enemy PWs under GPW and treatment of captured belligerent civilians under GCIV. During the Vietnam War, despite the temptation to turn captured Vietcong irregulars over to the Vietnamese for summary judicial action, the U.S. military treated captured enemy combatants under the provisions of GPW.[15] The interrogation manual used during this period, "Intelligence Interrogation," Field Manual 30–15, noted the possibility of host nation forces applying lower standards for interrogation of prisoners captured during internal armed conflict;[16] but the 1967 and 1969 manuals governing interrogation by U.S. forces applied the GPW standards strictly to PWs in international armed conflict and suggested use of a minimum humane treatment standard for insurgents in noninternational armed conflict, including an appendix that referred to common article 3 of the Geneva Conventions and its limitations on:

(a) Violence to life and person, in particular murder of all kinds, mutilation, cruel treatment and torture;

(b) Taking of hostages;

(c) Outrages upon personal dignity, in particular, humiliating and degrading treatment;

(d) The passing of sentences and the carrying out of executions without previous judgment pronounced by a regularly constituted court, affording all the judicial guarantees which are recognized as indispensable by civilized peoples.[17]

---

[14] U.S. Dep't of Army, Field Manual 30-15, Examination of Personnel and Documents, para. 30 (Sept. 1951).

[15] Major General George S. Prugh, Law at War: Vietnam 1964–73, at 66 (1975) ("The MACV policy was that all combatants captured during military operations were to be accorded prisoner of war status, irrespective of the type of unit to which they belonged.") The policy did not extend, however, to those who operated as terrorists, saboteurs or spies. *Id.*

[16] U.S. Dep't of Army, Field Manual 30-15, Intelligence Interrogation, para. 4-8 (July 1967) [hereinafter 1967 Interrogation FM] (Humane treatment of insurgent captives should extend far beyond compliance with Article 3.); U.S. Dep't of Army, Field Manual 30-15, Intelligence Interrogation, para. 66a. (Mar. 1969) ("…any insurgent taken into custody by host government security forces may not be protected by the Geneva Conventions, but will be subject to the internal security laws of the country concerning subversion and lawlessness. Action of U.S. Forces, however, will be governed by existing agreements with the host country and by the provisions of the Geneva Conventions in the treatment of insurgents, specifically by the provisions of Article 3 of the 1949 Geneva Conventions.")

[17] *See, e.g.,* 1967 Interrogation FM, *supra* note 16, Appendix D. Common article 3 refers to an article found in all the Geneva Conventions; it deals with rules applicable to "an armed conflict not of an international character." *See, e.g.,* GPW art. 3.

The 1973, 1978, and 1987 versions of the interrogation manual again adopted the standards included in GPW, which was based on humane treatment standards that can be traced to the Lieber Code. These manuals added general references to "international humanitarian law," the Uniform Code of Military Justice, FM 27–10, and the "prohibitions, limitations, and restrictions established by the Geneva Conventions of 1949 for the handling and treatment of personnel captured or detained by military forces."[18] The appendices of all three versions include a full version of common articles 2[19] and 3[20] of the Geneva Conventions, GPW article 4 (which defines the categories of persons who are entitled to treatment as PWs), GPW articles 13 (on humane treatment) and 17 (prohibiting coercion in questioning PWs), and GCIV article 31 (prohibiting coercion in questioning civilian detainees). The 1973, 1978, and 1987 versions of the field manual also expanded on the prohibition against the use of force against detainees and proscribed "brainwashing, mental torture, or any other form of mental coercion, to include drugs."[21] The 1987 version, modified in the face of allegations that U.S. military advisors condoned torture of prisoners during the civil war in El Salvador, added the requirement that advisors eschew "brutal methods" used by host country forces, remove themselves from the scene, and report in accordance with theater command directives.[22]

The same period of insurgency in Central America added some jurisprudence on humane treatment standards from the *Nicaragua* case before the International Court of Justice (ICJ). The court considered whether certain advice, including coercive interrogation methods contained in manuals allegedly provided to Contra rebels, was contrary to standards of customary "international humanitarian law." The ICJ noted that common article 3 was the "minimum yardstick" of conduct for military activities conducted during a noninternational armed conflict.[23] It also found that, under general principles of humanitarian law, the United States was bound to:

> …refrain from encouragement of persons or groups engaged in the conflict in Nicaragua to commit violations of common Article 3 of the four Geneva Conventions of 12 August 1949.[24]

---

[18] U.S. Dep't of Army, Field Manual 30-15, Intelligence Interrogation para. 1-8 (June 1973); U.S. Dep't of Army, Field Manual 30-15, Intelligence Interrogation para. 1-8 (Sept. 1978); U.S. Dep't of Army, Field Manual 34–52, Intelligence Interrogation.at. 1-1 (May 1987) [hereinafter 1987 Interrogation FM].

[19] Common article 2 refers to an article found in all of the Geneva Conventions; it defines the types of conflicts in which the Conventions apply.

[20] Common article 3 is discussed in note 17, *supra*.

[21] *See, e.g.*, 1987 Interrogation FM, *supra* note 18, at 1-1.

[22] *Id.* at 9-5.

[23] Military and Paramilitary Activities in and against Nicaragua (Nicar. v. U.S.), 1986 I.C.J. 14, 114 (June 27), *reprinted in* 25 I.L.M. 1023 (1986).

[24] *Id.* at 129.

The ICJ took note that a manual on "Psychological Operations in Guerrilla Warfare," the publication and dissemination of which the ICJ held the United States to be responsible for, advised certain acts the ICJ regarded as contrary to that article.

Although the United States did not consent to the jurisdiction of the ICJ in that case, and the ICJ's jurisprudence is not accepted as binding on the United States, references to this case and its finding continue in military doctrine and literature to the present day. The concept of "Civilian Protection Law," developed by then Major (now Colonel (Retired)) Richard Whitaker at the Army Judge Advocate General's School in the mid-1990s adopted this minimum standard,[25] echoing the words of Jean Pictet, the author of the official International Committee of the Red Cross (ICRC) Commentary on common article 3:

> It merely demands respect for certain rules, which were already recognized as essential in all civilized countries, and enacted in the municipal law of the States in question, long before the Convention was signed. What Government would dare to claim before the world, in a case of civil disturbances which could justly be described as mere acts of banditry, that, Article 3 not being applicable, it was entitled to leave the wounded uncared for, to inflict torture and mutilations and to take hostages?...no Government can object to respecting, in its dealings with internal enemies, whatever the nature of the conflict between it and them, a few essential rules which it in fact respects daily, under its own laws, even when dealing with common criminals.[26]

The Army regulations for treatment of captured personnel also maintained the GPW/GCIV approach throughout this period, with a "minimum humane treatment" standard echoing many of the provisions of common article 3. Army Regulations 633–50 (1963) and 190–8 (1982 and 1985), all entitled "Prisoner of War Administration, Employment and Compensation," contained guidance on the treatment standards for all detainees, no matter how characterized.[27] They prohibited inhumane treatment and quoted the nondiscriminatory treatment provisions of common article 3:

> Persons taking no active part in hostilities, including members of armed forces who have laid down their arms and those placed hors de combat by sickness, wounds, detention, or any other cause, shall in all circumstances be treated humanely,

---

[25] *See, e.g.*, Major Richard M. Whitaker, *Civilian Protection Law in Military Operations: An Essay*, ARMY LAW 3 (Sept. 1996).

[26] GWS COMMENTARY 50.

[27] U.S. DEP'T OF ARMY, REG. 633–50, PRISONER OF WAR ADMINISTRATION para. 4c(3). (Jan. 1963); U.S. DEP'T OF ARMY, REG. 190–8, PRISONER OF WAR ADMINISTRATION para. 1-5 (1 July 1982) [hereinafter 1982 AR 190-8]; U.S. DEP'T OF ARMY, REG. 190–8, PRISONER OF WAR ADMINISTRATION para. 1-5 (2 Dec. 1985) [hereinafter 1985 AR 190-8].

without any adverse distinction founded on race, colour, religion or faith, sex, birth or wealth, or any other similar criteria.[28]

The 1982 version of the Army regulation required punishment of PWs to be administered under due process of law and a "legally constituted court," echoing the "regularly constituted court" language of common article 3.[29] It also prohibited coercion and adopted the questioning standard from GPW art. 17:

> No physical or mental torture, nor any other form of coercion, may be inflicted on prisoners of war to secure from them information of any kind, whatsoever. Prisoners of war who refuse to answer may not be threatened, insulted, or exposed to unpleasant or disadvantageous treatment of any kind.[30]

The "prohibited acts" language in all three regulations is very similar to paragraph 1–5 of the existing 1997 version of AR 190–8 (provided in its entirety, below), mixing common article 3 language with some of the specific prohibitions from GPW.

During Operation Just Cause, in Panama in 1989, U.S. forces captured a number of "Dignity Battalion" members, irregular forces created by the Panamanian strongman General Noriega to supplement his military forces. These fierce fighters often wore civilian clothes and employed suicidal tactics,[31] and the conflict was described as an "internationalized" internal armed conflict, as the U.S. government was "providing a stable environment for the freely elected" government of Guillermo David Endara Galimany, the legitimately elected president of Panama.[32] Despite the potential confusion about the type of conflict and the status of the individuals, detainees were afforded treatment consistent with PW, and classified as civilian internees or prisoners of war.[33]

---

[28] Common article 3 is discussed, *supra*, in note 17 and accompanying text.

[29] 1982 AR 190–8, *supra* note 27, para. 1-5b.

[30] GPW art. 17. *Compare* GPW art. 17 *with* 1985 AR 190–8, *supra* note 27, para. 1-5d.

[31] Thomas Donnelly, Margaret Roth & Caleb Baker, Operation Just Cause: The Storming of Panama 310–11 (1991).

[32] *Id.* at ix. At the national level, the domestic legal authority and national policy justification for a conflict often conflicts with the law-of-war analysis under common articles 2 and 3 of the Geneva Conventions, which require, for the Geneva Conventions to apply, that there be an armed conflict, either an international conflict under common article 2 (i.e., an international armed conflict between States) to which all the Geneva Conventions apply, or a noninternational armed conflict (including, but not limited to, a civil war) to which only one article (common Article 3) applies under the Geneva Conventions. In the case of Panama, the national government provided numerous reasons for the intervention, including protection of nationals, protection of U.S. strategic interests in the Panama Canal, and the request of the Endara government (which was installed, on a U.S. military base, the night of the invasion). *Id.*

[33] Frederic L. Borch, Judge Advocates in Combat: Army Lawyers in Military Operations from Vietnam to Haiti 104 (2001).

Universal application of a PW standard continued, especially after the largely conventional "Gulf War," an international armed conflict in 1991 with Iraq over its invasion of Kuwait. The Army Regulation for detention was further strengthened in the 1990s, including introduction of provisions for an article 5 Tribunal, mandated by GPW art. 5 for detainees whose status was in "doubt."[34] The due process standard in the regulation, which was copied from article 5 Tribunal standards developed in U.S. Central Command regulations during the Gulf War,[35] was later cited by Justice O'Connor in her 2004 *Hamdi* opinion as reflecting "an appropriately authorized and properly constituted military tribunal" that might have met the minimum administrative due process standards that the Supreme Court believed must be provided to U.S. citizen detainees held as enemy combatants by U.S. forces to determine if they should continue to be held under the law of war.[36]

The 1997 version of AR 190–8 adds to the list of "prohibited acts" in a section of paragraph 1–5 several of the protections afforded by article 75 of Additional Protocol I[37] and articles 4–6 of Additional Protocol II, which provide equivalent "minimum humane treatment" standards to the humane treatment standards in common article 3.[38] The general protection policy contained in this regulation, still in effect today, is as follows:

1–5. General protection policy

a. U.S. policy, relative to the treatment of EPW [enemy Prisoners of War], CI [civilian internees] and RP [retained personnel—a special class of persons under GWS and GWS-Sea] in the custody of the U.S. Armed Forces, is as follows:

(1) All persons captured, detained, interned, or otherwise held in U.S. Armed Forces custody during the course of conflict will be given humanitarian care and treatment from the moment they fall into the hands of U.S. forces until final release or repatriation.

(2) All persons taken into custody by U.S. forces will be provided with the protections of the GPW until some other legal status is determined by competent authority.

(3) The punishment of EPW, CI and RP known to have, or suspected of having, committed serious offenses will be administered IAW due process of law and under legally constituted authority per the GPW, GC, the Uniform Code of Military Justice and the Manual for Courts Martial.

(4) The inhumane treatment of EPW, CI, RP is prohibited and is not justified by the stress of combat or with deep provocation. Inhumane treatment is a

---

[34] GPW art. 5. *See also* U.S. Dep't of Army, Reg. 190-8, Enemy Prisoners of War, Retained Persons, Civilian Internees and Other Detainees para. 1-6 (Oct. 1997) [hereinafter AR 190–8].

[35] U.S. Dep't of Defense, Conduct of the Persian Gulf War: Final Report to Congress, Appendix L, at L-3 (1992).

[36] Hamdi v. Rumsfeld, 542 U.S. 507, 538 (2004).

[37] AP II arts. 4–6.

[38] AR 190–8, *supra* note 34, para. 1-5.

serious and punishable violation under international law and the Uniform Code of Military Justice (UCMJ).

b. All prisoners will receive humane treatment without regard to race, nationality, religion, political opinion, sex, or other criteria. The following acts are prohibited: murder, torture, corporal punishment, mutilation, the taking of hostages, sensory deprivation, collective punishments, execution without trial by proper authority, and all cruel and degrading treatment.

c. All persons will be respected as human beings. They will be protected against all acts of violence to include rape, forced prostitution, assault and theft, insults, public curiosity, bodily injury, and reprisals of any kind. They will not be subjected to medical or scientific experiments. This list is not exclusive. EPW/RP are to be protected from all threats or acts of violence.

This mosaic of regulations and binding international law was cemented by the DoD policy on the Law of War, included in 1998 Department of Defense Directive 5100.77.[39] The directive, which was in effect when the GWOT begin in 2001, required military forces to:

> Ensure that the members of their Components comply with the law of war during all armed conflicts, however such conflicts are characterized, and with the principles and spirit of the law of war during all other operations.[40]

The Joint Chiefs of Staff Instruction to Combatant Commanders, implementing this DoD Directive, further directed forces in the field to comply with these provisions "unless otherwise directed by competent authorities."[41] The default position, for the U.S. military, at the beginning of the Global War on Terror, was to presumptively apply GPW or GCIV to captured individuals, and never violate the "General protection policy," modeled on common article 3 to the Geneva Conventions, in interrogation, or any other form of treatment.

The Development of New Interrogation and Treatment Standards

The law-of-war interrogation and treatment paradigm adopted for GWOT was changed substantially by several legal opinions prepared by the Justice Department's Office of Legal Counsel[42] and endorsed by the White House Legal Counsel, Alberto

---

[39] U.S. DEP'T OF DEFENSE, DIR. 5100.77, DOD LAW OF WAR PROGRAM (9 Dec. 1998).

[40] Id. para. 5.3.1.

[41] JOINT CHIEFS OF STAFF, INSTR. 5810.01B, THE DOD LAW OF WAR PROGRAM para. 5a (Aug. 1999).

[42] See Memorandum, U.S. Dep't of Justice Office of the Legal Counsel, to Counsel to the President, subject: Status of Taliban Forces under Article 4 of the Third Geneva Convention of 1949 (Feb. 7,

Gonzalez.[43] The legal discussion revolved around the "status" issue discussed in Chapter 5 and the application of article 4 of GPW to the Taliban and al-Qaeda. But there was also substantial discussion regarding the difficulty of interpreting the humane treatment standard contained in common article 3 and the application of the War Crimes Act (which included criminal sanctions for unspecified violations of common article 3) to U.S. officials.[44] Gonzales opined that the language of GPW is "undefined" in common article 3, as "it prohibits, for example 'outrages upon personal dignity' and 'inhuman treatment,'" which would possibly criminalize actions that might be needed "in the course of the war on terrorism."[45] Both the Secretary of State, Colin Powell, and his legal advisor, William Howard Taft, IV, tried to persuade the president that reciprocity and our "international legal obligations" militated toward application of the Geneva Conventions to the conflict in Afghanistan.[46] Powell emphasized that applying the Geneva Conventions to the conflict "provides the strongest legal foundation for what we intend to do," while preserving "our flexibility under both domestic and international law."[47] The arguments of the State Department were rejected in favor of vague standards of "humane treatment."

The president's "Military Order of November 13, 2001" mandated the following treatment of captured al-Qaeda terrorists responsible for the attacks on September 11th, those who "aided and abetted" them, and those who "knowingly harbored" them:

Any individual subject to this order shall be–

(a) Detained at an appropriate location designated by the Secretary of Defense outside or within the United States,

---

2002) (authored by Jay S. Bybee, Assistant Attorney General), *available at* http://www.fas.org/irp/agency/doj/olc/taliban.pdf. The Office of the Legal Counsel is charged with developing legal positions for the executive branch. This memorandum and others were prepared to establish the Bush administration's positions on the status of captured enemy combatants in the fight against the Taliban and al-Qaeda, as well as their treatment. *See also* Draft Memorandum, John Yoo, Deputy Assistant Attorney General, U.S. Department of Justice & Robert J. Delahunty, Special Counsel, U.S. Department of Justice, to General Counsel, U.S. Department of Defense, subject: Application of Treaties and Laws to al Qaeda and Taliban Detainees (Jan. 9, 2002), *available at* http://www2.gwu.edu/%7Ensarchiv/NSAEBB/NSAEBB127/02.01.09.pdf.

[43] Draft Memorandum, White House Legal Counsel to President George W. Bush, subject: Decision re Application of the Geneva Convention on Prisoners of War to the Conflict with Al Qaeda and the Taliban, at 2 (Jan 25, 2002) [hereinafter Legal Counsel Memorandum], *available at* http://www.washingtonpost.com/wp-srv/politics/documents/cheney_gonzales_addington_memo_jan252001.pdf.

[44] *Id.* at 3. *See* War Crimes Act, 18 U.S.C. § 2441 (1996).

[45] Legal Counsel Memorandum, *supra* note 43, at 3.

[46] *See* Memorandum, U.S. Sec. of State, to Counsel to the President and Asst. to the President for National Security Affairs, subject: Draft Decision Memorandum for the President on the Applicability of the Geneva Convention to the Conflict in Afghanistan (Jan. 26, 2002) [hereinafter Powell Memorandum], *available at* http://dspace.wrlc.org/doc/bitstream/2041/70953/00174_020126_001display.pdf; Memorandum, Legal Advisor, U.S. State Department, to Counsel to the President, subject: Comments on Your Paper on the Geneva Convention (Feb. 2, 2002), *available at* https://www.fas.org/sgp/othergov/taft.pdf. These and other internal U.S. government documents on this subject are reprinted in MARK DANNER, TORTURE AND TRUTH 88–95 (2004) [hereinafter DANNER].

[47] Powell Memorandum, *supra* note 46, at 3.

(b) Treated humanely, without any adverse distinction based on race, color, religion, gender, birth, wealth, or any similar criteria,

(c) Afforded adequate food, drinking water, shelter, clothing, and medical treatment,

(d) Allowed the free exercise of religion, consistent with the requirements of such detention,

(e) And detained in accordance with such other conditions as the Secretary of Defense may prescribe.[48]

The decision to apply only a vague "humane treatment" standard essentially abandoned (as a matter of law) the minimum standards of common article 3 and paragraph 1–5 of Army Regulation 190–8. The president's next declaration on this subject further muddied the waters and made the job of interpreting the law to be applied to the treatment of captured al-Qaeda and Taliban that much more difficult. On February 7, 2002, the [resident declared that the conflict with al-Qaeda was not governed by the Geneva Conventions and the Taliban were not covered by GPW, as they were found to be in violation of GPW art. 4, which required them to carry their arms openly, wear distinctive insignia, and comply with the law of war. He did, however, invoke the "principles of Geneva," stating that "[a]s a matter of policy, the United States Armed Forces shall continue to treat detainees humanely and, to the extent appropriate and consistent with military necessity, in a manner consistent with the principles of Geneva."[49]

The detailed debate over what standards did apply to interrogation of Taliban and al-Qaeda detainees continued at the national policy level, however. As early as December 2001, more than a month before the president signed his memorandum, the DoD's General Counsel's Office had already solicited information on detainee "exploitation" from the Joint Personnel Recovery Agency (JPRA), an agency whose expertise was in training American personnel to withstand interrogation techniques considered illegal under the Geneva Conventions.[50] These "counter-resistance techniques" were developed by instructors in the Survival, Escape, Resistance, and Evasion (SERE) Committee to condition U.S. military prisoners to resist torture and coercive techniques applied by enemy regimes in contravention of Geneva Convention standards. JPRA officials provided copies of the SERE techniques, including "waterboarding," to Defense Intelligence Agency (DIA) personnel and the DoD Deputy General Counsel for Intelligence, Richard Shiffrin.[51] The

---

[48] Military Order of November 13, 2001—Detention, Treatment and Trial of Certain Non-citizens in the War against Terrorism, 66 Fed. Reg. 57,833 (2001).

[49] Memorandum, President George W. Bush, to Vice President et al., subject: Humane Treatment of al Qaeda and Taliban Detainees (Feb. 7, 2002), *available at* http://www2.gwu.edu/~nsarchiv/NSAEBB/NSAEBB127/02.02.07.pdf.

[50] S. REP. NO. 110-54, at xiii (2008) [hereinafter Senate Inquiry], *available at* http://www.gpo.gov/fdsys/pkg/CPRT-110SPRT48761/pdf/CPRT-110SPRT48761.pdf.

[51] *The Treatment of Detainees in U.S. Custody: Hearings Before the Senate Comm. on Armed Services,* 110th Cong. 17 (2008) [hereinafter 17 June 2008 Senate Hearing] (Statement of Lieutenant Colonel

intent of the request was to "reverse engineer" the techniques in order to employ them on recalcitrant or uncooperative detainees at Guantanamo.[52]

In August 2002, John Yoo, a Deputy Assistant Attorney General at the OLC (writing for his boss, Jay Bybee), provided an opinion on permissible interrogation techniques to the General Counsel of the Department of Defense (DOD GC), William Haynes.[53] This infamous "Torture Memorandum," later repudiated[54] by Yoo's successors, provided broad latitude for the conduct of interrogations. Yoo's opinion required "specific intent" to disobey the law in order for the applicable law to be violated, which would presumably not be present for U.S. officials who relied on his opinion.[55] In addition, he interpreted the "severe pain and suffering" provision of 10 U.S.C. § 2340A to require "serious physical injury so severe that death, organ failure, or permanent damage resulting in a loss of significant body function will likely result" or "severe mental pain" that will only exist if there is "lasting psychological harm, such as seen in mental disorders like post-traumatic stress disorder."[56] Finally, Yoo posited that both "necessity" and "self-defense" would be available as a legal defense for anyone forced to use torture to determine key details of an impending al-Qaeda threat to national security.[57] This legal opinion, allegedly supported by other classified legal opinions on specified techniques,[58] laid the groundwork for a proposal for DoD personnel to employ interrogation techniques clearly banned by

---

Daniel J. Baumgartner), *available at* http://www.gpo.gov/fdsys/pkg/CHRG-110shrg47298/html/CHRG-110shrg47298.htm; *see also* Memorandum, Chief of Staff, JPRA to General Counsel, Dep't of Defense, subject: Exploitation (July 25, 2002), *extract available at* http://www.levin.senate.gov/imo/media/doc/supporting/2008/Documents.SASC.061708.pdf (Tab 1).

[52] Senate Inquiry, *supra* note 50, at xiv.

[53] *See* Memorandum, Assistant Attorney General, Office of Legal Counsel, U.S. Department of Justice, to Counsel to the President, subject: Standards of Conduct for Interrogation under 18 U.S.C. §§ 2340–2340A (Aug. 1, 2002) (authored by Jay Bybee and John Yoo) [hereinafter Yoo Memorandum], *available at* http://www2.gwu.edu/~nsarchiv/NSAEBB/NSAEBB127/02.08.01.pdf.

[54] Memorandum, Daniel Levin, Acting Assistant Attorney General, Office of Legal Counsel, U.S. Department of Justice, to Deputy Attorney General, subject: Legal Standards Applicable under 18 U.S.C. §§ 2340–2340a (Dec. 30, 2004) (authored by Jack Goldsmith), *available at* http://www.usdoj.gov/olc/18usc23402340a2.htm.

[55] Yoo Memorandum, *supra* note 53, section I.A.

[56] *Id.* section I.C.4.

[57] *Id.* section IV.

[58] Senate Inquiry, *supra* note 50, at xvi. *See* Memorandum for John Rizzo, Acting General Counsel of the Central Intelligence Agency, subject: Interrogation of Al Qaeda Operative (Abu Zubayda) (Aug. 1, 2002), *available at* http://www.justice.gov/olc/docs/memo-bybee2002.pdf. The description of specific techniques authorized in the Abu Zubayda case is chilling and eerily similar to techniques employed in several cases, discussed below:

> Finally, you would like to use a technique called the "waterboard." In this procedure, the individual is bound securely to an inclined bench, which is approximately four feet by seven feet. The individual's feet are generally elevated. A cloth is placed over the forehead and eyes. Water is then applied to the cloth in a controlled manner. As this is done, the cloth is lowered until it covers both the nose and mouth. Once the cloth is completely saturated and completely covers the mouth and nose, air flow is slightly restricted for 20 to 40 seconds due to the presence of the cloth. This causes an increase in

the Geneva Conventions and the "minimum humane treatment" provisions of common article 3.

Shortly after receiving these legal opinions from the OLC, Haynes visited the new detention facility at Guantanamo Bay Naval Station. He was concerned that the current interrogation techniques were not being used effectively.[59] He was accompanied by several senior administration attorneys, including the CIA Counsel, John Rizzo, and the Vice President's Counsel, David Addington.[60] At a meeting one week later, the Guantanamo staff discussed aggressive interrogation techniques, including sleep deprivation, death threats, and waterboarding, with Jonathan Fredman, the chief counsel for the CIA's Counter Terrorist Center; Fredman paraphrased the Yoo/Bybee Memo: "Severe physical pain is described as anything causing permanent damage to major organs or body parts...It is basically subject to perception. If the detainee dies, you're doing it wrong."[61] A group of Guantanamo behavioral scientists, who had attended SERE training at Fort Bragg several weeks previously, prepared a list of new interrogation techniques a week later.[62] The request included three categories of techniques, each more aggressive: Category I included yelling at the detainee, techniques of deception, and false flag (interrogators claiming to be from a harsh allied regime); Category II included stress positions, use of false documents, and up to 30 days of isolation, deprivation of auditory stimuli, prolonged interrogations, removal of comfort items (including religious items), changing hot rations to MREs ("meals ready to eat," which are standard U.S. military field rations), removal of clothing, forced grooming, and exploitation of detainee phobias (e.g., fear of dogs); and Category III, which included use of scenarios threatening death to the subject of interrogation or his family, exposure of the subject to cold weather or water, use of dripping water to induce "misperception of suffocation" (waterboarding), and use of "mild, non-injurious physical contact."[63]

Lieutenant Colonel (LTC) Diane Beaver, the Staff Judge Advocate for Joint Task Force 170 at Guantanamo, prepared a legal memorandum analyzing the "counter-resistance

---

the carbon dioxide level in the individual's blood. This increase in the carbon dioxide level stimulates increased effort to breathe. This effort plus the cloth produces the perception of "suffocation and incipient panic," i.e., the perception of drowning...

Id. at 3–4.

[59] 17 June 2008 Senate Hearing, *supra* note 51, at 27 (testimony of David Shiffrin).

[60] Senate Inquiry, *supra* note 50, at xvi.

[61] Counter Resistance Strategy Meeting Minutes (Oct. 24, 2002), *available at* http://www.levin.senate.gov/imo/media/doc/supporting/2008/Documents.SASC.061708.pdf (Tab 7, at 2–5). :John Fredman, in e-mail correspondence with one of the authors of this book, denies making this statement. But the similarity of the quoted remarks, operationalizing the Yoo memoranda, is striking.

[62] Senate Inquiry, *supra* note 50, at xvii.

[63] Memorandum, Director, J-2 to Commander, Joint Task Force 170, subject: Request for Approval of Counter-Resistance Strategies (Oct. 11, 2002), *available at* http://www.levin.senate.gov/imo/media/doc/supporting/2008/Documents.SASC.061708.pdf (attachment to Memorandum in Tab 8).

techniques," and the Joint Task Force Commander, Major General Dunleavy, forwarded the memo to United States Southern Command (SOUTHCOM) for review.[64] The legal memorandum, which incorporated the analysis of OLC on the definition of "torture," also discounted the application of Geneva Convention standards, common article 3, all human rights treaties to which the United States is a party, the Eighth Amendment, and the Uniform Code of Military Justice.[65] LTC Beaver did, however, caution that several of the techniques would be "assaults" under the UCMJ and would, therefore, require "immunity, in advance, from the convening authority for military members employing those techniques."[66] She recommended the techniques be approved with caution and oversight. As she testified in a Senate hearing on these techniques:

> I have repeatedly been asked whether I was pressured to write my October 2002 legal opinion. I felt a great deal of pressure, as did all of us at the facility. I felt the pressure of knowing that thousands of innocent lives might be lost if we got it wrong. I knew that honest, decent Americans would condemn our actions if we did not balance our efforts to protect them with due respect of the rule of law. I believed at the time, and still do, that such a balance could be reached if the interrogations were strictly reviewed, controlled and monitored. My legal opinion was not a blank check authorizing unlimited interrogations. Throughout the opinion, I emphasized the need for medical, psychiatric and legal reviews to be conducted prior to approval of these interrogation plans.[67]

The request to use aggressive interrogation techniques and LTC Beaver's memorandum were thoroughly reviewed at higher headquarters, despite Haynes's Senate testimony that he relied on the lieutenant colonel's opinion for his advice to the Secretary of Defense.[68] And Colonel (now retired) Manuel Superveille, the Staff Judge Advocate at U.S. Southern Command (which was responsible for operations at Guantanamo Bay Naval Station), prepared a detailed review of the proposal, concluding: the Category I techniques were permissible, with certain controls; the Category II techniques would violate GPW, and therefore should be sparingly used; and the Category III techniques violated common

---

[64] Memorandum, Commander, Joint Task Force 170 to Commander, United States Southern Command, subject: Counter-Resistance Strategies (Oct. 11, 2002), *available at* http://www.levin.senate.gov/imo/media/doc/supporting/2008/Documents.SASC.061708.pdf (Tab 8).

[65] Memorandum, Staff Judge Advocate, Joint Task Force 170, to Commander, Joint Task Force 170, subject: Legal Brief on Proposed Counter-Resistance Strategies (Oct. 11, 2002), *available at* http://www.levin.senate.gov/imo/media/doc/supporting/2008/Documents.SASC.061708.pdf (attachment to Memorandum in Tab 8).

[66] *Id.*

[67] Testimony of Diane Beaver, 17 June 2008 Senate Hearing, *supra* note 51, at 77.

[68] Senate Inquiry, *supra* note 50, at xix.

article 3 and various criminal statutes, including the torture statute.[69] U.S. Navy Captain (now a retired admiral) Jane Dalton, Legal Advisor to the Chairman of the Joints Chiefs of Staff, initiated a full "legal and policy" review of the request.[70] As a result, the service representatives, led by the International and Operational Law Divisions of the service Judge Advocate Generals, registered significant objection to the proposal. Colonel (now retired) John Ley, the Army Division Chief, indicated that the Category III techniques would violate the UCMJ and the torture statute. In addition, he noted the following:

> Regarding the Category II techniques, numbers 2 (prolonged use of stress positions), 5 (deprivation of light and auditory stimuli), and 12 (using individual phobias to induce stress), in my opinion, cross the line of "humane" treatment, would likely be considered maltreatment under Article 93 of the UCMJ, and may violate the Federal torture statute if it results in severe physical pain or suffering. Techniques 10 (removal of clothing) and 11 (forced grooming) are certainly permissible for health reasons, but are problematic and may be considered inhumane if done for interrogation purposes.[71]

The other service inputs were similar in their opposition to Category II and III techniques.[72]

Notwithstanding the legal concerns raised by the services, Haynes stopped the "legal and policy review."[73] After consulting with the Chairman of the Joint Chiefs of Staff, Captain Dalton, Deputy Secretary of Defense Wolfowitz, and Under Secretary of Defense for Policy Douglas Feith, he recommended approval of the Category I and II techniques and "use of mild, non-injurious physical contact" from Category III, noting that approval of other Category II techniques was "not warranted" at the time, as our

---

[69] Interview of Colonel Superveille by Richard Jackson, July 8, 2008. Lieutenant Colonel Beaver testified at the Senate Hearing that Colonel Superveille provided "no help" in reviewing her memorandum. Testimony of Lieutenant Colonel Diane Beaver, 17 June 2008 Senate Hearing, *supra* note 51, at 86. According to Colonel Superveille, however, his detailed memorandum to General Hill, the U.S. Southern Command Commander, has never been released and was incorporated, by reference, in General Hill's memorandum forwarding the request to the Chairman, Joint Chiefs of Staff. DANNER, *supra* note 46, at 179.

[70] Testimony of Jane Dalton, 17 June 2008 Senate Hearing, *supra* note 51, at 91 & 101.

[71] Memorandum, John Ley (Chief, International and Operational Law Division, U.S. Army Office of The Judge Advocate General) to Office of the Army General Counsel, subject: Review—Proposed Counter Review Techniques (undated), *available at* http://www.levin.senate.gov/imo/media/doc/supporting/2008/Documents.SASC.061708.pdf (attachment to Memorandum in Tab 12) last visited 24 June 2014. The Ley memorandum was attached to a November 2002 memorandum from the Assistant Deputy Chief for Operations and Plans, U.S. Army, to the Legal Counsel to the Chairman, Joint Chiefs of Staff, *available at* http://www.levin.senate.gov/imo/media/doc/supporting/2008/Documents.SASC.061708.pdf (Tab 12) last visited 24 June 2014.

[72] Senate Inquiry, *supra* note 50, at xix.

[73] Testimony of Jane Dalton, 17 June 2008 Senate Hearing, *supra* note 51, at 102.

forces are "trained to a standard of interrogation that reflects a tradition of restraint."[74] Secretary Donald Rumsfeld approved the list of interrogation techniques Haynes recommended, noting, "I stand for 8–10 hours a day. Why is standing limited to 4 hours?"[75]

The approval was transmitted to Guantanamo, where several of the techniques were used on at least one detainee, Mohammed al-Qahtani, the alleged "20th hijacker," who had been denied entry into the United States and returned to Afghanistan after the attacks of September 11, 2001.[76] Al-Qahtani was subjected to sleep deprivation for weeks on end, stripped naked, subjected to military working dogs and loud music, made to wear a leash, and told to perform dog tricks.[77] Alberto Mora, the Navy General Counsel, received "back-channel" reports in mid-December 2002 from Naval Criminal Investigative Service agents on the Criminal Investigation Task Force, who were shocked that detainees at Guantanamo were "being subjected to physical abuse and degrading treatment."[78] Mora consulted with the Army General Counsel, Steven Morello, who informed him that the Secretary of Defense had approved the techniques on December 2nd.[79] Mora concluded that, even if the approved techniques did not rise to the level of torture, they certainly consisted of "cruel, inhuman, and degrading treatment," a violation of common article 3 to the Geneva Conventions.[80] By threatening to provide a formal memorandum of non-concurrence to the action, Mora convinced DoD GC Haynes to prepare a memorandum for the Secretary of Defense rescinding the approval of December 2, 2002.[81]

This exchange did not conclude the "legal and policy review" of the techniques, however. The Secretary of Defense's rescission memo of January 15, 2003, also established a Legal Working Group to "assess legal, policy, and operational issues relating to the interrogations of detainees held by the U.S. Armed Forces in the war on terrorism."[82] John Yoo provided additional guidance (the "Yoo Memorandum") from OLC on March 14, 2003,

---

[74] William J. Haynes II, General Counsel, Memorandum for Secretary of Defense, subject: Counter-Resistance Techniques (Nov. 27, 2002), *available at* http://www.levin.senate.gov/imo/media/doc/supporting/2008/Documents.SASC.061708.pdf (Tab 15).

[75] *Id.*

[76] Bob Woodward, *Detainee Tortured, Says U.S. Official*, WASH. POST, Jan. 14, 2009, *available at* http://www.washingtonpost.com/wp-dyn/content/article/2009/01/13/AR2009011303372.html?hpid=topnews. *See also* Senate Inquiry, *supra* note 50, at xxii (concluding that "additional interrogation techniques," including sensory deprivation and "sleep adjustment" was approved for use on detainee Mohamedou Ould Slahi at Guantanamo).

[77] Senate Inquiry, *supra* note 50, at xxi.

[78] Memorandum, Navy General Counsel to Inspector General, Department of the Navy, subject: Statement for the Record—Office of General Counsel Involvement in Interrogation Issues 3 (July 7, 2004), *available at* http://www.newyorker.com/images/pdfs/moramemo.pdf [hereinafter Mora Memorandum].

[79] *Id.* at 6.

[80] Testimony of Alberto Mora, 17 June 2008 Senate Hearing, *supra* note 51, at 80.

[81] Mora Memorandum, *supra* note 78, at 14.

[82] Memorandum, Secretary of Defense to Commander, U.S. Southern Command, subject: Counter-Resistance Techniques (Jan. 15, 2003), *available at* http://www.levin.senate.gov/imo/media/doc/supporting/2008/Documents.SASC.061708.pdf (Tab 20).

which repeated much of what the first OLC memo (signed by Jay Bybee but authored by John Yoo) had said six months earlier.[83] Yoo essentially concluded that no domestic or international law constrained military interrogators:

> For the forgoing reasons, we conclude that the Fifth and Eighth Amendments do not extend to alien enemy combatants held abroad. Moreover, we conclude that different canons of construction indicate that generally applicable criminal laws do not apply to the military interrogation of alien unlawful combatants held abroad. Were it otherwise, the application of these statutes to the interrogation of enemy combatants undertaken by military personnel would conflict with the President's Commander-in-Chief power.
>
> We further conclude that [the Convention Against Torture] CAT defines U.S. international law obligations with respect to torture and other cruel, inhuman, or degrading treatment or punishment. The standard of conduct regarding torture is the same as that which is found in the torture statute, 18 U.S.C. §§ 2340–2340A. Moreover, the scope of U.S. obligations under CAT regarding cruel, inhuman, or degrading treatment or punishment is limited to conduct prohibited by the Eighth, Fifth, and Fourteenth Amendments. Customary international law does not supply any additional standards.
>
> Finally, even if the criminal prohibitions outlined above applied, and an interrogation method might violate these prohibitions, necessity or self-defense could provide justifications for any criminal liability.[84]

The Working Group, led by Air Force General Counsel Mary Walker, was severely constrained by the terms of the Yoo Memoranda; according to Mora, these memoranda "created the contours and boundaries for the working group."[85] Colonel Ley's concerns about military interrogators being prosecuted and about violations of international law's torture and "cruel, inhuman, and degrading treatment"[86] standards were completely marginalized. As a result, the conclusions were foreordained, despite the significant disagreement with the legal conclusions expressed by the Working Group members.[87]

---

83 Memorandum, John Yoo, Deputy Assistant General Counsel, Department of Justice Office of Legal Counsel, to William J. Haynes, General Counsel, Department of Defense, subject: Military Interrogation of Alien Unlawful Enemy Combatants Held Outside the United States (Mar. 14, 2003), *available at* http://ftp.fas.org/irp/agency/doj/olc-interrogation.pdf.

84 *Id*. at 81.

85 Testimony of Alberto Mora, 17 June 2008 Senate Hearing, *supra* note 51, at 145.

86 Convention against Torture and Other Cruel, Inhuman or Degrading Treatment or Punishment, Dec. 10, 1984, art. 16, S. Treaty Doc. No. 100-20 (1988), 1465 U.N.T.S. 85 (entered into force June 26, 1987). Nations are bound by the treaty to prohibit and criminally sanction torture, but only required to take other measures necessary to suppress cruel, inhuman, and degrading treatment.

87 Mora Memorandum, *supra* note 78, at 20.

On April 16, 2003, less than two weeks after the Working Group completed its report,[88] the Secretary authorized the use of 24 specific interrogation techniques for use at Guantanamo. While the authorization included such techniques as dietary manipulation, environmental manipulation, and sleep adjustment, it was silent on many of the techniques in the Working Group report.[89] Secretary Rumsfeld's memo said, however, that "[i]f, in your view, you require additional interrogation techniques for a particular detainee, you should provide me, via the Chairman of the Joint Chiefs of Staff, a written request describing the proposed technique, recommended safeguards, and the rationale for applying it with an identified detainee."[90]

Application of Policies in the Field

What did the president's declaration and the Secretary of Defense's interrogation memos mean for forces in the field? Was this balancing test—humane treatment, consistent with military necessity—an invocation of the "military necessity" defense that was rejected at Nuremburg?[91] Was the very constrained authorization of certain techniques a carte blanche for use of the techniques in the field? Most reasonable Judge Advocates, faced with uncertain guidance from the top, would stick with the clear doctrinal templates available in the Geneva Conventions, FM 27–10 (the Army manual on the Law of Land Warfare), AR 190–8 (the military's detainee regulation), and FM 34–52 (the Army's interrogation field manual). And most did, changing the approach only when directed to do so by "competent authority," per the regulatory guidance. For example, when faced with the prospect of receiving Taliban and al-Qaeda detainees in Guantanamo Bay Naval Base, in Cuba, in the first week of January 2002, the U.S. Southern Command Staff Judge Advocate consulted with the International Committee of the Red Cross (ICRC) and recommended application of the GPW standards to the development of the camp.[92] And the Commander of Joint Task Force 160 (the Task Force in Guantanamo responsible for care of the prisoners, as opposed to their interrogation, which was the responsibility of Joint Task Force 170), U.S. Marine Corps Brigadier General Michael

---

[88] Working Group Report on Detainee Interrogation in the Global War on Terrorism: Assessment of Legal, Historical, Policy, and Operational Considerations (Apr. 4, 2003), *available at* http://www.defenselink. mil/news/Jun2004/d20040622doc8.pdf (beginning on third page of this document).

[89] Memorandum, Secretary of Defense to Commander, U.S. Southern Command, subject: Counter-Resistance Techniques in the War on Terrorism (Apr. 16, 2003), *available at* http://www.levin.senate.gov/imo/media/ doc/supporting/2008/Documents.SASC.061708.pdf (Tab 23).

[90] *Id.*

[91] *See* U.S. v. List, 11 T.W.C. 759 (1950) (Hostage Case), XI Law Reports of Trials of War Criminals 40 (U.N. War Crimes Commission 1949).

[92] Interview with Colonel Manuel Superveille, in Karen J. Greenberg, *See Also When Gitmo Was (Relatively) Good*, Wash. Post, Jan. 25, 2009, at B1, *available at* http://www.washingtonpost.com/wp-dyn/content/ article/2009/01/23/AR2009012302313.html.

Lehnert, made a valiant effort to apply those portions of the conventions that ensured the "prisoners' safety and dignity." One of his attorneys, Lieutenant Colonel Timothy Miller, considered GPW his "working manual." And Lehnert directed his attorneys to study the 143 articles of the Prisoner of War Convention, "paying particular attention to Common Article 3," which resulted in an initial standard of care for the Guantanamo detainees that included ICRC oversight and, as far as practicable, GPW standards of treatment. These standards of treatment, with reasonable accommodations for imperative reasons of security, guided the housing of detainees at Guantanamo from the early days; but the treatment standards changed with Lehnert's departure in March 2002 and the initiation of interrogation-focused detention at Guantanamo.[93]

Some Judge Advocates in the field, when confronted with the "new paradigm" of a conflict that did not strictly apply either the higher standards of the Geneva Conventions or the more limited standards of common article 3, concluded that some of the aggressive techniques considered at the DoD level did not violate the Geneva "principle" of humane treatment invoked by the president. So the techniques approved at the DoD level for limited application at Guantanamo migrated to Afghanistan, and later to Iraq, without adequate legal oversight.[94] These amorphous standards were susceptible of abuse, resulting in numerous subsequent investigations of misconduct toward detainees in Afghanistan and, later, Iraq.[95]

Shortly after Rumsfeld approved aggressive interrogation techniques, in December 2002, the techniques became known in Afghanistan. Captain Carolyn Wood, the Officer-in-Charge of the Intelligence Section at Bagram Airfield in Afghanistan, said that she saw a PowerPoint presentation listing the aggressive techniques authorized by the Secretary in January 2003.[96] Despite the Secretary's January 15, 2003, rescission of authority for the use of the techniques at Guantanamo, his approval of the techniques six weeks earlier continued to influence the interrogation policies in the field.[97] Nine days after that rescission memorandum, on January 24, 2003, the Staff Judge Advocate for Combined Joint Task Force 180 (CJTF-180, which was the command then responsible for military operations in Afghanistan) produced an "interrogation techniques" memorandum that

---

[93] *Id.*

[94] FINAL REPORT OF THE INDEPENDENT PANEL TO REVIEW DoD DETENTION OPERATIONS 36 (Aug. 24, 2004) [hereinafter Schlesinger Report] ("In the initial development of these Secretary of Defense policies, the legal resources of the Services' Judge Advocates and General Counsels were not utilized to their fullest potential."), *available at* http://fl1.findlaw.com/news.findlaw.com/wp/docs/dod/abughraibrpt.pdf. *See also* Major General Fay, Investigating Officer, *AR 15-6 Investigation of the Abu Ghraib Prison and 205th Military Intelligence Brigade*, at 20 (Aug. 25, 2004) [hereinafter Fay Report] *available at* http://www.dod. gov/news/Aug2004/d20040825fay.pdf.

[95] *See* Tom Lasseter, *Day 2: U.S. Abuse of Detainees Was Routine at Afghanistan Base*, McCLATCHYDC (June 16, 2008) [hereinafter Lasseter], http://www.mcclatchydc.com/detainees/story/38775.html; *see also* Fay Report, *supra* note 94, at 22.

[96] Senate Inquiry, *supra* note 50, at xxii.

[97] *Id.*

authorized certain techniques approved in the earlier Secretary of Defense memorandum, including "removal of clothing" and "exploiting the Arab fear of dogs."[98] Soldiers who conducted interrogations at Bagram Air Base, north of Kabul, the capital of Afghanistan, also claimed that they had been authorized to provide "punishment blows" to detainees who were not cooperating with the interrogation.[99] When their abusive interrogation resulted in the death of the taxi driver Habibullah and others, their conduct was punished by military courts martial, however.[100] The misconduct of soldiers, in using unauthorized interrogation techniques or committing aggravated assault or murder, cannot be directly traced to the policy changes in Washington; but the abuse resulted, at least in part, "from misinterpretation of law or policy" and "confusion about what techniques were permitted."[101]

All of the investigations of the abuses at Abu Ghraib, including the overarching Schlesinger Report, which evaluated the involvement of the chain of command in the scandal, came to the same conclusion.[102] The first investigation, regarding alleged military police misconduct and conducted by Major General Antonio Taguba, concluded that between October and December 2003, there were numerous incidents of "sadistic, blatant, and wanton criminal abuses intentionally inflicted on several detainees";[103] he recommended criminal liability for those soldiers. Major General George Fay, who investigated the involvement of military intelligence interrogators, concluded that "most of the violent or sexual abuse occurred separately from interrogations and was not caused by uncertainty about law or policy. Soldiers knew they were violating approved techniques and procedures."[104] He also found that the Joint Intelligence Center (JIC) Commander, Colonel Thomas Pappas (assisted by the same Captain Wood who had been in Bagram), consented to "clothing removal and the use of dogs" without proper authorization from higher headquarters, but those actions did not cause the violent or sexual abuse at Abu Ghraib.[105]

In addition, the investigators reached several critical conclusions about the involvement of Judge Advocates and the application of Geneva Convention treatment standards to the military police and interrogation functions. Major General Taguba concluded that the Military Police Brigade Judge Advocate "lack[ed] initiative and

---

[98] Although the memorandum remains classified, portions of it were discussed in unclassified versions of the Fay Report, *supra* note 94. Senate Inquiry, *supra* note 50, at xxiii.

[99] Lasseter, *supra* note 95; *see also* TAXI TO THE DARK SIDE (documentary film by Alex Gibney, released by ThinkFilm January 18, 2008).

[100] Lasseter, *supra* note 95.

[101] Fay Report, *supra* note 94, at 22.

[102] *See* Schlesinger Report and Fay Report, *supra* note 94; *see also* Major General Taguba, Investigation of the 800th Military Police Brigade (Mar. 2004) [hereinafter Taguba Report], *available at* http://www.dod. mil/pubs/foi/operation_and_plans/Detainee/taguba/TAGUBA_REPORT_CERTIFICATIONS. pdf.

[103] Taguba Report at 16.

[104] Fay Report, *supra* note 94, at 11.

[105] *Id.* at 22.

was not willing to accept responsibility."[106] In his look at systemic issues, he concluded that it was "[c]ritical to have a dedicated senior Judge Advocate, with specialized knowledge and training in international and operational law to assist in the administration of detainee operations."[107] The Commander of Combined Joint Task Force 7 Lieutenant General Sanchez (CJTF-7 was responsible for U.S. military operations in Iraq in 2003–2004) had mandated GCIV treatment with advice from his attorney, the CJTF-7 Staff Judge Advocate Colonel Marc Warren, but Warren had authorized (for Sanchez's personal approval) some of the techniques mentioned in the Secretary of Defense's approval memorandum.[108] The approval and oversight mechanism created at CJTF-7 was never exercised, as subordinate commands never requested to use the techniques;[109] Major General Fay's investigation concluded, much like Major General Taguba's, that the abuses in interrogations would not have occurred if the directives in place had been followed and mission training was conducted.[110] But he cautioned that the clear application of Geneva Convention standards to detainee interrogation was essential; "Soldiers should never again be put in a position that potentially puts them at risk for non-compliance with the Geneva Conventions or the Laws of Land Warfare."[111]

Restoration of Standards

The development of policy and law continued, inexorably, "in the wake of the public disclosure of detainee abuse at Abu Ghraib."[112] It is undeniable that the investigations into

---

[106] Taguba Report, *supra* note 102, at 40.

[107] *Id*. at 21.

[108] Fay Report, *supra* note 94, at 25. *See also* Coalition Provisional Authority Memorandum 3, Criminal Procedures sec. 6 (June 27, 2004) ("The operation, condition and standards of any internment facility established by the MNF [Multi-National Force] shall be in accordance with Section IV of the Fourth Geneva Convention."), *available at* http://www.iraqcoalition.org/regulations/20040627_CPAMEMO_3_ Criminal_Procedures__Rev_.pdf. The CJTF-7 efforts to provide guidance on interrogation standards was also frustrated by the mixed messages emanating from the continuing efforts from the Secretary of Defense to improve interrogation (intelligence) output; Major General Miller's visit to Iraq at the end of August 2003 included a message to "get tough on detainees"; and the SERE instructors were, once again, involved in transferring SERE techniques to Iraq, at the request of an in-theater commander, in September 2003. Senate Inquiry, *supra* note 50, at xxiii. *But see* Memorandum, U.S. Department of Justice Office of Legal Counsel, to the Counsel to the President, subject: "Protected Person" Status in Occupied Iraq under the Fourth Geneva Convention (Mar. 18, 2004), *available at* http://www.usdoj.gov/olc/2004/gc4mar18. pdf (concluding there is no GCIV protection for non-Iraqi al-Qaeda operatives detained in Iraq).

[109] Colonel Pappas was reprimanded and fined under art. 15, Non-Judicial Punishment, of the Uniform Code of Military Justice, for failure to seek permission for the use of dogs as an interrogation technique. R. Jeffrey Smith, *Abu Ghraib Officer Gets Reprimand*, WASH. POST, May 12, 2005, A16, *available at* http:// www.washingtonpost.com/wp-dyn/content/article/2005/05/11/AR2005051101818.html.

[110] Fay Report, *supra* note 94, at 5.

[111] *Id*. at 6.

[112] Senate Inquiry, *supra* note 50, at xxv.

detainee abuse in Guantanamo, Afghanistan, and Iraq resulted in considerable policy discussion and, eventually, reaffirmation of the common article 3, GPW, and GCIV standards of treatment. For example, the involvement of JPRA, with their SERE techniques, abruptly stopped after the Abu Ghraib news broke and the JPRA issued policy guidance limiting support to interrogations.[113] The Army provided detailed guidance to interrogators on the application of common article 3, GPW, and GCIV to the interrogation function, filling the specific "legal void" created by the DoD interrogation policy by supplying Training Support Packages to the field and emphasizing the use of AR 190–8 and FM 34–52 as guidance, in the absence of specific combatant command direction to the contrary.[114] In messages intended to reinforce Major General Taguba's and Major General Fay's conclusions, the Army emphasized compliance with the "humane treatment" provisions of common article 3 and the prohibitions on coercion in GPW art. 17 and GCIV art. 31, respectively.[115] In lieu of substantive changes in policy at the DoD level, through doctrine, literature, and training guidance, the Army reinforced the Judge Advocate's role in training interrogators and military policemen, as well as the exercise of judgment in providing advice to the operational commander.[116]

Congress proposed the Detainee Treatment Act (DTA) to establish minimum standards of treatment for detainees.[117] But the DTA adopted the same "cruel, inhumane, or degrading" ("torture light") treatment standard John Yoo discussed in his 2002 and 2003 memos, adopting the Fifth, Eighth, and Fourteenth Amendments' jurisprudence on cruel, unusual, and inhumane treatment or punishment. As the "cruel and unusual punishment" standard was only applicable to sentenced criminals, and the Fourteenth Amendment only applied the law to the States, it added nothing to the equation. The resulting interpretation of policy relied on the Fifth Amendment "substantive due process" standard, which analyzed the importance of the governmental interest involved and balanced that with interrogators' conduct that must "shock the conscience," in the context of a dire threat to national security.[118] In the final analysis, the DTA had no effect on detainee treatment or interrogation policy.

DoD policy began to change significantly, however, in the fall of 2005. Haynes, the DOD GC, led a working group to determine the standards for "humane treatment,"

---

[113] *Id.*

[114] *See generally* Lieutenant Colonel Paul F. Kantwill, Captain Jon D. Holdway & Geoffrey S. Corn, *Improving the Fighting Position: A Practitioner's Guide to Operational Law Support to the Interrogation Process*, ARMY LAW. 12 (July 2005).

[115] *Id.* at 22.

[116] *Id.* at 26.

[117] Detainee Treatment Act of 2005, Pub. L. No. 109-148, § 1005(e), 119 Stat. 2680, 2742-44 [hereinafter DTA].

[118] MICHAEL GARCIA, CONG. RESEARCH SERV., RL32438. U.N. Convention against Torture (CAT): Overview and Application to Interrogation Techniques 6 (last updated Jan. 26, 2009), *available at* http://assets.opencrs.com/rpts/RL32438_20090126.pdf.

to be integrated in a revised DoD directive on the treatment of detainees. Its initial policy recommendation for adoption of common article 3 as the minimum standard of treatment was rejected by the White House.[119] While the Judge Advocate Generals of the military services supported the application of common article 3,[120] the Department of Defense adopted paragraph 1–5 of AR 190–8 as the standard of treatment in DoD Directive 2310.01E, *The Department of Defense Detainee Program*.[121] In the meantime, the Department of Defense published its directive for the Law of War, DoD Directive 2311.01A, which reiterated that, as a matter of DoD policy, the law of war was applicable to military operations "during all armed conflicts, however such conflicts are characterized, and in all other military operations."[122] It seemed to indicate that the default standard was the Geneva Convention standard of treatment, rather than the "minimum humane treatment standard" of common article 3.[123]

Just prior to the approval of the detainee directive, the Supreme Court issued its opinion in *Hamdan*,[124] affirming the value of common article 3 in establishing norms of conduct in the GWOT:

> The Court of Appeals thought, and the Government asserts, that Common Article 3 does not apply to Hamdan because the conflict with al Qaeda, being "international in scope," does not qualify as a " 'conflict not of an international character.' " 415 F.3d at 41. That reasoning is erroneous. The term "conflict not of an international character" is used here in contradistinction to a conflict between nations. So much is demonstrated by the "fundamental logic [of] the Convention's provisions on its application." *Id.*, at 44 (Williams, J., concurring). Common Article 2 provides that "the present Convention shall apply to all cases of declared war or of any other armed conflict which may arise between two or more of the High

---

[119] Jane Mayer, *The Memo: How an Internal Effort to Ban the Abuse and Torture of Detainees Was Thwarted*, New Yorker, Feb. 27, 2006, at 10.

[120] *See, e.g., Military Commissions in Light of the Supreme Court Decision in* Hamdan v. Rumsfeld: *Hearings Before the Senate Comm. on Armed Services*, 109th Cong. 17 (2006) (statement of Major General Scott C. Black, The Judge Advocate General, U.S. Army, regarding application of common article 3 standards to military operations), *available at* http://www.gpo.gov/fdsys/pkg/CHRG-109shrg35144/pdf/CHRG-109shrg35144.pdf.

[121] *Compare* para. 1-5, AR 190-8, *supra* note 34, with U.S. Dep't of Defense, Dir. 2310.01E, The Department of Defense Detainee Program, Enclosure A (Sept. 5, 2006) [hereinafter DoD Dir. 2310.01E].

[122] U.S. Dep't of Defense, Dir. 2311.01E, DOD Law of War Program (May 9, 2006).

[123] *Compare* Dick Jackson, Lieutenant Colonel Eric T. Jensen & Robert Matsuishi, *The Law of War after the DTA,* Hamdan, *and the MCA*, Army Law. 19 (Sept. 2007), *with* Major John T. Rawcliffe, *Changes to the Department of Defense Law of War Program*, Army Law. 23 (Aug. 2006). The authors of the former article endorsed Major Rawcliffe's conclusion that practitioners should "assume that Common Article 2 and similar triggers have been satisfied, to apply the law of war broadly, and to seek active involvement and consent from higher echelons of command when appropriate." Jackson et al. *supra* at 32.

[124] Hamdan v. Rumsfeld, 548 U.S. 557 (2006).

Contracting Parties." 6 U.S.T., at 3318 (Art. 2, GWS). High Contracting Parties (signatories) also must abide by all terms of the Conventions vis-a-vis one another even if one party to the conflict is a nonsignatory "Power," and must so abide vis-a-vis the nonsignatory if "the latter accepts and applies" those terms. *Ibid.* (Art. 2, GPW). Common Article 3, by contrast, affords some minimal protection, falling short of full protection under the Conventions, to individuals associated with neither a signatory nor even a nonsignatory "Power" who are involved in a conflict "in the territory of" a signatory. The latter kind of conflict is distinguishable from the conflict described in Common Article 2 chiefly because it does not involve a clash between nations (whether signatories or not). In context, then, the phrase "not of an international character" bears its literal meaning. See, e.g., J. Bentham, Introduction to the Principles of Morals and Legislation 6, 296 (J. Burns & H. Hart eds. 1970) (using the term "international law" as a "new though not inexpressive appellation" meaning "betwixt nation and nation"; defining "international" to include "mutual transactions between sovereigns as such"); AP COMMENTARY at 1351 ("[A] non-international armed conflict is distinct from an international armed conflict because of the legal status of the entities opposing each other").[125]

The Deputy Secretary of Defense immediately issued a memorandum to the services and the forces in the field to ensure that the minimum standards of common article 3 applied to all policies and directives.[126]

In September 2006, the DoD published DoD Directive 2310.01E. This directive provided the overarching DoD policy with respect to detainee operations. The revision set out policy guidance not only for detention operations in traditional conflicts, but also treatment standards for individuals detained in the GWOT, by incorporating the numerous lessons learned and taking into account the recommendations in the 12 major investigations of its detention operations conducted by the DoD.[127] The directive specifically incorporated references to common article 3 and provided that all detainees would be treated humanely and in accordance with U.S. law and the laws of war. Paragraph 4.2 of the directive specifically provided:

All persons subject to this Directive shall observe the requirements of the law of war, and shall apply, without regard to a detainee's legal status, at a minimum the

---

[125] *Id.* at 630–31.

[126] Memorandum, Deputy Sec'y of Defense to Sec'ys of Military Dep'ts et al., subject: Application of Common Article 3 of the Geneva Conventions to the Treatment of Detainees in the Department of Defense (July 7, 2006), *available at* http://www.defense.gov/pubs/pdfs/DepSecDef%20memo%20on%20common%20 article%203.pdf.

[127] Briefing by Charles "Cully" Stimson et al., *Department of Defense Directive on Detainee Operations, the Release of the Army Field Manual for Human Intelligence Collection and an Update on Military Commissions* (Sept. 7, 2006), *available at* http://2002-2009-fpc.state.gov/71958.htm.

standards articulated in Common Article 3 to the Geneva Conventions of 1949 [...], as construed and applied by U.S. law, and those found in Enclosure 4, in the treatment of detainees, until their final release, transfer out of DOD control, or repatriation. Note that certain categories of detainees, such as enemy prisoners of war, enjoy protections under the law of war in addition to the minimum standards prescribed in Common Article 3....[128]

In addition to the treatment standards of common article 3, enclosure 4 of the directive contained many other requirements, some of which exceeded the standards articulated in common article 3, that the DoD considered essential to ensure the humane care and treatment of detainees. For example, detainees were also entitled to "adequate food, drinking water, shelter, clothing, and medical treatment."[129] They will also be free to "exercise their religion, consistent with the requirements of detention."[130] Finally, paragraph E4.1.1.3 provided:

> All detainees will be respected as human beings. They will be protected against threats or acts of violence including rape, forced prostitution, assault and theft, public curiosity, bodily injury, and reprisals. They will not be subjected to medical or scientific experiments. They will not be subjected to sensory deprivation. This list is not exclusive.[131]

The release of this directive was an important step in ensuring that DoD detention policies complied with common article 3. It provided a baseline standard of treatment for all detainees. Its release, especially in combination with the subsequent issue of a new manual on interrogation, was widely perceived as a repudiation of the harsh interrogation tactics and treatment standards approved subsequent to the attacks of September 11th.[132]

The Army, which was designated Executive Agent for policy development and training of military police and military interrogators, next provided an updated version of the field manual for Internment and Resettlement Operations, FM 3–19.40, which relied on GPW and GCIV for the treatment standards of detainees, both prisoners of war and civilian internees.[133] The succeeding development in policy was the issuance

---

[128] DoD Dir. 2310.01E, *supra* note 121, para 4.2.

[129] *Id.* para. E4.1.1.3.

[130] *Id.*

[131] *Id.*

[132] Josh White, *New Rules of Interrogation Forbid Use of Harsh Tactics*, Wash. Post, Sept. 7, 2006, at A1, *available at* http://www.washingtonpost.com/wp-dyn/content/article/2006/09/06/AR2006090601947.html.

[133] U.S. Dep't of Army, Field Manual 3-19.40, Internment and Resettlement Operations Appendix C (July 21, 2006).

of the substantially revised "Interrogation Manual," Field Manual 2-22.3, "Human Intelligence Collector Operations,"[134] which the DTA had mandated to control interrogation standards.[135] The DTA mandate was a curious one, from a legal perspective, as it required military interrogators to comply with a doctrinal publication that was fungible and could be modified by the responsible service at any time. But the high profile of the manual and the requirement to consult with Congress made the publication of a revised FM 2–22.3 a significant event in the development of policy regarding interrogations.

The Field Manual included accumulated requirements, in law and policy, to maintain a minimum "humane treatment" standard, incorporating many of the lessons learned from the GWOT. The manual prohibits torture and cruel, inhuman, or degrading treatment, referencing the DTA and common article 3 for the minimum standard. But the manual also incorporates a single standard of treatment, based on GPW, for all detainees regardless of their status. It authorizes 18 interrogation techniques that, consistent with the DTA, are the only interrogation techniques authorized for any detainee, whether lawful or unlawful combatants. Applying the standards of article 17 of GPW, the manual bans coercive interrogation, the denial of basic rights, and the use of disparate treatment intended for the purpose of persuading a detainee to talk.[136] The only exception to the GPW standard is the use of isolation as an interrogation technique, but this technique is limited to "unlawful combatants," carefully controlled by the first General Officer in the chain of command, and limited to 30 days at a time.[137] With that one exception, the Field Manual restores the full Geneva Convention standard to interrogation.

An unfortunate coincidence overshadowed the publication of FM 2–22.3. The president announced that 16 "high-value detainees," kept in CIA custody to that point, were to be transferred to Guantanamo on the same day the field manual was published. In addition, the president announced his intent to continue the use of "aggressive interrogation techniques" for "unlawful combatants" in CIA custody. On July 20, 2007, the president issued Executive Order 13440, which purported to apply common article 3 standards to those techniques, when used by the CIA. The Army quickly announced that the Executive Order did not apply to its interrogation techniques; the Judge Advocate General took the unusual step, in a message to the field, of emphasizing that the treatment and interrogation standards detailed in DoD Directive 2310.01E and both Army field manuals for military police internment operations and interrogation

---

[134] U.S. Dep't of Army, Field Manual 2-22.3 (FM 34-52), Human Intelligence Collector Operations (Sept. 6, 2006) [hereinafter FM 2-22.3]. The new field manual replaced FM 34-52, but is much broader than FM 34-52 in its scope and application.

[135] DTA, *supra* note 117, § 1002(a).

[136] FM 2-22.3, *supra* note 134, para. 5-73.

[137] *Id.* Appendix M.

operations were controlling.[138] An Executive Order issued by President Obama shortly after his inauguration reversed that decision by President Bush and eliminated all doubt about the standard of treatment to be applied to detainees in military or CIA custody; he required future CIA interrogations to employ the techniques of interrogation outlined in Field Manual 2–22.3.[139]

President Obama also ordered the Secretary of Defense to certify that the treatment of detainees was consistent with the law enacted between 2005 and 2009, as well as the "humane treatment" standards, discussed above.[140] The Secretary of Defense appointed Admiral Walsh, the Vice Chief of Naval Operations, to review the treatment of detainees at Guantanamo and provide recommendations as to their treatment.[141] Admiral Walsh concluded that the Guantanamo detainees were being treated humanely, consistent with the legal regime established from 2005 to 2009, but while he observed that the detainees in Guantanamo were being treated consistent with the standards established by the Geneva Conventions, he recommended that the standards for treatment be viewed over time, defining what is humane in terms of "various factors, in a continuum, to assess what is humane ... over a long period of time."[142] In reality, the analysis of treatment standards at Guantanamo applied the more specific standards of treatment provided for prisoners of war or civilian internees, under the provisions of GPW or GCIV, respectively.[143]

---

[138] Dick Jackson & LTC Eric Jensen, *Common Article 3 and Its Application to Detention and Interrogation,* ARMY LAW. 69 (May 200).

[139] Exec. Order No. 13491, 74 Fed. Reg. 4893 (2009).

[140] Exec. Order. No. 13492, Sec. 6. 74 Fed. Reg. 4897 (2009).

[141] *See* REVIEW OF DEPARTMENT COMPLIANCE WITH PRESIDENT'S EXECUTIVE ORDER ON DETAINEE CONDITIONS OF CONFINEMENT (Feb. 23, 2009), *available at* http://www.defense.gov/pubs/pdfs/ review_of_department_compliance_with_presidents_executive_order_on_detainee_conditions_of_ confinementa.pdf. Navy Captain Patrick McCarthy (who had served previously as the Task Force Staff Judge Advocate) and Richard Jackson (one of the authors of this book) were detailed as legal advisors to Admiral Walsh.

[142] *Id.* at 72.

[143] *Id.* For example, the section of the report on "Sensory Deprivation—Solitary Confinement" cites GPW, articles 13, 17, 21, and 22, as well as GCIV, articles 27, 30–33, and 84, for the proposition that the Geneva Conventions provide for "individual or collective accommodations; and where possible, to group detainees by nationality, language, or custom. Except for disciplinary or penal sanctions, detainees may not be held in 'close confinement.'" The review concluded "[d]etainees in Guantánamo are never placed in solitary confinement or isolation. All detention spaces and cells have been built to support a program that enhances the safety and security of both detainees and staff members alike. All detention cells, except in Camp 7, permit easy communication and interaction with other detainees in adjoining cells." *Id.* at 45.

Conclusion

The treatment and interrogation standards to be applied in the Global War on Terror have come full circle. Beginning with the first set of policy discussions over interrogation techniques, prior to the President's Memorandum of February 7, 2002, the State Department and Defense Department attorneys with the experience in applying the law of war to military operations (and the judgment to see the consequences of applying a new standard) opposed limiting the application of the standards embodied in GPW and GCIV to detainees picked up on this "new battlefield." Even when these standards were not available as a matter of law (largely due to legal interpretations made by OLC or the White House), the GPW or GCIV standards were applied as a matter of policy in the field manuals developed and promulgated in the last several years. As the discussion above indicates, the available evidence suggests that, in policy discussions and battlefield application of the interrogation and treatment standards, Judge Advocates usually took the "high road" in offering advice to commanders, applying GPW or GCIV standards to the problems they encountered, and counseling caution in applying techniques that were close to the lines on torture and "cruel, inhumane, and degrading treatment."

In the policy discussions and field application of the law, three attempts by Army Judge Advocates to stop the inevitable slide of standards stand out. The first is Colonel John Ley's memorandum, in November 2002, opposing the Category II and III techniques for Guantanamo. The second is Colonel Manuel Superveille's assistance to General Lehnart, the CJTF-160 Commander at Guantanamo, in applying GPW standards to the new camp, with ICRC help. And the third is the decision, advised by Colonel Marc Warren to LTG Sanchez, the Commander of CJTF-7, to apply GCIV standards, protecting security detainees captured during the occupation of Iraq, as if they were "protected persons" and "civilian internees" under GCIV. The policy battles in Washington pale in comparison to the tough decisions made by soldiers in the field to stick to the moral high ground, except for a few isolated instances. The advice of each of these senior legal advisors, involved in both policy development and application of the policy on the battlefield, was essential to establish and maintain a Geneva Convention–based humane treatment approach that was consistent in most circumstances and resulted in a high standard of treatment across the GWOT battlefield.

But it was those isolated instances of criminal conduct that caused the light of day to shine on the deficiencies in military interrogation and treatment of detainees. Without the conclusions of investigating officers and the force of public opinion, the policy, which was limited in its formal application but insidious in its influence, could not have been changed. Thanks to the judgment of those senior officers, Major General Taguba and Major General Fay, and the Schlesinger Report, the reaffirmation of Geneva Convention–based treatment and interrogation standards was not long delayed.

The U.S. Army is left with the standards it began the War on Terror with—the minimum humane treatment standards of common article 3 as a legal baseline in all conflicts, supplemented, as a matter of policy, with the protections afforded by GPW and GCIV, to treat all those that are hors de combat (no longer taking an active part in hostilities) as decently and humanely as the conscience of our individual soldiers and the dictates of the public conscience demand.[144]

---

[144] Hague IV preamble (Martens Clause—"in cases not included in the regulations…the inhabitants and the belligerents remain under the protection and the rule of the principles of the law of nations, as they result from the usages established among civilized peoples, from the laws of humanity, and the dictates of the public conscience.")

5

Detention of Combatants and the War on Terror

by James A. Schoettler, Jr.

Introduction

In the conduct of an armed conflict, a State may not only kill or wound combatants fighting on behalf of its enemies, but also may capture and detain them until the end of the conflict.[1] Indeed, the legal justification for subjecting an enemy belligerent to direct attack terminates when the enemy belligerent (referred to in this chapter generically as a "combatant" without distinction, except as noted herein, between those who are permitted to engage in hostilities and those who are not) is no longer capable of fighting due to wounds, sickness, or where he or she has clearly signaled a desire to cease fighting. Accordingly, at that point, a State's only option to prevent that individual from continued participation in the conflict is capture and detention.

The principal sources of treaty law regarding the detention of enemy combatants in international armed conflicts are (1) Hague IV, (2) GPW, and (3) certain provisions of AP I. Together, these treaties define a highly protective regime that ensures that combatants who qualify as "prisoners of war" are humanely treated, protected from discrimination or persecution, and repatriated once hostilities are over. Importantly, persons who are treated as prisoners of war under these treaties cannot be prosecuted by the capturing State for belligerent acts that comply with the laws and customs of war, such as attacking lawful military objectives (no such protection is afforded to unprivileged belligerents even if they otherwise comply with the law of war). This protection against

---

[1] Hamdi v. Rumsfeld, 542 U.S. 507, 518 (2004) (plurality). Although he dissented from the plurality decision, Justice Thomas agreed that "the Federal Government has power to detain those that the Executive Branch determines to be enemy combatants." *Id.* at 589.

prosecution, typically called "combatant immunity," is an important protection under international law.

In the transnational armed conflict against al-Qaeda and associated forces,[2] however, belligerent acts are carried out by persons who do not satisfy the legal requirements for prisoner-of-war status under applicable treaties, such as GPW. In the first place, the conflict against al-Qaeda and associated forces is not considered by the United States to be an international armed conflict to which the Geneva Conventions apply in full, but rather a noninternational armed conflict to which the key Geneva Convention dealing with prisoners of war, GPW, does not apply (with the exception of one provision common to all the Geneva Conventions). Second, even if the Geneva Conventions did apply in full to the conflict with al-Qaeda, members of al-Qaeda and associated forces would still fail to qualify for prisoner-of-war status because of their failure to meet the specific requirements established in GPW (their failure to wear a fixed distinctive emblem recognizable at a distance or to carry their arms openly, and their association with an organization that does not operate pursuant to responsible command and that does not routinely comply with the laws and customs of war). Nonetheless, their actions can be as lethal and disruptive as those taken by a State's own military personnel, and therefore a State attacked by these individuals has just as strong an interest in neutralizing them, including by detaining them, as it would in neutralizing an enemy State's conventional military units. Yet, the law of war provides only limited guidance as to these individuals' status and treatment.

An important distinction between individuals who fall within the categories of combatants who, upon capture would be treated as prisoners of war under Hague IV, GPW, and the applicable provisions of AP I (hereinafter referred to as "lawful combatants" or "privileged belligerents") and those who engage in combatant activities but are not entitled to be treated as prisoners of war under the applicable treaties (hereinafter "unprivileged belligerents") is that unprivileged belligerents do not enjoy combatant immunity,[3]

---

[2] The concept of a "Global War on Terror" was widely used by the Bush administration to describe the conflict against al-Qaeda and groups affiliated with it, but has been de-emphasized by the Obama administration. *Compare* National Security Strategy of the United States of America (Sept. 2002) ("The United States of America is fighting a war against terrorists of global reach"), *available at* http://www.state.gov/documents/organization/63562.pdf *with* National Strategy for Counterterrorism (June 2011) ("The United States deliberately uses the word 'war' to describe our relentless campaign against al-Qa'ida... [but] we are not at war with the tactic of terrorism or the religion of Islam. We are at war with a specific organization—al-Qa'ida."). For ease of reference, we use the term "war on terror" in this chapter, without endorsing it as the correct way to view the conflict with al-Qaeda and associated groups.

[3] Under the LOAC, only State armed forces, members of certain militias, and citizens spontaneously rising up to resist invaders, in an international armed conflict who meet the requirements of GPW art. 4A(1), (2), (3), or (6), enjoy combatant immunity. *See* United States v. Lindh, 212 F. Supp. 2d 541, 552–58 (E.D. Va. 2002) (discussing "combatant immunity" in detail).

and can be prosecuted by the capturing State under its domestic law for any belligerent acts they have committed.[4] Thus, the unprivileged belligerent is not only subject to detention to prevent a return to hostilities like any privileged belligerent, he also is subject to criminal liability for his belligerent acts, even if those same acts would have been shielded from prosecution due to combatant immunity had they been committed by a privileged belligerent. Indeed, the criminal characterization of such a detainee's pre-capture conduct will often have a major impact on the nature of the detention and the attitude of the capturing State toward the prisoner.

Following the attacks on the United States on September 11, 2001 ("9/11"), the U.S. government invoked the law of war as a legal basis to detain and punish unlawful combatants in its conflict with al-Qaeda and the Taliban. Individuals suspected of being terrorists were seized both on and off "active battlefields" (a term ill-suited to the military response to transnational terrorism) and held by the U.S. military indefinitely pursuant to authorities derived from the law of armed conflict (LOAC). Without the protection of combatant immunity, these individuals are subject to prosecution under U.S. law for their terrorist activities, including not only attacks on civilians and civilian property but also belligerent acts against the forces of the United States and its allies. This certainly includes prosecution in U.S. civilian criminal courts, but also prosecution by military commission, although the scope of the crimes subject to the jurisdiction of military commissions is still being litigated.[5]

It is essential to emphasize that detention under the LOAC is not dependent upon prosecution and conviction for war crimes. As discussed further in this chapter, once it is established to the requisite legal standard of certainty that a captured individual is an enemy combatant participating in an armed conflict, he or she can be detained for the duration of that armed conflict.[6] Moreover, this right of preventive detention enjoys considerable support in international law and under U.S. law. Many of the individuals detained following the 9/11 attacks pursuant to this right of detention asserted in U.S. federal courts that they were not combatants, but rather civilians who, unless

---

[4] *Ex parte* Quirin, 317 U.S. 1, 31 (1942) ("Unlawful combatants are likewise subject to capture and detention, but in addition they are subject to trial and punishment by military tribunals for acts which render their belligerency unlawful.").

[5] See Chapter 6, *infra*, for discussion of military commissions litigation.

[6] Under the LOAC, detention is not limited to those who are combatants. GCIV also contemplates that in an international armed conflict, a State may "for imperative reasons of security" detain specific individuals. GCIV art. 78. Unlike the authority to detain combatants indefinitely, however, a determination to place an individual in detention for reasons of security is based upon the specific circumstances surrounding that individual rather than upon his or her status as a combatant or fighter. GCIV COMMENTARY at 367. Further, those held as security detainees have a right to periodic review of the basis of their detention. *See, e.g.*, GCIV art. 78 (providing for "periodical review, if possible every six months, by a competent body"). This security detention authority is discussed *infra* in the section entitled "Conduct and Detention."

charged with, and convicted of, crimes, should be freed.[7] Both substantive and procedural issues lay at the heart of these cases: substantively, these individuals challenged the legality of the enemy belligerent designation in the context of a counter-terrorism effort and, procedurally, they challenged the process by which this designation was made by the United States.

This chapter looks closely at the law applicable to the determination of a person's status as a combatant, the approach taken by the U.S. government to these status determinations in the transnational armed conflict against al-Qaeda and associated groups, the principal court decisions evaluating the U.S. government's approach, and the response of the executive and legislative branches to this litigation, including developments with respect to the rights of individuals held in long-term detention by U.S. forces outside the United States. In so doing, it provides insight into one of the most important questions affecting the detention of combatants, namely the determination of their status once captured.

Detention and the Terrorist-Belligerent in the War on Terror

Under the LOAC, the purpose of detention is to take the combatant off the battlefield[8] and to neutralize any threat he or she may pose to the capturing State and its forces.[9] Although detained combatants may be punished for acts committed before detention if those acts constitute crimes, the detention itself is not supposed to serve as punishment for those acts.[10] Indeed, the conflict that led to the combatant's detention is not a conflict against the combatant personally, but rather against the State or entity that he or she is fighting for. Thus, in the absence of proof that acts committed by the combatant were crimes, the combatant should be set free once the reason for his or her detention no longer applies (i.e., the conflict has ended).

This combatant detention paradigm formed the legal basis for the U.S. military to hold known or suspected foreign terrorists in indefinite military detention following the 9/11 attacks. Specifically, the U.S. government position is that the conflict between the United States and al-Qaeda and associated forces (including the Taliban) is an armed

---

[7] In one case, an individual claimed to enjoy protection as medical personnel, who, under applicable international law, should be released if not needed to perform medical duties. Al Warafi v. Obama, 716 F.3d 627, 629 (D.C. Cir. 2013).

[8] WILLIAM WINTHROP, MILITARY LAW AND PRECEDENTS 788 (2d ed. 1920).

[9] In re Territo, 156 F.2d 142, 145 ("The object of capture is to prevent the captured individual from serving the enemy. He is disarmed and from then on must be removed as completely as practicable from the front, treated humanely, and in time, exchanged, repatriated or otherwise released." (citations omitted)). See also Ali v. Obama, 736 F.3d 542, 545 (D.C. Cir. 2013) ("The purpose of military detention is to detain enemy combatants for the duration of hostilities so as to keep them off the battlefield and help win the war. Military detention of enemy combatants is a traditional, lawful, and essential aspect of successfully waging war.").

[10] Hamdi v. Rumsfeld, 542 U.S. at 518.

conflict, and accordingly the United States is legally empowered to hold the members of the enemy terrorist groups in that conflict for the duration of the conflict, just as it would be entitled to detain the members of an enemy armed force as prisoners of war in an international armed conflict. The U.S. government claims this authority as a necessary incident to the powers granted to the president by the Authorization for the Use of Military Force (AUMF) resolution, which was passed by Congress and signed by the president shortly after the 9/11 attacks,[11] and this position has been affirmed by both the Supreme Court[12] and Congress.[13]

To date, despite some setbacks in court, the executive, supported by Congress, has been successful in employing the combatant detention paradigm in the war on terror in order to detain terrorists who are part of al-Qaeda, the Taliban, and associated groups for the duration of the armed conflict. However, the use of the combatant paradigm to support long-term detention in the war on terror remains controversial and likely will continue to be criticized and opposed by those who believe the paradigm has been stretched beyond its legitimate limits under the LOAC.[14] Additionally, the paradigm has placed the United States at odds with foreign governments, who do not agree with the use of the combatant detention paradigm to hold terrorists indefinitely and this

---

[11] Authorization for Use of Military Force, Pub. L. 107–40, 115 Stat. 224 (2001) [hereinafter AUMF]. The AUMF authorizes the president "to use all necessary and appropriate force against those nations, organizations, or persons he determines planned, authorized, committed, or aided the terrorist attacks that occurred on September 11, 2001, or harbored such organizations or persons, in order to prevent any future acts of international terrorism against the United States by such nations, organizations or persons." Following the 9/11 attacks, the Bush administration asserted that "the Executive possesses plenary authority to detain pursuant to Article II of the Constitution." *Hamdi*, 542 U.S. at 516. The Supreme Court refused to decide this issue and instead relied on the AUMF as the source of its detention power. *Hamdi*, 542 U.S. at 517.

[12] *Hamdi*, 542 U.S. at 519 ("detention to prevent a combatant's return to the battlefield is a fundamental incident of waging war" that Congress "clearly and unmistakably authorized" in the AUMF). On the other hand, in an opinion handed down shortly before publication of the second edition of this book, a court in the United Kingdom held that the LOAC does not provide a basis for detention in a noninternational armed conflict. Mohammed v. Ministry of Defense, [2014] EWHC 1369 (QB) para. 257 (May 2, 2014) *available at* http://www.bailii.org/ew/cases/EWHC/QB/2014/1369.html.

[13] National Defense Authorization Act for Fiscal Year 2012, Pub. L. 112–81, § 1021(a), 125 Stat. 1562, *codified at* 10 U.S.C. § 801 note ("Congress affirms that the authority of the President to use all necessary and appropriate force pursuant to the Authorization for Use of Military Force (Public Law 107–40; 50 U.S.C. 1541 note) includes the authority for the Armed Forces of the United States to detain covered persons…pending disposition under the law of war.") [hereinafter FY12 NDAA].

[14] *See, e.g.*, the following posting on the website of the American Civil Liberties Union:

While the government has the right, under the laws of war, to detain prisoners captured on the battlefield until the end of hostilities, no president should have the power to declare the entire globe a war zone and then seize and detain civilian terrorism suspects anywhere in the world—including within the United States—and to hold them forever without charge or trial.

Am. Civ. Lib. Union, *Key Issues: Detention* (Dec. 26, 2013, 11:07 p.m.), https://www.aclu.org/national-security/detention.

disagreement has fueled criticism of the United States. Even where terrorists held by the United States come from countries that are allies in the armed conflict against al-Qaeda (particularly Australia, Canada, and the United Kingdom), concerns about that detention, including the length and basis of the detention as well as the treatment of their citizens during detention, may undermine support in those countries for cooperating with U.S. antiterrorism efforts.[15]

The U.S. government's position on the international law applicable to long-term detentions in the war on terror has also been controversial. From 2002 until 2006, the Bush administration asserted that the war on terror against al-Qaeda was an international armed conflict to which the four Geneva Conventions did not apply because al-Qaeda was not (and could not be) a State party to those treaties,[16] and that the specific provisions of GPW were inapplicable to members of the Taliban fighting against the United States in Afghanistan because they failed to qualify for POW status pursuant to the terms of that treaty.[17]

Following the decision of the Supreme Court in *Hamdan v. Rumsfeld*, which held, inter alia, that the war on terror was a noninternational armed conflict to which at least one article common to all Geneva Conventions ("common article 3") applied, the administration abandoned this earlier position and applied common article 3 to its detention operations as a matter of law.[18] However, while the Bush administration subsequently adopted (and the Obama administration continues to follow) policy directives that provide for a robust set of humanitarian protections that go well beyond the baseline

---

[15] In a recent study of U.S. relations with the United Kingdom, the Congressional Research Service noted:

> Although the overall intelligence and counterterrorism relationship is overwhelmingly positive, there have been some occasional tensions. The relationship was damaged by public accusations of British complicity in U.S.-led renditions and the alleged torture of terrorist suspects between 2002 and 2008.

Derek E. Mix, Cong. Res. Serv., RL33105, The United Kingdom and U.S.-U.K. Relations, 12 (2013).

[16] As a matter of treaty law, the provisions of the four 1949 Geneva Conventions, with the exception of article 3 common to all four conventions ("common article 3"), only apply in an international armed conflict between States who are party to the Geneva Conventions (each a "State Party") or a partial or total occupation of the territory of such a State Party by another State Party. AP I art. 1(4) does treat, as international armed conflicts, conflicts in "which peoples are fighting against colonial domination and alien occupation and against racist régimes in the exercise of their right of self-determination" under the U.N. charter. The United States objected to AP I in part because it believed this provision would grant combatant status under AP I to terrorist groups. Abraham D. Sofaer, *Agora: The U.S. Decision Not to Ratify Protocol I to the Geneva Conventions on the Protection of War Victims (Cont'd), The Rationale for the United States Decision*, 82 Am. J. Int'l L. 784, 786–87 (1988). It is doubtful that the war on terror would fall within the scope of conflicts covered by AP I art. 1(4), however.

[17] Matthew C. Waxman, *The Law of Armed Conflict and Detention Operations in Afghanistan*, in The War in Afghanistan: A Legal Analysis, 85 Int'l L. Stud. 343, 345–47 (Michael N. Schmitt ed., 2009) (explaining Bush administration rationale) [hereinafter Waxman].

[18] *Id.*

humanitarian protections found in common article 3,[19] the fact remains that common article 3 falls far short of providing the range of rights, privileges, and obligations applicable to POWs pursuant to the GPW. In the absence of comprehensive international law regulation of detention operations, any rights and privileges beyond those required by common article 3 (and where applicable, AP II) will be guided largely by national policies on detainee treatment, subject only to limitations or prohibitions on mistreatment imposed by domestic law,[20] plus whatever protections might be afforded under customary international law.[21]

---

[19] *See, e.g.*, U.S. Dep't of Def., Dir. 2310.01E, The Department of Defense Detainee Program (Sept. 5, 2006) (mandating treatment standards that include, but are not limited to, the requirements of common article 3) [hereinafter DoDD 2310.01E].

[20] Some domestic laws may be based on international obligations, such as the Convention against Torture, although the application of such treaties to conduct of a nation outside its own borders has been debated. *See, e.g.*, John B. Bellinger, III, Legal Adviser, U.S. Dep't of State, "Opening Remarks," Address at U.S. Meeting with U.N. Committee against Torture (May 5, 2006) (noting that the U.S. position is that its treatment of detainees at Guantanamo is governed by the law of armed conflict as the *lex specialis* governing detention operations), *available at* http://www.state.gov/j/drl/rls/68557.htm.

[21] It is not easy to determine with precision the rules of customary law that might apply to detention under the war on terror. Although AP II is widely regarded as a source of customary law for noninternational armed conflicts, AP II applies by its terms only to conflicts between a State Party and one or more dissident or armed groups, which, "under responsible command, exercise such control of part of its [the State Party's] territory as to enable them to carry out sustained and concerted military operations and to implement this Protocol." AP II art. 1(1). The war on terror has not met this threshold, at least since the Taliban was defeated in 2002, although in forwarding AP II to the Senate for ratification in 1987, President Reagan recommended that ratification be subject to an understanding that the United States would apply AP II to all conflicts to which common article 3 also applies. Message from the President of the United States Transmitting the Protocol Additional to the Geneva Conventions of August 12, 1949, and Relating to the Protection of Victims of Noninternational Armed Conflicts, Concluded at Geneva June 10, 1977, S. Treaty Doc. No. 100–2, VIII (Jan. 29, 1987) (reprinting letter from President Reagan dated Dec. 13, 1986). The Senate has yet to ratify AP II.

In 2011, the Obama administration stated that, although the United States has not ratified AP I, "[t]he U.S. Government will…choose out of a sense of legal obligation to treat the principles set forth in Article 75 [of AP I] as applicable to any individual it detains in an international armed conflict, and expects all other nations to adhere to these principles as well," thereby indicating that it treats article 75 as binding customary international law. "Fact Sheet: New Actions on Guantánamo and Detainee Policy" (Mar. 7, 2011), *available at* http://www.whitehouse.gov/the-press-office/2011/03/07/fact-sheet-new-actions-gu ant-namo-and-detainee-policy. The implications for the war on terror of the administration's position on article 75 is unclear. Article 75 is expressly applicable only to international armed conflicts, whereas the war on terror has been characterized as a noninternational armed conflict, particularly after the Supreme Court's *Hamdan* decision in 2006. Further, article 75 primarily deals with the treatment of an individual while detained and does not impose any express limitations on the power to detain, although article 75(3) does require that "[e]xcept in cases of arrest or detention for penal offences,… [the detained] persons shall be released with the minimum delay possible and in any event as soon as the circumstances justifying the arrest, detention or internment have ceased to exist," which depending upon the interpretation of the phrase "circumstances justifying the arrest, detention or internment" potentially could require release of a detainee even before the conflict has ceased. Because AP I applies only in international armed conflicts, it does not appear that the U.S. government's position includes extending the benefits of article 75 to detainees in noninternational armed conflicts such as the war on terror, although U.S. policy on detention in

Finally, the undefined scope and indeterminate length of the war on terror has also been a source of controversy. Detentions of terrorist belligerent operatives under the combatant paradigm have lasted for years, and could continue for decades, which raises concerns about when, if ever, the detainees will be released. On the other hand, the combatant paradigm will permit long-term detention only for so long as there is an armed conflict.[22] States have been tolerant of the U.S. detention of terrorists as part of the war on terror, in part because there has been an ongoing conflict in Afghanistan in which al-Qaeda and the Taliban continue to be active. As the presence of U.S. forces in Afghanistan declines and the U.S. combat role is diminished, however, it may be more difficult to argue that the conflict in which the detainees were captured continues. Although U.S. case law indicates that the "end of conflict" determination is left to the executive branch under U.S. law and is not subject to judicial review,[23] a determination that the conflict continues despite changing facts on the ground in Afghanistan may call into question, at least internationally, whether the continued use of the combatant paradigm to detain terrorists is supportable under international law. States may well become more vocal and active in the effort to stop the United States's continued use of the combatant paradigm in the war on terror, particularly if the United States no longer has combat troops or a combat role in Afghanistan.[24]

Although the conflict termination question is beyond the scope of this chapter, it must be understood that, even if it is determined that the conflict continues, any continued long-term detention related to the conflict will be difficult to justify in the first instance to the extent the procedures and standards used to determine an individual's combatant status do not appear to be regular and fair.

---

armed conflict appears to follow article 75, without distinction as to the type of conflict involved. *See* U.S. Dep't of Defense, Dir. 2311.01E, DoD Law of War Program, para. 4.1 (May 9, 2006) [hereinafter DoDD 2311.01E].

[22] Ali v. Obama, 736 F.3d at 545 ("military detention ends with the end of the war.").

[23] Ludecke v. Watkins, 335 U.S. 160, 170 (1948) ("These are matters of political judgment for which judges have neither technical competence nor official responsibility.")

[24] Neither the Bush nor Obama administrations tied their detention authority to the existence or intensity of the conflict in Afghanistan. In a speech in 2012, however, the General Counsel for the Department of Defense stated that "there will come a tipping point" at which, through the capture or killing of al-Qaeda and its affiliates, "the group is no longer able to attempt or launch a strategic attack against the United States," so further counter-terror efforts by the United States would no longer be considered an armed conflict. Jeh Charles Johnson, Gen'l Counsel, U.S. Dep't of Defense, "The Conflict against Al Qaeda and Its Affiliates: How Will It End?" Address at the Oxford Union, Oxford University (Nov. 30, 2012), *available at* http://www.lawfareblog.com/2012/11/jeh-johnson-speech-at-the-oxford-union/#_ftn22. "At that point we will also need to face the question of what to do with any members of al Qaeda who still remain in U.S. military detention without a criminal conviction and sentence [because] ... [in] general, the military's authority to detain ends with the 'cessation of active hostilities.'" *Id.* Thus, for the Obama administration at least, there is a possible end to hostilities that could lead to the need to release detainees who otherwise have not been charged or convicted of crimes.

Status and Detention

As a threshold matter, the LOAC rules applicable to a detained individual, including which treaty protections apply, and whether the individual is subject to prosecution for combatant activities, are determined by (1) whether there is an armed conflict (the LOAC applies only in situations of armed conflict or belligerent occupation), (2) the type of armed conflict (international versus noninternational), and (3) the relationship of the individual to the armed conflict (i.e., combatant, enemy civilian, or neutral citizen).

Historically, the LOAC consisted principally of rules for the conduct of conflicts between States in which the active participants were limited to citizens of each State fighting in military formations, that is, lawful combatants. Under these rules, non-combatants (i.e., civilians) were bystanders who were not involved in the conflict other than as potential victims.

In reality, however, civilians are far from bystanders, particularly in modern conflicts. Civilians produce the weapons and equipment that wars are fought with and the supplies that support the combatants, and, over the past one hundred years, their activities have moved closer and closer to the battlefield (or the battlefield has moved closer to them). Today, civilians transport military equipment and ammunition, service weapons, collect and interpret intelligence, and advise military commanders on military operations.

These are accepted roles for civilians supporting State armed forces in international armed conflicts, as reflected in treaty law that expressly applies to "persons who accompany the armed forces without actually being members thereof,"[25] who are accorded the same prisoner-of-war treatment under GPW as the armed forces of each of the belligerent nations.[26] However, in many conflicts, including, but not limited to the war on terror, individuals who might otherwise be considered civilians have taken up arms and conducted terrorist attacks, often as part of an armed group, using their civilian status as cover for their belligerent actions. Further, the targets of their attacks have not been limited to military objectives, but also included civilians and civilian objects, as part of a strategy to employ terror in connection with the conflict.

LOAC treaties were not drafted with transnational conflicts against nonstate terrorist groups in mind. The four 1949 Geneva Conventions were designed principally to provide detailed rules for international armed conflicts based on World War II experiences. Yet, the several decades that followed the end of World War II were characterized

---

[25] GPW art. 4A(4). *See also* Hague IV art. 13. No treaty specifically addresses the status of civilian senior leaders who also serve as the head of a nation's armed forces, but they certainly have been targeted in the same manner as combatants in recent conflicts. *See "Decapitation Strike" Was Aimed at Saddam*, CNN.COM (Mar. 20, 2003), http://www.cnn.com/2003/WORLD/meast/03/20/sprj.irq.target.saddam/.

[26] Individuals who accompany the forces and fall under GPW art. 4A(4) are still civilians and do not enjoy combatant immunity in the event they directly participate in hostilities, however.

by conflicts that did not comply with the World War II model. Conflicts resulting in, or resulting from, the breakup of Western European empires were most often guerrilla wars or "low intensity conflicts," in which one or both sides consisted of indigenous forces that often did not conform to the model of a modern Western army and who made up for a lack of fire power and resources with, inter alia, the use of force against their enemies that included indiscriminate attacks on civilians and civilian property.

In 1977, two treaties were opened for adoption, each of which supplemented the 1949 Geneva Conventions: AP I, which applies to international armed conflict, and a companion protocol, AP II, applicable to noninternational armed conflicts. These protocols expanded the scope of the conflicts that could be subject to the LOAC treaties. However, even under this expanded scope, the conflicts covered by these protocols generally fit one of two categories: (i) international armed conflicts between nations and other nations, or (ii) noninternational armed conflicts between a nation and a movement or organized force within its borders (or the borders of its colonies) or within territory occupied by it.[27]

The war on terror does not fit either of these categories, because it is neither a conflict among States nor a conflict within a single State. The terrorist enemy in the war on terror is ostensibly independent of any particular State, yet may have the capability to launch attacks as lethal as any State armed force, and can effectively project deadly force into third countries.[28] Further, the terrorist enemy may challenge or even supplant State authority in a country in which it is based to such an extent that it becomes the true power in that country (which arguably occurred in Afghanistan under the Taliban prior to 2002). Thus a conflict with a terrorist enemy of this type may not be an international armed conflict as traditionally conceived, but it may be a conflict on an international scale.

The regulation of combatants under the LOAC treaties is focused on the traditional category of combatants who would fight the wars covered by the treaties, that is, soldiers in State armed forces and militias, and resistance fighters.[29] All these categories envision fighters acting on behalf of a State and operating under responsible command (responsible in the sense of subordination to State authority and establishing the discipline necessary to comply with international law obligations). Further, only treaties dealing with international armed conflicts specifically provide for the treatment of combatants

---

[27] International jurisprudence has extended the LOAC governing noninternational armed conflicts to apply to conflicts between armed groups in certain situations. Prosecutor v. Tadic, Case No. IT-94-1-I, Decision on the Defence Motion for Interlocutory Appeal on Jurisdiction, ¶ 70 (Oct. 2, 1995) (holding that "an armed conflict exists whenever there is a resort to armed force between States or protracted armed violence between governmental authorities and organized armed groups or between such groups within a State").

[28] A good example, although not clearly within the ambit of the war on terror addressed in this chapter, is the terrorist attack in Mumbai in 2008.

[29] The treaties do include, as a category of lawful combatants fighting on behalf of a State in an international armed conflict, civilians who rise up spontaneously to repel an invasion of their country by another State. See, e.g., GPW art. 4A(6).

as prisoners of war. Treaty coverage of combatants who fight on behalf of a force that is neither sponsored by a State nor rebelling against a State is sparse.[30]

The traditional categories of combatants protected by the LOAC can be found in GPW. GPW affords prisoner-of-war treatment to the following specific six categories of persons, all of whom upon capture are considered "prisoners of war":

(1) Members of the armed forces of a Party to the conflict, as well as members of militias or volunteer corps forming part of such armed forces.

(2) Members of other militias and members of other volunteer corps, including those of organized resistance movements, belonging to a Party to the conflict and operating in or outside their own territory, even if this territory is occupied, provided that such militias or volunteer corps, including such organized resistance movements, fulfill the following conditions:
   (a) that of being commanded by a person responsible for his subordinates;
   (b) that of having a fixed distinctive sign recognizable at a distance;
   (c) that of carrying arms openly; and
   (d) that of conducting their operations in accordance with the laws and customs of war.

(3) Members of regular armed forces who profess allegiance to a government or an authority not recognized by the Detaining Power.

(4) Persons who accompany the armed forces without actually being members thereof, such as civilian members of military aircraft crews, war correspondents, supply contractors, members of labor units or of services responsible for the welfare of the armed forces, provided that they have received authorization from the armed forces which they accompany, who shall provide them for that purpose with an identity card.

(5) Members of crews, including masters, pilots and apprentices, of the merchant marine and the crews of civil aircraft of the Parties to the conflict, who do not benefit by more favorable treatment under any other provisions of international law.

(6) Inhabitants of a non-occupied territory, who on the approach of the enemy spontaneously take up arms to resist the invading forces, without having had time to form themselves into regular armed units, provided they carry arms openly and respect the laws and customs of war.[31]

Notably, the detention of individuals falling into the first five of these six categories is based not on their activities per se, but rather on their status in relation to the forces

---

[30] For example, AP II, which provides rules to regulate the conduct of certain noninternational armed conflicts, has only 28 articles compared to AP I's 102 articles.

[31] The six categories are set out in GPW art. 4A. They also are found in GWS art. 13 and GWS-Sea art. 13.

fighting on behalf of a State. For example, soldiers of all stripe and specialization in a State's armed forces fall under GPW art. 4A, including those who perform no direct combatant functions at all, such as personnel clerks.[32] Further, it is not necessary for a soldier to have participated in combat in order to fall under any of the first three categories that cover combatants.

The fourth and fifth categories cover individuals who are not part of the armed forces, but provide support to them. Individuals are included in this category on the basis of their status as supporting personnel, and not on the basis of the amount of support they provide. Indeed, in the fourth category, civilians are covered on the basis of their authorization from the State to accompany its armed forces, while under the fifth category, members of crews of merchant ships and civil aircraft that support these forces are covered based on their status as crew members of certain vessels and aircraft that serve the State.[33] Perhaps most important, although they may be detained as POWs upon capture (in order to prevent them from continuing to provide support to enemy armed forces), individuals in these two categories remain civilians and therefore, unlike their armed forces counterparts, they are not legally entitled to directly participate in hostilities prior to capture (nor can they be directly targeted). Only the sixth category under GPW, covering civilians who rise up to resist an invader (a *levée en masse*) relies upon the conduct of the individual involved in "spontaneously tak[ing] up arms to resist the invading forces" to determine whether he or she falls into that category.

Individuals falling within the six GPW categories are entitled to a number of protections, including the right to be interned, rather than confined;[34] to receive adequate food, clothing, shelter, medical treatment, and other benefits from the capturing State;[35] to be protected against all forms of abuse and coercion; and importantly to be released upon the conclusion of hostilities.[36] GPW also requires the capturing State to establish an official information bureau to collect, and report to the enemy State(s) (through intermediaries contemplated by the GPW), information about the fact of the capture of these individuals, and the state of their health, and to provide information on how they may be contacted.[37] Prisoners of war under the GPW are entitled to receive visits by the

---

[32] The first and second Geneva Conventions, GWS and GWS-Sea, provide that military doctors and other military personnel of a State's armed force who are exclusively engaged in medical or religious functions and are captured in connection with an international armed conflict cannot be made prisoners of war, but can be retained to perform medical and religious functions for prisoners of war if needed. GWS art. 28; GSW-Sea art. 37.

[33] Thus, passengers of such vessels and aircraft would not be included because they are not part of the crew. GPW COMMENTARY at 66.

[34] GPW art. 21.

[35] GPW art. 25–28 (food, clothing, and shelter), 30 (medical treatment), and 34–38 (religious, intellectual, and physical activities).

[36] GPW art. 118.

[37] GPW art. 122.

International Committee of the Red Cross or a neutral Protecting Power to ensure that the capturing State is fulfilling its treaty obligations under the GPW.[38]

There are important limitations on the scope of these protections under the GPW. First, they apply only to individuals falling within the six categories listed above. Thus, individuals who do not fit any of these categories are not protected by the GPW. Second, with the exception of common article 3, the protections under GPW apply only to prisoners taken by a State in an international armed conflict (including the military occupation of an enemy State). Thus, without limiting which protections might apply as a matter of customary law, the protections of GPW are not applicable, as a matter of treaty law, even to the six categories of individuals listed above if they are captured during a noninternational armed conflict, such as the war on terror.

The fact that an individual does not fall under one of the GPW categories does not mean that he or she cannot be detained.[39] Under international law, any person who is a combatant in an armed conflict against a State may be detained by that State for the duration of hostilities.[40] On the other hand, a State generally may not indefinitely detain persons who are not combatants,[41] even if they are citizens of an enemy State, absent an imperative security need.[42]

The Bush administration formally adopted in 2004 the following definition of enemy combatant for purposes of determining who may be detained at Guantanamo Bay, Cuba, ("Guantanamo") until the end of hostilities:

[A]n individual who was part of or supporting Taliban or al Qaeda forces, or associated forces that are engaged in hostilities against the United States or its

---

[38] GPW art. 125.

[39] LOAC treaties do not expressly authorize indefinite military detention in armed conflict. Rather, LOAC treaties primarily regulate the treatment of prisoners, requiring due process in determining whether they fall under the six categories in GPW and in prosecuting them for crimes. However, as the ICRC's Commentary to the GPW makes clear, there are other categories of individuals who can be detained in connection with an armed conflict that fall outside the six categories of persons covered by GPW. GPW COMMENTARY at 51 note 1. Further, article 44(4) of AP I also contemplates the possibility that a combatant may not qualify as a prisoner of war for purposes of GPW. AP COMMENTARY at 538.

[40] As recognized by the U.S. Supreme Court, the right to detain enemies is a "fundamental and accepted…incident to war." Hamdi v. Rumsfeld, 542 U.S. at 518.

[41] GPW art. 4A(4) permits civilians "who accompany the armed forces without actually being members thereof" to be detained as prisoners of war under GPW; this includes journalists embedded with enemy armed forces, contractors supporting enemy armed forces, and government employees and others attached to enemy armed forces in some capacity. GPW art. 4A(5) permits members of the crew of an enemy State's merchant marine or civil aircraft to be held as prisoners of war under the protection of the GPW in an international armed conflict.

[42] As previously stated, *supra* note 6, GCIV does permit an enemy civilian to be detained if he or she is a clear security threat. *See* GCIV art. 78 (permitting an occupying power to intern civilians where the occupying State "considers it necessary, for imperative reasons of security…."). However, unlike military detention of combatants, such detention is subject to periodic review to determine if the reasons for detention still apply. *Id.*

coalition partners. This includes any person who has committed a belligerent act or has directly supported hostilities in aid of enemy armed forces.[43]

In 2006, Congress adopted a similar definition of "unlawful enemy combatant" for purposes of establishing who could be tried by military commission under the Military Commissions Act ("MCA 2006"):

> (1) UNLAWFUL ENEMY COMBATANT.—(A) The term "unlawful enemy combatant" means—(i) a person who has engaged in hostilities or who has purposefully and materially supported hostilities against the United States or its co-belligerents who is not a lawful enemy combatant (including a person who is part of the Taliban, al Qaeda, or associated forces); or (ii) a person who, before, on, or after the date of the enactment of the Military Commissions Act of 2006, has been determined to be an unlawful enemy combatant by a Combatant Status Review Tribunal or another competent tribunal established under the authority of the President or the Secretary of Defense.[44]

A similar definition was adopted when the MCA was revised in 2009 ("MCA 2009"):

> (7) UNPRIVILEGED ENEMY BELLIGERENT.—The term "unprivileged enemy belligerent" means an individual (other than a privileged belligerent) who—(A) has engaged in hostilities against the United States or its coalition partners; (B) has purposefully and materially supported hostilities against the United States or its coalition partners; or (C) was a part of al Qaeda at the time of the alleged offense under this chapter.[45]

The above definitions in the 2006 and 2009 versions of the MCA established the categories of persons who are subject to jurisdiction of military commissions for their pre-capture war crimes (which, for purposes of the MCA, includes their participation in hostilities). Although neither version of the MCA was intended to establish criteria for detention, the category of persons subject to the U.S. government's authority to detain under the AUMF has been interpreted to be "no narrower" than the category of persons potentially subject to the jurisdiction of military commissions. Accordingly, any

---

[43] *See, e.g.*, Undersecretary of Defense for Policy, Department of Defense Order of July 9, 2004, *available at* http://www.defense.gov/news/jul2004/d20040707review.pdf. Only individuals who were not U.S. citizens were considered to be detainable at Guantanamo.

[44] Section 3, P.L. 109–366, 120 Stat. 2600, 2603, *codified at* 10 U.S.C. 948d (2006) [hereinafter MCA 2006].

[45] P.L. 111–84, 123 Stat. 2574, 2575 *amending* 10 U.S.C. § 948a *et seq.* (new definition is codified at 10 U.S.C. § 948a(7) (2012)).

captives falling within these MCA definitions would be subject to detention under the LOAC as interpreted by the United States.[46]

The definition adopted by Congress in the MCA 2009 mirrored a definition offered by the Obama administration in filings with the U.S. District Court for the District of Columbia in connection with cases brought in that court by detainees at Guantanamo who were seeking habeas review of their detention:

> The President has the authority to detain persons that the President determines planned, authorized, committed, or aided the terrorist attacks that occurred on September 11, 2001, and persons who harbored those responsible for those attacks. The President also has the authority to detain persons who were part of, or substantially supported, Taliban or al-Qaida forces or associated forces that are engaged in hostilities against the United States or its coalition partners, including any person who has committed a belligerent act, or has directly supported hostilities, in aid of such enemy armed forces.[47]

Careful examination of all of these definitions (i.e., the Bush administration definition, the MCA 2006 and MCA 2009 definitions, and the Obama administration definition) reveal that they share certain common elements and indicate that an individual can be considered a detainable combatant if he or she falls into one of three categories in connection with the war on terror:

(1) A person who has committed a belligerent act or engaged in hostilities in aid of the Taliban, al-Qaeda forces, or associated forces or against the United States or its coalition partners;

(2) A person who was directly supporting (or in the versions adopted beginning in 2009, "substantially supporting") the Taliban, al-Qaeda forces, or associated forces that are engaged in hostilities against the United States or its coalition partners; or

(3) A person who is a "part of" the Taliban, al-Qaeda forces, or associated forces that are engaged in hostilities against the United States or its coalition partners.

These are separate tests, meaning an individual only needs to fall into one of the three categories to be subject to the combatant paradigm.

---

[46] Al-Bihani v. Obama, 590 F.3d. 866, 872 (D.C. Cir. 2010). The AUMF does not expressly authorize detention, but both the Bush and Obama administrations, the courts, and Congress have stated that detention is one of the types of force that the president is authorized to use under the AUMF. *See, e.g.,* Respondents' Memorandum regarding the Government's Detention Authority Relative to Detainees Held at Guantanamo Bay, at 3, Hamlily v. Obama, 616 F. Supp. 2d 63 (D.D.C. 2009) (No. 05-0763(JDB)) [hereinafter March 2009 Memorandum]. Under recent legislation, Congress has confirmed that the AUMF includes the authority to detain. *See* FY12 NDAA, *supra* note 13.

[47] March 2009 Memorandum, *supra* note 46, at 2.

The first of the three categories focuses on the conduct of the individual in engaging in belligerent acts against the United States. The second category focuses on the role played by the individual in supporting the forces engaged in hostilities against the United States or directly or substantially supporting those forces. The third category focuses on whether the individual is a member of those forces. Arguably, this third, status-based category corresponds to the status basis for detention in three of the six categories of individuals covered by GPW.[48]

It also is important to note that the second of these three categories does not require that the individual actually engage in hostilities to be considered an enemy combatant for purposes of detention. Instead, the individual is subject to detention for acts of supporting the Taliban, al-Qaeda, or associated forces. These acts of support apparently do not have to rise to the level of belligerent acts or acts of hostilities, as those acts are covered by the first category.[49]

Finally, the third category, which covers all those who are "part of" the Taliban, al-Qaeda forces, or associated forces, does not expressly require that the individuals in this category have a combatant role in these organizations. Thus, those who perform important services for these nonstate armed groups, such as recruiting, logistical supply, or intelligence gathering, could be covered by this category (as well as the second category). Support services can be performed by civilians as well as by fighters, just as contractors and other civilians can be engaged to perform important support activities for States armed forces that also may be performed by soldiers. Detaining such support personnel does not offend the LOAC: GPW recognizes that civilians who accompany the armed forces of States without being members of those forces can be detained for the duration of hostilities as prisoners of war in an international armed conflict based on their status in providing support of those armed forces.[50]

---

[48] Two of the other categories in GPW art. 4A address civilians who accompany State forces or serve as crew on State vessels and aircraft, and could correspond to those providing direct or substantial support to State armed forces. A sixth category in GPW art. 4A, which deals with the *levée en masse*, is based on conduct.

[49] The fact that the second category does not require the individual to commit belligerent acts highlights that the definitions discussed here are directed at identifying who is detainable under the LOAC, but not necessarily who is targetable. Although the LOAC permits the targeting of the members of armed forces and armed groups, it prohibits attacks on others (i.e., civilians) "unless and for such time as they take a direct part in hostilities." AP I arts. 48, 51(3). Not all acts of support—even if they make a substantial contribution to the activities of an armed group—may qualify as direct participation in hostilities under the LOAC, at least in the view of international legal experts. *See* Nils Melzer, Interpretive Guidance on the Notion of Direct Participation in Hostilities under International Humanitarian Law 45 (2009) ("The notion of direct participation in hostilities refers to specific hostile acts carried out by individuals as part of the conduct of hostilities between parties to an armed conflict.")

[50] It is important to note, however, that individuals who accompany the armed forces but are not military members of those armed forces are still considered to be civilians for purposes of targeting under the LOAC. AP I art. 50(1) (including within the definition of "civilian," persons accompanying the armed forces who fall under AP I art. 4A(4).) This fact also reflects the potential complication of justifying the targeting of an individual based on the "support" prong of the combatant definition employed by the U.S. government for purposes of detention.

Conduct and Detention

The foregoing discussion has focused on the detention and prosecution of combatants and those directly supporting them. Yet, it is also possible that on the battlefield or in occupied territory, a commander may detain civilians who are neither combatants nor support personnel for enemy forces, but who nonetheless pose a security threat. Article 78 of GCIV specifically provides that, where a State occupies the territory of its enemy, it may "for imperative reasons of security" subject civilians in that territory to internment or assigned residence as a safety measure. Moreover, if a civilian is detained "as a spy or saboteur, or as a person under definite suspicion of activity hostile to the security of the Occupying Power," he or she may be deprived of "rights of communication" if "absolute military security so requires."[51] While this authority applies to occupied territory, it can apply by analogy to any area under military control during an armed conflict.

Detention under GCIV is not equivalent to detention under GPW. Combatants and others associated with combatant forces (covered by GPW) are presumed to represent an ongoing threat based on their status as combatants, while civilians (covered by GCIV) are presumed not to represent a threat absent individual conduct that can overcome this presumption for that individual, thereby justifying detention.

The presumption for combatants and those associated with combatant forces justifies detention upon capture as a means of removing them from the conflict for the duration of hostilities. In contrast, civilians are presumptively inoffensive, and therefore entitled to freedom unless and until their individual conduct rebuts the presumption by indicating that they represent a threat to the security of friendly forces. Unlike the status-based detention of the captured member of an enemy armed group (including detention of those members who perform support activities similar to the activities performed by civilians accompanying the armed forces who are detainable as prisoners of war under GPW), which continues until the end of hostilities, the conduct-based detention of civilians is justifiable only for so long as the civilian continues to represent a threat to the detaining power. This conduct-based detention standard imposes an obligation on the detaining power to evaluate on a case-by-case basis the nature of the risk posed by the individual civilian as a precondition to depriving the civilian of his or her liberty, and to periodically validate this determination.

Article 78 of GCIV requires that the decision to place an individual civilian into internment or assigned residence must be "made according to a regular procedure" that includes the right of appeal, with such appeals to be decided "with the least possible delay."[52] Further, if the decision to detain is upheld, "it shall be subject to periodical

---

[51] GCIV art. 5. GCIV art. 5 requires that these rights of communication be restored "at the earliest date consistent with the security of the State or Occupying Power, as the case may be."

[52] *Id.* art. 78.

review, if possible every six months, by a competent body set up by the [Occupying] Power."[53] No such right of appeal or "periodical review" exists under GPW or the LOAC generally for those detained as combatants.

These procedural requirements—and in particular the right of "periodical review"— mean that detention under GCIV is neither status-based, nor intended to be presumptively indefinite (i.e., for the duration of hostilities). Rather, it is only to last as long as required under the circumstances. Further, the decision to detain, and the length of that detention, hinge upon the security threat posed by the individual being detained. By contrast, under the combatant paradigm, once an individual is categorized as a combatant (including support personnel accompanying the combatant's armed group), he or she can be detained for the duration of hostilities, without further review, based solely on his or her status and the corresponding presumption of the continuing threat that all combatants pose to the detaining power. Even the protective requirements of GPW, which are applicable only to combatants who are privileged belligerents and civilians who accompany State armed forces or crews of State vessels and aircraft, do not include any express requirement to grant the prisoner of war an opportunity to appeal his or her status or to obtain any subsequent review of whether continued detention is required.

As a matter of treaty law, the provisions of GCIV dealing with detention are limited to individuals either in occupied territory or in the home territory of a belligerent State in an international armed conflict, and thus would not apply to a noninternational armed conflict, such as the war on terror (except as a matter of policy).[54] Further, the United States has interpreted GCIV to apply only to those who are residents of the occupied territory. Thus, when the United States was an occupier in Iraq from 2003 to 2004, the U.S. government took the position that although GCIV did apply to the occupation, non-Iraqi terrorists who entered occupied territory on their own initiative to carry out operations against U.S. forces fell outside the scope of these provisions because they were not truly individuals within the "core concern" of GCIV, but instead unprivileged belligerents in a separate "global armed conflict" against the occupying power.[55]

---

[53] *Id.* A similar right can be found in GCIV art. 43 regarding enemy civilians detained in a State's home territory.

[54] The United States has long recognized that GCIV can be applied, as a matter of policy, in any territory in which U.S. forces are present, even on a battlefield. *See* U.S. Dep't of Army, Field Manual 27-10, Law of Land Warfare, para. 352 (1956) [hereinafter FM 27-10] ("The rules set forth in this chapter apply of their own force only to belligerently occupied areas, but they should, as a matter of policy, be observed as far as possible in areas through which troops are passing and even on the battlefield.") Further, it is DoD policy to broadly apply the law of war in all military operations. *See* DoDD 2311.01E, *supra* note 21, at para. 4. However, a policy choice leaves open the possibility of a future change and therefore is not legally binding.

[55] Protected Person Status in Occupied Iraq under the Fourth Geneva Convention, 28 Op. O.L.C. 35, 60 (2004) (narrowly defining the scope of GCIV to exclude persons who voluntarily came into occupied territory from third countries to engage in combatant activities, such as "operatives of the al Qaeda terrorist organization who are not Iraqi nationals or permanent residents of Iraq" during the period in

Although not strictly applicable to the war on terror, Article 78 of GCIV nevertheless is useful as an example of rational and efficient procedural standards, based on international law, that can be used as a basis for establishing a process to periodically re-evaluate the continuing justification for continued detention of individual terrorists. The legal standards are not exacting—GCIV provides little guidance about the process itself other than requiring the "periodical review" to be conducted by a "competent body" that the occupying State establishes for itself. Even Article 75 of AP I, which regulates security detention in situations other than occupation, imposes only a few additional requirements that must be followed in determining whether to detain individuals and in periodically reviewing that detention.[56] Nevertheless, where long-term detention has become controversial, as at Guantanamo, implementing a periodic review process for detainees (including those held under the combatant paradigm) that would comply with Article 78 of GCIV supports the legitimacy of continued detention of those who still pose a threat and also facilitates the reduction of the detainee population (if the Article 78 process identifies prisoners who no longer pose a threat and therefore can be released) before the end of hostilities. It is not surprising, therefore, that the United States has provided for periodic reviews of the detainees it holds to determine whether and when they can be released, despite being enemy combatants, even where such reviews are not required as a matter of law.[57]

Detention Determinations

An individual detained by a State in connection with an armed conflict has a significant stake in the determination of his or her status. If the individual can demonstrate that he or she is not a combatant or has not engaged in conduct justifying detention, the detaining State may release the detainee. Indeed, if the individual can show that he or she is not a combatant, but rather is a civilian who can only be held administratively for reasons of security, the detainee may have rights under international law to a "periodical review" of the basis for detention that would not be available if the detainee were considered a combatant. On the other hand, even if the individual is determined to be a combatant, the

---

which the United States was an occupying power, as such persons did not "find themselves" in occupied territory but rather had elected to come there), *available at* http://www.justice.gov/olc/opiniondocs/op-olc-vo28-p0035.pdf.

[56] AP I art. 75(3) provides:

Any person arrested, detained or interned for actions related to the armed conflict shall be informed promptly, in a language he understands, of the reasons why these measures have been taken. Except in cases of arrest or detention for penal offences, such persons shall be released with the minimum delay possible and in any event as soon as the circumstances justifying the arrest, detention or internment have ceased to exist.

[57] *See, e.g.*, discussion of Administrative Review Board process, *infra* notes 141–142, and accompanying text.

individual will want to argue that he or she should be treated as a prisoner of war who is entitled to the protections afforded by GPW. In all these cases, the process by which the status determination will be made is critically important to the individual, as it will determine his or her entitlement to protection under the LOAC.

Before turning to a more detailed discussion of the procedures that have been applied by the United States in making detention determinations in the war on terror, it is useful to consider what international law requires, in order to put the U.S. procedures into a broader context and to provide a basis to compare them to international standards. It is also helpful to consider how the U.S. procedures in the war on terror compare to the U.S. implementation of the LOAC standards prior to 9/11.

I. LOAC TREATY REQUIREMENTS

There is surprisingly little guidance in the GPW on the question of status determinations.[58] Article 5 of GPW directs that "[s]hould any doubt arise as to whether persons, having committed a belligerent act and having fallen into the hands of the enemy, belong to any of the categories in Article 4 [the applicable article regarding the persons covered by GPW], such persons shall enjoy the protection of the present Convention until such time as their status has been determined by a competent tribunal."[59] Although the rule provides for the protection of the GPW as the default in cases of doubt, it does not stipulate which person or entity is to make the decision whether or not such doubt exists. The decision about the existence of doubt is critically important to the detainee, because the detainee's entitlement to a tribunal (at least under GPW in an international armed conflict) depends upon the existence of doubt as to his or her status. The absence of guidance on the question of determinations of doubt leaves enormous latitude for different practices among the various States who are party to the GPW, as individual States could leave the decision as to doubt to the low level command of the capturing unit, who may have an incentive to hold an individual in order to minimize the risk of error in releasing a potential belligerent, or could require such authority to be exercised by higher levels, away from the pressures of the battlefield. In either case, the States would be complying with the GPW.

Article 45 of AP I eliminates the possibility that a detainee could be denied a tribunal to determine his or her prisoner-of-war status on the grounds that there is no doubt that he or she is eligible for it. Article 45 provides that any person who takes part in

---

[58] As stated, *supra* notes 51–53 and accompanying text, for security detainees under GCIV art. 78, the only requirement imposed by GCIV is that the decision to detain and intern or place in assigned residence must be made "according to a regular procedure" and, although the decision can be appealed, there is no particular body identified to which appeals are to be made. Article 78 does require that the "periodical review" be conducted by a "competent body," however.

[59] GPW art. 5.

hostilities and is then detained by an adverse Party is presumed to be a prisoner of war if he or she claims that status.[60] Thus, the only way to deny prisoner-of-war status to such an individual is to convene a tribunal to determine his or her status. However, not all States are party to AP I, including the United States, and thus the *legal* entitlement of detainees to a tribunal to determine their status is not universal, even in international armed conflict.

Also missing from article 5 of the GPW is any detail about the nature of the tribunal that will make the status determination in cases of doubt.[61] This lack of detail is arguably helpful to implementation of Article 5, as it affords each State party to the GPW the flexibility to adopt procedures commensurate with the circumstances in which article 5 is to be applied. For example, it would be difficult to follow a very formal procedure on the battlefield, where there may be large numbers of detainees, and where the armed forces of the capturing State are operating under austere conditions. On the other hand, formal procedures could be followed where the number of detainees is limited and they are being held at locations suitable for such procedures.[62] Therefore, the flexibility provided by the generality of the language used in the article is practical. However, the point here is that, as a matter of law, absolutely nothing in the GPW guides the capturing State in fashioning its procedure.[63]

Article 45 of AP I, which relates to the detention of persons who have taken a direct part in hostilities in an international armed conflict, provides no additional detail regarding the tribunal process. However, it does provide that even if prisoner-of-war status is denied, the individual is still entitled to the protections of article 75 of AP I, which applies to all persons detained in connection with an international armed conflict

---

[60] AP I art. 45(1). In U.S. practice, determinations about the status of a detainee may be revisited at various points as the individual is moved from the battlefield to a detention facility. *See* JOINT CHIEFS OF STAFF, JOINT. PUB. 3–63, DETAINEE OPERATIONS at VII-2 (2008), *available at* http://www.dtic.mil/doctrine/new_pubs/jp3_63.pdf. *See also* note 84, *infra*.

[61] The International Committee of the Red Cross (ICRC)'s Commentary on the GPW, which is influential (albeit not binding) on how States interpret their obligations under the GPW and related law-of-war treaties, notes that, in earlier drafts of article 5, it was initially proposed by the ICRC to have the status determination made by a "responsible authority." Concerns about leaving this important decision to an individual led the drafters to replace the phrase with "military tribunal" and later with "competent tribunal," which was ultimately adopted. GPW COMMENTARY at 77.

[62] The length and consequences of detention might also influence the degree of formality in any procedures adopted by a State to implement the "tribunal" requirement. Detentions that are anticipated to last only a very short time before release would seem to merit a less formal procedure as compared to detentions that could last indefinitely or that might also be accompanied by prosecution for the detainee's belligerent acts.

[63] The ICRC Commentary's view of the meaning of the reference to a tribunal tilts toward the more formal:

> The matter should be taken to a court, as persons taking part in the fight without the right to do so are liable to be prosecuted for murder or attempted murder, and might even be sentenced to capital punishment.

Id.

subject to AP I, and affords the detainee essential protections of humanitarian treatment and due process in case of criminal prosecution (but also does not provide any detail about the tribunal that will make administrative detention determinations).[64]

Like article 5 of GPW, article 45 of AP I includes the same presumption that a detainee whose status is in doubt is entitled to prisoner-of-war treatment until a tribunal determines otherwise. However, there is a notable difference between the presumptions in the two articles. In article 5 of GPW, it is only individuals who have "committed a belligerent act" who are afforded the presumption. The reason, which is not addressed in the International Committee of the Red Cross (ICRC)'s Commentary to GPW, appears to be that a person committing a belligerent act has at least established, by that act, that he or she is a combatant. The only question then is whether he or she belongs in one of the categories of combatants protected by GPW.

By contrast, article 45 of AP I affords this presumption to any person who "takes part in hostilities" and claims that he or she qualifies as a prisoner of war. The phrase "takes part in hostilities" is broad and could include persons committing acts that are not clearly "belligerent" in that they do not involve the use of arms or otherwise are not easily recognized as combatant activities, but are nonetheless directly related to the hostilities. By expanding the protection of GPW to include all individuals who "take part" in hostilities and claim prisoner-of-war status, AP I expands the numbers of individuals who are presumed to be prisoners of war absent a determination by a tribunal under GPW art. 5 that they are not. As the ICRC Commentary on AP I notes:

> [T]he capture can occur in conditions when the captor has no way of finding out whether or not the person concerned is a prisoner of war, or perhaps in circumstances which give him some indication, but no proof on this point. This provision has therefore introduced a system of legal presumptions in favour of the prisoner. If the captor wants to contest such a presumption, it is up to him to present evidence that the person concerned is not a prisoner of war....[65]

Thus, as noted above, all the detainee has to do under AP I is claim prisoner-of-war status, and then the burden falls on the captor to establish that a detainee is not entitled to that status.

The United States has not ratified AP I and has identified various aspects of its provisions that are unacceptable because they would afford prisoner-of-war status to persons and groups that the United States does not believe should be given such treatment. However, the United States has not objected to certain principles reflected in article 45, including the principle that where there is doubt as to the status of a detainee, he or she

---

[64] AP II arts. 4–6 provide similar protections in noninternational armed conflicts.

[65] AP COMMENTARY at 547.

should be accorded prisoner-of-war treatment until that doubt is resolved.[66] Indeed, it is U.S. policy, as expressed in Army Regulation (AR) 190–8, that "all persons taken into custody by U.S. forces will be provided the protections of the GPW until some other legal status is determined by competent authority."[67]

2. U.S. IMPLEMENTATION OF TREATY REQUIREMENTS

The United States has implemented article 5 of GPW in a manner that provides more due process protections than is required by GPW or AP I. The U.S. military services, with the U.S. Army acting as Executive Agent for the Department of Defense (DoD) on detainee matters, have promulgated AR 190–8, which although an Army Regulation, also falls within the regulation series of each of the other services (U.S. Air Force, Marine Corps, and Navy). AR 190-8 includes procedures for the tribunals required by article 5, GPW, and therefore establishes the baseline for what is required to make a status determination under the LOAC.

The current version of AR 190–8 was promulgated in 1997, based in part on lessons learned in the Gulf War and in prior conflicts. It provides for tribunals consisting of three commissioned officers, one of whom must be in the grade of Major (or its Navy equivalent) or higher, assisted by a recorder, which the regulation says "preferably" should be a judge advocate (i.e., a military lawyer).[68] The tribunal's procedure includes a number of due process protections, including notifying the detainee of his or her rights at the beginning of the tribunal's hearings and granting the detainee the right to attend all open hearings (hearings may be closed where open hearings would "compromise security"), to question witnesses, and to have the assistance of an interpreter. The detainee may testify or otherwise address the tribunal, but may not be compelled to do so.

The tribunal decides, by majority vote and applying a "preponderance of the evidence" standard, whether the detainee is an "[i]nnocent civilian who should be immediately returned to his home or released"; a prisoner of war under GPW, who will be accorded prisoner-of-war status; a civilian who should be detained "for reasons of operational security" or "probable cause incident to criminal investigation"; or a person with some other

---

[66] Michael J. Matheson, *Session One: The United States Position on the Relation of Customary Law to the 1977 Protocols Additional to the 1949 Geneva Conventions*, 2 AM. U. J. INT'L L. & POL'Y 419, 425–26 (1987) (remarks of Deputy Legal Advisor, U.S. Department of State).

[67] U.S. DEP'T ARMY, REG. 190-8 ENEMY PRISONERS OF WAR, RETAINED PERSONNEL, CIVILIAN INTERNEES AND OTHER DETAINEES, para. 1–5.a.(2) (1997) [hereinafter AR 190–8].

[68] Although not required by AR 190–8, military lawyers could serve as the three members of the tribunal, and in some cases this occurred in recent U.S. operations where article 5 tribunals have been required. *See* U.S. ARMY CENTER FOR LAW AND MILITARY OPERATIONS, FORGED IN THE FIRE: LEGAL LESSONS LEARNED DURING MILITARY OPERATIONS 1994–2008, at 33–34 (2008) [hereinafter FORGED IN THE FIRE 2008].

status detainable under the LOAC.[69] There is no specific category for a combatant who does not qualify as a prisoner of war under GPW, but presumably the category of "civilian" held either for reasons of security or as a criminal suspect includes combatants who are not entitled to prisoner-of-war status or combatant immunity.[70] These individuals are not entitled to protection under GPW, although they would benefit from the protections afforded to internees under GCIV if they are considered "protected persons" (which, as noted earlier, may be interpreted narrowly).[71]

A written report of the proceedings is prepared and forwarded to a higher headquarters for legal review within three days after the tribunal's decision is completed. The record of every proceeding resulting in a determination denying prisoner-of-war status is reviewed for legal sufficiency by the legal office of the general officer who convened the tribunal.[72]

Although extensive, the procedures adopted by the United States in AR 190-8 do not accord a detainee the full panoply of rights that could have been granted in light of the significant interest the detainee may have in either (1) proving that he or she is an innocent civilian entitled to be released or, if that is not possible, at least (2) securing

---

[69] AR 190–8, *supra* note 67, para. 1-6.e.(10). The tribunal may also determine that the person is a member of certain categories of "retained personnel," that is, medical or religious personnel who are part of an enemy armed force or the staff of voluntary aid societies who work with the enemy armed force. *Id.*, para. 1–6e.(10) (b). These categories of non-combatants are to be "repatriated as soon as military requirements permit" if not needed to minister to the medical or religious needs of other prisoners. *Id.* para. 3–15.w.

[70] Chapters 5–7 of AR 190–8, *supra* note 67, describe the "internment" of persons considered to be "civilian internees" or "CI," which the regulation defines as "[a] civilian who is interned during armed conflict or occupation for security reasons or for protection or because he has committed an offense against the detaining power." *Id.* Glossary, Section II. Under the terms of GCIV, CIs are entitled to treatment similar to that accorded to prisoners of war under GPW. The applicability of the CI category is unclear. AR 190–8 para. 6–2.a(2) provides that only civilian persons entitled to "protected status" who meet the requirements set forth in GCIV will be classified as CI. GCIV only explicitly protects enemy civilians in occupied territory and in the home territory of a belligerent, and indeed the applicable provisions of AR 190–8 suggest that its provisions on CI are directed only toward civilians in those specific circumstances. *Id.*, para. 5–1.c. Thus, it is not explicitly clear that the provisions of AR 190–8 regarding CI apply to persons detained in other areas (e.g., on a battlefield), such as an unprivileged enemy combatant, who is determined not to be either a prisoner of war entitled to protection under GPW or an innocent civilian entitled to be released. Nevertheless, consistent with the policy in FM 27–10, *supra* note 54, of applying key LOAC protections broadly, U.S. policy is to apply to all detainees, "without regard to a detainee's legal status," a minimum humane treatment standard that includes the provisions of common article 3 plus some enhancements. DoDD 2310.01E, *supra* note 19, para. 4.2 & enclosure 4. Thus, uncertainty as to status under AR 190-8 does not justify affording the detainee lesser treatment than DoDD 2310.01E requires.

[71] As indicated in note 55, *supra*, during the occupation of Iraq by U.S. forces, the Department of Justice's Office of Legal Counsel defined the phrase "find themselves in the hands of a Party" very narrowly, to exclude, inter alia, citizens of third countries who voluntarily came into occupied territory to engage in belligerent activities against the occupying power.

[72] An important element of the procedure under AR 190–8 is that tribunals can only be convened by a commander exercising "general courts-martial convening authority," which is generally reserved to higher-ranking general officers or admirals. AR 190–8, *supra* note 67, para. 1–6.d.

prisoner-of-war status under GPW (and hence the protection of combatant immunity) rather than being treated as an unprivileged belligerent. Indeed, in Vietnam, U.S. military authorities issued directives that required the tribunals to consist of three officers, generally military lawyers, assisted by a nonvoting counsel who handled administrative tasks, including advising the detainee of his rights, arranging for witnesses, presenting evidence, and preparing the report of the tribunal's proceedings.[73] The detainee was permitted to be present at all open sessions of the tribunal, to testify, and to have the assistance of an interpreter.[74]

Unlike the procedures in AR 190–8 (which do not include a right to counsel), the detainee in the Vietnam War procedure could select his own counsel, including a fellow detainee to help him, but if he failed to appoint someone, a military lawyer familiar with the Geneva Conventions was appointed for him.[75] Counsel for the detainee had a number of rights, including conferring with the detainee, and examining and presenting (and cross-examining) witnesses and testimony on the detainee's behalf.[76] The tribunal would decide by vote, in a closed session, whether the detainee was a prisoner of war, and a record would be prepared for further review, particularly in cases where the tribunal determined that the detainee was not entitled to prisoner-of-war status.[77]

The extensive procedures used in Vietnam reflected a broader U.S. policy of liberally granting prisoner-of-war status to combatants, other than those engaged in terrorism, spying, or sabotage.[78] The policy was driven in part by the reality that the government of South Vietnam did not have the resources and facilities to try and punish as civil defendants those who engaged in belligerent acts, but did not qualify as prisoners of war.[79] The policy was also driven by the belief that humane treatment accorded to captured North Vietnamese and Vietcong forces would be reciprocated by the North Vietnamese and

---

[73] U.S. Mil. Assistance Cmd, Vietnam, Dir. 20-5, Inspections and Investigations Prisoners of War—Determination of Eligibility, para. 6.e. (1968) in III U.S. Dep't of Army, Report of the Department the Army Review of the Preliminary Investigations into the My Lai Incidents at Exhibit D-42 (1970), *available at* http://www.loc.gov/rr/frd/Military_Law/pdf/RDAR-Vol-IIIBook1.pdf. According to the directive, in all cases, at least one of the members of the tribunal was required to be a judge advocate or other military lawyer familiar with the Geneva Conventions. *Id.* Annex A, para. 3.

[74] *Id.* Annex A, paras. 7, 10 & 12.

[75] *Id.* Annex A., para. 8.

[76] *Id.* Annex A, para. 9.

[77] *Id.* Annex A, para. 14.

[78] George S. Prugh, Law at War: Vietnam 1964–1973, at 66 (1975) ("The MACV policy was that all combatants captured during military operations were to be accorded prisoner-of-war status, irrespective of the type of unit to which they belonged. Terrorists, spies and saboteurs were excluded from consideration as prisoners of war.")

[79] *Id.* ("By broadly construing Article 4 [GPW], so as to accord full prisoner-of-war status to Viet Cong Main Force and Local Force troops, as well as regular North Vietnamese Army troops, any Viet Cong taken in combat would be detained for a prisoner-of-war camp rather than a civilian jail.")

Vietcong who captured Americans.[80] As noted by a senior military lawyer, who was the chief military legal advisor to the U.S. military forces in Vietnam from 1964 to 1966:

> U.S. policy was to do all in its power to alleviate the plight of American prisoners. It was expected that efforts by the United States to ensure humane treatment for Vietcong and North Vietnamese Army captives would bring reciprocal benefits for American captives.[81]

As the foregoing suggests, the procedures were tailored to Vietnam and were not applicable to U.S. military operations generally. In subsequent conflicts, it was left to commanders at the theater level or lower to determine what procedures would be used to make status determinations. As a result, in those conflicts, U.S. military officials used more informal procedures that were better suited to the circumstances of the conflict.[82] Further, the procedures for article 5 tribunals that eventually were set out in AR 190–8 in the 1990s provide a bottom-line standard to be applied, with the potential for more elaborate procedures on a case-by-case basis.[83]

As an obligation under international law, article 5 has proven to be sufficiently flexible for the United States to tailor its implementation to meet the circumstances on the ground.[84]

---

[80] *Id.* at 62–63 ("In the south, where the government of South Vietnam had tried and publicly executed some Viet Cong agents, there had been retributory executions of Americans by Viet Cong. In the north,... Hanoi repeatedly threatened to try United States pilots in accordance with Vietnamese laws, but never carried out this threat.")

[81] *Id.* The article 5 tribunals held in Vietnam are also described in FRED L. BORCH, JUDGE ADVOCATES IN COMBAT: ARMY LAWYERS IN MILITARY OPERATIONS FROM VIETNAM TO HAITI 20–21 (2001) [hereinafter JUDGE ADVOCATES IN COMBAT].

[82] For example, in U.S. operation "Just Cause" in Panama in December 1989, U.S. Army Major (later Colonel) Richard B. Jackson (one of the coauthors of this book) developed a procedure to deal in a short time with the classification of a large number of Panamanian prisoners taken by U.S. forces:

> Reaffirming that Article 5 of the GPW Convention required that a three-person tribunal determine the status of detainees, Jackson, along with a representative of the camp commander and a military intelligence officer, began the process of sorting out the individuals in question. In determining their status, Major Jackson and the two other officers acted as a de facto Article 5 tribunal, examining any paperwork accompanying the detainees and questioning the individuals concerned when necessary.

> *Id.* at 104. Although this procedure did not employ all the formalities of the procedures used in Vietnam, it nonetheless met the requirements of article 5, GPW. Further, the procedure allowed Major Jackson and his colleagues to reduce from 4100 to 100 the number of individuals who required continued detention and greatly facilitated repatriation and release of the others. *Id.* at 105.

[83] In practice, commanders have varied the procedures to fit the specific situation while still complying with the regulation's requirements.

[84] In addition, in the case of captures made on a battlefield, U.S. military practice is that the article 5 tribunal is typically only a part of a lengthy screening process that begins with a determination by a commander at the time of capture on the battlefield, based on evidence on the ground, and continues as the detainee is processed by military authorities as he or she is moved to more centralized internment facilities away from the battlefield. *See* Brief for the Respondents at 3, Hamdi v. Rumsfeld, 542 U.S. 528 (2004), 2004 WL

Importantly, however, article 5's requirement that, in cases of doubt, a person must be treated as a prisoner of war until a tribunal determines otherwise, means that there should be little risk that an individual will be afforded less rights than he or she is entitled to under international law.[85] On the other hand, where the capturing State concludes there is no doubt and that State is not a party to AP I, article 5 is not applicable and provides no protection against an erroneous conclusion.[86] Further, neither article 5 of GPW nor AP I apply in noninternational armed conflicts, and therefore there is scant authority in LOAC treaties to require a procedure for status determinations. Instead, the detainee must rely on domestic law, customary law, and ultimately, the policies of the detaining power for procedures that ensure his or her status is correctly determined.

Detention as a Method of Warfare in the War on Terror

The scale and lethality of the attacks on the United States on September 11, 2001, led the U.S. government to view as an armed conflict the United States's struggle with the terrorist elements that launched the attacks and the nations that harbored them. In his statement of September 11th on the attacks, the president said: "The United States will hunt down and punish those responsible for the cowardly acts," adding "[o]ur military around the world is on high alert status...." On September 14, 2001, the president declared a national emergency to respond to "the continuing and immediate threat of further attacks on the United States" and authorized the call to duty of reserve military personnel.[87]

On September 18, 2001, citing the "threat to the national security and foreign policy of the United States posed by these grave acts of violence," both houses of Congress approved the AUMF, which authorized the president to "use all necessary and appropriate force against those nations, organizations, or persons he determines planned, authorized, committed, or aided the terrorist attacks that occurred on September 11, 2001, or

---

724020 (U.S.) [hereinafter "Government Response Brief in Hamdi"] ("Those taken into U.S. control [in the conflict in Afghanistan] are subjected to a multi-step screening process to determine if their continued detention is necessary.")

[85] In the past decade or so, U.S. military lawyers have "used an informal screening process to make the initial determination whether to release a detainee or to conduct an Article 5 tribunal if classification was not possible after initial screening," FORGED IN THE FIRE 2008, *supra* note 68, at 33. This approach is not precluded by either GPW or AR 190-8.

[86] As noted, supra *note* 60 and accompanying text, AP I art. 45 changes the burden/presumptions regarding prisoner-of-war status in cases of doubt, by requiring the detaining State to treat a detainee as a prisoner of war if he or she claims such status, at least until a tribunal determines that the detainee has another status. The United States is not a party to AP I, but even if it were, AP I would not apply to the noninternational armed conflict with al-Qaeda, because AP I applies only to international armed conflicts.

[87] Proclamation No. 7463, 66 Fed. Reg. 48,199 (2001). This national emergency remains in effect. Continuation of the National Emergency with Respect to Certain Terrorist Attacks, 78 Fed. Reg. 56,581 (2013).

harbored such organizations or persons, in order to prevent any future acts of international terrorism against the United States by such nations, organizations or persons."[88]

On October 7, 2001, the president announced military operations against al-Qaeda training camps and Taliban military installations in Afghanistan, noting that "[t]oday we focus on Afghanistan, but the battle is broader. . . . In this conflict, there is no neutral ground."[89]

That detention and prosecution of terrorists as unlawful combatants would be a key element of the war on terror was made clear with the issuance of the president's Military Order of November 13, 2001.[90] Finding that, among other things, "[i]nternational terrorists, including members of al Qaida, have carried out attacks . . . on a scale that has created a state of armed conflict that requires the use of the United States Armed Forces," section 2(a) of the order authorized the Secretary of Defense to detain any individual who is not a U.S. citizen with respect to whom the president made the following determinations:

(1) there is reason to believe that such individual, at the relevant times,

    (i) is or was a member of the organization known as al Qaida;

    (ii) has engaged in, aided or abetted, or conspired to commit, acts of international terrorism, or acts in preparation therefor, that have caused, threaten to cause, or have as their aim to cause, injury to or adverse effects on the United States, its citizens, national security, foreign policy, or economy; or

    (iii) has knowingly harbored one or more individuals described in subparagraphs (i) or (ii) of subsection 2(a)(1) of this order; and

(2) it is in the interest of the United States that such individual be subject to this order.[91]

The order authorized not only detention, but also prosecution of the detained individuals by military commission.[92]

---

[88] AUMF, *supra* note 11, at § 2(a). The AUMF declared that it constituted specific statutory authorization within the meaning of section 5(b) of the War Powers Resolution, which relates to the need for congressional authority for any extended involvement of U.S. forces in hostilities. Thus, as the title suggested, Congress in passing the AUMF was authorizing the use of military force to fight terrorists. The president signed the AUMF the same day it was passed by Congress.

[89] George W. Bush, Address to the Nation on Operations in Afghanistan (Oct. 7, 2001), *in* SELECTED SPEECHES OF PRESIDENT GEORGE W. BUSH 2001–2008, at 75, 76, *available at* http://georgewbush-whitehouse. archives.gov/infocus/bushrecord/documents/Selected_Speeches_George_W_Bush.pdf.

[90] Military Order of November 13, 2001—Detention, Treatment and Trial of Certain Non-Citizens in the War against Terrorism, 66 Fed. Reg. 57,833 (2001) [hereinafter Military Order].

[91] *Id.* sec. 2. Although detention is authorized under the Military Order, few detainees were actually designated as subject to the Military Order for purpose of detention. JENNIFER K. ELSEA & MICHAEL J. GARCIA, CONG. RES. SERV., RL33180, ENEMY COMBATANT DETAINEES: HABEAS CORPUS CHALLENGES IN FEDERAL COURTS DETENTIONS 10 n.63 (last updated Apr. 5, 2010), *available at* http://assets.opencrs. com/rpts/RL33180_20100405.pdf. Rather, such detention generally occurs under the authority granted in the AUMF, which courts have interpreted to include the right to detain.

[92] Military Order, *supra* note 90, sec. 4.

The order directed that the detained individuals be:

(a) detained at an appropriate location designated by the Secretary of Defense outside or within the United States;

(b) treated humanely, without any adverse distinction based on race, color, religion, gender, birth, wealth, or any similar criteria;

(c) afforded adequate food, drinking water, shelter, clothing, and medical treatment;

(d) allowed the free exercise of religion consistent with the requirements of such detention; and

(e) detained in accordance with such other conditions as the Secretary of Defense may prescribe.[93]

The order also directed that regulations to be prescribed by the Secretary of Defense would provide for "a full and fair trial, with the military commission sitting as the triers of both fact and law."[94] It also provided that military tribunals would have exclusive jurisdiction with respect to offenses by the detainees, and that detainees would not have the privilege to seek any remedy or maintain any action, or to have others seek a remedy or maintain an action on the individual's behalf, in any U.S. or foreign court or any international tribunal.[95]

The U.S. military did not, however, need the military order to authorize detention of battlefield combatants. It already enjoyed that right under the law of war. However, the order significantly expanded the authority to detain by including a potentially broader category of individuals who may not have committed belligerent acts, but who supported or aided those committing or preparing to commit such acts, or who harbored such individuals. Also, the detention authority granted under the order was not limited to any particular theater of operations, and potentially included any person in the world who was not a U.S. citizen and with respect to whom the president had made the required determinations.

Given the authority granted to the DoD to try detainees by military commission, it was clear that detention was not simply to take these individuals off the battlefield, but also to prosecute them for war crimes. An important question in implementing this strategy was whether the detainees would be entitled to prisoner-of-war status under GPW. Were they to have prisoner-of-war status, the United States would have been prohibited from

---

[93] *Id.* sec. 3.

[94] *Id.* sec. 4. The provisions of the military order related to military commissions were superseded by Executive Order 13425, which implemented provisions of MCA 2006, *supra* note 44. Executive Order 13425 of February 14, 2007, "Trial of Alien Unlawful Enemy Combatants by Military Commission," 72 Fed. Reg. 7737 (2007).

[95] Military Order, *supra* note 90, sec. 7.

trying detainees for any activities that complied with the law of war, such as attacking military installations or military personnel, as the combatant immunity enjoyed by prisoners of war would shield them from prosecution for such acts.[96] Furthermore, use of military commissions may have been improper, as the GPW requires trial by the same tribunals used to try the detaining power's own armed forces (in the case of the United States, these are courts-martial or trials in civilian courts). On the other hand, if they were not prisoners of war and did not enjoy combatant immunity, the detainees could be prosecuted for belligerent acts, even against military personnel and military targets, and there would be no bar to the creation and use of military commissions to adjudicate war crimes charges.

The issue of the application of the GPW in the war on terror first arose with respect to the conflict in Afghanistan, where initially it was anticipated that U.S. military operations would yield detainees who would be held under the Geneva Conventions.[97] In early 2002, however, the Justice Department's Office of Legal Counsel (OLC) concluded that neither the Taliban nor al-Qaeda fighters could qualify for prisoner-of-war status under GPW.[98] GPW did not apply to the conflict with al-Qaeda as a matter of law, because, according to article 2 of GPW, GPW applies only in conflicts between "two or more of the High Contracting Parties" to the GPW. Al-Qaeda is not a State, nor does it belong to a State. Further, al-Qaeda fighters did not meet the requirements of any of the categories of prisoners covered by GPW.[99] They were not members of a regular armed force of a State, nor do they qualify as a volunteer force, militia, or organized resistance force under GPW. This latter conclusion was based on two determinations. First, al-Qaeda was not an organization that was in any way subordinate to or acting exclusively on behalf of the Taliban, but instead was simply using Afghanistan (and by implication the Taliban) as a safe haven from which to prepare and launch attacks against worldwide targets. Second, they did not meet the treaty's requirements that such forces distinguish themselves from civilians by wearing uniforms or insignia, carrying their arms openly, and obeying the laws of war.

Taliban fighters, on the other hand, did fight on behalf of a State Party to the GPW (Afghanistan) but, like al-Qaeda fighters, they did not come within any of the categories of prisoners covered by GPW. The Taliban lacked an organized command structure, with responsibility for subordinates, and was dominated by al-Qaeda. Taliban fighters

---

[96] Even if he or she had combatant immunity, however, the detainee could be tried for offenses that violated the LOAC, such as intentionally attacking civilians.

[97] Waxman, *supra* note 17, at 345 ("Shortly before conventional operations began, US military commanders in charge of Afghanistan operations issued an order instructing that the Geneva Conventions were to be applied to all captured individuals.")

[98] *See* Department of Justice, Office of Legal Counsel, Memorandum Opinion for Alberto R. Gonzales, Counsel to the President, and William J. Haynes II, General Counsel of the Department of Defense, *"Application of Treaties and Laws to al Qaeda and Taliban Detainees"* (Jan. 22, 2002), *available at* http://www.justice.gov/olc/docs/memo-laws-taliban-detainees.pdf.

[99] *See supra* note 31 and accompanying text for these categories.

did carry their arms openly and in some cases had a tribal flag, but they otherwise did not distinguish themselves from civilians. Further, as an organization, the Taliban routinely disregarded law-of-war obligations, did little to distinguish between civilians and combatants in hostilities, and in fact intentionally killed civilians and committed other atrocities. For these and other reasons, the OLC concluded that there were sufficient factual grounds for the president to determine that the GPW did not apply to any member of al-Qaeda or the Taliban.[100]

On February 7, 2002, the White House announced that the president had made a determination that the "Geneva Convention will apply to the Taliban detainees, but not to the al Qaeda international terrorists," adding that:

> Taliban detainees are not entitled to POW [prisoner of war] status. To qualify as POWs under Article 4, al Qaeda and Taliban detainees would have to have satisfied four conditions: They would have to be part of a military hierarchy; they would have to have worn uniforms or other distinctive signs visible at a distance; they would have to have carried arms openly; and they would have to have conducted their military operations in accordance with the laws and customs of war.
>
> The Taliban have not effectively distinguished themselves from the civilian population of Afghanistan. Moreover, they have not conducted their operations in accordance with the laws and customs of war. Instead, they have knowingly adopted and provided support to the unlawful terrorist objectives of the al Qaeda.[101]

The president's determination served two purposes. First, it affirmed that even though the Taliban did not qualify for prisoner-of-war status, the Geneva Conventions did apply to the conflict. This had the important effect of underscoring that the United States expected any members of regular forces taken during the conflict, including U.S. soldiers, to be treated as prisoners of war. Second, by categorically determining that al-Qaeda and Taliban fighters did not qualify for prisoner-of-war status, the president eliminated any "doubt" as to their status and thereby any need to hold tribunals to make individual determinations of their status under article 5 of the GPW. Had such a determination not been made, then a Taliban prisoner would have been given the benefits of

---

[100] *See* Department of Justice, Office of Legal Counsel, Memorandum Opinion for the Counsel to the President, "Status of Taliban Forces under Article 4 of the Third Geneva Convention of 1949" (Feb. 7, 2002), *available at* http://www.fas.org/irp/agency/doj/olc/taliban.pdf.

[101] L. Ari Fleischer, Statement by the Press Secretary on the Geneva Convention, (Feb. 7, 2002), Digest of United States Practice in International Law 2002, *available at* http://www.state.gov/s/l/38727.htm (White House Press Secretary announcement of President Bush's determination concerning the legal status of Taliban and al-Qaeda detainees.)

GPW, at least until a tribunal was convened and determined that he was not a prisoner of war.[102]

At the time of the announcement, the administration emphasized, as a matter of U.S. policy, the treatment accorded al-Qaeda and Taliban prisoners would be substantially similar to what they would have received if held as prisoners of war under GPW. Indeed, a fact sheet issued on the date of the president's announcement noted:

> The detainees will receive much of the treatment normally afforded to POWs by the [GPW]. However, the detainees will not receive some of the specific privileges afforded to POWs, including:
> - access to a canteen to purchase food, soap, and tobacco
> - a monthly advance of pay
> - the ability to have and consult personal financial accounts
> - the ability to receive scientific equipment, musical instruments, or sports outfits[103]

Yet there were significant differences between receiving protection under GPW as a matter of law as opposed to receiving its benefits as a matter of policy. First, without prisoner-of-war status, the detainees would not enjoy combatant immunity; they could be treated as unlawful combatants and therefore were subject to prosecution for belligerent acts against U.S. and coalition forces. Second, any favorable protection they enjoyed was provided only as a matter of policy, not law, except to the extent treatment was mandated by U.S. domestic law, meaning that it could be modified as the president may determine necessary. Thus, the president's February 7, 2002, determination stated "[a]s a matter of policy, the United States Armed Forces shall continue to treat detainees humanely and, *to the extent appropriate and consistent with military necessity*, in a manner consistent with the principles of [the Geneva Conventions]."[104]

The transfer of detainees to the U.S. naval station at Guantanamo, pursuant to the president's military order, quickly drew petitions for writs of habeas corpus challenging both the detention of detainees as unlawful combatants and their possible trial by military commission, rather than prosecution in U.S. civilian courts.[105] The U.S. government opposed these petitions on the grounds that the writ of habeas

---

[102] This was never even an option for al-Qaeda fighters, because the president had already determined that the GPW did not apply to the conflict with al-Qaeda.

[103] Fact Sheet: Status of Detainees at Guantanamo (Feb. 7, 2002), *available at* http://www.presidency.ucsb.edu/ws/index.php?pid=79402.

[104] *See* Memorandum, President George W. Bush, to Vice President et al, subject: Humane Treatment of al Qaeda and Taliban Detainees (Feb. 7 2002), *available at* http://www2.gwu.edu/~nsarchiv/NSAEBB/NSAEBB127/02.02.07.pdf (emphasis added).

[105] One of the first petitions was filed by a coalition of clergy, lawyers, and professors (including former Attorney General Ramsey Clark) in January 2002. *See* Order to Show Cause re Jurisdiction, Coalition of

corpus did not apply in Guantanamo because it lay outside the sovereign territory of the United States. The government relied principally on *Johnson v. Eisentrager*,[106] a U.S. Supreme Court decision handed down after World War II. The Court in *Eisentrager* ruled that German citizens convicted by a U.S. military commission and imprisoned in an Allied-controlled prison in Landsberg, Germany, for war crimes committed in China did not have the right under the U.S. Constitution to pursue a habeas claim in a U.S. court. Important to the Court in this decision was that the prisoners "at no relevant time were within any territory over which the United States is sovereign, and the scenes of their offense, their capture, their trial and their punishment were all beyond the territorial jurisdiction of any court of the United States."[107] In reaching this holding, the Court noted that granting the writ to the prisoners would involve a considerable burden on U.S. military authorities to transport them to the United States to appear in U.S. courts. The Court also pointed out that the writ "since it is held to be a matter of right, would be equally available to enemies during active hostilities...and would hamper the war effort and bring aid and comfort to the enemy."[108] In the Court's view, such trials would "diminish the prestige of our commanders, not only with enemies but with wavering neutrals" and "divert his efforts and attention from the military offensive abroad to the legal defensive at home."[109]

A detailed account of the litigation of these habeas corpus cases—an account that is still evolving—falls outside the scope of this chapter. Ultimately, however, conflicting outcomes in appellate courts led the U.S. Supreme Court in 2004 to grant certiorari in two cases involving detainees that significantly changed U.S. law and policy regarding detention of enemy combatants.

In *Rasul v. Bush*,[110] the Court held that the U.S. District Court for the District of Columbia had jurisdiction to hear habeas corpus petitions filed under 28 U.S.C. § 2241 (the habeas statute) and other statutory authorities on behalf of 12 Kuwaitis and two Australians[111] held in Guantanamo who sought to challenge their continued detention as combatants. After examining the legal status of Guantanamo and the authority exercised by the U.S. government there, the Court found that although not technically within the sovereign territory of the United States, Guantanamo was under the

---

Clergy v. Bush, 2002 WL 1377710 (C.D. Cal. 2002) (noting that a petition for writ of habeas corpus was filed by petitioners on January 20, 2002).

[106] 339 U.S. 763 (1950).

[107] *Id.* at 776.

[108] *Id.* at 779.

[109] *Id.* The Court also noted that such litigation would create "a conflict between judicial and military opinion highly comforting to enemies of the United States" but without any reciprocal benefit for U.S. soldiers given the absence of the writ of habeas corpus in most foreign legal systems. *Id.*

[110] 542 U.S. 466 (2004).

[111] Two U.K. petitioners' appeals were originally included, but were rendered moot when they were released.

"exclusive jurisdiction and control" of the United States. Therefore, the holding in *Eisentrager* was not controlling and the District Court could entertain habeas petitions from detainees to challenge the legality of their detention in Guantanamo.[112] The Court further held that with respect to non-habeas claims brought by Guantanamo detainees regarding their detention, "nothing in *Eisentrager* or in any of our other cases categorically excludes aliens detained in military custody outside the United States from the 'privilege of litigation in U.S. courts.' "[113]

Having opened the door in *Rasul* to detainees' court challenges to their detention in Guantanamo, the Court in a separate decision addressed the substantive and procedural due process rights of an American citizen detained as a combatant. Two key issues in the case were, first, did U.S. law provide a substantive legal basis for his detention, and second, what process was he due before he was subjected to that legal detention authority? In *Hamdi v. Rumsfeld*,[114] which was handed down on the same day as *Rasul*, Justice O'Connor, writing for a plurality of the Court (although it is important to note that these aspects of her opinion were implicitly endorsed in Justice Thomas's dissent), affirmed that "[t]he capture and detention of lawful combatants, and the capture, detention, and trial of unlawful combatants, by 'universal agreement and practice' are 'important incident[s] of war....' "[115] The plurality also found that Congress, in authorizing the president's use of "necessary and appropriate force" under the AUMF, had necessarily authorized the detention of terrorists, because "detention to prevent a combatant's return to the battlefield is a fundamental incident of waging war...."[116] Thus, the combined impact of the plurality opinion and Justice Thomas's dissent indicating that the president's authority as commander in chief to order Hamdi's detention was beyond question, created a clear holding that detention of the petitioner, Yaser Hamdi, an American citizen who allegedly had been fighting for the Taliban in Afghanistan, was legally authorized pursuant to the LOAC once it was demonstrated that he was an enemy combatant.[117] While Hamdi challenged his detention on the ground that the indefinite duration of the war on terror meant that his detention might also be indefinite, the Court found that, because there was still active combat ongoing in Afghanistan,[118]

---

[112] *Id.* at 484.

[113] *Id.*

[114] 542 U.S. 507 (2004) (plurality).

[115] *Id. at* 518 (citing *Ex parte* Quirin, 317 U.S. 1, 30 (1942).

[116] *Id. at* 519.

[117] *Id.* ("There is no bar to this Nation's holding one of its own as an enemy combatant.") For this purpose, the Court adopted the definition of "enemy combatant" proffered by the U.S. government, that is, "an individual who...was 'part of or supporting forces hostile to the United States or coalition partners' in Afghanistan and who 'engaged in an armed conflict against the United States.' " *Id.* at 516.

[118] Hamdi was released to Saudi Arabia in 2004 on condition he renounce his American citizenship. *Hamdi Voices Innocence, Joy about Reunion*, CNN.com (Oct. 14, 2004), *available at* http://www.cnn.com/2004/WORLD/meast/10/14/hamdi/.

the detention of an individual "legitimately determined" to be an enemy combatant was authorized at least until active hostilities had ceased.[119]

At the same time, the plurality emphasized "a state of war is not a blank check for the President when it comes to the rights of the Nation's citizens."[120] Thus, procedural due process required that Hamdi be afforded the opportunity to challenge his detention before a neutral decision-maker under the writ of habeas corpus. The question was what due process standards applied to that challenge. On this issue, the government argued, among other things, that (1) any right to an individual determination of prisoner-of-war privileges under article 5 of the GPW had been foreclosed by the president's conclusive determination that al-Qaeda and Taliban fighters were not entitled to such privileges; (2) a sworn affidavit presented by the government to the District Court regarding Hamdi's activities in Afghanistan, along with his acknowledged presence in the area, were sufficient to support detention; (3) as a captured enemy combatant, Hamdi did not enjoy a right to counsel to "plot a legal strategy to secure his release," particularly when a right of access to counsel would interfere with "the military's compelling interest in gathering intelligence"; and (4) requiring further factual development regarding the enemy combatant determination would present formidable constitutional and practical difficulties, given the ongoing hostilities, and would demoralize U.S. troops called to account for their actions.[121]

Explicitly or implicitly rejecting the government's arguments, Justice O'Connor noted that the habeas statute's minimum due process requirement included giving the detainee "some opportunity to present and rebut facts."[122] Accordingly, Justice O'Connor "easily rejected" the argument that a habeas determination could be made "as a matter of law, without further hearing or factfinding necessary."[123] Such a determination also could not be made under a highly deferential "some evidence" standard, which effectively would amount to relying exclusively on the government's evidence.[124]

However, Justice O'Connor disagreed with the District Court's conclusion that "the appropriate process would approach the process that accompanies a criminal trial," with the potential for "quite extensive discovery."[125] Instead, although Hamdi was entitled to "notice of the factual basis for his classification" and "a fair opportunity to rebut the factual assertions before a neutral decisionmaker,"[126] "enemy combatant proceedings could be tailored to alleviate their uncommon potential to burden the Executive at a time of ongoing

---

[119] The Court in *Hamdi* noted that "indefinite detention for purposes of interrogation is not authorized." 542 U.S. at 521.

[120] *Id.* at 536.

[121] Government Response Brief in Hamdi, *supra* note 84, at 9–12.

[122] 542 U.S. at 526.

[123] *Id.*

[124] *Id. at* 527.

[125] *Id. at* 528.

[126] *Id. at* 533. Justice O'Connor characterized these as "core elements" of the petitioner's rights. *Id.*

military conflict."[127] Thus, "hearsay may need to be accepted as the most reliable evidence," and a rebuttable presumption in favor of government evidence might be provided.[128]

As to the question of whether the petitioner had a right to counsel in habeas proceedings, however, the Court held that he "unquestionably" had such a right.[129] (On the other hand, the Court did not expressly decide the question of whether a detainee has a right to counsel in proceedings under article 5 of GPW to determine his or her status, and the U.S. government has interpreted the *Hamdi* decision not to require that a right to counsel be granted in military proceedings to determine the detainee's status.[130])

In *Hamdi*, the Court clearly sought to articulate a flexible approach to due process that would minimize interference with ongoing military operations in deference to the administration's concerns about the impact of habeas review on its ability to prosecute the war on terror. Justice O'Connor's plurality opinion also clarified that the procedural protections did not apply to "initial captures" on the battlefield, but rather only when a decision is being made to continue the detainee's captivity. Yet, the opinion also was clear that the judiciary would play a significant role in combatant status determinations:

> While we accord the greatest respect and consideration to the judgments of military authorities in matters relating to the actual prosecution of a war, and recognize that the scope of that discretion necessarily is wide, it does not infringe on the core role of the military for the courts to exercise their own time-honored and constitutionally mandated roles of reviewing and resolving claims like those presented here.

Thus, the Bush administration policy on war-on-terror detainees, including most importantly the categorical denial of any right for enemy combatants in the war on terror to challenge their status, had to be modified to account for the results of both *Rasul* and *Hamdi*.[131]

---

[127] *Id.*

[128] *Id.* at 534.

[129] *Id.* at 539.

[130] In the Combatant Status Review Tribunals described, *infra* notes 132–140 and accompanying text, no right to legal counsel was provided, although the detainee was assigned a commissioned officer to act as his or her personal representative.

[131] Although detainees did not have a right to challenge their detention at the time *Rasul* and *Hamdi* were handed down, in early 2004 (i.e., prior to the date of these decisions) the DoD issued a fact sheet indicating that it had put in place administrative procedures, including an internal DoD review panel, to assess whether a detainee should be moved to Guantanamo or released, and that further assessments were made even after the arrival of the detainee at Guantanamo, to determine if the detainee could be released or transferred to his government. *See* U.S. Dep't of Defense, Fact Sheet: Guantanamo Detainees, Feb. 20, 2004, *available at* www.defenselink.mil/news/Feb2004/d20040220det.pdf.[hereinafter February 2004 DoD Fact Sheet]. The DoD also announced an initiative to formalize the process and to create a review board that would consider individual detainees for release. *See* Secretary Rumsfeld Remarks to Greater Miami Chamber of Commerce, Feb. 13, 2004, *available at* http://www.defenselink.mil/transcripts/

Executive Branch Response

While Justice O'Connor's plurality opinion in *Hamdi* focused upon the rights of a citizen detainee held in the United States, it was obvious that extending analogous procedures to noncitizen detainees at Guantanamo could mitigate future risk of judicial invalidation of military detention review procedures, with the logic being that if *Hamdi* set the bar for what was required for a U.S. citizen detainee, the same bar should be adequate for the noncitizen detainees in Guantanamo. Accordingly, shortly after the *Hamdi* and *Rasul* decisions were handed down, the administration responded by adopting a process for detainees in Guantanamo that was consistent with the *Hamdi* standards. This process resulted in two levels of review.

The first level of review was a Combatant Status Review Tribunal (CSRT) process to determine "whether the detainee is properly detained as an enemy combatant,"[132] employing a definition of "enemy combatant" similar to the one offered by the government in its brief in *Hamdi*,[133] which was adopted by Justice O'Connor in her opinion.[134]

---

transcript.aspx?transcriptid=2075. On May 18, 2004, the DoD announced that the Secretary of Defense had established an administrative review procedure to consider early release of detainees "captured in the Afghan theater" and held at Guantanamo. U.S. Dep't of Defense, Review Procedures Announced for Guantanamo Detainees, May 18, 2004, *available at* http://www.defenselink.mil/releases/release. aspx?releaseid=7386. In its announcement, the DoD noted:

> The release of enemy combatants prior to the end of a war is a significant departure from past U.S. wartime practices. Enemy combatants are detained for a very practical reason: to prevent them from returning to the fight. That's why the law of war permits their detention until the end of an armed conflict. Although the global war on terror is real and ongoing, DoD has decided as a matter of policy to institute these review procedures. This process will assist DoD in fulfilling its commitment to ensure that no one is detained any longer than is warranted.

Id.

132 Dep'y Sec. of Defense, Memorandum for the Secretary of the Navy, subject: Order Establishing Combatant Status Review Tribunal (July 7, 2004), *available at* http://www.defense.gov/news/jul2004/d20040707review.pdf [hereinafter CSRT Order]. On July 29, 2004, the Secretary of the Navy issued procedures to implement the CSRT Order. Combatant Status Review Tribunal Process Sec'y of Navy, Memorandum: Implementation of Combatant Status Review Tribunal Procedures for Enemy Combatants detained at Guantanamo Naval Base, Cuba, Enclosure (1) (July 29, 2004), *available at* http://www.defense.gov/news/jul2004/d20040730comb.pdf. The DoD announced in March 2005 that it had completed CSRTs for all Guantanamo detainees. Defense Department Special Briefing on Combatant Status Review Tribunals (Mar. 29, 2005), *available at* http://www.defense.gov/transcripts/transcript. aspx?transcriptid=2504.

133 Government Response Brief in Hamdi, *supra* note 84, at 3 (quoting from the February 2004 DoD Fact Sheet, *supra* note 131).

134 542 U.S. at 516 ("[The Government] has made clear, however, that, for purposes of this case, the 'enemy combatant' that it is seeking to detain is an individual who, it alleges, was 'part of or supporting forces hostile to the United States or coalition partners' in Afghanistan and who 'engaged in an armed conflict against the United States' there.")

Justice O'Connor had mentioned in the *Hamdi* plurality opinion that "the standards we have articulated could be met by an appropriately authorized and properly constituted military tribunal," and referred to the fact that such tribunals already existed in AR 190–8. Accordingly, the CSRT was modeled after the tribunal under AR 190–8, with "three neutral commissioned officers" to hear the evidence and a recorder ("preferably a judge advocate," as stipulated under AR 190–8) to handle administrative tasks, although there were some significant differences in the CSRTs as compared to the AR 190-8 tribunal. First, the detainee whose case was to be reviewed by the CSRT was entitled to advance notice of the "unclassified factual basis" for his designation as an enemy combatant.[135] Second, in addition to the recorder, one of the CSRT members was required to be a judge advocate (i.e., military lawyer).[136] Third, the detainee was entitled to be represented by a non-lawyer military officer acting as "personal representative." The personal representative had the right to review any "reasonably available" evidence and to share any unclassified evidence with the detainee.[137] Fourth, the convening authority for the CSRT was not a military commander, but rather an appointee of the Secretary of the Navy.[138] Fifth, hearsay evidence was permitted "taking into account the reliability of such evidence in the circumstances."[139]

In making its determination, the CSRT was to apply a "preponderance of the evidence" standard, which was the same standard employed in tribunals under AR 190-8. In addition, there was a "rebuttable presumption" in favor of the government's evidence.[140]

The second level of review was the Administrative Review Board (ARB), which was established "to assess annually the need to continue to detain each enemy combatant during the course of the current and ongoing hostilities."[141] Like the CSRT, the ARB consisted of three officers; but, unlike the CSRT, there was no requirement for a lawyer to be a member,[142] although a lawyer was to advise the ARB. As in the case of the CSRT, the detainee was to be given the assistance of a non-lawyer military officer, as well as a

---

[135] CSRT Order, *supra* note 132, para. g(1).

[136] *Id.* para. e.

[137] *Id.* para. c.

[138] *Id.* para. f.

[139] *Id.* para. g(9).

[140] *Id.* para. g(12).

[141] Dep'y Sec'y Defense, Order, subject: Administrative Review Procedures for Enemy Combatants in the Control of the Department of Defense at Guantanamo Bay Naval Base, Cuba, para. 1 (May 11, 2004), *available at* http://www.defenselink.mil/news/May2004/d20040518gtmoreview.pdf. An ARB process had already been announced before either *Hamdi* or *Rasul* was handed down. *See supra* note 131. However, in response to these cases, it was necessary for the DoD to first implement a procedure to allow detainees an opportunity to challenge the lawfulness of their detention at Guantanamo. Thus, the ARB was not a review of the CSRT decisions per se, but rather a supplemental review to consider whether an individual determined by a CSRT to be an enemy combatant nonetheless could be released because he or she was no longer a threat.

[142] *Id.* para. 2.B.ii. At least one member must be an officer "experienced in the field of intelligence." *Id.*

summary of the evidence. The detainee was permitted to present to the Review Board information about "why he is no longer a threat to the United States and its allies in the ongoing armed conflict against al Qaida and its affiliates and supporters, why it is otherwise appropriate that he be released, or any other relevant information." The ARB made its recommendation on retention to a designated civilian official or "DCO," who was to be "a presidentially-appointed Senate-confirmed civilian in the DoD whom the Secretary of Defense has designated to operate and oversee the administrative review process."

Taken together, although they shared some common elements, these procedures far exceeded anything required by article 5 of GPW, AP I, or AR 190–8. In some respects, the CSRT procedures bore a resemblance to the procedures used in Vietnam, albeit without the right to counsel. Importantly, with the ARB procedures, the detainees were given an annual "relook" to determine whether there was a need to continue to detain them. The "relook" was more akin to the "periodical review" provided for civilian security internees under article 78 of GCIV and was beyond anything required under applicable law-of-war treaties dealing with combatants.

However, there were still grounds to question whether the procedures truly satisfied what the *Hamdi* plurality outlined as a meaningful opportunity to challenge the basis of detention before a "neutral decision maker." First, the tribunals consisted of military officers selected to review the case for the DoD, which was the same organization that had decided to detain the individuals in the first place. Second, although the Court had held that Hamdi unquestionably had a right to the assistance of counsel, none was provided in the CSRT process. Third, the procedures included presumptions in favor of the government that might be difficult to overcome, including the rule that certain evidence could be withheld from the detainee on the grounds that it was not "reasonably available."[143] Finally, there was no explicit right of appeal to a civilian or even a military appellate court.

---

[143] In one of the few cases to be brought to the D.C. Circuit under the Detainee Treatment Act, Pub. L. No. 109–148, Sec. 1005, 119 Stat. 2739, 2740 (2005) (amending 28 U.S.C. § 2241 (2005)) [hereinafter DTA], the D.C. Circuit held that the government was required to provide the Circuit Court with more than just the evidence provided to the CSRT. Bismullah v. Gates, 501 F.3d 178 (D.C. Cir.), *reh'g denied*, 503 F.3d 137 (D.C. Cir. 2007), *reh'g en banc denied* Bismullah v. Gates, 514 F.3d 1291 (D.C. Cir. 2008). In an opinion concurring in the denial of the rehearing *en banc* requested by the government regarding the scope of the evidence the government was required to provide to the D.C. Circuit, Chief Judge Ginsburg noted various limitations of the CSRT:

> Unlike the final decision rendered in a criminal or an agency proceeding, which is the product of an open and adversarial process before an independent decision maker, a CSRT's status determination is the product of a necessarily closed and accusatorial process in which the detainee seeking review will have had little or no access to the evidence the Recorder presented to the Tribunal, little ability to gather his own evidence, no right to confront the witnesses against him, and no lawyer to help him prepare his case, and in which the decision maker is employed and chosen by the detainee's accuser.

Despite the more detailed procedures for status determinations under the CSRT process, courts continued to accept habeas petitions regarding challenges to combatant status determinations, as well as to military commission procedures. In response, Congress passed the Detainee Treatment Act of 2005 (DTA). Section 1005 of the DTA amended the habeas statute to preclude courts from taking jurisdiction of petitions from detainees regarding detention at Guantanamo. Instead, the U.S. Court of Appeals for the D.C. Circuit was given exclusive authority to review final decisions of the CSRTs, but only with respect to two issues:

(i) whether the status determination of the Combatant Status Review Tribunal with regard to such alien was consistent with the standards and procedures specified by the Secretary of Defense for Combatant Status Review Tribunals (including the requirement that the conclusion of the Tribunal be supported by a preponderance of the evidence and allowing a rebuttable presumption in favor of the Government's evidence); and

(ii) to the extent the Constitution and laws of the United States are applicable, whether the use of such standards and procedures to make the determination is consistent with the Constitution and laws of the United States.[144]

In 2006, the Supreme Court, in *Hamdan v. Rumsfeld*,[145] held, inter alia, that Congress had not intended the DTA to require dismissal of habeas challenges by detainees at Guantanamo (in the case of Hamdan, the challenge was to a military commission's authority to try him) already pending at the time the DTA was passed. In response, the president requested, and Congress passed, another amendment to the federal habeas statute, this time contained in the MCA 2006.[146] While the primary focus of the MCA 2006 was to provide a statutory basis for trial of terrorist belligerents by military commission (thereby curing the legal defects in the authorization for military commissions

---

Id. at 1296. These concerns about the CSRT were cited by Justice Kennedy in the Supreme Court's decision in *Boumediene v. Bush*, which held that Guantanamo detainees had a constitutional right to pursue habeas petitions to challenge their detention. 553 U.S. 723, 785 (2008) ("Although we make no judgment as to whether the CSRTs, as currently constituted, satisfy due process standards, we agree with petitioners that, even when all the parties involved in this process act with diligence and in good faith, there is considerable risk of error in the tribunal's findings of fact.")

[144] DTA, *supra* note 143, § 1005(e)(2)(C). The DTA provisions related to habeas review were amended by the MCA 2006, *supra* note 44, § 7. After the Supreme Court held in *Boumediene* that the provision of the MCA 2006 that suspended the right of Guantanamo detainees to bring habeas petitions in District Court to challenge their detention was unconstitutional, the D.C. Circuit held that the DTA's limited direct appeal to the D.C. Circuit of CSRT decisions was integrally connected with the invalidated provision of MCA 2006, and therefore the D.C. Circuit was without jurisdiction to hear appeals under the DTA. Bismullah v. Gates, 551 F.3d 1068, 1075 (D.C. Cir. 2009). Accordingly, appeal of CSRT determinations under the DTA has been supplanted by the more fulsome habeas petitions permitted by *Boumediene*.

[145] 548 U.S. 557 (2006).

[146] *See supra* note 44.

that led the *Hamdan* Court to invalidate military commissions based on Military Order Number 1), this amendment retroactively stripped detainees at Guantanamo of any claim to a statutory right to habeas corpus, thereby preventing the judiciary from applying the federal habeas statute to any writ filed by a Guantanamo detainee, no matter when it was filed. Specifically, the amendment barred all habeas challenges, "by or on behalf of an alien detained by the United States who has been determined by the United States to have been properly detained as an enemy combatant or is awaiting such determination."[147] This provision of the MCA 2006 applied not only to challenges to CSRT determinations brought by detainees at Guantanamo, but also to any enemy combatant determination made worldwide regarding persons in the custody of the United States.

As a result of MCA 2006, which denied them the ability to challenge their detention under the habeas statute, Guantanamo detainees were left to assert a constitutional right to habeas corpus review in order to secure judicial review of the legality of their continued detention. As a result, although the Court in prior cases had avoided the question of whether there was a constitutional right to pursue the writ, by relying instead on the federal habeas statute, the constitutional question could no longer be avoided once MCA 2006 stripped the detainees of any rights under the habeas statute. The Court addressed this question head-on in *Boumediene v. Bush*. In a contentious 5-4 holding, the Court concluded that alien enemy combatant detainees held in Guantanamo did indeed enjoy a constitutional right of habeas corpus, and that the habeas-stripping provisions of the DTA and MCA 2006 amounted to an unconstitutional suspension of the writ.[148] On the question of the availability of the constitutional right,[149] the Court

---

[147] MCA 2006, *supra* note 44, section 7(a). This provision of MCA 2006 also amended 28 U.S.C. § 2241(e) to bar courts from considering "any other action against the United States or its agents relating to any aspect of the detention, transfer, treatment, trial, or conditions of confinement of an alien who is or was detained by the United States and has been determined by the United States to have been properly detained as an enemy combatant or is awaiting such determination." Although the Supreme Court in *Boumediene* held unconstitutional the denial to Guantanamo detainees of the writ of habeas corpus to challenge their detention (as codified in 28 U.S.C. § 2241(e)(1)), lower courts have held that this did not affect the validity of this separate MCA 2006 provision (as codified in 28 U.S.C. § 2241(e)(2)) barring other actions by detainees to challenge other aspects of their detention, transfer, treatment, trial, or conditions of confinement. Hamad v. Gates, 732 F.3d 990, 993 (9th Cir. 2013) (concluding that 28 U.S.C. § 2241(e)(2) barred claims for damages arising from former detainee's detention and treatment by the United States); Al-Zahrani v. Rumsfeld, 684 F. Supp. 2d 103, 109 (D.D.C. 2011) (citing cases, "[t]his Court joins the chorus in concluding that Boumediene did not invalidate § 2241(e)(2)"); Khadr v. Bush, 587 F. Supp. 2d 225, 235–36 (D.D.C. 2008).

[148] 553 U.S. at 792. Article I, Section 9, Clause 2 of the U.S. Constitution provides: "The privilege of the Writ of Habeas Corpus shall not be suspended, unless when in Cases of Rebellion or Invasion the public Safety may require it."

[149] In Rasul v. Bush, 542 U.S. 466, 504 (2004), the Court similarly found that the fact Guantanamo was not sovereign U.S. territory did not preclude detainees from seeking a writ of habeas corpus under the habeas statute. In *Boumediene*, the Supreme Court affirmed that, even after Congress had withheld the statutory habeas right from the Guantanamo detainees under MCA 2006, they still had a constitutional right to the writ.

held that although Guantanamo was outside the sovereign territory of the United States, the reach of the constitutional right of habeas corpus was not determined by formal sovereignty over the territory where the detainee was held, but rather by a case-by-case factual determination involving the examination of "at least" three factors: "(1) the detainees' citizenship and status and the adequacy of the process through which that status was determined; (2) the nature of the sites where apprehension and then detention took place; and (3) the practical obstacles inherent in resolving the prisoner's entitlement to the writ."[150] Weighing these factors in the case before it, the Court found that the constitutional right to the writ of habeas corpus extended to aliens held as enemy combatants at Guantanamo.

Once it determined the Guantanamo detainees had a constitutional right to habeas review, the Court required that any substitute for review in a District Court had to provide substantively the same or better rights than the detainee would have in a traditional review in federal courts. The Court rejected the government's argument that the CSRT process or the right to appeal the CSRT's findings to the D.C. Circuit under the DTA provided an adequate substitute for traditional habeas proceedings before a federal judge. The Court recognized that a CSRT provided "some process," but the CSRT hearings "are far more limited, and...fall well short of the procedures and adversarial mechanisms that would eliminate the need for habeas corpus review."[151] Among the deficiencies of the CSRT process was the absence of any right to legal counsel or even an advocate of any kind, the lack of access to all evidence relied upon to detain the suspect, and the liberal use of hearsay evidence (which meant that the "opportunity to question witnesses is likely to be more theoretical than real.")[152] The limited opportunity to appeal CSRT decisions to the D.C. Circuit under the DTA also was not a sufficient substitute for habeas, because (1) the DTA limited the scope of the D.C. Circuit's review, (2) the D.C. Circuit did not expressly have the authority to order the release of a detainee in the event detention was found to be unauthorized, and (3) the detainee did not have an opportunity to present evidence discovered after the CSRT proceedings were complete.[153]

The Court concluded that the CSRT process and the limited appeal to the D.C. Circuit under the DTA were both expressly intended by the administration and

---

[150] 553 U.S. at 766. The Court based its ruling in part on Johnson v. Eisentrager, 339 U.S. 763 (1950), a post–World War II decision in which the Court held that German prisoners of war tried by U.S. military commission in China and imprisoned in occupied Germany did not have a right to pursue a writ of habeas corpus to challenge their detention. Previously, however, *Eisentrager* had been cited for the proposition that aliens tried and imprisoned outside the territorial limits of the United States could not seek the writ, which was the formalistic approach rejected by the Court in *Boumediene*.

[151] 553 U.S. at 766–767.

[152] *Id.* at 767, 781. The Court noted that the personal representative in a CSRT was explicitly not a detainee's advocate.

[153] *Id.* at 787–92.

Congress to provide less due process than a traditional habeas proceeding. In the case of the CSRT process, this was a fatal flaw: "[E]ven when all the parties involved in this [CSRT] process acted with diligence and in good faith, there is considerable risk of error in the tribunal's finding of fact."[154] As for the limited appeal to the D.C. Circuit under the DTA, the Court said it might interpret away some of the defects it found in the appeals process, but that would simply restore the very right to habeas review that Congress clearly intended to deny the detainee. Rather than affording the legislation an interpretation that it "cannot bear," the Court held it to be an unconstitutional suspension of the writ.

The Court qualified its opinion by adding that "[o]ur holding…should not be read to imply that a *habeas* court should intervene the moment an enemy combatant steps in a territory where the writ runs." It also did not reject the CSRT process, holding instead that "[t]he Executive is entitled to a reasonable period of time to determine the detainee's status before a court entertains that detainee's habeas corpus petition."[155] The Court also noted that "accommodations" could be made to reduce the burdens of habeas proceedings and to protect sources and methods of intelligence gathering.[156]

Nonetheless, the Court was far less deferential than it had been in *Hamdi* to the executive branch's concerns regarding interference with national security interests:

Security subsists, too, in fidelity to freedom's first principles. Chief among these are freedom from arbitrary and unlawful restraint and the personal liberty that is secured by adherence to the separation of powers.[157]

The Court was clearly troubled by the fact that the administration had held the detainees in confinement for years without any confirmation of the legality of their detention by any court. In the Court's view, separation of powers under the Constitution required a judicial determination of legality to "vindicate[]" the exercise of the Executive's war powers in detaining these individuals. The Court ominously warned that, although short conflicts in the past had made it possible to leave the "outer boundaries" of these powers undefined, the "Court might not have this luxury" if the war on terror proved to be even more lengthy. Therefore, it invited the administration and Congress to "engage in a genuine debate about how best to preserve constitutional values while protecting the Nation from terrorism."[158]

---

[154] *Id.* at 785.

[155] *Id.* at 795.

[156] *Id.* at 795–796.

[157] *Id.* at 797.

[158] *Id.* at 798.

Subsequent Litigation

The decision in *Boumediene* effectively put an end to the administration's attempts to preclude full habeas review of detentions of individuals held at Guantanamo. Lower courts responded with "admirable dispatch" (in the words of the D.C. Circuit)[159] to consider the habeas petitions that had been moving slowly through the District Court for the District of Columbia since 2002. Beginning in July 2008, a massive effort was launched by the District Court for the District of Columbia to provide habeas review for all of the Guantanamo detainees still seeking it. In response, the administration assembled large teams of government lawyers to devote themselves full-time to the task of collecting and presenting the evidence required to respond to the habeas petitions, and arguing the cases in court. District Court judges in the post-*Boumediene* habeas proceedings required disclosure of an extensive amount of information to support the factual basis for the detention, as well as all statements of the detainee and any reasonably available exculpatory evidence.

Various decisions were reached by judges in the District Court for the District of Columbia beginning in late 2008, with mixed results for the U.S. government. These decisions set the stage for appeals to the D.C. Circuit, where that court was expected to resolve key issues, including the standard to be applied by the courts subordinate to the D.C. Circuit for determining who was properly subject to detention at Guantanamo.

In *al-Bihani v. Obama*, a decision issued in early 2010, the D.C. Circuit brought a substantial amount of uniformity to the interpretation of the scope of the U.S. government's detention authority by upholding all aspects of the government's definition of who was detainable under the AUMF.[160] Specifically, the D.C. Circuit held that:

> Al-Bihani is lawfully detained whether the definition of a detainable person is, as the district court articulated it, "an individual who was part of or supporting Taliban or al Qaeda forces, or associated forces that are engaged in hostilities against the United States or its coalition partners," or the modified definition offered by the government that requires that an individual "substantially support" enemy forces.[161]

The D.C. Circuit based its conclusion solely on the terms of the AUMF, which authorized the president to use "necessary and appropriate force against those nations, organizations, or persons he determines planned, authorized, committed, or aided the

---

[159] Al-Bihani v. Obama, 590 F.3d 866, 869 (D.C. Cir. 2010) [hereinafter *Al-Bihani I*].

[160] *Id.* at 870 ("In this decision, we aim to narrow the legal uncertainty that clouds military detention.")

[161] *Id.* at 872.

terrorist attacks that occurred on September 11, 2001." The court noted that in *Hamdi*, the Supreme Court had ruled that "necessary and appropriate force" included "the power to detain combatants subject to such force."[162] The D.C. Circuit also noted that in both the MCA 2006 and the MCA 2009, Congress had adopted a definition of individuals who could be tried by military commission, which included those who "purposefully and materially" supported hostilities against the United States or its coalition partners. In the D.C. Circuit's view, "logically" the category of individuals subject to the U.S. government's detention authority is "no narrower than is covered by its military commission authority."[163]

The D.C. Circuit also rejected al-Bihani's argument that international law, including the Geneva Conventions, limits the scope of the government's detention authority:

> We reiterate that international law…do [*sic*] not limit the President's detention power in this instance.[164]

This latter conclusion—ostensibly unnecessary to the D.C. Circuit's decision to deny the writ—was actually at odds even with the definition of unprivileged enemy belligerent that the government had submitted to the District Court in March 2009. This definition, according to the government, was "derived from the AUMF, which empowers the President to use all necessary and appropriate force to prosecute the war, in light of law-of-war principles that inform the understanding of what is 'necessary and appropriate.' "[165] For the D.C Circuit, reliance on international law was irrelevant; the authority to detain was determined solely by reference to domestic law:

> [W]hile the international laws of war are helpful to courts when identifying the general set of war powers to which the AUMF speaks, *see Hamdi,* 542 U.S. at 520, 124 S. Ct. 2633, their lack of controlling legal force and firm definition render their use both inapposite and inadvisable when courts seek to determine the limits of the President's war powers. Therefore, putting aside that we find Al-Bihani's reading of international law to be unpersuasive, we have no occasion here to quibble over the intricate application of vague treaty provisions and amorphous customary principles. The sources we look to for resolution of Al-Bihani's case are the sources courts always look to: the text of relevant statutes and controlling domestic caselaw.[166]

---

[162] *Id.* (citing Hamdi v. Rumsfeld, 542 U.S. at 519).

[163] *Id.* at 872. These definitions can be found in the text accompanying notes 44 and 45, *supra.*

[164] *Al-Bihani I, supra* note 159, at 873.

[165] March 2009 Memorandum, *supra* note 46, at 3.

[166] *Al-Bihani I, supra* note 159, at 871–72. The strength of this statement was diluted somewhat by an unusual memorandum from seven judges of the D.C. Circuit, sitting *en banc*, that accompanied an order denying a rehearing *en banc* of the D.C. Circuit's conclusions regarding international law. Al-Bihani v. Obama,

Not surprisingly, given the breadth of the D.C. Circuit's opinion, all of the habeas challenges of Guantanamo detainees reviewed by the D.C. Circuit, including those that the government lost in the District Court before *al-Bihani* was handed down and subsequently appealed, have been decided in favor of the government. Further, the D.C. Circuit's rulings in favor of the government on the burden of persuasion and evidentiary standards to be applied in the habeas cases unquestionably facilitated the government's ability to prevail in even the most hotly contested Guantanamo cases.[167]

Judicial Review of Overseas Military Detention outside Guantanamo

Boumediene's extension of the constitutional right to the writ of habeas corpus was limited to alien detainees at Guantanamo. However, the "factors" test adopted by the Court provides a basis for the potential extension of the holding to aliens detained in other locations, most notably Afghanistan. Perhaps unsurprisingly, this led to an attempt in 2009 to invoke *Boumediene* to support just such an expansion of habeas review to noncitizen detainees held by the U.S. military in locations outside the United States other than Guantanamo, an effort that met with initial success in the District Court but was subsequently reversed on appeal.[168]

---

619 F. 3d. 1 (D.C. Cir. 2010). In that memorandum, the seven judges explained that these conclusions were not necessary to decide the case. The three other judges (Brown, Kavanaugh, and Williams) who issued the original opinion submitted separate statements. Judge Brown's statement (which concurs with the memorandum from the seven judges) criticized the *en banc* decision and the statement of the other two judges, saying "their cumulative effect is to muddy the clear holding of *Al-Bihani* that international law as a whole does not limit the AUMF's grant of war powers." *Id.* at 2. Judge Kavanaugh's statement (which also concurs with the memorandum) offers a lengthy and scholarly explanation in support of his view that while "the Executive Branch within its constitutional and statutory bounds may decide, as a matter of international obligation or policy, to follow non-self-executing treaties and customary-international-law norms," Congress did not incorporate those norms into the AUMF. *Id.* at 52. Therefore, "[i]n asking us to nonetheless rely on international-law principles to order Al-Bihani's release from U.S. military custody, the argument of Al-Bihani and amici contravenes bedrock tenets of judicial restraint and separation of powers." *Id.* at 53. Finally, Judge Williams (who does not expressly concur or dissent from the memorandum) in his statement agrees in part with Judge Kavanaugh, but disagrees with Judge Kavanaugh's view to the extent Kavanaugh would hold that international law cannot affect a statute's interpretation. *Id.*

167 For a detailed and insightful discussion of the decisions of the District Court for the District of Columbia and the D.C. Circuit since *Boumediene*, including rulings on key issues such as the burden of proof, the use of hearsay evidence, and other matters, *see* BENJAMIN WITTES, ROBERT M. CHESNEY & LARKIN REYNOLDS, THE EMERGING LAW OF DETENTION 2.0: THE GUANTANAMO HABEAS CASES AS LAWMAKING (2012), *available at* http://www.brookings.edu/~/media/research/files/reports/2011/5/guantanamo%20wittes/05_guantanamo_wittes.pdf.

168 Al Maqaleh v. Gates, 604 F. Supp. 2d 205 (D.D.C. 2009) [hereinafter *Al Maqaleh I*] *rev'd* 605 F.3d 84 (D.C. Cir. 2010) [hereinafter *Al Maqaleh II*].

In *Al Maqaleh v. Gates*,[169] the District Court for the District of Columbia, applying the *Boumediene* analysis to habeas corpus petitions filed by four noncitizen detainees held at the Bagram Air Field in Afghanistan, held that three of the four detainees had a constitutional right to the protection of the Suspension Clause.[170] This led to the conclusion that the District Court could entertain their petitions notwithstanding the provision of MCA 2006 that stripped the court of jurisdiction under the habeas statute.

Applying the analysis from *Boumediene*, the District Court in *al Maqaleh* used the following six-factor test (derived from the three factors used in *Boumediene*) to make a determination with respect to the four detainees: "(1) the citizenship of the detainee; (2) the status of the detainee; (3) the adequacy of the process through which the status determination was made; (4) the nature of the site of apprehension; (5) the nature of the site of detention; and (6) the practical obstacles inherent in resolving the petitioner's entitlement to the writ."[171] However, noting the multiple references in the *Boumediene* decision to concern about the length of time that the detainees had been held, the District Court also identified a seventh factor that "tacitly informed *Boumediene's* analysis as well: the length of a petitioner's detention without adequate review."[172] Because the Supreme Court had not specifically called the length of detention a separate factor, the District Court would not consider it separately but noted that the detention's length may "shade" the six factors the District Court is required to consider under the *Boumediene* analysis.[173]

The District Court's analysis produced some interesting observations on the application of the *Boumediene* factors. For example, while it found the "status of the detainee" factor to provide little guidance on the question whether petitioners had a constitutional right to the writ of habeas corpus, it noted that "the breadth of the definition of 'enemy combatant' utilized by respondents underscores the need for a meaningful process to ensure that detainees are not improperly classified as enemy combatants."[174] The District Court also found it relevant that the detainees had been brought ("rendered") to the detention facility in Afghanistan, which made them "qualitatively different" than detainees from other countries captured in Afghanistan, which is "a theater of war, where the Constitution arguably may not reach."[175] For the District Court, "[s]uch rendition resurrects the same specter of limitless Executive power the Supreme Court sought to guard

---

[169] *Al Maqaleh 1, supra* note 168.

[170] The District Court also considered other arguments from the fourth detainee, but ultimately denied his habeas petition. Wazir v. Gates, 629 F. Supp. 2d 63 (D.D.C. 2009).

[171] *Al Maqaleh I, supra* note 168, at 215.

[172] *Id. at* 216.

[173] *Id. at* 217.

[174] *Id. at* 220–21.

[175] *Id. at* 220.

against in *Boumediene*—the concern that the Executive could move detainees physically beyond the reach of the Constitution and detain them indefinitely."[176]

The most significant factors relied on by the District Court to justify its conclusion were the site of detention, the process used to make the detention decision, and the practical obstacles inherent in resolving the petitioner's entitlement to the writ. With respect to the site of detention, the District Court asked whether the prison in Bagram Air Field was more like Guantanamo, with respect to which the Court in *Boumediene* had held that U.S. courts had jurisdiction to entertain habeas petitions, or more like Landsberg prison in occupied Germany, with respect to which the Court in *Eisentrager* had found habeas in U.S. courts to be inapplicable.[177] Applying an "objective degree of control" test in measuring whether the United States exercised sufficient control to apply the constitutional right to the writ, the District Court held that "Bagram lies much closer to Guantanamo than to Landsberg."[178]

More relevant to the subject of this chapter, the District Court held that the process for making "enemy combatant" determinations at Bagram Air Field was "less sophisticated and more error prone" than the CSRT procedure at Guantanamo.

> Unlike a CSRT, where a petitioner has access to a "personal representative," Bagram detainees represent themselves. Obvious obstacles, including language and cultural differences, obstruct effective self-representation by petitioners such as these. Detainees cannot even *speak* for themselves; they are only permitted to submit a written statement. But in submitting that statement, detainees do not know what evidence the United States relies upon to justify an "enemy combatant" designation—so they lack a meaningful opportunity to rebut that evidence. Respondents' far-reaching and ever-changing definition of enemy combatant, coupled with the uncertain evidentiary standards, further undercut the reliability of the... [Bagram tribunal's] review. And, unlike the CSRT process, Bagram detainees receive no review beyond... [the Bagram tribunal] itself.[179]

Declining to state what would constitute an adequate process sufficient to "stave off the reach of the Suspension Clause to Bagram," the District Court held that the process then in use at Bagram was not adequate.[180]

---

[176] *Id. at* 220–21.

[177] In *Eisentrager*, which was decided several years after the end of World War II, the Supreme Court rejected habeas petitions from German prisoners who had been tried in China for belligerent acts committed in China against Allied forces after the surrender of Germany to the Allies and, without entering U.S. territory, were transferred to a U.S.-operated military prison in Landsberg, Germany, to serve out their sentences. For discussion of *Eisentrager, see supra* notes 106–109 and accompanying text.

[178] *Al Maqaleh I, supra* note 168, at 225.

[179] *Id.* at 227.

[180] *Id.* Significant changes reportedly were made to the review process at Bagram after the District Court issued this decision. For a discussion of these changes, *see* Lt. Col. Jeff A. Bovarnick, *Detainee Review*

In assessing the sixth factor—practical obstacles to application of the writ—the District Court took into account the security issues ("Bagram…is under constant threat by suicide bombers and other violent elements"[181]), but noted that the United States had "near-total control over Bagram" and that "the military exercises such control at any military base it establishes…which has allowed the United States to convene wartime tribunals during previous conflicts…with far greater process than the…process at Bagram."[182] The District Court also recognized the challenge of collecting evidence under battlefield conditions, but said it "was not persuaded that those difficulties rise to the level that precludes application of the Suspension Clause or bars petitioners from access to habeas review."[183] The District Court's willingness to minimize the practical obstacles to extending the writ to a detention facility in a war zone highlighted the overriding importance to the District Court of the duration of detention and the likelihood of erroneous status determinations, to the outcome of its analysis of the petitioners' entitlement to the writ of habeas corpus.[184]

In response to a government appeal, the D.C. Circuit reversed and held that the District Court did not have jurisdiction to consider the petitions for habeas corpus.[185] Applying the Supreme Court's reasoning in *Boumediene*, the D.C. Circuit rejected the government's argument that *Boumediene* established a bright-line test that would extend the constitutional right to petition for habeas corpus only to territories over which the United States had de jure sovereignty (such as the territory of the United States itself) or de facto sovereignty (such as Guantanamo).[186] Thus, the D.C. Circuit could not decide the case solely with reference to the control exercised by the U.S. government over the Bagram airbase. Rather, the D.C. Circuit held that it was required to apply the

---

Boards in Afghanistan: From Strategic Liability to Legitimacy, ARMY LAW., June 2010, at 20–35 [hereinafter Bovarnick].

[181] *Al Maqaleh I, supra* note 168, at 228 (citations omitted).

[182] *Id.*

[183] *Id.* at 229. The District Court was not at all persuaded that habeas proceedings would actually interfere with military operations:

> Although logistical issues have certainly been presented, the hearings and related proceedings are going forward with the burdens on the government falling mainly on the lawyers and administrative personnel involved, not on those who would otherwise be on the battlefield.

Id. at 228. The District Court also noted that the impact of practical obstacles was ameliorated by the requirement that a "reasonable amount of time" should be allowed as a buffer before "meaningful review" is required, but added that "[s]uch a reasonable time period elapsed for these detainees, like those at Guantanamo, many years ago." *Id.* at 229.

[184] One obstacle that the District Court considered to be determinative was the fact that one of the detainees was an Afghan citizen. The District Court found that the potential friction with the Afghan government that might result from the release of an Afghan detainee was in fact an overriding "practical obstacle" to extending the writ to such a detainee. *Id.* at 229–30.

[185] *Al Maqaleh II, supra* note 168, at 87.

[186] *Id.* at 94.

Boumediene factors on a case-by-case basis to determine whether the writ extended to petitioners at Bagram.

The D.C. Circuit relied not only on *Boumediene*, but also on *Eisentrager*.[187] The Circuit Court noted that *Eisentrager* was not overruled in *Boumediene*, but rather "reinforced."[188] Accordingly, the D.C. Circuit applied each of the *Boumediene* factors to the petitioners in custody in Afghanistan by evaluating whether their situation was closer to the facts in *Eisentrager*, in which the Supreme Court held that there was no jurisdiction to entertain the habeas petitions, or to the facts in *Boumediene*, where it held that there was. Under such a comparison, the first factor, "the citizenship and status of the detainee and the adequacy of the means of the process through which that status determination was made," tended to favor taking jurisdiction over the *al Maqaleh* petitions. This was because, although the citizenship and status of the petitioners in *al Maqaleh*, *Boumediene*, and *Eisentrager* were similar (enemy alien), the process used to determine the combatant status of the *al Maqaleh* petitioners was weaker than in *Boumediene*, where the petitioners' status had been determined by a CSRT (which afforded detainees greater due process than the process used in Afghanistan at the relevant time) or in *Eisentrager*, where the petitioners' status had been determined by a military commission (thus, giving the petitioners in that case an even greater amount of due process).[189] Accordingly, the D.C. Circuit held that the first factor supported the availability of the writ of habeas corpus for the *al Maqaleh* petitioners.[190]

As to the second factor, "the nature of the sites where apprehension and then detention took place," however, the D.C. Circuit held that this factor weighed "heavily in favor of the United States" (and against extension of the writ) because U.S. control over Bagram was more akin to the U.S. control of Landsberg prison in *Eisentrager* and much weaker than U.S. control over Guantanamo in *Boumediene*:

> While it is true that the United States holds a leasehold interest in Bagram, and held a leasehold interest in Guantanamo, the surrounding circumstances are hardly the same. The United States has maintained its total control of Guantanamo Bay

---

[187] For discussion of *Eisentrager, see supra* notes 106–109 and accompanying text. In *Boumediene*, the Supreme Court rejected a "formalistic" interpretation of *Eisentrager*, that is, that the habeas petitions in *Eisentrager* were dismissed simply because the petitioners were confined outside of sovereign U.S. territory. 553 U.S. at 762. Instead, the *Boumediene* Court pointed to broad language in the *Eisentrager* opinion concerning the impact of extending the Suspension Clause on military operations and other factors as a basis for concluding that the *Eisentrager* decision was based on an evaluation of various factors, including, but not limited to, U.S. sovereignty. *Id. at* 766.

[188] *Al Maqaleh II, supra* note 168, at 98.

[189] *Id.* at 95–96.

[190] *Id.* at 96. It should be noted that although U.S. citizenship is an important factor in extending the constitutional right to the writ of habeas corpus to detainees outside the United States, it does not mean that review will lead to meaningful relief even for U.S. citizens being held abroad by the U.S. government, as demonstrated in the *Munaf* case discussed *infra*, note 202.

for over a century, even in the face of a hostile government maintaining *de jure* sovereignty over the property. In Bagram, while the United States has options as to duration of the lease agreement, there is no indication of any intent to occupy the base with permanence, nor is there hostility on the part of the "host" country. Therefore, the notion that *de facto* sovereignty extends to Bagram is no more real than would have been the same claim with respect to Landsberg in the *Eisentrager* case. While it is certainly realistic to assert that the United States has *de facto* sovereignty over Guantanamo, the same simply is not true with respect to Bagram.[191]

The third factor, "'the practical obstacles inherent in resolving the prisoner's entitlement to the writ,'" also weighed "overwhelmingly" in favor of the United States. In reaching this conclusion, the D.C. Circuit was strongly influenced by the fact that "Bagram, indeed the entire nation of Afghanistan, remains a theater of war." Thus, the situation in al Maqaleh was more clearly comparable to the situation in *Eisentrager* (i.e., occupied post–World War II Germany). The D.C. Circuit noted that "all of the attributes of a facility exposed to the vagaries of war are present in Bagram."[192] Indeed, among the facts recited by the D.C. Circuit at the beginning of the option was that:

> Afghanistan remains a theater of active military combat. The United States and coalition forces conduct "an ongoing military campaign against al Qaeda, the Taliban regime, and their affiliates and supporters in Afghanistan." These operations are conducted in part from Bagram Airfield. Bagram has been subject to repeated attacks from the Taliban and al Qaeda, including a March 2009 suicide bombing striking the gates of the facility, and Taliban rocket attacks in June of 2009 resulting in death and injury to United States service members and other personnel.[193]

The Court noted that a factor weighing in favor of the United States is the fact that the petitioners are being held "in the sovereign territory of another nation, which itself creates practical difficulties," and which called for caution in extending constitutional protections to individuals held on Afghan territory, given that "[t]he United States holds the detainees pursuant to a cooperative arrangement with Afghanistan...."[194] Thus, "[w]hile we cannot say that extending our constitutional protections to the detainees

---

[191] *Al Maqaleh II, supra* note 168, at 97.

[192] *Id.*

[193] *Id.* at 88. The D.C. Circuit also pointed out that "[w]hile the United States provides overall security to Bagram, numerous other nations have compounds on the base" and "[s]ome of the other nations control access to their respective compounds." *Id.*

[194] *Id.* at 99.

would be in any way disruptive of that relationship, neither can we say with certainty what the reaction of the Afghan government would be."[195]

In its opinion, the D.C. Circuit noted that the three *Boumediene* factors were not exclusive,[196] and there might be cases in which other factors could be important. Thus, "[w]e do not ignore the arguments of the detainees that the United States chose the place of detention" and thus might have chosen to transfer the petitioners to Bagram to evade judicial review.[197] In the D.C. Circuit's view,

> Perhaps such manipulation by the Executive might constitute an additional factor in some case in which it is in fact present.

The Court rejected the petitioners' claims of manipulation as "unsupported by the evidence" and "not supported by reason" because it "would have required the military commanders or other Executive officials making the situs determination to anticipate the complex litigation history set forth above and predict the *Boumediene* decision long before it came down."

Nevertheless, the petitioners in *al Maqaleh* later pressed this very claim at the District Court, although the claim ultimately was rejected on appeal.[198] Having already decided in its earlier opinion that U.S. courts did not have habeas jurisdiction at the detention facility in Afghanistan, the D.C. Circuit looked only for whether circumstances "have changed so drastically that we must revisit" the earlier opinion.[199] Reviewing each of the *Boumediene* factors in turn, the D.C. Circuit found no basis to change its earlier *al Maqaleh* opinion.[200] In a footnote, the Circuit Court explained its caution, suggesting that it will be difficult to expand habeas jurisdiction to reach detainees held anywhere outside the United States other than Guantanamo, absent additional guidance from the Supreme Court:

> Boumediene marked the first time in our constitutional history that aliens held outside the sovereign territory of the United States were accorded any

---

[195] *Id.*

[196] The *Boumediene* Court had only said that "at least" three factors were relevant. 553 U.S. at 727.

[197] *Al Maqaleh II, supra* note 168, at 98.

[198] Al Maqaleh v. Hagel, No. 12–5404, 2013 WL 6767861 (D.C. Cir. Dec. 23, 2013) [hereinafter *Al Maqaleh III*]. The opinion addressed in a consolidated fashion several separate appeals that had been argued together. *Id.* at *1. Among the claims made by the petitions was that new evidence indicated that the United States intended to remain at Bagram indefinitely, that obstacles to conducting habeas proceedings were less severe than the *Al Maqaleh II* court believed, that the United States detained the petitioners at Bagram in order to evade the habeas jurisdiction of federal courts, and that the propriety-of-detention determination procedures used at Bagram were inadequate. *Id.* at *4. Additionally, one detainee argued that his infancy weighed in favor of extending the writ. *Id.*

[199] *Id.*

[200] *Id. at *6–*16.

constitutional protection. Boumediene, 553 U.S. at 770.... As a novel constitutional development, we are loath to expand Boumediene's reach without specific guidance from the Supreme Court, particularly where expansion would carry us further into the realm of war and foreign policy.[201]

Despite the petitioners' lack of success in the *al Maqaleh* litigation, the rejection of bright-line tests in *Boumediene* means that noncitizens held by U.S. forces outside the United States have greater opportunity to seek judicial review of their detention than previously under *Eisentrager*. Certainly, as the *al Maqaleh* litigation shows, the writ of habeas corpus will not apply everywhere, and indeed, as the language in the most recent D.C. Circuit decision in the *al Maqaleh* litigation indicates, the prospects for success in many cases will be poor. Nevertheless, the case-by-case nature of the *Boumediene* factors suggests that the U.S. government has to be prepared to face court challenges, if only because any case may be different on one or more of the *Boumediene* factors, particularly as the U.S. combat role in Afghanistan winds down. Even if the government is successful in such future litigation, the mere fact that the government must respond to efforts to apply the *Boumediene* analysis to detentions outside of Guantanamo means that courts could have an ongoing role in scrutinizing military activities. Indeed, Judge Williams, in an opinion concurring in the denial of *en banc* review of the D.C. Circuit's *Bihani* decision, offered this observation:

> [U]nder *Boumediene,* Article III courts evaluate the propriety of the detention of non-U.S. nationals. In doing so they necessarily pass judgment on the admissibility of evidence collected on the battlefield, and thus on the propriety of the methods used for such collection. District courts have been doing so regularly since *Boumediene.* They therefore monitor, and to a degree supervise, the battlefield conduct of the U.S. military. But that is a consequence of *Boumediene,* in which the federal judiciary assumed an entirely new role in the nation's military operations....

In short, the *Boumediene* Court's "practical considerations and exigent circumstances" approach to determining the definition and reach of the writ of habeas corpus has eliminated any clear geographic bright line as to where the writ does not apply.[202] Certainly,

---

[201] *Id.* n.16.

[202] Where the detainee is an American citizen, the writ is certainly going to apply without regard to geographic limitations. For example, in Munaf v. Geren, 128 S. Ct. 2207 (2008), a decision handed down the same day as *Boumediene,* the Court upheld the jurisdiction of U.S. federal courts to entertain habeas petitions filed by two American citizens held overseas by American soldiers subject to a U.S. chain of command even though the U.S. forces held the two individuals pursuant to U.S. obligations as part of a multinational force. The Court stressed that U.S. forces were still subject to U.S. command and that the individuals were U.S. citizens. However, the Court dismissed the petitions because they were not

the lack of a bright-line test increases uncertainty for commanders in the field, who need to pay greater attention to collection of evidence to respond to later judicial inquiries into a detention decision.[203] The LOAC has never before contemplated this type of judicial scrutiny.[204]

Response to Litigation

As of the end of 2013, the net result of litigation in U.S. courts regarding detention in the war on terror is a mixed bag for detainees. A subset of the detainees—those held in Guantanamo—have established a constitutionally protected right to the writ of habeas corpus to challenge the basis for their detention. However, none of these detainees has successfully challenged the substantive authority by which they are detained—as enemy belligerents pursuant to the law of armed conflict and the AUMF in the ongoing armed conflict with al-Qaeda and associated forces. Indeed, in some ways, *Boumediene* was a pyrrhic victory, as there have been no decisions in favor of granting that writ since the D.C. Circuit handed down its *al Bihani* decision in early 2010. Further, as the *al Maqelah* litigation showed, detainees held in foreign locations other than Guantanamo have been unsuccessful in their efforts to extend the writ to other detention facilities outside of the United States.

None of the Supreme Court's decisions held that any of the Geneva Conventions or other law of war treaties were self-executing, or otherwise specifically limited executive branch discretion. While in *Hamdan v. Rumsfeld*, the Court held that a military commission lacked jurisdiction to try an enemy combatant because it did not comply, inter alia, with common article 3 of the Geneva Conventions,[205] the Court cited to common article 3 only because the legislative authorization for military commissions relied upon by the government[206] specifically referred to the "law of war." Absent the

---

challenges to unlawful detention by the United States, but rather an attempt to prevent transfer of the detainees to Iraqi authorities in connection with Iraqi criminal proceedings.

[203] Possibly in response to the District Court's analysis in *Al Maqaleh I*, the DoD did take steps in 2009 to improve the process for making the enemy combatant determination in Afghanistan. *See* Bovarnick, *supra* note 180, at 9 (describing the changes made).

[204] At this point, the focus of judicial review is clearly upon long-term detention, and it does not yet appear that the courts would engage in extensive judicial inquiry into short-term battlefield detention. *See* Hamdi v. Rumsfeld, 542 U.S. at 534 ("The parties agree that initial captures on the battlefield need not receive the process we have discussed here; that process is due only when the determination is made to *continue* to hold those who have been seized.")

[205] Hamdan v. Rumsfeld, 548 U.S. at 631–632. The decision was extremely important because it was confirmation that common article 3 applied and guaranteed certain humane treatment standards for the detainees as a matter of international law. Common article 3 does not limit or affect U.S. authority to hold the detainees as enemy combatants, however.

[206] The provision relied upon in *Hamdan* was article 21 of the Uniform Code of Military Justice (codified at 10 U.S.C. § 821 (2012). Article 21 provides that "[t]he jurisdiction [of] courts-martial shall not be construed

specific reference to the "law of war" in the statute, it is questionable whether the Court would have treated any of the Geneva Conventions as directly applicable.[207] Moreover, in adopting MCA 2006[208] in response to *Hamdan*, Congress specifically prohibited the use of the Geneva Conventions or any of its protocols (e.g., AP I) as a "source of rights"

---

as depriving military commissions...of concurrent jurisdiction in respect of offenders or offenses that by statute or by the law of war may be tried by such...commissions." Accepting that UCMJ art. 21 authorized military commissions, the Court held that "compliance with the law of war is the condition upon which the authority set forth in Article 21 is granted." 548 U.S. at 628. As the Geneva Conventions were part of the law of war, then any applicable provision of the Geneva Conventions applied to the military commissions. Although the parties disputed whether the war on terror was a type of conflict falling under the Geneva Conventions, the Court found that "there is at least one provision of the Geneva Conventions that applies here even if the relevant conflict is not one between signatories," that is, common article 3, which prohibits "the passing of sentences and the carrying out of executions without previous judgment pronounced by a regularly constituted court affording all the judicial guarantees which are recognized as indispensable by civilized peoples." *Id*. at 629–30 (quoting common article 3). Yet it is clear from the opinion that the Court only looked to common article 3 because of the reference to "the law of war" in the legislation. Indeed, although a portion of Justice Stevens' opinion (joined in this case by only three other Justices) identifies AP I art. 75 as potentially applicable as customary law, the applicability of such customary law could only stem from the reference in the legislation to the "law of war." It is not clear that Justice Stevens would have looked to customary law if the statute had not referred to the law of war.

[207] An interesting development in the habeas litigation is the use of Army Regulation (AR) 190–8 as the foundation for legal challenges to detention. Although styled as a "regulation," AR 190–8, inter alia, "provides policy, procedures, and responsibilities for the administration, treatment, employment, and compensation of enemy prisoners of war (EPW), retained personnel (RP), civilian internees (CI) and other detainees (OD) in the custody of U.S. Armed Forces." AR 190–8, *supra* note 67, at para. 1-1.a. It also states that it "implements international law, both customary and codified, relating to EPW, RP, CI, ODs which includes those persons during military operations other than war." *Id*. at para. 1-1.b. It also cites the four Geneva Conventions as the "principal treaties relevant to this regulation...." *Id*. It does not distinguish between international armed conflicts (to which the four Geneva Conventions apply in full) and noninternational armed conflicts (to which only common article 3 applies). It also refers to customary international law, which would apply to both types of conflicts.

In Al Warafi v. Obama, 716 F.3d 627 (D.C. Cir. 2013), the D.C. Circuit held that, although section 5 of the MCA 2006 (codified at 28 U.S.C. § 2241 note) prohibits invoking the Geneva Conventions as a source of rights in any action or proceeding (including a habeas proceeding) to which the United States is a party, AR 190–8 "is domestic U.S. law, and in a habeas proceeding such as this, a detainee may invoke [AR 190–8]...to the extent that the regulation explicitly establishes a detainee's entitlement to release from custody." 716 F.3d at 629. On that basis, the D.C. Circuit analyzed, as relevant to the detainee's petition, "those aspects of the Geneva Conventions that have been expressly incorporated into" AR 190–8. *Id*. Warafi alleged that he was entitled to be released because he fit the definition of Retained Personnel (RP) under GWS who can only be detained for so long as they are needed to serve the medical or religious needs of other detainees. *Id*. The D.C. Circuit considered his claim, but nonetheless rejected it on the facts. *Id*. at 632. The case was unusual in a number of respects, including the fact that at the time Warafi was alleged to be part of the Taliban at a time when the Taliban arguably was the government of Afghanistan, and therefore the conflict with Afghanistan was an international armed conflict to which the Geneva Conventions did apply. However, the decision does indicate that in some limited circumstances, the Geneva Conventions could be directly applicable to a detainee's status determination through AR 190–8, regardless of the type of conflict involved.

[208] 120 Stat. 2631–2632, *codified at* 28 U.S.C. § 2241 note (2006).

in any habeas or other civil proceeding in which the United States or its agent is a party. Thus, to the extent a detainee had any right to challenge his or her detention, he or she had to base that challenge on U.S. law, rather than international law.[209]

While not promoting the direct application of LOAC treaties under U.S. law, the litigation spurred efforts by both Congress and the administration to strengthen the legal underpinnings for long-term detention in the war on terror and to improve the procedures used to make enemy combatant (or unprivileged enemy belligerent) determinations. For example, the DoD did take steps in 2009 to improve the process for making the enemy combatant determination in Afghanistan, which had been found to be weak by the District Court in the first *al Maqaleh* decision.[210] The final product of this effort was a process that looks remarkably similar to that used in Guantanamo, which includes periodic reviews.

Further, the Obama administration took steps to strengthen the processes used to evaluate whether to continue to hold long-term detainees. In March 2011, the president issued an executive order requiring a periodic review of the detention of individuals held in Guantanamo, to determine whether continued detention of each individual is justified "to protect against a significant threat to the security of the United States."[211] In some respects this determination mirrored the "periodical review" under article 78 of GCIV,[212] but with an important difference: section 1 of the Executive Order states that the periodic review process in the order was established "as a discretionary matter" as part of "the executive branch's continued, discretionary exercise of existing detention authority in individual cases," and thus was not adopted as a matter of legal obligation. Therefore, the reliance on policy rather than law that the Bush administration followed with respect to detainees continues.

---

[209] An attempt by the former leader of Panama, whose incarceration by the United States for drug crimes was held to be subject to the GPW because he was captured by U.S. forces during the 1989 invasion of that country, to use the GPW to oppose his extradition to France, was rejected in 2009 by the 11th Circuit. Noriega v. Pastrana, 564 F.3d 1290 (11th Cir. 2009), *cert. denied*, 130 S. Ct. 1002 (2010). In a vigorous dissent to the Supreme Court's denial of certiorari, Justice Thomas, joined by Justice Scalia, noted that a question that the Court had left open in its prior decisions was "whether the Geneva Conventions are self-executing and judicially enforceable" and asserted that this issue, if decided by the Court, could help guide lower courts in handling future detainee cases. 130 S. Ct. at 1009.

[210] *See* Bovarnick, *supra* note 180, at 9 (describing the changes made). Under the revised procedures, a detainee's status is subject to determination by a "Detainee Review Board" or "DRB," which has replaced the Unlawful Enemy Combatant Review Boards (UECRBs) that had been in use at the time of the initial *al Maqaleh I* decision. In *al Maqaleh III, supra* note 198, the D.C. Circuit noted that "the DRB procedures are undoubtedly more akin to traditional habeas proceedings than were the UECRB procedures." 2013 WL 6767861 at *9.

[211] Executive Order 13567, "Periodic Review of Individuals Detained at Guantánamo Bay Naval Station Pursuant to the Authorization for Use of Military Force," 3 C.F.R. 227 (2012), *reprinted in* 10 U.S.C. § 801 note (2012).

[212] Discussed, *supra* notes 51–53 and accompanying text.

Congress has taken measures to shore up the legal authority supporting use of the combatant paradigm to justify detention in the War on Terror. In section 1021 of the National Defense Authorization Act for Fiscal Year 2012 (the "FY12 NDAA"), Congress adopted the administration's 2009 definition of "unprivileged enemy belligerent" in confirming that the scope of the president's detention authority under the AUMF in all cases includes the authority for the Armed Forces of the United States to detain persons falling within that definition "pending disposition under the law of war." Among the options for "disposition under the law of war" is "[d]etention under the law of war without trial until the end of the hostilities authorized by the Authorization for Use of Military Force."[213] In enacting section 1021, Congress was careful to confirm that the section did not "limit or expand the authority of the President or the scope of the Authorization for Use of Military Force" but rather confirmed the scope of existing authority.[214] It therefore eliminated any doubt as to the legislative foundation for the president's authority to detain unprivileged enemy belligerents for the duration of hostilities in the war on terror, while also not expanding that detention authority.

In the FY12 NDAA, Congress adopted a new statutory protection for long-term detainees that represents a fundamental change to the process of status determinations for those held under the AUMF outside the United States or Guantanamo. Section 1024 of the FY12 NDAA directed the Secretary of Defense to adopt procedures for status determinations of individuals held in long-term detention under the AUMF that, for the first time, include the following requirements:

(1) A military judge shall preside at proceedings for the determination of status of an unprivileged enemy belligerent.

(2) An unprivileged enemy belligerent may, at the election of the belligerent, be represented by military counsel at proceedings for the determination of status of the belligerent.[215]

These requirements do not apply to those detainees who already have the right to pursue a habeas petition to challenge their detention.[216] This excludes, as a consequence, the detainees at Guantanamo, but not the detainees in Afghanistan, such as the petitioners in *al Maqaleh*. How the provision will impact detainees in Afghanistan is unclear. The Conference Report on the FY12 NDAA emphasizes that "this provision is prospective" and therefore "the Secretary of Defense is authorized to determine the extent, if any, to which such procedures [required by section 1024] will be applied to detainees for whom status determinations have already been made prior to the date of the

---

[213] FY12 NDAA, *supra* note 13, § 1021(c).

[214] *Id.* § 1021(d).

[215] *Id.* § 1024(b).

[216] *Id.* § 1024(c).

enactment of [the FY12 NDAA]." The Conference Report further stipulates that in the procedures to implement section 1024, the Secretary of Defense will have the authority to define what constitutes "long-term" detention for the purposes of section 1024, and that, in the case of the detainees in Afghanistan, it is expected that the requirements of section 1024 would not be triggered by the first review of the status of the detainee (in Afghanistan, this is typically made within 60 days after capture), but rather a subsequent review, which could be made months after the first review.[217] Further, in his statement upon signing the FY12 NDAA, President Obama registered his objection to section 1024 and stated:

> Going forward, consistent with congressional intent as detailed in the Conference Report, my Administration will interpret section 1024 as granting the Secretary of Defense broad discretion to determine what detainee status determinations in Afghanistan are subject to the requirements of this section.[218]

In a report submitted to Congress (as required by the FY12 NDAA) in April 2012, the DoD adopted a limited approach to implementation of section 1024.[219] Noting that it only holds unprivileged enemy belligerents pursuant to the AUMF at Guantanamo and the Detention Facility in Parwan, Afghanistan ("Parwan"), the DoD stated that the section 1024 procedures would apply only to those held in the Parwan Detention Facility as habeas review already was available to the detainees at Guantanamo. Further, consistent with the Conference Report's description of section 1024 as being "prospective," the procedures in the DoD report would not apply to "any detainees transferred to the custody and control of the Government of Afghanistan pursuant to the Memorandum of Understanding of March 9, 2012."[220] Under the terms of that Agreement and subsequent agreements, the United States turned over control of the Parwan Detention Facility to the government of Afghanistan. Thus, the population of U.S.-held detainees in Afghanistan has dropped dramatically, and going forward, U.S forces are obligated to turn over to the Afghans any new Afghan detainee

---

217   H.R. Rep. 112-329, at 697 (2011).

218   Press Release, President Barack Obama, Statement by the President on H.R. 1540 (Dec. 31, 2011), http://www.whitehouse.gov/the-press-office/2011/12/31/statement-president-hr-1540.

219   "Department of Defense Report on the Procedures for Unprivileged Enemy Belligerent Status Determinations" (Mar. 2012), attached as enclosure with Letter from Sec'y of Defense, to Chairman, Committee on Armed Services, U.S. Senate (Apr. 5, 2012) [hereinafter Section 1024 Report] (on file with authors).

220   Memorandum of Understanding between the Islamic Republic of Afghanistan and the United States of America on Transfer of U.S. Detention Facilities in Afghan Territory to Afghanistan, Mar. 9, 2012, *available at* http://mfa.gov.af/en/news/7671. For a summary of recent developments in the handover of detainees to Afghan control, *see* JENNIFER K. ELSEA & MICHAEL J. GARCIA, CONG. RES. SERV., RL42143, THE NATIONAL DEFENSE AUTHORIZATION ACT FOR FY2012 AND BEYOND: DETAINEE MATTERS 4–5 (Jan. 27, 2014), *available at* http://www.fas.org/sgp/crs/natsec/R42143.pdf.

within 96 hours of capture.[221] However, as of December 2013, "United States forces in Afghanistan still continue to detain approximately 53 third-country nationals under the 2001 Authorization for the Use of Military Force (Public Law 107-40), as informed by the law of war."[222] The United States' proposed disposition of these remaining individuals has not yet been publicly clarified, and there is now a pressing need to determine whether (and if so, how) these individuals will continue to be detained once the U.S. combat role in Afghanistan ends.

In terms of the implementation of section 1024, the third-country nationals now in detention by U.S. forces could be candidates for a review under this section. However, according to the report by the administration on section 1024, it is to be implemented in two steps that on their face are likely to delay implementation. As the first step, a determination must be made by U.S. authorities in Afghanistan whether section 1024 applies to each detainee.[223] Then, as the second step, the section 1024 review itself will take place at some point after the initial applicability determination occurs.

By the terms of the DoD's section 1024 procedures, the time between capture and the applicability determination could be up to 18 months. Further, once the applicability determination is made, the time before an actual section 1024 review occurs could be up to another 18 months. Thus, it might take up to 36 months before a newly captured individual would receive a section 1024 review. A detainee now in U.S. custody should get more expedited review, but still could wait for 18 to 36 months before having a review under section 1024, depending upon how quickly the applicability determination is made.[224] Although the DoD has not offered any public explanation of the extended timeline, it is likely that it was intended to provide a cushion of time before section 1024

---

[221] Press Release, President Barack Obama, Message to the Congress—Report Consistent with the War Powers Resolution (Dec. 13, 2013), http://www.whitehouse.gov/the-press-office/2013/12/13/message-congress-report-consistent-war-powers-resolution.

[222] *Id.*

[223] The initial determination would be made as part of a review of the detainee's case by a Detainee Review Board (DRB) or similar review. Section 1024 Report, *supra* note 219, second page. *See* Bovarnik, *supra* note 180, for more detail about the DRB process implemented by the United States in Afghanistan since 2009 for the review of detainees held at the Bagram Theater Detention Facility and later the Detention Facility in Parwan. *See also* Respondent's Motion to Dismiss Amended Petitions for Writs of Habeas Corpus (filed May 19, 2011), Al Maqaleh v. Gates, 899 F. Supp. 2d 10 (D.D.C. 2012), *available at* http://www.lawfareblog.com/wp-content/uploads/2011/07/64-main.pdf.

[224] In addition, although under the DRB procedure, a detainee's case is reviewed every six months to consider, first, whether the detainee qualifies as an unprivileged enemy belligerent who can be detained, and second, whether his or her detention continues to be justified based on the threat posed by the detainee, after a section 1024 review is held and a military judge determines that the detainee is an unprivileged enemy belligerent, the DRB review need not be held as frequently and the review need consider only the threat posed by the detainee. This is consistent with the treatment of detainees at Guantanamo where, following a determination of enemy combatant status, further reviews consider only whether the threat posed by the detainee justifies continued detention. Exec. Order No. 13,567, 47 Fed. Reg. 13277 (2011) (establishing an annual periodic review process for Guantanamo detainees).

reviews could begin, presumably to allow the United States an opportunity to dispose of the non-Afghan detainees in a manner that does not subject their detention to section 1024 review.

Despite the limitations on the section 1024 reviews that are likely to result from the U.S. government's procedures and in particular its protracted timelines, section 1024 is an important new development for applying the enemy-combatant paradigm to the detention of individuals who do not qualify for protection under GPW or GCIV.[225] While courts have accepted that indefinite military detention of enemy combatants is an incident of armed conflict (reflected, inter alia, in the reasoning of the plurality in *Hamdi*), there nevertheless have been recurring concerns in various court decisions that the military's administrative processes for determining whether an individual qualifies as an enemy combatant (including CSRTs and the review boards in Afghanistan) is prone to error.[226]

In the case of the detainees at Guantanamo, the Supreme Court, applying its three-factor test in *Boumediene*, addressed these doubts by extending to the detainees a constitutional right to challenge the legality of their detention through the writ of habeas corpus. Even though the *Boumediene* test, as subsequently applied by the D.C. Circuit, did not yield habeas jurisdiction for detainees in Afghanistan, the D.C. Circuit did acknowledge, at least in its original decision in the *al Maqaleh* case, that the procedures used in Afghanistan to make enemy combatant status determinations were inferior to the CSRTs that the Supreme Court had found to be inadequate in *Boumediene*.[227] Had the other factors in the *Boumediene* test outweighed the concerns of the D.C. Circuit with avoiding interference with the military situation in Afghanistan, the decision of the District Court, which would have extended the right to habeas review to detainees in Afghanistan, might have been upheld. However, if section 1024 reviews were

---

[225] *See* Geoffrey S. Corn & Peter A. Chickris, *Unprivileged Belligerents, Preventive Detention and Fundamental Fairness: Rethinking the Review Tribunal Representational Model*, 11 SANTA CLARA J. INT'L L. 99, 102 (2012) ("the provision for a right to legal representation for individuals subjected to detention is perhaps the most profound shift in detention policy since September 11, 2001").

[226] For example, in *Boumediene*, the Court observed:

> They [the Petitioners] have been afforded some process in CSRT proceedings to determine their status; but, unlike in Eisentrager..., there has been no trial by military commission for violations of the laws of war. The difference is not trivial. The records from the Eisentrager trials suggest that, well before the petitioners brought their case to this Court, there had been a rigorous adversarial process to test the legality of their detention.
>
> ...
>
> In comparison the procedural protections afforded to the detainees in the CSRT hearings are far more limited, and, we conclude, fall well short of the procedures and adversarial mechanisms that would eliminate the need for habeas corpus review.

553 U.S. at 767.

[227] As noted, *supra* note 210, the D.C. Circuit had more positive statements to make about the review procedures now being used in Afghanistan.

available, including the right to representation by military counsel and a hearing before a military judge, the case for rejecting a further extraterritorial extension of *Boumediene* likely would be much stronger because section 1024 provides a much stronger substitute for habeas review than any of the procedures applied previously during the war on terror.

Given the pace with which the United States is winding down its detention activities in Afghanistan, it is not clear that section 1024 reviews will occur there. From the perspective of the development of the law and procedure applicable to detention, it is unfortunate that section 1024 will not be tested, as a section 1024 review might significantly improve the perceptions of governments, organizations, and the public generally of the procedural and substantive fairness of the status determination process, by granting the long-term detainee representation by a military lawyer, and review by a military judge, each of whom is familiar with the law and practice of armed conflict. Arguably, section 1024—which, as part of the FY12 NDAA, now is part of the status determination process for all long-term detainees held under the AUMF who do not already have a right to petition for habeas corpus in U.S. civilian courts—will help address concerns about the risk that U.S. military procedures will produce erroneous status determinations and may well save the U.S. government considerable effort in defending those procedures to courts and others in the future. Indeed, the U.S. government should consider incorporating the requirements of section 1024 into its standard procedures for status determinations of long-term detainees in conflicts, particularly where the status under the LOAC of the enemy forces is subject to doubt.[228]

---

[228] The requirements of section 1024 would have no place in a conflict involving a clash of State armed forces, whose members are prisoners of war who, if captured, enjoy the protection of the GPW and combatant immunity, except perhaps with respect to determinations of the combatant status of armed groups participating in the conflict.

6

Trial and Punishment for Battlefield Misconduct

by Dru Brenner-Beck

The terms "war crime" and "terrorism" share common connections: they both refer to the unjustified infliction of suffering, both connote the victimization of the innocent, and both trigger criminal sanction. But these two terms also differ in certain legally substantial ways. Perhaps the most important difference is the source of law that operates to condemn these crimes. War crimes are quintessential international law violations—crimes that are defined by international law and subject to criminal sanction either through international tribunals or domestic tribunals invoking the substance of international law. Terrorism, in contrast, although ostensibly universally condemned, is primarily the subject of domestic law and subject to criminal sanction as the result of domestic criminal prohibition.

Prior to September 11th, these distinctions had virtually no practical significance: war crimes and terrorism were distinctly defined and prosecuted as discrete classes of crime. This changed, however, when President Bush issued Military Order of November 13, 2001 providing that certain noncitizen members of al-Qaeda and other noncitizens whom the president had reason to believe were involved in international terrorism or who knowingly harbored such persons would be detained by the United States and, if tried, would be tried by military commission.[1] Pursuant to this order, the Secretary of Defense issued Military Commission Order No. 1 in 2002, which established the procedure for military commissions,[2] and Military Commission Instruction No. 2 ("MCI 2"),

---

[1] Military Order of November 13, 2001, *Detention, Treatment, and Trial of Certain Non-citizens in the War against Terrorism*, 66 Fed. Reg. 57833 (Nov. 16, 2001) [hereinafter Military Order of November 13, 2001].

[2] U.S. Dep't of Defense, Military Commission Order No. 1 (Mar. 21, 2002), *available at* http://www.defense.gov/news/mar2002/d20020321ord.pdf.

which established the crimes that would be triable by military commission.[3] Although terrorism was not included among the list of war crimes included in the instruction,[4] MCI 2 specifically included "Terrorism" as among other offenses that were triable by military commission.[5]

By subjecting acts of terrorism to the jurisdiction of what had up to that time been understood as a "law of war" court, the president initiated one of the most controversial debates related to the U.S. struggle against transnational terrorism.[6] Could the conduct of terrorists violate the laws and customs of war? Could terrorism itself be characterized as a war crime? Could the jurisdiction of a "war court" be extended to acts of terrorism? If terrorists were to be tried by such courts, would they be entitled to invoke the fundamental trial rights guaranteed by the law of armed conflict (LOAC) to challenge procedures of the court? Did these defendants have a right to judicial review of their challenges? And finally, what were the sources and limits, if any, on congressional authority to include terrorism offenses in the jurisdiction of military courts? Is congressional authority limited to its powers to define and punish "Offences against the Law of Nations,"[7] or can other constitutional provisions also support congressional expansion of military tribunal jurisdiction?

The debate related to all of these questions unfolded in the months and years following the creation of the military commissions, and continues today. As a result, the commissions themselves went through a fairly radical transformation—at least procedurally. Substantively, however, the basic proposition that provided the impetus for the president's initial order—that acts of transnational terrorism could constitute war crimes triable by military commission, or in the alternative, could fall within the scope of another category of offenses triable by military commission—remained essentially unaltered. This assertion of jurisdiction, however, has been subject to continued legal challenges as members of al-Qaeda convicted by military commission for terrorism-type offenses, such as the provision of material support for terrorism or conspiracy, contest

---

[3] U.S. Dep't of Defense, Military Commission Instruction No. 2 (Apr. 20, 2003), 32 C.F.R. pt. 11 (2012) [hereinafter MCI 2].

[4] *Id.* § 11.6 (b)(1). However, many terrorist acts would be covered by the war crimes included in the list (such as attacking civilians).

[5] *Id.* § 11.6 (b)(2).

[6] Jennifer K. Elsea, Cong. Res. Serv., R41163, The Military Commissions Act of 2009 (MCA 2009): Overview and Legal Issues (May 13, 2013) ("The use of military commissions to try suspected terrorists has been the focus of intense debate (as well as significant litigation) since President Bush in November 2001 issued his original Military Order (M.O.) authorizing such trials"), *available at* http://www. fas.org/sgp/crs/natsec/R41163.pdf. *See generally* Geoffrey S. Corn, *Hamdan, Lebanon, and the Regulation of Hostilities: The Need to Recognize a Hybrid Category of Armed Conflict*, 40 Vand. J. Transnat'l L. 295, 299–300 (2007) (defining transnational armed conflict as "a term used to represent the extraterritorial application of military combat power by the regular armed forces of a state against a transnational non-state armed enemy.")

[7] U.S. Const. art. I, § 8, cl. 10.

the legitimacy of both the charges and the forum, in the appeals of their convictions before the U.S. Court of Appeals for the D.C. Circuit. At the time of the writing of this text, the D.C. Circuit Court of Appeals has ruled that solicitation and material support for terrorism are not war crimes under international law. Accordingly, these charges cannot be tried by military commission if the criminal acts upon which the charges are based occurred prior to the enactment of the 2006 Military Commissions Act (2006 MCA).[8] The validity of conspiracy charges is unclear. Six of the seven judges in the recent D.C. Circuit *en banc* review in Al-Bahlul v. United States upheld the legitimacy of conspiracy charges based on pre-2006 conduct, but based their conclusions on very different rationales.[9] Because plain error review formed the basis of the majority's opinion, the court failed to provide useful precedent for future cases. Thus, thirteen years after the attacks of September 11th, and eight years after the passage of the 2006 MCA, the question of whether conspiracy was a crime triable by military commission prior to enactment of the 2006 MCA that expressly codified it as such,[10] as well as the ultimate

---

[8] P.L. 109-366, 120 Stat. 2600, codified at 10 U.S.C. § 948a et seq. (2006) [hereinafter 2006 MCA]; In *Hamdan v. United States*, 676 F.3d 1238, 1252–53 (D.C. Cir. 2012) [hereinafter *Hamdan II*], the D.C. Circuit interpreted the MCA to not authorize prosecution of conduct that was not a war crime under international law when committed, specifically in that case, conspiracy and material support of terrorism. However, in *Al-Bahlul v. United States*, No. 11-1324, 2014 WL3437485 (D.C. Cir. Jul. 14, 2014) [hereinafter *Al-Bahlul*], the D.C. Circuit, sitting en banc, overruled *Hamdan II*'s conclusion that the 2006 MCA did not authorize retroactive prosecution for pre-2006 MCA conduct. Rather, applying the Ex Post Facto Clause of the U.S. Constitution (which the government had conceded applied to Guantanamo military commissions), the court vacated al-Bahlul's conviction on charges of material support for terrorism and solicitation, two charges based on conduct that predated the 2006 MCA. However, applying the Ex Post Facto clause to al-Bahlul's conviction for conspiracy, the court held that it was not plain error to conclude that conspiracy was triable by law-of-war military commissions prior to enactment of the 2006 MCA, and therefore upheld al-Bahlul's conviction for that offense. The court majority applied a "plain error" analysis because it concluded that al-Bahlul had not raised the ex post facto issue during his trial, a conclusion disputed by the remaining three of the *en banc* judges. Thus, the court left considerable uncertainty as to the outcome if the ex post facto issue had been fully litigated at trial. As of July, 17, 2014, the *en banc* decision in the *Al Bahlul* case is *available at* http://images.politico.com/global/2014/07/14/bahlulenbancopn.pdf (last visited July 15, 2014).

[9] Although the five of the seven judges considering al-Bahlul's appeal concluded that in light of *Boumediene v. Bush,* 553 U.S. 723 (2008), the Ex Post Facto Clause does apply at Guantanamo, two judges disagreed. However, because the government had conceded its application, the majority opinion assumed, without deciding, that the Ex Post Facto Clause applied. Additionally, although two of the judges applying de novo review, concluded that conspiracy "had long been an offense triable by military commission, including at the time of Bahlul's conduct in 2001," the majority held that al-Bahlul had waived his ex post facto issue when he did not raise it at trial. The majority upheld the conspiracy conviction only under plain error review, meaning that it was not "plain error" to convict Al-Bahlul on those charges despite his waiver.

[10] The charges in *Al-Bahlul* and *Hamdan II* involved pre-2006 MCA conduct. The question of whether post-2006 MCA conduct can be tried as a statutory offense under the MCA prospectively, even if not a crime under international law, remains open. However, referred charges against Abd Al Hadi Al-Iraqi, currently pending trial by military commission, will directly raise the issue of the validity of conspiracy charges that post-date the October 17, 2006, entry into force of the 2006 MCA. See "Referred Charges" dated 6/02/2014 in United States v. al-Hadi, *available at* http://www.mc.mil/Portals/0/pdfs/alIraqi/Hadi%20Al%20Iraqi%20Referred%20Charge%20Sheet.pdf.

question of how to determine whether a crime may be tried by military commission at all, remain, for various reasons, unresolved. [11]

There is nothing fundamentally irrational or controversial about the use of military courts to try war crimes. The very notion of the war crime is derived from a history of "warriors judging warriors" in military courts vested with such jurisdiction. A primary purpose of such tribunals was "to compel compliance with the laws and customs of war."[12] Indeed, the advent of civilian international tribunals vested with jurisdiction over such crimes is a relatively new phenomenon. What is unclear, however, is how this historically valid use of military "war courts" can be reconciled with the designation of the struggle against terrorism as an armed conflict—a lack of clarity that becomes particularly profound in the context of criminal prosecutions. For the United States, procedural obligations related to the use of military tribunals to try terrorism offenses have been defined by a combination of the Supreme Court decision in *Hamdan v. Rumsfeld* [*Hamdan I*],[13] the subsequent evolving statutory framework for military commissions detailed by Congress in the 2006[14] and 2009[15] Military Commissions Acts ("2006 MCA" and "2009 MCA" respectively), and continuing judicial review and clarification of the results of military commission proceedings. Substantive clarity, however, has remained elusive. Although the 2006 MCA, as amended by the 2009 MCA, purports to define with precision those offenses validly subject to the jurisdiction of military commissions, internal inconsistencies in the statute, coupled with continuing *ex post facto* and other judicial challenges to military commission subject matter jurisdiction, have contradicted this congressional purpose.

This chapter will explore the issues surrounding the use of courts whose jurisdiction is derived from the LOAC for the trial of operatives captured in the course of the armed struggle against transnational terrorism. It will assert why such use can and should be

---

[11] None of the opinions in *Al Bahlul* tethered the validity of the conspiracy charge exclusively to its status as a war crime under international law, muddying the waters further. *See Al-Bahlul, supra* note 8, at *54 (Kavanaugh, J., concurring in the judgment in part and dissenting in part). The ultimate validity of pre-2006 MCA conspiracy charges in future commissions trials where the issue is raised by defendants remains uncertain for a variety of reasons. First, the plain error review used by the majority provided no guidance to the government going forward on how pre-2006 charges will be judged—through the international law of war; through the international law of war supplemented with the domestic U.S. common law of war; or through the new theory of preexisting federal criminal offenses providing legitimacy for charges before military commissions. Second, only seven of the D.C. Circuit judges considered this appeal, with four newly appointed judges not participating. Finally, the court in *Al-Bahlul* decided neither the question of the applicability of the Ex Post Facto Clause nor determined which body of law was referred to in 10 U.S. Code § 821, leaving these two critical questions for future resolution.

[12] Geoffrey Corn, *Taking the Bitter with the Sweet: A Law of War Based Analysis of the Military Commission*, 35 STETSON L. REV. 811, 814–15 (2006).

[13] Hamdan v. Rumsfeld, 548 U.S. 557 (2006) [hereinafter *Hamdan I*].

[14] 2006 MCA, *supra* note 8.

[15] P.L. 111-84, 123 Stat. 2190, 2574 *amending* 10 U.S.C. § 948a *et seq.* [hereinafter 2009 MCA].

considered legitimate, but also how this legitimacy is contingent on respecting substantive and procedural limitations that are inherent in the LOAC. Although the debate on the legitimate use of such tribunals will no doubt continue for some time, it seems increasingly apparent that if the characterization of the struggle against terrorism as an armed conflict is valid, there is no logical reason that individuals who transgress certain fundamental LOAC norms should be immune from the jurisdiction of military tribunals simply because their misconduct is subject to the concurrent jurisdiction of civilian courts.

The Jurisdiction Created by "Any" Armed Conflict

Although application of LOAC principles as a matter of policy may provide regulatory solutions to many operational issues, it cannot provide a legal basis for the war crimes prosecution of individuals captured during these operations. War crimes prosecutions are based on a legally simple but factually complex jurisdictional predicate: a violation of proscriptions established by the international law of armed conflict.[16] Accordingly, any war crimes allegation must rest on a two-prong foundation: first, that the LOAC applied at the time of the alleged misconduct; and second, that the defendant's acts or omissions violated a proscription established by that law.

The president's decision in November 2001 to order the establishment of military commissions for the trial and punishment of captured terrorist operatives was a clear indication that the United States considered the struggle against al-Qaeda to be an "armed conflict" sufficient to trigger LOAC application. In his Order, the president explicitly asserted this conclusion when he determined:

> International terrorists, including members of al Qaida, have carried out attacks on United States diplomatic and military personnel and facilities abroad and on citizens and property within the United States on a scale that has created a state of armed conflict that requires the use of the United States Armed Forces.[17]

And that:

> To protect the United States and its citizens, and for the effective conduct of military operations and prevention of terrorist attacks, it is necessary for individuals subject to this order pursuant to section 2 hereof to be detained, and, when tried, to be tried for violations of the laws of war and other applicable laws by military tribunals.[18]

---

[16] 2006 MCA, *supra* note 8, § 948d.

[17] Military Order of November 13, 2001, *supra* note 1, § 1(a).

[18] *Id.* § 1(e).

While this Order and the trials it generated would ultimately lead the Supreme Court to rule that the trial structure created by the president violated both domestic and international law, nothing in that decision challenged the basic jurisdictional premise reflected in these excerpts.[19] Indeed, by focusing on the procedural defects of the military commission instead of on any jurisdictional defect, *Hamdan I* was, if anything, an implicit endorsement of these conclusions.[20] There may be rational explanations for why the Court seemed to avoid any meaningful critique of the jurisdictional foundation of trial of al-Qaeda terrorists as war criminals—first among these the apparent concession of jurisdiction by Hamdan's lawyers. In its opinion, the Court noted that "[Petitioner] concedes that a court-martial constituted in accordance with the Uniform Code of Military Justice (UCMJ)…would have authority to try him."[21] Because such court-martial jurisdiction could be based only on applicability of the law of war to Hamdan, this one sentence reveals that the jurisdiction for trying Hamdan as a war criminal was never challenged by his lawyers. Nonetheless, the Court's focus on the lack of a clear statutory basis for the use of military commissions against international terrorists in the Global War on Terror was not lost on Congress, which almost immediately following the Court's decision adopted the president's initial jurisdictional determinations in the form of the Military Commissions Act of 2006.

According to this statute:

> This chapter establishes procedures governing the use of military commissions to try alien unlawful enemy combatants engaged in hostilities against the United States for violations of the law of war and other offenses triable by military commission.[22]

Similar language was used in the 2009 MCA.[23]

In each version of the Military Commissions Act, Congress emphasized that the offenses created by the statute were not new and had always been subject to trial by military commission—clearly reflecting the congressional view that both the 2006 and 2009 MCA had merely codified existing war crimes.[24]

---

[19] *See Hamdan I, supra* note 13, at 593–94 (2006) (noting that the Court assumes that the Authorization for the Use of Military Force activated the president's war powers and that those powers included the power to convene military commissions in appropriate circumstances, subject to applicable provisions of the Uniform Code of Military Justice).

[20] *Id.*

[21] *Id.* at 567.

[22] 2006 MCA, *supra* note 8, § 948b(a).

[23] The 2009 MCA amended section 948b(a), as follows:

> This chapter establishes procedures governing the use of military commissions to try alien unprivileged enemy belligerents for violations of the law of war and other offenses triable by military commission.

[24] 2006 MCA, *supra* note 8, § 950p(b); 2009 MCA, *supra* note 15, § 950p(d); *but see Al-Bahlul, supra* note 8, at *5–*8, *10 (The "2006 MCA unambiguously authorizes Bahlul's prosecution for the charged offenses

Thus, from the outset of the Global War on Terror, the struggle against transnational terrorism has been treated by the United States as an armed conflict triggering LOAC obligations. This determination is critical, for it provides the jurisdictional basis for designating acts and omissions of terrorist operatives as "war crimes." This treatment of terrorism as a war crime is no less controversial today than it was on the day the president issued his military order, and only time will tell if such an approach to both LOAC applicability and individual responsibility will gain wider acceptance in the international community. At a more immediate level, however, we must critique the subordinate issues created by this invocation of the LOAC: What is the legitimate scope of criminal jurisdiction derived from a transnational armed conflict, and what, if any, procedural protections does the LOAC demand for any person subject to trial for violating the LOAC?

This chapter will focus on these two issues as they relate to the trial of nonstate actors captured by the United States in the struggle against terrorism. It is based on the assumption that the acts or omissions forming the basis for war crimes charges leveled against these detainees did in fact occur within the context of a noninternational "transnational" armed conflict. Any assumption that these acts or omissions were not committed in connection with an armed conflict would totally invalidate such charges. And, although most of the alleged misconduct subject to characterization as war crimes addressed in this chapter is also subject to domestic (and perhaps international) criminal jurisdiction, in keeping with the focus of this text, treatment of such jurisdiction is left to other scholars. Our focus is therefore clear: If the struggle against transnational terrorism is an armed conflict, what war crimes liability does this fact legitimately create, and what minimum procedural protections must be respected in trials of such war crimes?

Jurisdiction Derived from Transnational Armed Conflict.

The law of armed conflict is and has always been inherently responsive to the changing realities of warfare. In a very real sense, rules developed for the regulation of armed hostilities are never truly validated or discredited until they are tested in the "battle laboratory."[25] It is therefore unsurprising that some of the most significant developments in the law have occurred in the aftermath of wars. Most experts—indeed many laymen—could identify the post–World War II war crimes trials as marking one of

---

[conspiracy, material support for terrorism, and solicitaton] based on pre-2006 conduct," requiring analysis of Bahlul's ex post facto argument.).

[25] *See generally* LESLIE C. GREEN, THE CONTEMPORARY LAW OF ARMED CONFLICT 59–61 (2d ed. 2000); *see also* INT'L & OPERATIONAL LAW DEP'T, THE JUDGE ADVOCATE GENERAL'S SCHOOL, U.S. ARMY, LAW OF WAR WORKSHOP DESKBOOK (Brian J. Bill ed., 2004).

these landmark developments. It was not, however, until the end of the Cold War that the concept of international criminal responsibility of individuals for violations of the laws and customs of war came to full fruition. In response to the brutal internal conflict that broke out in the former Yugoslavian republic of Bosnia-Herzegovina, the United Nations established the first ad hoc international war crime tribunal since the end of World War II.[26] Like its predecessors from that war, the International Criminal Tribunal for the Former Yugoslavia, or ICTY, was tasked with holding accountable individuals who had committed, among other offenses, serious violations of the laws and customs of war. Unlike its predecessors, however, the ICTY would ultimately conclude that its jurisdiction was not limited to offenses committed in the context of an inter-state armed conflict. Instead, for the first time in history, the concept of individual criminal responsibility for violating the international laws of war would extend into the realm of intra-state, or noninternational armed conflict (NIAC).[27]

In light of the brutality historically associated with internal armed conflicts, this extension seemed pragmatic and justified. Nonetheless, it was then and remains today regarded as a landmark development in the law of armed conflict. Added to this extension of jurisdiction was an expanded scope of norms applicable to this realm of armed conflict. In its first opinion, the ICTY determined that many norms of the law that had been developed to regulate the methods and means of warfare in international armed conflicts had "migrated" into the realm of NIACs.[28] This new development established both enhanced accountability for individuals participating in these noninternational armed conflicts and significantly expanded regulation of NIACs in general.

The jurisprudence of the ICTY and its sister tribunal, the International Criminal Tribunal for Rwanda (ICTR), unleashed a new wave of LOAC development that finally addressed the reality that the regulation of hostilities and the protection of victims of hostilities must be driven first and foremost by the existence of armed conflict, irrespective of its characterization as international or noninternational in nature.[29] In fact, in the years following the ICTY's first decision of *Prosecutor v. Tadic*[30] a remarkable shift in the law

---

[26] S.C. Res. 827, U.N. Doc. S/RES/827 (May 25, 1993), *available at* http://www.icty.org/x/file/Legal%20 Library/Statute/statute_827_1993_en.pdf.

[27] The Tribunal's statute covers, inter alia, crimes against humanity "committed in armed conflict, whether international or internal in character." Updated Statute of the International Criminal Tribunal for The Former Yugoslavia, Sept. 2008, art. 5, *available at* http://www.icty.org/x/file/Legal%20Library/Statute/ statute_sept08_en.pdf.

[28] *See* Prosecutor v. Tadic, Case No. IT-94–1, Decision on the Defence Motion for Interlocutory Appeal on Jurisdiction (Appeals Chamber, Int'l Crim. Trib. for the Former Yugoslavia Oct. 2, 1995), *available at* http://www.icty.org/x/cases/tadic/acdec/en/51002.htm [hereinafter Tadic Jurisdiction Decision].

[29] *See generally* S.C. Res. 955, U.N. Doc. S/RES/955 (Nov. 8, 1994), *available at* http://69.94.11.53/ENGLISH/ Resolutions/955e.htm.

[30] Prosecutor v. Tadic, Case No. IT-94–1, Judgment (Appeals Chamber, Int'l Crim. Trib. for the Former Yugoslavia July 15, 1999), *available at* http://www.icty.org/x/cases/tadic/acjug/en/tad-aj990715e.pdf [hereinafter Tadic Appeals Chamber Judgment].

occurred. Prior to that decision, the law of noninternational armed conflict was understood as a minor offshoot of the law of international armed conflict, focused almost exclusively on the most fundamental protections of individuals who were not participating in hostilities.[31] Today, the understanding is inverse: the fundamental norms applicable to both types of armed conflict have become in large measure synonymous, and it is the disparities between applicable law that have become minor. The operative word is of course "norms," for the treaty rules established to regulate international armed conflicts, such as the bulk of the Geneva Conventions, cannot simply be extended to the realm of noninternational armed conflict by fiat. But because so many of these rules and those of other LOAC treaties reflect underlying norms of operational conduct, the difference between the two types of armed conflict have become virtually transparent at the operational level.[32]

These developments of the law also planted the seed for another step forward in the realm of individual responsibility: extending war crimes liability to transnational terrorist operatives. Once the president determined that the United States was engaged in an armed conflict, the extension of international criminal responsibility to noninternational armed conflict became the logical focal point for a new approach for prosecuting terrorists. This intersection of war crimes jurisdiction and a revised assessment of the nature of the struggle against transnational terrorism is manifested in the president's Military Order establishing the military commissions, when he determined it was necessary:

> . . . for individuals subject to this order pursuant to section 2 hereof to be detained, and, when tried, to be tried for violations of the laws of war and other applicable laws by military tribunals.[33]

An analogous invocation of jurisdiction and liability derived from the LOAC also lies at the core of both Military Commissions Acts,[34] and has already been the basis for several trials and convictions of al-Qaeda operatives.[35]

---

[31] *See* GWS COMMENTARY at 19–23. A similar Commentary was published for each of the four Geneva Conventions. Because articles 2 and 3 are identical—or common—to each Convention, however, the substance of the Commentary for these articles generally is identical in each of the four Commentaries.

[32] The most significant exception to this trend is qualification for status as a prisoner of war and the accordant combatant immunity derived from that status. This status is and will almost certainly continue to be restricted to State-sponsored belligerents involved in international armed conflicts. *See* Major Geoffrey S. Corn & Major Michael L. Smidt, *"To Be or Not to Be, That Is the Question," Contemporary Military Operations and the Status of Captured Personnel*, ARMY LAW. 1 (June 1999); *see also* International Criminal Court, Elements of Crimes (2011) (listing elements of war crimes recognized for both international and noninternational armed conflict, which although largely similar are not identical), *available at* http://www.icc-cpi.int/nr/rdonlyres/336923d8-a6ad-40ec-ad7b-45bf9de73d56/0/elementsofcrimeseng.pdf.

[33] Military Order of November 13, 2001, *supra* note 1.

[34] *See, e.g.*, 2009 MCA, *supra* note 15, § 948b(a) ("violations of the law of war and other offenses triable by military commission").

[35] As of the date this text was completed, the website of the Office of Military Commissions shows five military commissions trials that have been completed (United States v. Muhammed, United States v. Hicks,

If, as the president and Congress have concluded, the armed component of the struggle against transnational terrorism is an armed conflict, then there does seem to be a legitimate basis to subject terrorist operatives to war crimes jurisdiction. Once this extension of war crimes jurisdiction to transnational armed conflict is understood as the foundation for trying terrorists (a proposition rejected by many experts in the field), it becomes necessary to determine what range of offenses legitimately can be derived from applying international armed conflict norms to NIACs. In addition, if the LOAC is the source of jurisdiction upon which trial and punishment of terrorist operatives is derived, then it becomes equally essential to determine whether and to what extent the LOAC provides procedural protections that must be respected in this adjudication process.

The scope of criminal prohibition derived from the LOAC is not unlimited. International law does not countenance bringing charges before a military tribunal for any crime selected or created by the president or his or her subordinate officers. Even Congress is arguably limited in the range of offenses it may properly designate as war crimes under the jurisdiction of military tribunals. Instead, international law limits war crime jurisdiction to violations of the LOAC applicable to the conflict in which the alleged misconduct occurred.[36] Although this may seem axiomatic, the nature of offenses established for trial by military commission—both by the Department of Defense in MCI 2 and by Congress in the Military Commissions Acts—was not necessarily consistent with this jurisdictional limit. Instead, the range of offenses reflected a combination of proscriptions derived from the law of international armed conflict, the law of noninternational armed conflict, and domestic prohibitions against terrorism.

United States v. Khadr, United States v. al Qosi, and United States v. Hamdan). An extensive set of filings and other relevant documents is available on the Military Commissions website at http://www.mc.mil/CASES.aspx.

[36] In a 2012 case it was the conclusion that the international law of war was the relevant yardstick against which to measure criminal liability for actions that occurred prior to the passage of the 2006 MCA that led the D.C. Circuit to conclude that material support for terrorism was not a viable charge in military tribunals, at least for those defendants whose acts occurred prior to its passage. *See Hamdan II, supra* note 8, at 1248 ("The Supreme Court's precedents tell us: The 'law of war' referenced in 10 U.S.C. § 821 is the international law of war."). However, in a more recent case, while acknowledging that Supreme Court precedent and scholarly analysis supported the conclusion in *Hamdan II* that "the 'law of war' as used in section 821 is a term of art that refers to the international law of war," an *en banc* panel of the D.C. Circuit also recognized that "section 821 might not be so limited," and might include the common law of war developed in U.S. military tribunals, as argued by the government, and accepted by two of the *en banc* judges. *Al-Bahlul, supra* note 8, at *15. Because of these legitimate differences in analysis, the majority determined that Al-Bahlul's convictions for conspiracy were not plain error. *Id.* at *15 ("Ultimately we need not resolve *de novo* whether section 821 is limited to the international law of war. It is sufficient for our purpose that, at the time of the appeal, the answer to that question is not obvious.... As seven justices did in Hamdan, we look to domestic wartime precedent to determine whether conspiracy has been traditionally triable by military commission. That precedent provides sufficient historical pedigree to sustain Bahlul's conviction on plain-error review.") (citation omitted). Nevertheless, because the *en banc* court did not decide the issue, the holding in *Hamdan II* remains as circuit precedent, albeit a weakened one.

This limitation on the exercise of war crimes jurisdiction by U.S. military tribunals (to include commissions) is reflected in the U.S. Uniform Code of Military Justice ("Code").[37] Although the Code allows for the use of military tribunals to try captured enemy personnel for pre-capture misconduct, it explicitly limits that jurisdiction to violations of the laws and customs of war.[38] This authorization for the use of military tribunals as venues for the trial and punishment of alleged war crimes committed by *any* person is consistent with the historic interrelationship between military tribunals and the LOAC. As the U.S. Supreme Court recognized in its *Hamdan I* decision, this history provides a solid foundation for the use of military courts to try war crimes.[39] However, by implication, this historical rule also limits the jurisdiction of such tribunals over enemy personnel's pre-capture offenses to acts or omissions that violate the laws and customs of war, a conclusion that was equally central to an earlier Supreme Court decision endorsing the use of military tribunals for war crimes prosecutions, *Ex parte Quirin*.[40] As the Court noted in that opinion:

> We have no occasion now to define with meticulous care the ultimate boundaries of the jurisdiction of military tribunals to try persons according to the law of war ... *We hold only that those particular acts constitute an offense against the law of war which the Constitution authorizes to be tried by military commission.*[41]

Accordingly, in relation to individuals associated with al-Qaeda, this source of jurisdiction may be legitimately asserted only for a very narrow category of offenses derived from violations of the LOAC rules and norms applicable to noninternational armed conflict in which al-Qaeda operatives participate. The most significant source of liability would be violations of the principle of humanity as reflected in common article 3[42] and Additional Protocol II.[43] These treaty provisions impose the universal obligation that all participants in armed conflict treat individuals not actively participating in hostilities humanely. The provisions therefore provide a basis for establishing criminality that is broad enough in scope to sanction almost all conduct that would fall under the broad definition of terrorism for the simple reason that acts of terror are presumptively directed against non-combatants. These treaty provisions would certainly provide a legitimate basis for holding individuals associated with the attacks of September 11th accountable

---

[37] 10 U.S.C. §§ 801–946 (2012) [hereinafter UCMJ].

[38] *Id.* at § 818 ("General courts-martial also have jurisdiction to try any person who by the law of war is subject to trial by a military tribunal and may adjudge any punishment permitted by the law of war.").

[39] *Hamdan I, supra* note 13, at 595–604.

[40] *Ex parte* Quirin, 317 U.S. 1 (1942).

[41] *Id.* at 45–46 (emphasis added).

[42] *See* GWS art. 3, GWS-Sea art. 3, GPW art. 3 and GCIV art. 3 [hereinafter common article 3].

[43] AP II arts. 4, 5 & 7.

for their actions. As reflected in both common article 3[44] and Additional Protocol II,[45] this principle prohibits murder, torture, or other cruel, inhumane, or degrading treatment of persons taking no active part in hostilities.[46]

The principle reflected in common article 3 establishes a norm from which to derive a legal basis for prosecution before any forum empowered by international law to enforce the LOAC, including military tribunals. Common article 3's humane treatment mandate represents a "compulsory minimum"[47] standard of conduct for any and all participants in any armed conflict—not necessarily as a matter of treaty obligation,[48] but as a principle of customary international law. This conclusion is only reinforced by the fact that humane treatment represents the very purpose of the Geneva Conventions.[49] Violations of the LOAC based on the principles reflected in this article could therefore encompass the taking of airline passengers as hostages; the targeting of structures filled with civilians or, in the language of the law, the targeting of "persons taking no active part in hostilities"; the terrorizing of the civilian population; and the killing of the thousands of innocent civilians on September 11th. No additional "positive legislation" is required. International law proscribes the conduct of the September 11th terrorists; and those who planned, encouraged, and supported them violated these minimum standards of conduct that must be respected during any armed conflict.[50]

---

[44] The provision is referred to as "common" article 3 because it is found in each of the four Geneva Conventions.

[45] AP II art. 4.

[46] Similar principles are reflected in the definitions of war crimes included in the Rome statute authorizing the creation of the International Criminal Court.

[47] Tadic Jurisdiction Decision, *supra* note 28, at para. 37.

[48] It is certainly plausible to assert the applicability of common article 3, and not merely the principles reflected therein, to any armed conflict not of an international character, even if not occurring in the territory of a High Contracting Party. *See* Derek Jinks, *September 11 and the Laws of War*, 28 YALE J. INT'L L. 1, 2 (2003) (citing Harold Hongju Koh, *The Spirit of the Laws*, 43 HARV. INT'L L.J. 23, 26 (2002)). In this regard, it is also worth noting that the subject of the binding nature of common article 3 has been a significant issue for the International Committee of the Red Cross (ICRC). In fact, in the September–October 1978 edition of the INTERNATIONAL REVIEW OF THE RED CROSS, the ICRC along with the League of Red Cross Societies published the *Fundamental Rules of Humanitarian Law Applicable in Armed Conflicts*, 206 INT'L REV. RED CROSS 247 (1978), *available at* http://www.loc.gov/rr/frd/Military_Law/pdf/ RC_Sep-Oct-1978.pdf. The ICRC and the League of Red Cross Societies, while emphasizing the informal nature of the rules, noted the rules "state in a condensed form the very essence of international humanitarian law applicable in armed conflicts." *Id.*

[49] Common article 3, *supra* note 42.

[50] It is the opinion of these authors that the offense of "unlawful belligerency" would be both much more difficult to sustain and unnecessary to charge, due to the clear applicability of common article 3 as a basis for criminal prosecution under international law. The essence of a charge of "unlawful belligerency" is that an individual engaged in armed conflict without combatant immunity. In support of this offense, there has been much said and much written about the "four criteria" from the Geneva Prisoner of War Convention's article 4 that must be satisfied by conflict participants to be entitled to be a prisoner of war protected by GPW. However, the criteria relied upon to assert that members of al-Qaeda and the Taliban engaged in unlawful belligerency—that they failed to carry arms openly, wear fixed insignia recognizable from a distance, operate under effective command, and comply with the law of war—are requirements that three of

Additional Protocol II is an equally significant source of definition for the principles applicable to NIACs.[51] As of the date of publication of this book, 167 States were parties to this treaty.[52] Although this treaty is by its terms applicable only to certain internal armed conflicts, it also can be viewed as a reflection of underlying principles applicable to any NIAC. It therefore seems reasonable to refer to the definition of the principle of humanity contained in this treaty as an additional indication of the scope of this obligation.

Like common article 3, article 4 of Additional Protocol II[53] imposes upon participants in a NIAC the general obligation to treat humanely individuals affected by the armed conflict who are not actively participating in hostilities. And, like common article 3, Article 4 of the treaty expressly defines activities that are per se inconsistent with this obligation. However, article 4 is more extensive in this respect than common article 3. This additional illumination of the scope and content of the humane treatment obligation adds several potentially viable sources of criminal liability derived from violations of this basic principle. Among these are pillage, slavery, sexual assaults, and remarkably, acts of terrorism. Although terrorism is not defined, the ICRC Commentary indicates that article 4's intent was to prohibit attacks directed against civilians.[54]

Attacks intended to spread terror among the civilian population are also prohibited by article 13 of AP II:

Article 13—Protection of the civilian population
1. The civilian population and individual civilians shall enjoy general protection against the dangers arising from military operations. To give effect to this protection, the following rules shall be observed in all circumstances.

---

the four Geneva Conventions (GWS, GWS-Sea, and GPW) only expressly refer to with respect to conflicts of an international (State versus State) character, and not to internal armed conflicts.

Thus, while these criteria are used to determine when a member of an insurgent or militia group becomes entitled to status as an enemy prisoner of war under GPW, neither treaty nor customary international law confer prisoner-of-war status (and the accompanying combatant immunity) on non-State combatants in a noninternational armed conflict, regardless of their uniform or conduct. Accordingly, it is difficult to understand how engaging in hostilities against other combatants while in civilian clothes during a noninternational armed conflict per se amounts to an offense under international law absent perfidious conduct. There simply is no requirement to be in uniform because there is no benefit of combatant immunity associated with wearing a uniform. It seems that the true objection to the conduct of al-Qaeda and the Taliban was not so much who they were, but what they did. Their attacks on civilians were certainly unlawful under common article 3, and it is this provision of the law of war that should form the basis for any subsequent prosecution.

[51] *See* Geoffrey S. Corn, Hamdan, *Fundamental Fairness, and the Significance of Additional Protocol II*, Army Law. 1 (Aug. 2006).

[52] *See* International Committee of the Red Cross International Humanitarian Law database: States Party and Signatories by Treaty, *available at* http://www.icrc.org/applic/ihl/ihl.nsf/Treaty.xsp?documentId=AA0C5BCBAB5C4A85C12563CD002D6D09&action=openDocument (last visited June 25, 2014).

[53] AP II art. 4.

[54] AP Commentary at 1375.

2. The civilian population as such, as well as individual civilians, shall not be the object of attack. *Acts or threats of violence the primary purpose of which is to spread terror among the civilian population are prohibited.*[55]

The ICRC Commentary provides the following explanation of the emphasis of this prohibition:

"Acts or threats of violence the primary purpose of which is to spread terror among the civilian population are prohibited." Attacks aimed at terrorizing are just one type of attack, but they are particularly reprehensible....

Any attack is likely to intimidate the civilian population. The attacks or threats concerned here are therefore those, the primary purpose of which is to spread terror, as one delegate stated during the debates at the Conference.[56]

The collective effect of these treaty provisions is to offer more precise meaning to the principle of humanity as it relates to all armed conflicts. These provisions, including the substance of common article 3, if not applicable to such armed conflicts as a matter of treaty obligation, nonetheless serve as reflections of the LOAC principles applicable to all conflicts as a matter of customary law. They offer a viable source of obligation for all individuals engaged in armed conflict—to include members of transnational armed entities such as al-Qaeda. Accordingly, they provide a source of subject matter jurisdiction that is broad enough in scope to allow for the prosecution of members of al-Qaeda without resort to principles of criminal responsibility derived from the law of international armed conflict or domestic law. Thus, the most appropriate charge available for the military prosecution of a terrorist operative could generally follow this example:

The Charge: Violation of the Laws of War
The Specification: In that, (name of individual), a member of an armed organization engaged in armed conflict against the United States, did, at or near (location) on or about (date), engage in conduct in violation of the principle of (humanity, distinction, prohibition against the use of specific weapons), to wit: participating in an attack directed against civilians (and) (or) civilian objects (with the intent of terrorizing the population).

Simple, clear, and supported by the law of armed conflict, charges alleging violations of the basic principles of this law offer the most legitimate jurisdictional basis for trial of al-Qaeda operatives before a military tribunal, including a military commission.

---

[55] AP II art. 13 (emphasis added).
[56] AP Commentary at 1453.

Another source of proscription ostensibly applicable to noninternational armed conflict are those fundamental LOAC norms that have, in the language of the ICTY, "migrated" from the realm of international armed conflict to NIACs. These norms extend beyond the humane treatment obligation to regulate methods and means of warfare. Prohibitions against deliberate targeting of civilians or civilian property, launching attacks expected to produce excessive incidental injury to civilians and civilian objects, use of indiscriminate weapons, and use of weapons calculated to cause unnecessary suffering would all fall into this category.[57] In addition, LOAC prohibitions against perfidy and treachery, such as feigning surrender or misuse of a protected emblem in order to launch attacks, are also applicable to NIACs.[58] Accordingly, violation of these norms in the context of noninternational armed conflict provides an equally legitimate basis for war crimes accountability of transnational terrorist operatives.

If the subject-matter jurisdiction of the military commission established first by President Bush in the Military Order of November 13, 2001, and subsequently by Congress through the 2006 MCA (as later amended by the 2009 MCA) had been limited to the offenses discussed above, much of the criticism of the commissions would have been averted. This is because objections to jurisdiction would have been focused on the debate over the legitimacy of characterizing the struggle against terrorism as an armed conflict. However, this was not the case. Instead, expanding the range of offenses available to military prosecutors beyond this limited source of international proscription exacerbated the criticism of the legitimacy of the commissions' jurisdiction. The questionable nature of this expansion is exemplified by three offenses that have been central to the military commissions' process: murder in violation of the laws of war,[59] material support for terrorism,[60] and inchoate conspiracy.[61]

Few would debate that murder in violation of the laws of war should be subject to criminal sanction. In fact, any deliberate killing that is not justified by the LOAC should be considered murder.[62] In this regard, the title of the offense is misleading, for it suggests that it is the law of war that renders a killing unlawful. In reality, all killings are unlawful unless they are authorized pursuant to the LOAC,[63] even when

---

[57] *See generally* AP I arts. 35, 51–52.

[58] *See* JEAN-MARIE HENCKAERTS & LOUISE DOSWALD-BECK, CUSTOMARY INTERNATIONAL HUMANITARIAN LAW, VOLUME I: RULES 58, 59, 65 (2005) [hereinafter CUSTOMARY LAW STUDY][recognizing limited categories of perfidy in noninternational armed conflict and that "the elements of the crime of treacherously killing or wounding were identical in international and noninternational armed conflict"); *see also* ICC Statute, article 8(2)(e)(ix), *available at* http://www.icc-cpi.int/NR/rdonlyres/EA9AEFF7-5752-4F84-BE94-0A655EB30E16/0/Rome_Statute_English.pdf.

[59] 2006 MCA, *supra* note 8, § 950v(b)(15); 2009 MCA, *supra* note 15, § 950t(15).

[60] 2006 MCA, *supra* note 8, § 950v(b)(25); 2009 MCA, *supra* note 15, § 950t(25).

[61] See MCI 2, *supra* note 3, § 6(C)(6); 2006 MCA, *supra* note 8, § 950v(29); 2009 MCA, *supra* note 15, § 950t(28).

[62] However, the source of criminal liability may lie solely in domestic criminal law, rather than in the international law of war.

[63] Or other source of law.

committed by belligerents in an armed conflict.[64] But this incongruity reveals what is so troubling about this offense. This offense is a derivative of an offense originally established by MCI 2: Murder by an Unprivileged Belligerent.[65] Under this offense, any killing by a belligerent who does not qualify for prisoner-of-war status (if captured in an international armed conflict) is treated as a violation of the LOAC, per se, and therefore murder. This is reflected in the following explanation for this offense contained in the original 2007 Manual for Military Commissions ("the 2007 Manual"), the regulatory implementation of the 2006 MCA: "For the accused to have been acting in violation of the law of war, the accused must have taken acts as a combatant without having met the requirements for lawful combatancy...."[66] This critical foundation for the prosecution

---

[64] In the words of Telford Taylor, a prosecutor at the Nuremburg Tribunals: "What is a 'war crime'? To say that it is a violation of the laws of war is true, but not very meaningful. War consists largely of acts that would be criminal if performed in a time of peace—killing, wounding, kidnapping, destroying or carrying off other people['s] property. Such conduct is not regarded as criminal if it takes place in the course of war, because the state of war lays a blanket of immunity over the warriors...But the area of immunity is not unlimited, and its boundaries are marked by the laws of war. Unless the conduct in question falls within those boundaries, it does not lose the criminal character it would have should it occur in peaceful circumstances. In a literal sense, therefore, the expression 'war crime' is a misnomer, for it means an act that remains criminal even though committed in the course of war, because it lies outside the area of immunity prescribed by the laws of war." Telford Taylor, *War Crimes, in* WAR, MORALITY, AND THE MILITARY PROFESSION 415–16 (Malham M. Wakin ed., 1979).

[65] MCI 2, *supra* note 3, § 6(B)(3).

[66] U.S. Dep't of Defense, The Manual for Military Commissions IV-11 (2007), available at http://www.defenselink.mil/pubs/pdfs/The%20Manual%20for%20Military%20Commissions.pdf [hereinafter 2007 Manual]. Nevertheless, both Omar Khadr and David Hicks filed appeals of their convictions with the Court of Military Commission Review in late 2013 based on the D.C. Circuit's decision and reasoning in *Hamdan II*. In these appeals, both Khadr and Hicks argue that material support for terrorism, under *Hamdan II*, is not an international war crime, and as such is not a valid charge before the Military Commission. Khadr also argues that murder in violation of the law of war and spying are likewise not international war crimes. Both Khadr and Hicks argue that because their appeal attacks the jurisdiction of the military commissions that tried them, any appeal waiver is invalid. Both of these appeals were stayed by the court pending the D.C. Circuit's *en banc* decision in *United States v. Al-Bahlul. See* Posting of Marty Lederman, The Khadr Appeal [UPDATE: and the Hicks Appeal], Just Security Blog (Nov. 11, 2013), *available at* http://justsecurity.org/3088/khadr-appeal/ (last visited July 4, 2014) (the blog entry contains links to the appellate briefs, which are not yet available on the military commissions website). *See also* www.mc.mil. On June 30, 2014, Khadr filed a subsequent motion seeking immediate determination of his appeal based upon a memorandum written by the Department of Justice's Office of Legal Counsel (OLC), in which the OLC rejected the view that "any hostile acts performed by unprivileged belligerents are *for that reason* violations of the laws of war." This U.S, government position, Khadr argued, undermines the basis for his conviction for murder in violation of the laws of war. *See* Motion to Lift Stay of Proceedings and Vacate Appellant's Convictions, June 30, 2014, in *United States v. Omar Khadr*, CMCR Case No. 13-005, *available at* http://www.lawfareblog.com/wp-content/uploads/2014/07/US-v-Khadr-Motion-to-Lift-Stay-June-30-2014.pdf (citing to the United States Office of Legal Counsel Memorandum, *Re: Applicability of Federal Criminal Laws and the Constitution to Contemplated Lethal Operations Against Shaykh Anwar al-Aulaqi* (July 16, 2010), at 33, n.44, *available at* http://www.lawfareblog.com/wp-content/uploads/2014/06/6-23-14_Drone_Memo-Alone.pdf) (last visited July 5, 2014)). Immediately after the U.S. response contending that the OLC memorandum applied only to state actors, the court denied the motion to vacate. *See* Posting of Sam Morison, The Drone Memo Makes It Clear: Khadr's Conviction Lacks Legal Foundation, to Lawfare Blog, http://www.

of individuals for war crimes alleged to have occurred in the context of the transnational armed conflict against al-Qaeda is also reflected in this excerpt from the 2007 Manual:

> It is generally accepted international practice that unlawful enemy combatants may be prosecuted for offenses associated with armed conflicts, such as murder; such unlawful enemy combatants do not enjoy combatant immunity because they have failed to meet the requirements of lawful combatancy under the law of war.[67]

The theory of war crimes liability reflected in the excerpt is both overbroad and imprecise in the context of a NIAC. Contrary to the assertion, there is no such "general acceptance" in the context of a NIAC. Instead, the assertion that operating without privilege renders the belligerent conduct of an individual a violation of *international* law has only been asserted in the context of international armed conflict (this theory is ostensibly derived from the U.S. Supreme Court's *Ex parte Quirin*[68] decision, which upheld the trial of German saboteurs for the war crime of "unlawful belligerency" during the Second World War). Even in this context that assertion of liability has never been universally or even widely endorsed. But even assuming *arguendo* the legitimacy of this theory of war crimes liability in the context of international armed conflict, there is simply no precedent for extending the theory to noninternational armed conflict. Indeed, such an extension produces an anomaly: because a nonstate belligerent can never enjoy "lawful" belligerent status, the offense imposes *international* legal sanction without a complementary *international* legal reward. In this regard, the underlying rationale supporting the Supreme Court's endorsement of this offense in *Quirin*—to "incentivize" operating as a lawful belligerent—is nullified when the theory is extended to NIACs.

This does not, of course, mean that the 2007 Manual was incorrect to suggest that unlawful enemy combatants do not enjoy combatant immunity. But by mixing the benefits of status with the consequence of participation in NIACs, the 2007 Manual distorts the impact of failing to qualify for combatant immunity. Nonstate belligerents cannot qualify for this immunity, a privilege reserved for State armed forces engaged in international armed conflicts. But this does not result in the conclusion that acting as a belligerent without qualification for combatant immunity is ipso facto a war crime. Instead, it simply permits the application of domestic criminal jurisdiction to the acts and omissions of the belligerent. In short, the lack of combatant immunity subjects him or her to the criminal jurisdiction of the State against which this conduct occurs, for violations under the laws of that State, which for such a combatant could include murder, assault, arson, kidnapping, etc.[69]

---

lawfareblog.com/2014/07/the-drone-memo-makes-it-clear-khadrs-conviction-lacks-legal-foundation/ (July 14, 2014) (last visited July 16, 2014).

[67] 2007 Manual, *supra* note 66.

[68] *Ex parte* Quirin, 317 U.S. 1 (1942).

[69] Or theoretically, an appropriate exercise of extraterritorial criminal jurisdiction by another State.

In order to qualify as a war crime, those acts or omissions must violate not only applicable domestic law (such as prohibitions against murder, assault, arson, kidnapping, mayhem, etc.), but also *international* law, or more specifically the LOAC. And here the over-breadth of the theory is exposed, for there is simply no basis to assert that the mere participation in a NIAC by a nonstate actor violates international law. Instead, those individuals become *internationally* liable for their acts or omissions only when those acts or omissions violate norms of conduct applicable to this type of armed conflict. Why would the ICTY and the ICTR have ever even bothered to assess which norms of conduct had migrated from international to noninternational armed conflict if participation in the conflict by a nonstate actor was itself a "war crime"? The answer is clear: operating without the privilege of combatant immunity does not automatically result in *international* criminal responsibility for belligerent actions.

Because the 2006 MCA applies to both al-Qaeda and Taliban personnel, and because the U.S. government treated the armed conflict with Afghanistan as "international," it is possible that this offense was originally intended to apply only to international armed conflicts. Such a limited application would at least preserve symmetry between international benefit and international sanction. This has not, however, been confirmed by practice, or subsequent statutory or regulatory definition.[70] Instead, military prosecutors have used this offense to charge captured al-Qaeda operatives, reflecting a particularly problematic but central theory to the extension of war crimes liability to transnational armed conflict. Additionally, despite vigorous academic dispute over the validity of this charge, Congress in the 2009 MCA retained it as a listed offense.[71] The commentary to the offense of murder in violation of the law of war in both the 2010 and 2012 versions of the Manual for Military Commissions reflects the intent of the Department of Defense to uncouple this offense from its recognition under the international law of war and continue its use to try members of al-Qaeda before military commissions.[72]

---

[70] The 2009 MCA uses the term "unprivileged enemy belligerent," which includes, in part, anyone who engaged in hostilities against the United States purposively and materially supported hostilities against the United States, or who is a part of al-Qaeda at the time of the alleged offense, a change from the 2006 MCA's use of the term "unprivileged enemy combatant," which included, in part, any person who had engaged in hostilities or purposively and materially supported hostilities against the United States or its co-belligerents who is not a lawful enemy combatant "including a person who is part of the Taliban, al Qaeda, or associated forces." *Compare* 2009 MCA, *supra* note 15, § 948a(7) *with* 2006 MCA, *supra* note 8, § 948a(1).

[71] *See* 2009 MCA, *supra* note 15, § 950t(15).

[72] *See, e.g.*, U.S. Dep't of Defense, Manual for Military Commissions, IV-11, (2012), *available at* http://www.mc.mil/Portals/0/pdfs/2012ManualForMilitaryCommissions.pdf (stating the following in discussing the offenses of intentionally causing serious bodily injury, murder in violation of the law of war, destruction of property in violation of the law of war, and spying, respectively:

c. *Comment*. For purposes of offenses (13), (15), (16), and (27) in part IV of this Manual (corresponding to offenses enumerated in paragraphs(13), (15), (16), and (27) of §950t of title 10, United States Code), an accused may be convicted in a military commission for these offenses if the commission finds that the accused employed a means (e.g. poison gas) or method (e.g. perfidy) prohibited by the law of war;

In 2010, Omar Khadr pled guilty to murder in violation of the law of war for the battlefield killing of an American soldier. The plea was made pursuant to a pretrial agreement limiting his sentence and incorporating a requirement that he would be repatriated to Canada to serve any portion of his sentence in excess of one year.[73] As discussed, the offense to which Khadr pled guilty does not exist under international law, specifically the LOAC, and although it could be prosecuted under the appropriate domestic criminal law, its prosecution in a military tribunal is subject to considerable controversy. Subsequent appeals attempts by Khadr are discussed infra in note 99.

Perhaps even more problematic is the designation as a war crime of "material support for terrorism," another offense central to the U.S. military trial of captured terrorist operatives. Unlike murder in violation of the law of war, there is not even an international armed conflict precedent for this offense. Instead, including material support for terrorism (and other terrorism offenses) within the subject-matter jurisdiction of the military commission, a tribunal that the Supreme Court recognized in its *Hamdan I* opinion exists for the sole purpose of adjudicating war crimes allegations, seems motivated by the desire to avoid bringing such cases to trial in civilian courts. Although this may be both logical and even legitimate from a national security policy perspective, it does not comport with the subject-matter limitations historically associated with military war crimes tribunals. In at least two military commission cases held in 2007

---

intentionally attacked a "protected person" or "protected property" under the law of war; or engaged in conduct traditionally triable by military commission (e.g. spying; murder committed while the accused did not meet the requirements of privileged belligerency) **even if such conduct does not violate the international law of war**) [emphasis added].

[73] In 2010, Omar Khadr pled guilty to murder in violation of the laws of war for the killing of SFC Christopher Speer by throwing a hand grenade in the aftermath of a firefight between U.S. soldiers and an al-Qaeda cell in Afghanistan of which he was a member. Although sentenced to 40 years confinement, his sentence was limited by the pretrial agreement in the case to eight years confinement. The pretrial agreement also required waiver of his appellate rights. *See* in United States v. Khadr—"Referred Charges dated 04/24/2007," AE001, *available at* http://www.mc.mil/Portals/0/pdfs/Khadr/Khadr%20(AE001).pdf); "Khadr Military Commission Approved Pretrial Agreement," dated 10/13/2010 AE341, *available at* http://www.mc.mil/Portals/0/pdfs/Khadr/Khadr%20(AE341).pdf; "U.S. and Canadian Diplomatic Notes Dated 10/23/2010," AE342, *available at* http://www.mc.mil/Portals/0/pdfs/Khadr/Khadr%20(AE342).pdf; and "Panel Members Sentencing Worksheet," dated 10/30/2010, AE380, *available at* http://www.mc.mil/Portals/0/pdfs/Khadr/Khadr%20(AE380).pdf. Documents for his trial *available at* http://www.mc.mil/CASES.aspx. In addition to the controversy over the charge of murder in violation of the law of war, the prosecution of Omar Khadr incited additional challenges as he was estimated to be 15 at the time of the offense. The UCMJ does not include minimum age requirements for its jurisdiction, largely because the enlistment requirements largely comport with the age of majority. This area was not addressed in either version of the Military Commissions Act, and remains a source of international condemnation. *See* Statement by UNICEF Executive Director, Anthony Lake, on the case of Guantanamo Bay detainee, Omar Khadr, May 26, 2010, http://www.unicef.org/lac/media_17960.htm; Warren Richey, *"Child Soldier" Pleads Guilty at Guantanamo, Averting a Trial*, CHRISTIAN SCI. MONITOR, Oct. 25, 2010, *available at* http://www.csmonitor.com/USA/Justice/2010/1025/Child-soldier-pleads-guilty-at-Guantanamo-averting-a-trial.

and 2010, defendants have pled guilty to charges of material support and conspiracy to provide material support pursuant to pretrial agreements in their cases.[74] Because these pretrial agreements contained waivers of appellate review, the legitimacy of these charges were not reviewed by either the Court of Military Commissions Review or the U.S. Court of Appeals for the D.C. Circuit. In 2012, in a review of Salim Hamdan's ultimate conviction by military commission, however, the D.C. Circuit held that material support for terrorism was not a war crime under the international law of war at the time of Hamdan's conduct. Both Hicks and Khadr have subsequently filed appeals based on *Hamdan II* contesting their convictions.

The inclusion of inchoate conspiracy as a charge before the military commissions is equally problematic.[75] In *Hamdan I*, Justice Stevens, writing for a plurality, concluded

---

[74] *See* in United States v. David Hicks—"Referred Charges," dated 3/1/2007 (AE002), *available at* http://www. mc.mil/Portals/0/pdfs/Hicks/Hicks%20(AE002).pdf; "Offer of a Pretrial Agreement and Appendix A to Offer of a Pretrial Agreement," dated 3/26/2007 (AE027), *available at* http://www.mc.mil/Portals/0/pdfs/ Hicks/Hicks%20(AE027).pdf, "U.S. v. Hicks Military Commission Sentence Worksheet (Filled Out by Members)," dated 3/30/2007 (AE026), *available at* http://www.mc.mil/Portals/0/pdfs/Hicks/Hicks%20 (AE026).pdf; and in United States v. Al-Qosi,—"Referred Charges," dated 1/8/2009 (AE031), *available at* http://www.mc.mil/Portals/0/pdfs/alQosi/Al%20Qosi%20(AE031).pdf; "Pre-Trial Agreement (Sealed)," dated 6/14/2010 (AE089), *available at* http://www.mc.mil/Portals/0/pdfs/alQosi/Sealed.pdf; "Appendix A (Sealed)," dated 6/14/2010 (AE090), *available at* http://www.mc.mil/Portals/0/pdfs/alQosi/Sealed. pdf; "Stipulation of Fact," dated 7/7/2010 (PE1), *available at* http://www.mc.mil/Portals/0/pdfs/alQosi/ Al%20Qosi%20(PE1).pdf; "Official Authenticated Transcript, Pages 303–619" dated 9/29/2010, *available at* http://www.mc.mil/Portals/0/pdfs/alQosi/Al%20Qosi%20(Transcript%20Pages%20303-619). pdf (pretrial agreement includes waiver of appellate rights and collateral attack); "Sentencing Worksheet," dated 8/9/2010 (AE110), *available at* http://www.mc.mil/Portals/0/pdfs/alQosi/Al%20Qosi%20(AE110). pdf). More case information *available at* http://www.mc.mil/CASES.aspx. Australian observers of the Hicks trial were highly critical of the proceedings, calling it "shambolic" and "a charade." *See* Lex Lasry, *Summary of the Report of the Independent Observer for the Law Council of Australia*, July 24, 2007, *available at* http://australiansall.com.au/archive/post/david-hicks-v-the-united-states/. Additionally, upon his return to Australia, David Hicks, in violation of his plea agreement, wrote a tell-all book on his detention and trial at Guantanamo Bay, entitled My Journey. The Australian government was unsuccessful in its attempt to enforce the "Son-of-Sam" provision of Hicks's plea agreement. *See* Louise Hall & Paul Bibby, *David Hicks to Keep All Profits from Guantanamo Tell-All Book*, Sydney Morning Herald, July 24, 2012, *available at* http://www.smh.com.au/national/david-hicks-to-keep-all-profits-from-tellall-gua ntanamo-book-20120724-22lq2.html. Al-Qosi, a Sudanese al-Qaeda member, pled guilty in his 2010 military commission trial to conspiracy and providing material support to terrorism. He received as sentence of 14 years confinement, with the portion above two years suspended in accordance with his plea agreement. Two years later, in 2012, he was transferred to Sudan. *See* Carol Rosenberg, *Convicted al Qaida Operative Released from Guantánamo, Repatriated to Sudan in Plea Deal*, Miami Herald, July 10, 2012, *available at* http://www.miamiherald.com/2012/07/10/2890308/convicted-al-qaida-operative-released.html.

[75] *See* MCI 2, *supra* note 3, § 6(C)(6) (the elements of the conspiracy charge included in MCI No. 2 are that:

> (1) The accused entered into an agreement with one or more persons to commit one or more substantive offenses triable by military commission or otherwise joined an enterprise of persons who shared a common criminal purpose that involved, at least in part, the commission or intended commission of one or more substantive commissions triable by military commission; (2) the accused knew the

that conspiracy did not historically constitute an offense against the law of war.[76] In Justice Stevens's view, absent congressional identification of conspiracy as an "Offence[] against the Law of Nations," the precedent for such an offense in the law of war must be "plain and unambiguous."[77] Such an exacting standard was required, according to the plurality, to avoid "concentrating in military hands a degree of adjudicative and punitive power in excess of that contemplated either by statute or by the Constitution."[78] In coming to his conclusion that the charge of conspiracy was not supported by such precedent,

---

unlawful purpose of the agreement, or the common criminal purpose of the enterprise and joined it willfully, that is, with the intent to further the unlawful purpose; and (3) One of the conspirators or enterprise members, during the existence of the agreement or enterprise, knowingly committed an overt act in order to accomplish some objective or purpose of the agreement or enterprise).

[76] *Hamdan I, supra* note 13, at 600, 611. *See also id.* at 599–602. Relying on the authoritative treatise, MILITARY LAW AND PRECEDENTS, by Col. William Winthrop, "the Blackstone of Military Law" [hereinafter WINTHROP], Justice Stevens outlined four preconditions for the exercise of jurisdiction of a law of war military commission of the type convened to try Hamdan. In relevant part, these preconditions are: (1) the offense must be committed within the field of command of the convening commander, which he equated to the "theater of war" (place restriction); (2) the offense charged must have been committed within the period of war and the military commission could not try offenses committed either before or after the war (time restriction); (3) the law-of-war tribunal may only try "individuals of the enemy's army who have been guilty of illegitimate warfare or other offences in violation of the law of war . . ."; and (4) the tribunal may try only "[v]iolations of the laws and usages of war cognizable by military tribunals only." *Id.* at 597–98. By categorizing these preconditions as the necessary jurisdictional elements to ensure that "a military necessity exists to justify the use of this extraordinary tribunal," *id.* at 598, Justice Stevens raised questions on the time and place requirements of the jurisdictional test for Hamdan, but he focused the inquiry on the validity of the charge of conspiracy under the laws of war.

Another military commissions defendant, Abd al-Rahim Hussein Muhammed Abdu Al-Nashiri, the alleged mastermind of the attempted bombing of the USS *The Sullivans*, and the bombing of the USS *Cole*, has challenged the jurisdiction of his trial by military commission, both at trial and by collateral attack, contending that the alleged offenses were not committed during time of war. *See* Al-Nashiri v. MacDonald, 2012 WL 1642306 (W.D. Wash. May 10, 2012) [hereinafter Al-Nashiri], 2013 WL 6698066 (9th Cir. Dec. 20, 2013)(affirming dismissal). Al-Nashiri has raised these claims anew in a habeas challenge to his commission trial, discussed *infra* in note 132.

[77] *Hamdan I, supra* note 13, at 601–02 ("There is no suggestion that Congress has, in exercise of its constitutional authority to 'define and punish . . . Offences against the Law of Nations,' U.S. Const., Art. I, § 8, cl. 10, positively identified 'conspiracy' as a war crime. As we explained in *Quirin,* that is not necessarily fatal to the Government's claim of authority to try the alleged offense by military commission; Congress, through Article 21 of the UCMJ, has 'incorporated by reference' the common law of war, which may render triable by military commission certain offenses not defined by statute. *When, however, neither the elements of the offense nor the range of permissible punishments is defined by statute or treaty,* the precedent must be plain and unambiguous.") (emphasis added) (internal citations omitted). In this quote the Court also referred specifically to other statutory authorities that either allowed trial by military tribunal or defined "war crimes," strengthening the inference that such a congressional determination would be due more deference than the unilateral presidential determination that was the basis of the charge in *Hamdan. See Hamdan I, supra* note 13, at 602 n.33 ("Cf. 10 U.S.C. § 904 (making triable by military commission the crime of aiding the enemy); § 906 (same for spying); War Crimes Act of 1996, 18 U.S.C. § 2441 (2000 ed. and Supp. III) (listing war crimes); Foreign Operations, Export Financing, and Related Programs Appropriations Act, 1998, § 583, 111 Stat. 2436 (same).")

[78] *Id.* at 602.

Justice Stevens examined traditional sources of customary international law such as historical military commissions proceedings, relevant international treaties, and authoritative treatises[79] to determine if "[a]t a minimum, the Government [made] a substantial showing that the crime for which it seeks to try a defendant by military commission is acknowledged to be an offense against the law of war."[80] Although vehemently contested by Justice Thomas in dissent, Justice Stevens, in a portion of the opinion joined by three other justices, concluded that the charge of conspiracy was not supported by such clear precedent. Justice Breyer, however, in his separate concurrence, suggested that the president could return to Congress to seek the authorizations determined to be lacking in the UCMJ.[81]

President Bush did exactly that. Despite the plurality's conclusion that conspiracy did not historically constitute a war crime under the law of war, Congress included specific proscriptions against conspiracy and material support for terrorism in the 2006 MCA among 28 substantive offenses triable by military commission.[82] In enacting the 2006 MCA, Congress indicated that its provisions codified only offenses that had traditionally been triable by military commissions, and did not establish new crimes,[83] indicating, at least in the view of Congress, that conspiracy and material support for terrorism did constitute preexisting offenses under the laws of war.[84] Such a conclusion, however, is subject to considerable controversy under international law.

---

[79] *Id.* at 603–04.

[80] *Id.* at 608. (quoting *Ex parte* Quirin, 317 U.S. 1, 30 (1942) for the proposition that an offense triable by military commission need not be defined by statute. Justice Stevens, indicated that "[w]hen, however, neither the elements of the offense nor the range of permissible punishments is defined by statute or treaty, the precedent must be plain and unambiguous.").

[81] *Id.* at 636.

[82] 2006 MCA, *supra* note 8, § 950v(b)(28) (2006) ("Any person subject to this chapter who conspires to commit one or more substantive offenses triable by military commission under this chapter, and who knowingly does any overt act to effect the object of the conspiracy, shall be punished, if death results to one or more of the victims, by death or such other punishment as a military commission under this chapter may direct, and, if death does not result to any of the victims, by such punishment, other than death, as a military commission under this chapter may direct."). The 2007 Manual for Military Commissions listed the elements of the offense as:

> (1) The accused entered into an agreement with one or more persons to commit one or more substantive offenses triable by military commission or otherwise joined an enterprise of persons who shared a common criminal purpose that involved, at least in part, the commission or intended commission of one or more substantive offenses triable by military commission; (2) The accused knew the unlawful purpose of the agreement or the common criminal purpose of the enterprise and joined willfully, that is, with the intent to further the unlawful purpose; and (3) The accused knowingly committed an overt act in order to accomplish some objective or purpose of the agreement or enterprise.

2007 Manual, *supra* note 66, IV-20 to IV-21. *See also* 2006 MCA, *supra* note 8, § 950v(b)(25) (material support for terrorism).

[83] 2006 MCA, *supra* note 8, § 950p(a).

[84] *Id.* §§ 950v(b)(25) & 950v(b)(28). Both offenses were also included in the 2009 MCA. 2009 MCA, *supra* note 15, §§ 950t(25) & 950t(29).

In his military commission trial initiated under the new procedural provisions of the 2006 MCA, Hamdan asserted that because both conspiracy and material support were not violations of customary international law, the military commissions still lacked jurisdiction to try him.[85] Osama bin Laden's propagandist, Ali Hamza Abdul Suliman al-Bahlul, made substantially the same arguments in the appeal of his commission trial.[86] Earlier military commissions, reinitiated after the passage of the 2006 MCA, relied heavily on charges of material support for terrorism and conspiracy, but because these trials involved guilty pleas that required waiver of appellate rights, appellate evaluation of the validity of inchoate conspiracy and material support as charges was delayed until appeal in Hamdan's and al-Bahlul's proceedings.[87] Although challenges to the legitimacy of these charges under the international law of war were brought to the attention of Congress during its consideration of amendments to the MCA, in passing the 2009 MCA Congress retained murder in violation of the law of war, material support for terrorism, and conspiracy as specified charges under the 2009 MCA.[88]

Recall that in order to qualify as a war crime, the acts or omissions that constitute the offense must violate *international* law, or more specifically the law of war ("LOAC"). Even prior to the 2006 MCA, article 21 of the UCMJ[89] recognized that military commissions had jurisdiction over violations of the "law of war." As the D.C. Circuit has instructed, the law of war referenced in article 21 is the international law of war.[90]

Arguably, Congress could prospectively include other statutory offenses in the jurisdiction of military commissions, similar to the long-standing statutory authorizations to try espionage or aiding and abetting the enemy in military commissions. However, military commission jurisdiction over murder in violation of the law of war, material support for terrorism, and conspiracy were only specifically authorized by statute in the 2006 MCA. Although the prospective effect of this statutory authorization can be challenged as beyond the scope traditionally allowed under international law of war for military commissions, it has been argued that its domestic effect can be upheld as a valid exercise of congressional and presidential war powers, in much the same way that espionage and aiding and abetting the enemy charges have been upheld.[91]

---

[85] *See Hamdan II, supra* note 8, at 1244.

[86] *See* Petitioner's Brief, Al-Bahlul v. United States, 2012 WL 761316 (D.C. Cir. Mar. 9, 2012).

[87] *See* trial record of United States v. Hicks and United States v. al-Qosi, *available at* http://www.mc.mil/CASES.aspx.

[88] *See* 2009 MCA, *supra* note 15, §§ 950t(15), 950t(25) & 950t(29).

[89] UCMJ, *supra* note 37, § 821. Military commissions could also try charges of espionage and aiding the enemy under specific long-standing statutory authorization contained in the UCMJ. *Id.* §§ 902, 904.

[90] *See Hamdan II, supra* note 8, at 1241 (citing *Ex parte* Quirin, 317 U.S. 1, 27–30, 35–36); *see also Al-Bahlul, supra* note 8 (because the *en banc* decision did not decide the question of what body of law section 821 refers to, or overrule that portion of the *Hamdan II* decision, *Hamdan II*'s holding that "law of war" as used in § 821 was a term of art that meant the international law of war remains undisturbed, although weakened).

[91] Challenges to both these offenses have had little success in appeals to the U.S. Court of Military Commissions Appeals. Unsurprisingly, the judges on that court concluded that great deference was

However, charges based on conduct that predated the passage of the 2006 MCA, such as those brought against Hamdan and Al-Bahlul, are subject to challenge under the Ex Post Facto Clause (U.S. Const. art. I § 9, cl. 3), which prohibits Congress from passing laws, particularly criminal laws, with retroactive effect. Reflecting the international principle of legality, this prohibition has been categorized as "ancient as the law itself."[92] Included within common article 3's basic protections, applicable under *Hamdan I* to military commissions, this principle has been recognized by the International Committee of the Red Cross as customary international law applicable to all armed conflicts:

> Rule 101. No one may be accused or convicted of a criminal offence on account of any act or omission which did not constitute a criminal offense under national or international law at the time it was committed; nor may a heavier penalty be imposed than that which was applicable at the time the criminal offence was committed.[93]

After concluding in *Hamdan v. United States* [*Hamdan II*][94] that Congress did not intend the 2006 MCA to have retrospective effect,[95] and thus avoiding the "serious" Ex Post

---

due Congress's decision to include an offense within the Commission's jurisdiction, at its apogee when Congress was exercising its war powers, and acting in concert with the executive, and that the exercise of jurisdiction for these offenses was therefore valid. *See* United States v. Hamdan, 801 F. Supp. 2d 1247, 1264–70 (U.S. Ct. Mil. Comm'n Rev. 2011) *rev'd Hamdan II, supra* note 8, at 1241; United States v. Al-Bahlul, 820 F. Supp. 2d 1141, 1172 (U.S. Ct. Mil. Comm'n Rev. 2011) (applying *Hamdan's* substantial showing requirement, but granting great deference to Congress's specific statutory scheme, to include name of the offense, elements, forum, and applicable rules/procedures, if Congress's determination that certain acts constitute offenses under the law of nations is consistent with international law), *vacated* Al-Bahlul v. United States, 2013 WL 297726 (D.C. Cir. Jan. 25, 2013). *See also Hamdan II, supra* note 8, at 1246 (outlining U.S. position that congressional authority to define military commission's jurisdiction can be supported under Congress's Article I war powers, which are not constrained by international law) and 1247 n.6 (in which Judge Kavanaugh alone "would conclude that Congress has authority under Article I, § 8 to establish material support for terrorism as a war crime that, when committed by an alien, may be tried by military commission." For Judge Kavanaugh, these independent authorities would, because they are not limited by international law, allow the United States to be a leader in the development of international law, "not just a follower."); *see also Al-Bahlul, supra* note 8, at *64 (Kavanaugh, J., concurring in the judgment in part and dissenting in part)(same).

92 Dash v. Van Kleeck, 7 Johns. 477, 503 (N.Y. 1811) (Kent, C.J.) ("It is a principle in the English common law, as ancient as the law itself, that a statute, even of its omnipotent parliament, is not to have a retrospective effect."); *see also Al-Bahlul, supra* note 8, at *40 (Rogers, J., concurring in the judgment in part and dissenting) ("*Ex post facto* laws are 'contrary to the great first principles of the social compact,' Calder, 3 Dall. at 388 (opinion of Chase, J.), and are 'condemned by the universal sentence of civilized man' as 'oppressive, unjust, and tyrannical,' Ogden v. Saunders, 25 U.S. 213 266 (1827).").

93 CUSTOMARY LAW STUDY, *supra* note 58, RULE 101 at 371–72 (reflecting fundamental principles of *nullum crimen sine lege* and *nulla poena sine lege* (no crime without law, and no punishment without law)).

94 *Hamdan II, supra* note 8.

95 The D.C. Circuit emphasized that its retroactivity conclusion was based on the statutory interpretation of the MCA, not on any constitutional restrictions on congressional power. *See Hamdan II, supra* note 8, at 1241, 1246 ("consistent with Congress's stated intent and so as to avoid a serious Ex Post Facto Clause

Facto issue, the D.C. Circuit analyzed Hamdan's material support for terrorism convictions with this constraint in mind. In *Al-Bahlul v. United States*, the D.C. Circuit, sitting *en banc*, overruled this determination, deciding Congress in passing the 2006 MCA unambiguously intended to legislate retroactively. Nevertheless the court came to the same ultimate conclusion. The *en banc* court determined that to survive an ex post facto challenge, the charged crime had to have existed prior to the 2006 MCA.[96]

In *Hamdan II*, the court concluded that congressional ability to "codify" existing law of war crimes, and thereby avoid a serious ex post facto issue, depended on the war crimes' prior existence under the international law of war,[97] incorporated by article 21 of the UCMJ, the only statute recognizing the existence of military commissions at the time of Hamdan's alleged criminal conduct from 1996 to 2001.[98] Finding no support for material support for terrorism as an international war crime in relevant international treaties, customary international law as evidenced by treaties creating international criminal tribunals, international criminal tribunal jurisprudence, or commentaries on international law, the court vacated Hamdan's convictions for that offense.[99]

---

issue, we interpret the Military Commissions Act of 2006 not to authorize *retroactive* prosecution of **crimes** that were not prohibited as **war crimes** triable by military commission under U.S. law at the time the conduct occurred") (emphasis added). *See also* 2006 MCA, *supra* note 8, § 950p ("(a) Purpose—The provisions of this subchapter codify offenses that have traditionally been triable by military commissions. This chapter does not establish new crimes that did not exist before its enactment, but rather codifies those crimes for trial by military commission. (b) Effect—Because the provisions of this subchapter (including provisions that incorporate definitions in other provisions of law) are declarative of existing law, they do not preclude trial for crimes that occurred before the date of the enactment of this chapter."); 2009 MCA, *supra* note 15, § 950p(d) ("Because the provisions of this subchapter codify offenses that have traditionally been triable under the law of war or otherwise triable by military commission, this subchapter does not preclude trial for offenses that occurred before the date of the enactment of this subchapter, as so amended.")

[96] *Al-Bahlul, supra* note 8, at *5–*8 (overruling *Hamdan II*'s statutory holding that the 2006 MCA did not apply retroactively).

[97] *Hamdan II, supra* note 8, at 1241 (citing *Ex parte* Quirin, 317 U.S. 1, 27–30, 35–36) and 1246 (citing *Hamdan I, supra* note 13, at 602, 610 and *Quirin*).

[98] *Hamdan II, supra* note 8, at 1248 ("[W]e interpret the Military Commissions Act of 2006 so that it does not authorize *retroactive* prosecution for conduct committed before enactment of that Act unless the conduct was already prohibited under existing U.S. law as a war crime triable by military commission. In this case, therefore, Hamdan's conviction stands or falls on whether his conduct was prohibited by the pre-existing statute, 10 U.S.C. § 821, at the time he committed the conduct.")

[99] *Hamdan II, supra* note 8, at 1251–52; *see also Al-Bahlul, supra* note 8, at *18–*20 (no pre-2006 material support for terrorism offense applicable to Al-Bahlul's conduct.) Same for solicitation. *Id.* at *20–*21. Both Omar Khadr and David Hicks filed appeals of their convictions with the Court of Military Commission Review in late 2013 based on the D.C. Circuit's decision and reasoning in *Hamdan II*. In these appeals, both Khadr and Hicks argue that material support for terrorism, under *Hamdan II*, is not an international war crime, and as such is not a valid charge before the Military Commission. Khadr also argues that murder in violation of the law of war and spying are likewise not international war crimes. Both Khadr and Hicks argue that because their appeals attack the jurisdiction of the military commissions that tried them, any appeal waiver is invalid. Both of these appeals were stayed by the court pending the D.C. Circuit's *en banc* decision in *United States v. Al-Bahlul. See* Posting of Marty Lederman, The Khadr Appeal [UPDATE: and

In coming to this conclusion, the D.C. Circuit rejected the government's contention that U.S. Civil War military commission precedents created a U.S. "common law of war" that supported the existence of both the offense of material support for terrorism and its amenability to trial by military commission prior to 2006.[100] The court also rejected the U.S. government's contention that aiding and abetting an international war crime is a recognized war crime akin to material support for terrorism.

In its decision, the court restricted the U.S. government to the actual offense charged, rather than to offenses arguably encompassed by the charged conduct.[101] This highlights one of the recurring issues in evaluating congressional definition of international war crimes under the MCA—what is the scope of the search for analogous international war crimes? Should it be formalistic or functional?[102] The formalistic approach focuses on the existence

---

the Hicks Appeal], Just Security Blog (Nov. 11, 2013), *available at* http://justsecurity.org/3088/khadr-appeal/ (last visited July 4, 2014) (the blog entry contains links to the appellate briefs that are not, as of July 17, 2014, available on the military commissions website). *See also* www.mc.mil. On June 30, 2014, Khadr filed a subsequent motion seeking immediate determination of his appeal based upon a memorandum written by the Department of Justice's Office of Legal Counsel (OLC), in which the OLC rejected the view that "any hostile acts performed by unprivileged belligerents are *for that reason* violations of the laws of war." This U.S. government position, Khadr argued, undermines the basis for his conviction for murder in violation of the laws of war. *See* Motion to Lift Stay of Proceedings and Vacate Appellant's Convictions, June 30, 2014, in *United States v. Omar Khadr*, CMCR Case No. 13-005, *available at* http://www.lawfareblog.com/wp-content/uploads/2014/07/US-v-Khadr-Motion-to-Lift-Stay-June-30-2014.pdf (citing to the United States Office of Legal Counsel Memorandum, *Re: Applicability of Federal Criminal Laws and the Constitution to Contemplated Lethal Operations Against Shaykh Anwar al-Aulaqi* (July 16, 2010), at 33, n.44, *available at* http://www.lawfareblog.com/wp-content/uploads/2014/06/6-23-14_Drone_Memo-Alone.pdf) (last visited on July 5, 2014)).

[100] The U.S. government raised and expanded this U.S. common law of war argument in its appeal of the D.C. Circuit's order vacating al Bahlul's conviction for conspiracy to commit a violation of the law of war. Brief for the United States, *Al Bahlul v. United States*, 2013 WL 3479237 (D.C. Cir. July 10, 2013). The majority in that case declined to decide the issue, holding that its unsettled state made the answer to the question "not obvious" such that Al-Bahlul's conspiracy convictions could be sustained on plain error review. *See Al-Bahlul, supra* note 8, at *14–*17.

[101] *Hamdan II, supra* note 8, at 1252 ("But Hamdan was not charged with aiding and abetting terrorism or some other similar war crime. He was charged with material support for terrorism. And as the Government acknowledges, aiding and abetting terrorism prohibits different conduct, imposes different mens rea requirements, and entails different causation standards than material support for terrorism. If the Government wanted to charge Hamdan with aiding and abetting terrorism or some other war crime that was sufficiently rooted in the international law of war (and thus covered by 10 U.S.C. § 821) at the time of Hamdan's conduct, it should have done so."); *see also* CUSTOMARY LAW STUDY, *supra* note 58, at 372 (2005) (Interpretation to Rule 101, stating that "criminal law must not be extensively construed to an accused's detriment, for instance by analogy...").

[102] Although the due process concerns over any variance between the offense charged and the offense upheld as extant in the international law of war limit an appellate court's retrospective analysis of the offense under international law, prospective tailoring of MCA offenses by the government to match those recognized under the international law of war would not pose similar concerns. Thus, rather than charging material support to terrorism, the government could appropriately charge aiding and abetting the commission of a war crime, or could tailor a conspiracy charge to include only conspiracy as a mode of liability for a completed war crime, similar to internationally recognized joint criminal enterprise liability. *See also*

of the exactly labeled offense in the international law of war,[103] an approach similar to that taken by the D.C. Circuit in *Hamdan II*. Alternatively, a principled approach using "a functional nexus entail[ing] an analogy between the underlying *conduct at issue* in past proceedings and the *conduct alleged* in current trials"[104] could legitimately form the basis for a congressional determination of the existence of an offense under the international law of war, a conclusion due deference by reviewing courts. Because the legitimacy of military tribunals rests on the existence of a war crime under international law, the principled tracing of the conduct at issue to the conduct tried in past international law of war tribunals more appropriately recognizes and defers to Congress's role in "defining" such offenses.[105]

Although the D.C. Circuit in *Hamdan II* focused on the differing elements of proof for material support for terrorism and aiding and abetting (an analogous crime), rather than the label or even the similarity of an offense under international law, the court's conclusion that material support was not an international law war crime from 1996 to 2001 at the time of Hamdan's conduct was unquestionably correct.

Evaluation of al-Bahlul's appeal of his conspiracy convictions is more complicated. The U.S. government has defended al-Bahlul's convictions for conspiracy by supporting the existence of inchoate conspiracy under the U.S. common law of war, a theory that has little support in *Quirin* or the Supreme Court's *Hamdan I* decision. Although Hamdan prevailed in his appeal in *Hamdan II* because of the lack of support for material support for terrorism as an offense under the international law of war, conspiracy has a more complicated history in past international criminal tribunal practice. The theory of joint criminal enterprise (JCE), forming at least a potential basis to appropriately charge a conspiracy-like offense,[106] existed in the international law of war during the applicable time prior to the enactment of the 2006 MCA.

Al-Bahlul, supra note 8, at *44–*52 (Brown, J., concurring in the judgment in part and dissenting in part) (extensive discussion of parameters of the Define and Punish power, arguing for "tremendous deference" to Congress's determinations).

[103] Peter Margulies, *Defining, Punishing, and Membership in the Community of Nations: Material Support and Conspiracy Charges in Military Commissions*, 36 FORDHAM INT'L L.J. 1, 66–67 (2013) [hereinafter Margulies].

[104] *Id.* at 9; *see also Al-Bahlul, supra* note 8, at *50–*51 (Brown, J. concurring in the judgment in part and dissenting in part).

[105] Margulies, *supra* note 103, at 72–77. It also comports with the principle of legality, as development of international criminal law is allowed, but is limited to changes that are foreseeable. *See* CUSTOMARY LAW STUDY, *supra* note 58, at 372 ("[T]he principle of legality allows courts to gradually clarify the rules of criminal liability through judicial interpretation from case to case, 'provided that the resultant development is consistent with the essence of the offense and could reasonably be foreseen.'"); *but see Al-Bahlul, supra* note 8, at *45–*52 (Brown, J., concurring in the judgment in part and dissenting in part) (extensive discussion of Define and Punish power subject only "to the limits which restrain any regime premised on natural law and dedicated to the protection of natural rights").

[106] Margulies, *supra* note 103, at 86–87. If the conspiracy offense is charged with sufficient specificity to allege a violation of a JCE to commit a substantive offense, such an offense would exist under the international law of armed conflict applicable to NIACs.

Although the 2006 MCA includes inchoate conspiracy[107] as an offense against the law of war, inchoate conspiracy is generally not recognized as an international war crime. Prosecutors at the International Military Tribunal at Nuremburg, the International Military Tribunal for the Far East, and the national criminal tribunals under the World War II allies' Control Council Law No. 10 refused to treat conspiracy as "a discrete substantive offense"[108] under the law of war, with the only exception being conspiracy to commit a crime against peace. Recent international criminal tribunals created to address war crimes in the context of NIACs, such as the ICTY and the ICTR, have also rejected inchoate conspiracy for war crimes or crimes against humanity. Finally, the Rome Statute, creating the International Criminal Court in 1998, also refused to adopt conspiracy as a war crime.[109] Only conspiracy to commit genocide has been recognized as an international crime.

Both the ICTY and ICTR have recognized JCE as a theory of liability, however, in the context of both an international armed conflict and a NIAC. JCE establishes criminal liability when a substantive war crime is committed pursuant to a common plan or scheme with a shared criminal intent.[110] Some have argued that the specifics of the conspiracy charge against al-Bahlul (i.e., the specific conduct charged and found by the military commission panel) is equivalent to JCE for the substantive war crimes listed in his charge sheet, despite its being charged under the label of inchoate conspiracy as defined in the 2006 MCA.[111] A core issue is the meaning of 10 U.S. Code section 821, which refers

---

[107] Inchoate conspiracy is unique to Anglo-American law, and criminalizes the agreement to commit a crime, requiring no completed act for a conviction.

[108] See Brief of Amici Curiae International Law Scholars in Support of Petitioner on *En Banc* Review at 8, Al Bahlul v. United States, 2013 WL 2484580, No. 11-1324 (D.C. Cir. June 10, 2013) [hereinafter International Law Scholars Amicus Brief].

[109] The United States had a significant role in developing the list of war crimes in the Rome Statute. *See* PROPOSALS FOR REFORM OF THE MILITARY COMMISSION SYSTEM, Hearing Before the H. Subcomm. on the Constitution, Civil Rights, and Civil Liberties, of the H. Comm on the Judiciary, 111th Cong. 103 (2009) (prepared statement of David J.R. Frakt).

[110] Under this theory, an individual is guilty of participation in a JCE if he intentionally aids a common plan that results in a completed war crime. International tribunals have recognized that conspiracy as a mode of liability for a completed war crime precisely tracks the elements of JCE. *See* International Law Scholars Amicus Brief, *supra* note 108, at 6.

[111] Under this argument, the conviction can be sustained so long as any errors in the sentencing instructions were harmless and did not affect al-Bahlul's substantive rights. *See id.* at 6 (citing Tadic Appeals Chamber Judgment, *supra* note 30, at paras. 196, 199; and Prosecutor v. Brdanin, Case No. IT-99-36A, Judgment, at paras. 404, 410 (Appeals Chamber, Int'l Crim. Trib for the Former Yugoslavia Apr. 3, 2007)); Margulies, *supra* note 103, at 86–87; *but see* Alexandra Link, Note, *Trying Terrorism: Joint Criminal Enterprise, Material Support, and the Paradox of International Criminal Law*, 34 MICH. J. INT'L L. 439 (2013) (questioning persuasive authority of ICTY's JCE analysis). *See also* International Law Scholars Amicus Brief, *supra* note 108, at 6 (A comparison of the conduct charged in al-Bahlul's charge sheet and the military commission's factual findings could form the basis of sustaining his convictions under a functional approach should the appeals court determine that the charged conduct does amount to a violation of the international law of war. At least in theory, a court of appeals could uphold his convictions under JCE for

to "offenses that by statute or the law of war may be tried by military commissions", with the question being whether the phrase "law of war" refers to the international law of war (i.e., the LOAC) or a variant of the law of war developed under domestic U.S. common law and practice. Rather than provide guidance on which body of law is applicable, the D.C. Circuit, in a recent *en banc* decision, acknowledged both views on the law referenced by section 821 and, although upholding al-Bahlul's conspiracy conviction under a "plain error" review,[112] did not definitively decide the issue of which law is applicable in the 2006 MCA.[113]

Several issues remain unresolved, and remain unanswered in the *en banc* decision, as they are not relevant to al-Bahlul's case. One such issue, whether conspiracy as a form of liability, which has a long history in the international law of war, can form the basis for liability for other substantive offenses in the MCA is currently being litigated in Al-Nashiri's military commission.[114]

---

the substantive offenses of murder of protected persons, attacking civilian persons, and attacking civilian objects, all found by the al-Bahlul panel to have been the object of the criminal agreement between al-Bahlul and members of al-Qaeda, regardless of its labeling, so long as al-Bahlul's substantive rights are not affected by any variance between the panel's legal instructions and charging language and the substantive offenses under the law of war. Such tailoring at the appellate stage will require that the variances amount to harmless error.)

[112] *Al-Bahlul, supra* note 8, at *17. Plain error review was key to the D.C. Circuit's upholding of Al-Bahlul's conspiracy convictions, both in its evaluation of what law underlay section 821 (either the international law of war or the U.S. common law of war), and in its alternative holding that a preexisting federal statute, 18 U.S.C. section 2332(b), had already criminalized conspiracy outside the United States to kill a U.S. national. Under plain error review, the D.C. Circuit held that, as section 2332(b) encompassed Al-Bahlul's criminal conduct, the change in forum from an Article III court to a military commission effected by the 2006 MCA did not amount to a plain ex post facto violation. Under plain error review, the court also declined to decide what body of law was referred to in section 821, deciding only that the unsettled nature of the issue rendered the charging of Al-Bahlul based on the U.S. common law of war "not plain error." *Id.* at *15.

[113] Three judges on the *en banc* panel (Kavanaugh, Brown, and Rogers) expressed "serious doubts about the majority opinion's suggestion that the Ex Post Facto Clause may allow military commissions to retroactively prosecute crimes that were previously triable as federal crimes in federal court even when they were not previously triable by military commission. Can Congress, consistent with the Ex Post Facto Clause, really just pull out the federal criminal code and make offenses retroactively triable before military commissions?" Judge Kavanaugh found this suggestion to be unsupported by precedent, scholarly commentary, or legislative history. *Id.* at *67 (Kavanaugh, J., concurring in the judgment in part and dissenting in part). Additionally, with the significant procedural and evidentiary differences between Article III courts and military commissions under the 2006 MCA, this suggestion is subject to considerable dispute. *See id.* at *41 (Rogers, J. concurring in the judgment in part and dissenting).

[114] *See* United States v. Al-Nashiri—"Government Response to Defense Renewed Motion to Dismiss the Charge of Conspiracy," dated 1/25/2013 (AE048D) (in its response, the United States contends that although a stand-alone conspiracy is not an international war crime, conspiracy as a mode of liability has a long history in international law, and as such with minor conforming changes, the charge sheet will continue to provide notice to Al-Nashiri of his liability under this theory, and does not expose him to conviction for any additional offense), *available at* http://www.mc.mil/Portals/0/pdfs/alNashiri2/Al%20Nashiri%20II%20(AE048D)_Part1. pdf; http://www.mc.mil/Portals/0/pdfs/alNashiri2/Al%20Nashiri%20II%20(AE048D)_Part2.

These issues, however, highlight more fundamental legal questions over the proper jurisdiction of military commissions and congressional power. First, it is unclear what degree of deference will be given by a court to a congressional determination that a crime is "sufficiently rooted" in the international law of war to be prescribed as a codification of an existing international war crime and used to punish conduct that predates the congressional enactment—as in *Hamdan II* and *Al-Bahlul*—of the 2006 MCA. Although Congress may have the power to criminalize conduct, its power to subject an offense to trial before a military commission is limited, at least according to a plurality of the Supreme Court,[115] by the content of the law of war, as part of the law of nations. This international law of war is the source of congressional authority under the Define and Punish Clause, but to what extent is it also a constraint on its exercise? Hamdan claimed that "Congress's authority under the Define and Punish Clause is limited to proscribing offenses that are already illegal under international law."[116] But, given the evolving and uncertain nature of international law, is Congress limited to defining "Offences under the Laws of Nations" to those that have achieved universal acceptance and agreement, the standard enunciated by the Supreme Court in *Hamdan I* and *Quirin* to determine which offenses are triable before a military commission as violations of the law of war? Or does Congress have some flexibility under the Define and Punish Clause to clarify uncertain customary norms that have not yet crystalized fully by defining this conduct as a war crime? If so, what are the limits to this discretion, and what deference is to be given to such a congressional determination? Justice Stevens's plurality opinion in *Hamdan I* at least implies that a differing standard might apply to explicit congressional statutory definition of a law-of-war offense than that applied to a bare presidential assertion of that same authority, as does Justice Kennedy's concurrence in that case.[117] Nevertheless, courts still retain the responsibility to proclaim what the law is, and to do so must evaluate the same treaty and customary international law sources ostensibly

---

pdf; http://www.mc.mil/Portals/0/pdfs/alNashiri2/Al%20Nashiri%20II%20(AE048D)_Part3.pdf; http://www.mc.mil/Portals/0/pdfs/alNashiri2/Al%20Nashiri%20II%20(AE048D)_Part4.pdf; *see also* "Defense Renewed Motion to Dismiss the Charge of Conspiracy," dated 1/11/2013 (AE048C), *available at* http://www.mc.mil/Portals/0/pdfs/alNashiri2/Al%20Nashiri%20II%20(AE048C).pdf.

[115] *Hamdan I, supra* note 13, at *595–618; *but see Al-Bahlul, supra* note 8, at *45–*52 (Brown, J., concurring in the judgment in part and dissenting in part). Although Judge Brown's separate opinion in *Al-Bahlul* addressed this issue in depth, it provided no resolution. Additionally, the plain error review conducted by the D.C. Circuit cast doubt on *Hamdan II*'s determination that the law of war under section 821 was the international law of war, although it did not overrule that holding.

[116] *Hamdan II, supra* note 8, at 1246.

[117] *Hamdan I, supra* note 13, at 655 (J. Kennedy, concurring in part) ("In light of the conclusion that the military commissions at issues are unauthorized, Congress may choose to provide further guidance in this area. Congress, not the Court, is the branch in the better position to undertake the 'sensitive task of establishing a principle not inconsistent with the national interest or with international justice.'" (citations omitted))

consulted by Congress to determine the content of the international law of war, and thus the proper scope of military commission jurisdiction.

Second, in his plurality opinion in *Hamdan I,* Justice Stevens further emphasized that limitations on military commission jurisdiction were essential to ensuring constitutional limits on the accumulation of power in military hands.[118] Does the historical limitation of the jurisdiction of law-of-war commissions to offenses under the international law of war[119] pose structural constitutional constraints on Congress's power prospectively to enlarge its jurisdiction? Responding to Hamdan's claims on appeal, the U.S. government argued that his focus on the Define and Punish Clause alone was misplaced—that Congress had independent authority under "the Declare War Clause and other war clauses in Article I, as supplemented by the Necessary and Proper Clause to establish military commissions to try an enemy's war crimes,"[120] a power, the government claimed, that was not "constrained by the evolving and often difficult to discern standards of international law."[121] The D.C. Circuit, in its resolution of Hamdan's appeal, however, declined to answer this antecedent question, relying instead on its conclusion that Congress in passing the 2006 MCA, "did not authorize retroactive prosecution for conduct that was committed before the Act's enactment and was not prohibited by U.S. law at the time the conduct occurred."[122] In its revision of the Manual for Military

---

[118] *Id.* at 602 ("To demand any less [than a clear and unambiguous precedent] would be to risk concentrating in military hands a degree of adjudicative and punitive power in excess of that contemplated either by statute or by the Constitution. Cf. Loving v. United States, 517 U.S. 748, 771, 116 S. Ct. 1737, 135 L. Ed. 2d 36 (1996) (acknowledging that Congress "may not delegate the power to make laws"); Reid [v. Covert], 354 U.S. [1] at 23–24, 77 S. Ct. 1222 [1957] ('The Founders envisioned the army as a necessary institution, but one dangerous to liberty if not confined within its essential bounds'); The Federalist No. 47, p. 324 (J. Cooke ed. 1961) (J. Madison) ('The accumulation of all powers legislative, executive and judiciary in the same hands...may justly be pronounced the very definition of tyranny')."); *see also* Al-Bahlul, *supra* note 8, at *45–*52 (Brown, J., concurring in the judgment in part, dissenting in part) (The Framers placed the ability to define offenses against the laws of nations with Congress, and their determinations are subject only to limited judicial review and due "tremendous deference.").

[119] This jurisdiction also includes certain long-standing statutory offenses such as spying and aiding the enemy.

[120] *Hamdan II, supra* note 8, at 1246. The government raised the arguments in the Al-Bahlul appeal. In that case, the *en banc* court remanded the case to the original panel for an initial determination on these other issues. *See Al-Bahlul, supra* note 8, at 53 (These issues are: whether Congress exceeded its Article I, s. 8 authority by defining crimes punishable by military commission that are not offenses under the international law of war; whether Congress violated Article III by vesting military commissions with jurisdictions to try crimes that are not offenses under the international laws of war; whether his convictions violate the First Amendment; and whether the 2006 MCA discriminates against aliens in violation of the equal protection component of the Due Process Clause.)

[121] *Hamdan II, supra* note 8, at 1246.

[122] *Id.* at 1246–47; *but see id.* at 1247 n.6 (Judge Kavanaugh alone would have held that Congress's Article I war powers were not "defined or constrained by international law" arguing that the "United States may be a leader in the international community, not just a follower, when Congress authorizes war against a terrorist organization or makes crimes such as material support for terrorism war crimes triable by

Commissions in 2010, and again in 2012, the Department of Defense explicitly decoupled military commissions' jurisdiction from the international law of war for certain offenses, to include intentionally causing serious bodily injury, murder in violation of the law of war, destruction of property in violation of the law of war, and spying.

The standard of near universal acceptance and agreement enunciated in both *Hamdan I* and *Quirin* requires military commissions[123] to frame their charges within the limits of war crimes established by treaty law and customary international law. Evaluation of the legitimacy of a congressional statutory definition would likely involve a similarly rigorous inquiry. Untethering Congress's discretion from the international law of war would, however, raise considerable questions about the legitimacy of trials by military commissions under international law, and could have the perverse effect of subjecting U.S. military personnel to similarly subjective interpretations of criminal liability for military operations.[124] Such untethering also would at least raise significant separation-of-powers issues upon which our constitutional scheme depends.[125]

Finally, in *Hamdan I,* Justice Stevens, in addition to questioning the appropriateness of conspiracy as an international war crime, also raised, but did not address, several other constraints on the jurisdiction of law-of-war military commissions—those of time and place.[126] As discussed previously, military commission jurisdiction is premised on a central assumption—that the acts or omissions forming the basis for war crimes charges leveled against detainees in the "GWOT" did in fact occur within the context of a noninternational "transnational" armed conflict. Thus, the NIAC (recognized by the Supreme Court in *Hamdan I*) must exist in time and place to validate such charges. These inquiries, by their nature, become intertwined. The current theater of war is defined by the threat posed by the transnational global organized armed force we

---

military commission." (emphasis added)). The statutory holding on the retroactive effect of the 2006 MCA was explicitly overruled in *Al-Bahlul. Al-Bahlul, supra* note 8, at *5.

[123] Under article 21 of the UCMJ, *supra* note 37, § 821; *see also* article 18 of the UCMJ, *id.,* § 818 ("General courts-martial also have jurisdiction to try any person who by the law of war is subject to trial by a military tribunal and may adjudge any punishment permitted by the law of war.")

[124] *See* Brief of Amici Curiae Professors David Glazier and Gary Solis in Support of Petitioner and Reversal, Al-Bahlul v. United States, 2013 WL 2484579, No. 11-1324 (D.C. Cir. June 10, 2013).

[125] *See* Brief of National Institute of Military Justice as Amici Curiae in Support of Petitioner, Al-Bahlul v. United States, 2013 WL 894499, No. 11-1324 (D.C. Cir. Mar. 16, 2012) (arguing that the Constitution's jury trial protections pose separate limitations on military commissions' jurisdiction. *Ex parte* Quirin, 317 U.S. 1 (1942) recognized a limited exception for enemy belligerents charged with international war crimes); *see also Al-Bahlul, supra* note 8, at *37 (Rogers, J., concurring in the judgment in part, dissenting in part) (The implications for separations of powers raised by military commissions are of the "highest order.")

[126] *Hamdan I, supra* note 13, at 597–98 (citing WINTHROP, *supra* note 76; Justice Stevens's plurality decision described four preconditions for the exercise of a law-of-war commission: first, personal jurisdiction over the defendant; second, subject-matter jurisdiction over the offense; third, the offense must have been committed within the theater of war (a place restriction); and finally, "the offense charged must have been committed within the period of the war,… [n]o jurisdiction exists to try offenses committed either before or after the war.").

face—a conclusion that is not universally accepted and that may become less compelling as the intensity of the GWOT diminishes.[127] The place requirement will also become increasingly contentious as the "hot" war in Afghanistan draws down and is terminated. The termination of hostilities in Afghanistan, with its concentrated U.S. combat forces, will contribute to lessening the evidence of the intensity of the overall hostilities arguably necessary to constitute a NIAC, transnational or otherwise. Attempts to assert jurisdiction to punish offenses that occur in other geographic areas lacking the presence of U.S. armed forces, or which occurred prior to September 11th, will have to meet the time and place preconditions for the assertion of military commission jurisdiction described by the *Hamdan I* plurality.

The conclusion of hostilities has been recognized as a political question likely to draw deference from reviewing courts,[128] but the commencement of armed conflict in the GWOT is a more complicated issue. It is not clear that any "armed conflict" existed prior to the attacks of September 11th, certainly not one with the requisite intensity under international law.[129] In the MCA, recognizing the prerequisite of the existence of an "armed conflict" for the assertion of jurisdiction over war crimes under international law, Congress included the requirement that the offense "took place in the context of and was associated with hostilities," as an element of every offense listed in the MCA. In addition to being a jurisdictional requirement, because it is an element of every offense, the U.S. government bears the burden of proof on this issue. One current commission defendant, Abd al-Rahim Hussein Muhammed Abdu Al-Nashiri, accused of planning the attempted bombing of the USS *The Sullivans* in January 2000, the completed bombing of the USS *Cole* in October 2000, and the completed bombing of the French tanker L/V Limburg in October 2002, is contesting the jurisdiction of his military commission on this basis. In a collateral attack on his commission trial, attacking both the time and

---

[127] In *Tadic*, the ICTY concluded that "an armed conflict exists whenever there is a resort to armed force between States *or protracted armed violence between governmental authorities and organized armed groups or between such groups within a State.*" Tadic Jurisdiction Decision, *supra* note 28, at para. 70 (emphasis added). *See also* Kenneth Anderson, *Targeted Killing and Drone Warfare: How We Came to Debate Whether There Is a "Legal Geography of War,"* American University Washington College of Law Research Paper No. 2011-16 (2011). As a shorthand test for a NIAC, some have argued that the intensity of the fighting and the level of organization of the parties involved are what determines the existence of a NIAC. *See* Lawfareblog.com, Guest Post, Daniel Cahen, Legal Advisor to the ICRC's Regional Delegation for the United States and Canada, *Guest Post from the ICRC's Daniel Cahen Responding to My Post on Syria/LOAC, available at* http://www.lawfareblog.com/2012/07/guest-post-from-the-icrcs-daniel-cahen-responding-to-my-post-on-syrialoac/ (last visited June 25, 2014).

[128] *See* Hamdi v. Rumsfeld, 542 U.S. 507, 588 (2004); Ludecke v. Watkins, 335 U.S. 160 (1948); *see generally* MARY L. DUDZIAK, WAR TIME: AN IDEA, ITS HISTORY, ITS CONSEQUENCES (2013).

[129] Even the Military Order of November 13, 2001 includes wording that does not specifically delimit the precipitating events leading to the U.S. military response—generally referring to attacks abroad and in the United States, "in light of grave acts of terrorism, and threats of terrorism, *including* the attacks of September 11, 2001." Military Order of November 13, 2001, *supra* note 1, § 1(b) (emphasis added).

place aspects of the existence of hostilities, Al-Nashiri filed a petition in federal district court seeking a declaration that his military commission trial lacked jurisdiction because the charges against him "did not occur, as a matter of law, in the context of, and [were] not associated with hostilities."[130] In this filing, Al-Nashiri contended that no hostilities or armed conflict existed between al-Qaeda and the United States in Yemen until, at the earliest, September 2003, when the president filed a filed a War Powers Resolution report notifying Congress that "for the first time that the United States had undertaken military operations against al-Quaida (*sic*) and other international terrorists in the Horn of Africa region, including Yemen."[131] This allegation attacks both the time and place requirement for military commission jurisdiction. Concluding that Al-Nashiri could contest the military commission's jurisdiction as part of his trial, the District Court dismissed Al-Nashiri's collateral challenge for lack of jurisdiction.[132] That dismissal was upheld by the U.S. Court of Appeals for the Ninth Circuit.[133] The temporal and geographic nature of the charged offenses thus implicate not only the government's burden to prove every element of every offense, but also the jurisdiction of the military commission itself.[134] As the GWOT continues to change, increased challenges to the jurisdiction of military commissions can be expected.

Although this chapter focuses on military commissions as the means to ensure accountability for war crimes in this new transnational NIAC, the availability and viability of Article III courts to prosecute violations of the law of war *and* federal criminal statutes such as material support for terrorism and conspiracy may become more critical as the end of the long-lasting war on terrorism occurs at some point in the

---

[130] *See* Al-Nashiri, *supra* note 76 (order granting motion to dismiss for lack of jurisdiction).

[131] *Id.* at 6.

[132] *Id.* at 18 (dismissed because the court lacked jurisdiction under section 7 of the 2006 MCA, and sovereign immunity of the United States. Nothing prevented Al-Nashiri from raising his jurisdictional argument with the military commission, or appealing that issue to an Article III court consistent with the MCA.)

[133] Al-Nashiri v. MacDonald, 2013 WL 6698066 (9th Cir. Dec. 20, 2013).

Al-Nashiri has subsequently raised this issue in a habeas challenge to his ongoing military commissions trial, again contesting the validity of military commission jurisdiction based on temporal and geographic limitations to trial by military commission. See Motion for Preliminary Injunction, Document 228, in Al-Nashiri v. Obama, No: 1:08-cv-01207-RWR, Misc. No. 08-mc-442 (TFH)(D.D.C. May 1, 2014), available at http://www.lawfareblog.com/wp-content/uploads/2014/05/Motion-for-a-PIJ-April-21-2014.pdf (last visited on 28 June 28, 2014), and Aaccompanying Memorandum of Law, Document 229 in Al-Nashiri v. Obama, id. at *8, available at https://docs.google.com/file/d/0B0Q208mqTlrzbWt5cXBRT21RMWs/edit?pli=1(last visited June 28, 2014)["Every public record on the legal status of events in Yemen at that time [between 2000 and 2002, but predominantly in 2000] not only fails to show the existence of hostilities, but demonstrates the unambiguous determination by the political branches that events in Yemen were governed by the laws of peace, not the laws of war."].

[134] Although not directly raised in *Hamdan II*, the temporal aspect of military commission jurisdiction is tangentially touched on by focusing on the relevant period of Hamdan's charged conduct between 1996 and 2001. This is likely to be another constraint on military commissions' assertion of jurisdiction over conduct that occurred in the period before the attacks of September 11th and the passage of the AUMF.

future. In 2009, Ahmed Khalfan Ghailani was transferred from Guantanamo Bay to stand trial in the Southern District of New York for his role in the 1998 East Africa Embassy bombings. Although the outcome of his 2010 trial has been subject to criticism, Ghailani was sentenced to life imprisonment for his conviction for conspiring to damage or destroy U.S. property in the bombings. The outcome of the trial, which has been used to impugn the ability of Article III courts to try "terrorism" offenses, is controversial because Ghailani was acquitted of 276 counts of murder and attempted murder, largely because evidence obtained by, or as result of, torture was excluded from the trial. Protection against evidence obtained from torture, however, is not unique to Article III courts, and does not implicate their viability as a forum to try alleged war criminals. Although the Presidential Military Order of November 13, 2001 did not exclude evidence obtained by torture as long as it "had probative value to a reasonable person,"[135] subsequent legislation—the 2006 and 2009 MCAs—has resulted in statutory prohibitions similar to that applicable in federal courts and courts-martial.[136] Even prior to these statutory changes, ethical professional behavior on the part of military and civilian attorneys involved in military commissions has resulted in the inability to prosecute Guantanamo detainees because substantiated allegations of torture and cruel and inhumane treatment tainted evidence necessary to obtain convictions.[137] On at least one occasion, the Commissions Convening Authority refused to refer charges against a detainee, Mohammed al-Qahtani, the alleged 20th hijacker, because of substantiated allegations of torture.[138] Significant issues concerning torture alleged to have occurred

---

[135] Military Order of November 13, 2001, *supra* note 1, § 4(c)(3).

[136] *Compare* 2009 MCA, *supra* note 15, § 948r(a) ("Exclusion of Statements Obtain [*sic*]] by Torture or Cruel, Inhuman, or Degrading Treatment—No statement obtained by the use of torture or by cruel, inhuman, or degrading treatment (as defined by section 1003 of the Detainee Treatment Act of 2005 (42 U.S.C. 2000dd)), whether or not under color of law, shall be admissible in a military commission under this chapter, except against a person accused of torture or such treatment as evidence that the statement was made.") *with* 2006 MCA, *supra* note 8, § 948r(a)–(c) ("(a) In General.—No person shall be required to testify against himself at a proceeding of a military commission under this chapter. (b) Exclusion of Statements Obtained by Torture.—A statement obtained by use of torture shall not be admissible in a military commission under this chapter, except against a person accused of torture as evidence that the statement was made. (c) Statements Obtained before Enactment of Detainee Treatment Act of 2005,—A statement obtained before December 30, 2005 (the date of the enactment of the Defense Treatment Act of 2005) (*sic*) in which the degree of coercion is disputed may be admitted only if the military judge finds that—(1) the totality of the circumstances renders the statement reliable and possessing sufficient probative value; (2) the interests of justice would best be served by admission of the statement into evidence; and (3) the interrogation methods used to obtain the statement do not amount to cruel, inhuman, or degrading treatment prohibited by section 1003 of the Detainee Treatment Act of 2005.")

[137] *See* JESS BRAVIN, THE TERROR COURTS, ROUGH JUSTICE AT GUANTANAMO BAY (2013); David Cole, *Torture Makes Justice Impossible*, L.A. TIMES, Dec. 3, 2005, *available at* http://www.commondreams.org/views05/1203-27.htm.

[138] *See* Bob Woodward, *Guantanamo Detainee Was Tortured, Says Official Overseeing Military Trials*, WASH. POST, Jan. 14, 2009, *available at* http://www.washingtonpost.com/wp-dyn/content/article/2009/01/13/AR2009011303372.html

as part of the Central Intelligence Agency's Rendition, Detention, and Interrogation (RDI) program at black sites worldwide have permeated the ongoing military commission trials of Al-Nashiri and Khalid Sheik Mohammed and the remaining four 9/11 defendants. Thus, the result of the Ghailani federal trial should not be seen as an indictment of the ability of federal courts to try these offenses, but rather as a consequence of earlier U.S. government decisions to allow torture or cruel and inhumane treatment of detainees. If material support for terrorism and inchoate conspiracy continue to exist as the most potent charges with which to combat international terrorism, then Article III courts may be in a better position to prosecute these offenses in light of the results of *Hamdan II*. While Article III courts provide an alternative forum for the prosecution of less controversial international war crimes even while military commissions remain available, they assuredly provide the only available forum after the termination of hostilities ends the jurisdiction of military commissions, at least as to any offenses occurring after the termination of hostilities.

The transnational armed conflict chapter in the history of war crimes has only just begun to be written. In fact, only time will tell whether the experience of the military commission is a draft that will be relegated to the international law trash bin, or the initiation of a further extension of individual criminal responsibility in the realm of armed conflict. If it is to be the latter, then precision in the application of the doctrine and caution in its extension must be the defining characteristics of national invocation of this international source of criminal liability. In this regard, the U.S. experiment has been both a success and a failure, but it ultimately does suggest that the continuing trend toward characterizing the armed component of the struggle against transnational terrorism as armed conflict will require the international community to come to terms with the difficult challenges that have been confronted by the participants in the military commission process.

The discussion above of the role of Congress in defining these offenses raises one additional consideration. Congress is expressly vested by the Constitution with the authority to "define and punish…Offenses against the Law of Nations."[139] Because of this, there is a plausible argument that Congress is justified in including, within the category of war crimes, offenses that lie in the proverbial twilight zone between armed conflict and transnational terrorism. This argument certainly seems to have persuaded the military judges who have continually rejected challenges to the subject-matter jurisdiction of the commission, although it has had less success, at least as to such retrospective "definition," before the D.C. Circuit,[140] While such an exercise of constitutional authority does not, of course, automatically produce legitimacy at the international level, the reaction

---

[139] U.S. Const. art. 1, § 8, cl. 10.

[140] *See Hamdan II, supra* note 8; Al-Bahlul Vacating Order, Al-Bahlul v. United States, 2013 WL 297726 (D.C. Cir. Jan. 25, 2013) (vacating Al-Bahlul's convictions for conspiracy, solicitation, and material support for terrorism, under rationale of *Hamdan II*).

of reviewing courts and future political leaders to this trend may impact both international acceptance of this theory and its adoption in the future by other States. As a result, in spite of the intense criticism the jurisdiction of the military commission has generated, it may be the first step in a reassessment of the scope of war crimes liability in relation to terrorism. The degree of deference accorded by reviewing courts to congressional action in this area, and their choice in the formality or functionality of the test to identify analogous offenses under the international laws of war, will have long-lasting effects on the development of U.S. law in this area.

Procedural Aspects of Trial of Terrorists by Military Courts

Unlike substantive jurisdiction, discussed above, where clarity is lacking for LOAC prosecutions of transnational terrorists, procedural limitations affecting the exercise of jurisdiction are clearer. Prior to the U.S. Supreme Court's ruling in *Hamdan I*[141] and the subsequent passage of the 2006 MCA,[142] the military commissions process was insufficient to guarantee the basic necessary procedures to ensure fair trials. In fact, the Court in *Hamdan I* stated quite clearly that "[t]he procedures that the Government has decreed will govern Hamdan's trial by commission violate [fundamental guarantees]." However, in response to *Hamdan I*, Congress's passage of the 2006 MCA provides a commissions process containing the necessary procedural limitations to provide fair trials, although both the procedures and their implementation continued to draw criticism. Additional procedural protections, added with the passage of the 2009 MCA, have addressed many of these concerns. Criticism, however, continues on their implementation in ongoing military commission proceedings.

Establishing procedures that provide for a legitimate tribunal under international law is a component of the principle of humane treatment, a principle reflected in several significant treaty provisions related to punishing violations of the law of armed conflict. Common article 3 is the starting point of these treaty provisions. Among its basic protections, it prohibits "the passing of sentences and the carrying out of executions without previous judgment pronounced by a regularly constituted court affording all the judicial guarantees which are recognized by civilized peoples."[143] In *Hamdan I*, the Supreme Court embraced this standard and specifically stated, "Common Article 3, then, is applicable here and, as indicated above, requires that Hamdan be tried by a 'regularly constituted court affording all the judicial guarantees which are recognized as indispensable by civilized peoples.'"[144]

---

[141] *See Hamdan I, supra* note 13.

[142] 2006 MCA, *supra* note 8, § 948b(a).

[143] *See supra* note 42.

[144] *See Hamdan I, supra* note 13, at 631–32.

Common Article 3's "non-exclusive" enunciation of humane treatment requires only a "regularly constituted" tribunal but does not expressly clarify the elements of one. However, both Additional Protocol I and Additional Protocol II have provisions that clarify common article 3's requirement. Article 75 of Additional Protocol I was drafted for the specific purpose of supplementing the explanation of humane treatment provided in common article 3.[145] According to Article 75:

> No sentence may be passed and no penalty may be executed on a person found guilty of a penal offence related to the armed conflict except pursuant to a conviction pronounced by an impartial and regularly constituted court respecting the generally recognized principles of regular judicial procedure....[146]

Justice Stevens's plurality in the *Hamdan I* decision spoke approvingly of article 75 as a standard for further enunciation of common article 3's standard:

> Inextricably intertwined with the question of regular constitution is the evaluation of the procedures governing the tribunal and whether they afford "all the judicial guarantees which are recognized as indispensable by civilized peoples." Like the phrase "regularly constituted court," this phrase is not defined in the text of the Geneva Conventions. But it must be understood to incorporate at least the barest of those trial protections that have been recognized by customary international law. Many of these are described in Article 75 of Protocol I to the Geneva Conventions of 1949, adopted in 1977. Although the United States declined to ratify Protocol I, its objections were not to Article 75 thereof. Indeed, it appears that the Government "regards the provisions of Article 75 as an articulation of safeguards to which all persons in the hands of an enemy are entitled."[147]

Analogous language was also included in Additional Protocol II, the treaty developed to supplement the law applicable to conflicts not of an international character. According

---

[145] The ICRC Commentary to article 75 states:

> The wording of this introductory sentence is based on Common Article 3. However, Article 3 refers to a "regularly constituted court," while this paragraph uses the expression "impartial and regularly constituted court." The difference is slight, but it emphasizes the need for administering justice as impartially as possible, even in the extreme circumstances of armed conflict, when the value of human life is sometimes small. Article 3 relies on the "judicial guarantees which are recognized as indispensable by civilized peoples," while Article 75 rightly spells out these guarantees. Thus this article, and to an even greater extent, Article 6 of Additional Protocol II "(Penal prosecutions)," gives valuable indications to help explain the terms of Article 3 on guarantees.

AP COMMENTARY at 878.

[146] *See* AP I art. 75(4).

[147] *See Hamdan I, supra* note 13, at 633 (citations omitted).

to article 6 of that treaty, "[n]o sentence shall be passed and no penalty shall be executed on a person found guilty of an offence except pursuant to a conviction pronounced by a court offering the essential guarantees of independence and impartiality."[148] As with article 75 of Additional Protocol I, there is no evidence to support the conclusion that this provision was considered objectionable by the United States.

Specifically, the plurality held that the military commissions as then constituted "dispense[d] with the principles, articulated in Article 75 and indisputably part of the customary international law, that an accused must, absent disruptive conduct or consent, be present for his trial and must be privy to the evidence against him."[149] The Court was also very concerned about the wholesale disregard for evidentiary protections in the military commissions order. These failings of the military commissions were sufficient to make them violative of the international standard and an unacceptable procedural method for trying transnational terrorists for war crimes. To remedy this failing, the Supreme Court announced that the procedural requirements of a fair trial would be met by reference to the Uniform Code of Military Justice and its provisions for courts-martial. As the Court stated, "[a]t a minimum, a military commission can be 'regularly constituted' by the standards of our military justice system only if some practical need explains deviations from court-martial practice."[150] Where following such standards was impracticable, evidence to support that assertion would need to be presented.[151]

Given that guidance by the Supreme Court, the president, and Congress went to work to produce an amended tribunal process that would comport with customary international law. The result was the 2006 MCA. This Act was passed to amend the military commissions process and to overcome the problems highlighted by the Supreme Court in prior commissions. The 2006 MCA took into account many of the criticisms of the Supreme Court and established the procedures, in compliance with international law, to try those under its jurisdiction. Despite this continued improvement, criticism, particularly in the areas of admission of evidence obtained by torture, ultimately resulted in additional changes to the MCA in 2009.

In response to the Supreme Court's comment on regularly constituted courts and the UCMJ, the 2006 MCA stated: "The procedures for military commissions set forth in this chapter are based upon the procedures for trial by general courts-martial under chapter 47 of this title (Uniform Code of Military Justice)."[152] The statute further asserted "[a] military commission established under this chapter is a regularly constituted court affording all the necessary 'judicial guarantees which are recognized as indispensable

---

[148] AP II art. 6 (2).

[149] *See Hamdan I, supra* note 13, at 634.

[150] *See id.* at 632–33.

[151] *See id.* at 622–24.

[152] 2006 MCA, *supra* note 8, § 948b(c).

by civilized peoples' for purposes of common Article 3 of the Geneva Conventions."[153] Although this assertion is not necessarily accepted, particularly by those facing military commissions, and will likely be tested in the U.S. judicial process, the statement's presence in the statute makes clear that the United States accepts the standard of common article 3 as the basis for procedural fairness in the trials of transnational terrorists.

The 2006 MCA responded to the specific objections to the military commissions' process in *Hamdan I*, though again with varying acceptance by academics and practitioners. In responding to the requirement that the accused be present at trial, section 949a(b)(1)(B) of the 2006 MCA mandated that "[t]he accused shall be present at all sessions of the military commission (other than those for deliberations or voting), except when excluded under section 949d of this title."[154] Section 949d(b) of the 2006 MCA states: "Except as provided in subsections (c) and (e), all proceedings of a military commission under this chapter, including any consultation of the members with the military judge or counsel shall—(A) be in the presence of the accused, defense counsel, and trial counsel, and (B) be made part of the record."[155] Subsection (c) exempts the deliberations on guilt or innocence by the members of the commission (the jury), and subsection (e) allows the judge to "exclude the accused from any portion of a proceeding upon a determination that, after being warned by the military judge, the accused persists in conduct that justifies exclusion from the courtroom—(1) to ensure the physical safety of individuals; or (2) to prevent disruption of the proceedings by the accused."[156] These provisions, although altered slightly in the 2009 MCA,[157] retained the accused's right to be present at all sessions of the military commission, other than members' deliberations and voting, unless excluded because of disruptive behavior as outlined above.[158] These provisions represent a significant reversal from prior commissions practice and are in line with federal court practice in this area.

An accused's access to the evidence against him was also one of the failings of the previous commissions process as noted by the Supreme Court. The 2006 MCA attempted to strike a balance between the need for the United States to maintain its national security information and the principle of providing legitimate information to the accused to

---

[153] *Id.* § 948b(f).

[154] Identical language is included in the 2009 MCA, *supra* note 15, § 949a(b)(2)(B).

[155] 2006 MCA, *supra* note 8, § 949d(b).

[156] *Id.* § 949d(e).

[157] 2009 MCA, *supra* note 15, § 949b(2)(B).

[158] The 2009 MCA retained the basic right of the accused to be present at all sessions of the military commission, *id.* § 949a(b)(2)(B), and required that all sessions without members be "conducted in the presence of the accused, defense counsel, and trial counsel, and shall be made part of the record." *Id.* § 949d(a)(2). Although this provision is narrower than the provision in the 2006 MCA, applying only to sessions without members, the general right of the accused to be present at all proceedings under section 949a(b)(2)(B) continues to operate even for sessions with members, and the exclusion provision in section 949d(d), identical to section 949d(e) of the 2006 MCA, continues to apply to all sessions, with and without members. *See* 2009 MCA, *supra* note 15, § 949d.

allow him to prepare his defense. Again, the final resolution of these provisions will likely be the subject of further litigation, but the statute's language is an important insight into what the U.S. government views as the limits of what it can withhold from the accused. For example, 2006 MCA § 949d(f) contains the provisions on protection of classified information and allows the government to protect the disclosure of "sources, methods, or activities by which the United States acquired the evidence if the military judge finds that (i) the sources, methods, or activities by which the United States acquired the evidence are classified, and (ii) the evidence is reliable."[159] The judge may require the trial counsel to produce an unclassified summary if practicable. In the 2009 MCA, Congress incorporated provisions that were largely based on the Classified Information Procedures Act, applicable in Article III courts.[160] These changes reflect congressional intent to bring this aspect of the military commissions process into line with the procedures used in Article III courts.[161] Nevertheless, disputes continue in ongoing military commissions on the ability of the commission to exclude the accused from any proceedings, specifically in interlocutory hearings involving allegations of torture arising from the RDI program.[162]

Finally, in dealing with the Supreme Court's concern about evidentiary protections in general, and the issue of coerced evidence specifically, the 2006 MCA again tried to strike a balance. The 2006 MCA excluded all evidence obtained by torture, but allowed coerced statements made prior to December 30, 2005 (the date the Detainee Treatment Act[163] came into force) if the military judge found that "(1) the totality of the

---

[159] 2006 MCA, *supra* note 8, § 949d(f)(2)(B).

[160] 2009 MCA, *supra* note 15, §§ 949p-1 through p-7.

[161] *Id.* § 949p-1(d) ("CONSTRUCTION OF PROVISIONS.—The judicial construction of the Classified Information Procedures Act (18 U.S.C. app.) shall be authoritative in the interpretation of this subchapter, except to the extent that such construction is inconsistent with the specific requirements of this chapter."). These provisions incorporate much of the case law and practice of federal court judges, and include the ability to conduct ex parte hearings with either party to discuss potential classified information issues; require the military judge to issue a protective order to protect all classified information, even that learned outside of the discovery process; allow the military judge to order alternatives to full disclosure of classified information; require the government to provide a declaration invoking the national security privilege; provide explicit authority for the use of alternatives to full disclosure of classified information at trial; provide for interlocutory appeal by the United States for issues involving forced disclosure of classified information; and allow closure of the courtroom.

[162] Continued litigation has occurred on this provision over the government's contention that it can exclude the accused from pretrial interlocutory matters involving classified information, particularly discussion of the alleged torture undergone by the detainees, and to their presence during future suppression hearings. The government contended that the accused could be excluded and that any right to presence in pretrial motions would have to be determined on a case-by-case basis. *See* Khalid Shaikh Mohammad et al. (2), Argument on AE136 Government's Memorandum of Law Regarding Accused Presence in Closed Proceedings, "Unofficial/Unauthenticated Transcript of Motions Hearing Dated 6/19/2013 from 9:05 AM to 12:19 PM" at 3397–449, *available at* http://www.mc.mil/Portals/0/pdfs/KSM2/KSM%20II%20 (TRANS19June2013-AM).pdf.

[163] Detainee Treatment Act of 2005, Pub. L. No. 109–148, §§ 1001–1005, 119 Stat. 2739–744.

circumstances renders the statement reliable and possessing sufficient probative value; and (2) the interests of justice would best be served by admission of the statement into evidence."[164] For evidence obtained by coercion after December 30, 2005, a third element is also required: "the interrogation methods used to obtain the statement do not amount to cruel, inhuman, or degrading treatment prohibited by section 1003 of the Detainee Treatment Act of 2005."[165]

This was one of the most hotly debated provisions in the 2006 MCA legislation and continued to draw the focus and criticism of experts in the field after its passage. Although all questioning has some degree of coercion inherent to it, potentially allowing evidence that was obtained by cruel, inhuman, or degrading treatment did not find much support among those most vocal about the MCA The resistance to this bifurcated standard resulted in a far different provision in the 2009 MCA.[166] In its 2009 revision of the MCA, Congress excluded any statement obtained by torture or by cruel, inhuman, or degrading treatment, regardless of the date obtained (widening both the date and nature of the coerced statement).[167] Attempting to align the admission of other statements of the accused, often taken on the battlefield with its inherent coercive atmosphere, Congress also excluded other statements by the accused, unless the military judge finds that "(1) the totality of the circumstances renders the statement reliable and possessing sufficient probative value; and...[it is either]...incident to lawful conduct during military operations at the point of capture or during closely related active combat engagement, and the interests of justice would best be served by admission of the statement into evidence; or...the statement was voluntarily given."[168] By incorporating

---

[164] 2006 MCA, *supra* note 8, § 948r(c).

[165] *Id.* § 948r(d).

[166] Significant testimony was taken by both the House and Senate in an attempt to balance the exclusion of statements obtained by torture and cruel, inhuman, and degrading treatment with the exigencies of battlefield capture and admission of statements taken in that inherently coercive environment. In section 948r(c), Congress made the military judge the gatekeeper on the admissibility of "other statements of the accused." Thus, through the application of a tailored voluntariness standard, the military judge would play an important role in striking the appropriate balance, admitting battlefield statements only if found to be "in the interests of justice," or otherwise voluntary. *See* 2009 MCA, *supra* note 15, § 948r(c); *see also* PROPOSALS FOR REFORM OF THE MILITARY COMMISSION SYSTEM, Hearing Before the H. Subcomm. on the Constitution, Civil Rights, and Civil Liberties, of the H. Comm on the Judiciary, 111th Cong. (2009); LEGAL ISSUES REGARDING MILITARY COMMISSIONS AND THE TRIAL OF DETAINEES FOR VIOLATIONS OF THE LAW OF WAR, Hearing Before the S. Comm. on Armed Services, 111th Cong. (2009).

[167] 2009 MCA, *supra* note 15, § 948r(a).

[168] *Id.* § 948r(c). The standard of voluntariness is defined in section 948r(d) ("In determining for purposes of subsection (c)(2)(B) whether a statement was voluntarily given, the military judge shall consider the totality of the circumstances, including, as appropriate, the following: (1) The details of the taking of the statement, accounting for the circumstances of the conduct of military and intelligence operations during hostilities. (2) The characteristics of the accused, such as military training, age, and education level. (3) The lapse of time, change of place, or change in identity of the questioners between the statement sought to be admitted and any prior questioning of the accused.")

this tailored voluntariness standard, Congress attempted to meet *Hamdan I's* require-ment that any variance from the rules that apply in regular courts-martial must be based on a determination that they are impracticable.[169] The 2009 amendments to the MCA arguably bring the procedures far closer to those that apply in both courts-martial and Article III trials, with exceptions for the specific circumstances of battlefield captures.[170]

Despite these ongoing debates as to the specific procedural limitations on military commissions, the process in the United States has made clear that the international legal standards for such tribunals rest on common article 3, article 75 of Additional Protocol I, and article 6 of Additional Protocol II. Though there may still be differences as to the specific application of those standards, the standards are clear and the detail will likely become further refined as the commissions process continues.

Conclusion

In the wake of current U.S. practice since 2001, it seems clear that because the fight against transnational terrorism is an armed conflict, transnational terrorists detained in the conduct of that fight are legitimately subject to trial by military commission for war crimes committed in connection with that conflict. Once detained, they accrue custom-ary and treaty law rights, including those found in common article 3 and its compan-ion provisions in AP II. These provisions provide not only procedural but substantive limitations to jurisdiction and determine the basic rights that all such detainees have in any prosecution. The U.S. practice in this area is instructive, especially with regard to procedural limitations, where there is little doubt that the current commissions process will refine those rights with significant clarity.

Where substantive jurisdiction is the issue, it is still unclear how the United States practice will resolve. It seems clear that under the 2009 MCA, the U.S. military is pros-ecuting terrorists for crimes that are not traditional international law crimes, though they are domestic crimes. Recent appellate decisions by the D.C. Circuit recognize and enforce the traditional restriction on the jurisdiction of law of war military commis-sions; unfortunately, the recent *en banc* decision in *United States v. Al-Bahlul*, rather than providing clarity, has further confused the laws governing the validity of the use

---

[169] *See Hamdan I, supra* note 13, at 622.

[170] The 2009 MCA also made specific improvements in the admission of hearsay evidence, with the 2009 MCA allowing the admission of hearsay evidence not otherwise admissible under the rules of evidence applicable in trial by general court-martial, only after the military judge determines (1) that the statement is offered as evidence of a material fact and is probative, (2) that direct testimony is not available as a practi-cal matter, and (3) that the general purposes of the rules of evidence and the interests of justice would be best served by its admission. 2009 MCA, *supra* note 15, § 949a(d)(3)(D)(ii). This was a significant improve-ment from the "reasonable man" standard of relevance in the 2006 MCA, and more closely reflects deter-minations that exact adherence to the procedures in general courts-martial are impractical—the standard enunciated in *Hamdan I*.

of military commissions to try violators of the law of war. The resolution of the interconnection between these two sources of law (domestic and international) and their application to the armed conflict against transnational terrorists undoubtedly deserve continuing observation and analysis, to include potential resolution of these issues by the Supreme Court. As elegantly stated in *Boumediene v. Bush*: "The laws and Constitution are designed to survive, and remain in force, in extraordinary times. Liberty and security can be reconciled; and in our system they are reconciled within the framework of the law."[171]

---

[171] Boumediene v. Bush, 553 U.S. 723, 798 (2008).

7

Battlefield Perspectives on the Laws of War

by Michael W. Lewis

Introduction

Any genuine understanding of the role of the law of war in the struggle against transnational terrorism begins with an appreciation of the unique context in which the law of war operates. The previous chapters have focused primarily on the strategic level of war. At that level, time, space, and the nature of operational challenges allow for a robust role for both law and lawyers. As my coauthors have illustrated, while fidelity to the core principles of the law is a universal element of disciplined military operations, application of the principles in these contexts involves a high degree of complexity.

The student of the law must, however, always be aware of the reality that the strategic and operational complexity of law must somehow effectively translate into practical application. At the tactical "point of execution" level, military personnel risk their lives and take the lives of others, based upon instantaneous decisions that seldom allow for reflection or consideration, let alone the benefit of timely legal advice. For the law of war to be meaningful it must function effectively at this level. To make it effective at this level, the process of translating the complex legal mandates from the strategic level into practical parameters is critical. This process involves a "distillation" of the complex and comprehensive legal regimes described in previous chapters into workable operational principles. Making this process work is one of the great challenges facing the law of war.

This chapter will examine some of the complex challenges facing international humanitarian law (IHL) (also commonly referred to as the "law of armed conflict" or simply the "law of war") and its tactical implementation and how those challenges are overcome in the current environment. It is understandably difficult for rules drafted over 60 years ago and last amended over 35 years ago to keep pace with the changes in both the means and methods of warfare that have occurred since then. Although the Bush administration's characterization of the Geneva Conventions as "quaint" was both politically misguided and improperly demeaning of the importance that IHL has in the current international order, an appreciation of the challenges associated with tactical execution will reveal that there was a kernel of truth to the statement that bears examination. The aspirational nature of many of Geneva's provisions (for example the requirement that the detaining state pay prisoners of war and provide them with a canteen at which they can spend their money)[1] have always required the exercise of judgment in their interpretation and enforcement. And it is the soundness of that judgment that has always been at the core of whether IHL is operationally, rather than merely notionally, effective.

The nature of warfare means that IHL can only be effective if it is instilled in the combatants involved in armed conflict. If the goal is to protect civilians, for example, then for the combatant, the 159 articles and 19,899 words of the Fourth Geneva Convention must be distilled into a few core principles. These principles must be basic enough to be easily understood by young men and women who may have limited educational backgrounds. More important, the principles must be clear enough to meaningfully influence their actions. The challenge for military commanders and their legal advisors has been to agree on what those core principles must be, and to frame them in a way that effectively constrains behavior in an environment that is peculiarly unsuited to restraint.

It must always be remembered that at the ultimate point of execution, law is competing with a number of other priorities in the minds of each combatant. As one special forces officer put it when discussing the role of law-of-war issues in combat preparation and planning: "There are things that can get you killed, and there are things that can end your career. We spent a lot more time worrying about the former."[2] This is not to say that the things that can end your career, such as failing to comply with the law of war, are not a concern for combatants. But compliance with the law of war is not principally based on a fear of the professional consequences for failing to comply. Instead, most effective law-of-war compliance arises from a belief that the rules governing warfare are beneficial for the combatant.

This core understanding, that for law to be effective in constraining warriors it is best for it to be viewed as beneficial by warriors rather than merely punitive, should be kept in mind when considering how law is best applied to the battlefield. How is law most effectively injected into combat? What external factors predictably influence this effectiveness? And how should this process of operationalization inform conclusions about law's likely successes and limitations in the war on terror?

---

[1] *See* GPW art. 54, 58–68.

[2] Interview by Professor Lewis with former Navy SEAL Lieutenant J. D. Denney [hereinafter Denney Interview].

As this chapter will illustrate, the answers to these questions depend upon the type of combat forces involved, the tactics they employ, and, perhaps most important, the type of support they receive. The level of interaction between combat units and their support units—not only legal support units but also other support units such as intelligence—is critical to effectively bringing law to the battlefield, particularly in as disaggregated a conflict as the war on terror. This chapter will also illustrate why members of military units engaged in combat are simultaneously both more and less susceptible to changes in "senior direction" with regard to law of war issues than the other parts of the military, such as interrogators or prison guards, who are involved in the war on terror. In some ways, executive branch claims of legal exceptionalism with respect to the war on terror and the continual emphasis on the "unique" nature of the conflict and the enemy may have undermined the culture of compliance that had come to define the armed forces. But in other ways, the insular nature of the combat arms, which may have impeded the process of bringing law to the battlefield in the past, also served to insulate the gains that law had made in recent decades within the combat arms from such executive branch claims.

What should also be taken from this narrative are the two critical elements in the analysis of the role of law in this struggle. The first is how the applicability of core law-of-war principles, most often communicated to combatants through rules of engagement, reinforces the base premise of this text: that warriors need rules. The second is how this process reflects an essential aspect of tactical application of the law of war: the requirement for simplicity, confidence, and clarity. This chapter will address these issues by examining law's application to both aviation and ground forces in the war on terror. Although each of these forces faces unique challenges in how to most effectively inject law into the combat environment, their respective approaches to these challenges display some common characteristics that are critical to understanding how the success of this endeavor can be achieved.

Successfully altering or regulating the behavior of any organization is heavily dependent upon understanding the culture and structure of that organization.[3] This is certainly true of the military. The success of injecting law into the combat environment is tied to bridging gaps in understanding between lawyers and combatants and getting the buy-in from the most influential combatants. It is impossible for an expert in one area (such as law) to truly understand the perspective of an expert in another field (such as combat). However, there are certain key individuals in combat units or organizations that individual combatants turn to when they have questions about direction from experts outside of their field.[4] Those at the top of this influence hierarchy for combatants

---

[3] *See* Laura Dickinson, *Military Lawyers on the Battlefield: An Empirical Account of International Law Compliance*, 104 Am. J. Int'l L. 1, 6–9 (2010) (describing organizational theory literature and the factors that determine how effectively behavior can be altered within organizations) [hereinafter Dickinson].

[4] *See id.* at 8. (describing the factors that make "compliance agents" most effective at affecting change in the culture of an organization). In the experience of Professor Lewis, junior officers in his F-14 squadron looked

have a tremendous influence on what that group values and how that group behaves. Although rank is a somewhat reliable proxy for "influence hierarchy" in a strongly hierarchical organization such as the military, it is not a definitive measure of influence. Other factors, such as perceived combat proficiency, also matter in establishing an individual's place in the influence hierarchy. The key to influencing combatants' behavior toward compliance with the law of war lies in identifying those at the top of the relevant influence hierarchy and then getting those individuals to understand, internalize, and support such compliance. Significantly, once the influencers understand and internalize the value of compliance, it becomes very difficult to dislodge the mindset favoring compliance within the organization subject to that individual's influence.[5]

Air Support

I. PRE-9/11 DEVELOPMENTS

An understanding of aviation's role in the war on terror must begin with the strategic changes that occurred in the 1991 Gulf War, and the technological developments that have happened since. Strategy and technology complemented each other in a way that moved law closer to the battlefield than at any other time in history. Although it should be acknowledged that the practical value of law's ascendancy has not been without its critics, there can be little question that law is now more integrated into aerial bombardment than ever before.

In late 1990 and early 1991, during the run-up to the Gulf War, there were competing strategic views of air power's optimum employment. On one side were the advocates of the Air-Land Battle strategy,[6] which viewed air power in a critical supporting role for ground operations. For them, victory was achieved when "a 19 year old with a rifle" was standing on the ground that needed to be occupied. On the other side were advocates of "effects-based targeting" who believed that a modern war could be won almost exclusively from the air.[7]

This idea was not new. Strategic air-power advocates from Douhet and Mitchell to Goering, Harris, and LeMay had all believed that air power could apply decisive,

---

to tactically proficient mid-grade officers (O-4s or O-5s) for guidance on how legal terms such as "hostile intent" or "hostile act" were to be understood operationally, which made them the most effective "compliance agents" if they accepted the culture changes being instilled.

[5] *See* Dickinson, *supra* note 3, at 14.

[6] "Air-Land Battle" was a U.S. military doctrine used, beginning in the late 1970s, in planning for an armed conflict with the Soviet Union in Europe. *See* John L. Romjuc, *The Evolution of the Airland Battle Concept*, AIR U. REV. (May–June 1984), *available at* http://www.airpower.maxwell.af.mil/airchronicles/aureview/1984/may-jun/romjue.html.

[7] *See* Michael W. Lewis, *The Law of Aerial Bombardment in the 1991 Gulf War*, 97 AM. J. INT'L L. 481, 484–87 (2003) [hereinafter Gulf War].

conflict-terminating pressure on the civilian population, the military command structure, and the political leadership. Not only had these older air-power advocates seemingly been proven wrong by the Second World War, but their attempts at proving their strategy killed hundreds of thousands of civilians in Rotterdam, London, Coventry, Hamburg, Dresden, Berlin, Tokyo, and dozens of other cities around the globe. As a result, air-power advocacy seemed almost antithetical to the law of war.

But 1991 changed that. The development of precision-guided munitions and aircraft that could deliver them accurately from relatively safe altitudes allowed air power to apply intense pressure to infrastructure, communications, and the military and political command structure without risking the lives of a substantial number of aircrew, or killing large numbers of civilians. This was significant for the law of war because the nature of the targets selected by "effects-based targeting" invited a much higher level of legal and political scrutiny. Most of the targets were "dual use" targets that had both military and civilian applications. Electrical power grids, radio and telecommunication networks, oil and gasoline storage and processing facilities, and transportation infrastructure were all targeted in order to degrade the cohesion and operating capacity of the Iraqi Army in Kuwait. Such targets required much greater legal oversight than more traditional Air-Land Battle targets such as troop concentrations, military supply depots, military airfields, antiaircraft batteries, prepared defensive positions, etc.

Although the doctrine of proportionality, previously discussed in detail in Chapter 3, applies to all attacks, most Air-Land Battle targets did not require an extensive proportionality analysis. Unless the targets were located in or near a civilian population center, in which case the likelihood of civilian casualties was based upon the accuracy and payload of the weapon, their exclusively military nature made it unnecessary to balance the military advantage gained against the cost to civilians of destroying the target. However, the "dual use" nature of so many targets in the 1991 Gulf War meant that a system had to be developed for a large number of targets to receive proportionality consideration on a daily basis.[8] This process, and the way it was implemented, had a profound effect on the long-term consolidation of law's place in air operations.

The targeting cell, which selected targets, determined the order in which they were struck, and assigned the weapons systems to strike them, was composed of a group of officers. Most of them were pilots, but the targeting cell also contained some intelligence officers and legal officers, tasked with implementing the air commander's broad strategic goals. During Desert Storm, the cell produced the Master Attack Plan for each day's air operations, which included the targets, and aircraft and weapons to be used to strike those targets. These targets and weapons systems were reviewed by the legal officer before the daily Air Tasking Order, which assigned each of the missions to various squadrons, was approved. As the war unfolded, the targeteers relied upon intelligence

---

[8] *See id.* at 487–502.

assessments to update, revise, and reprioritize their target lists. The regular interaction among targeteers, legal officers, and intelligence officers resulted in a mutual understanding of each group's goals and concerns, which stretched far beyond the month-and-a-half long conflict in 1991. As this mutual understanding and cooperation among the legal, intelligence, and targeting communities became institutionalized in the following years, it created a self-reinforcing dynamic that enhanced law's effective impact on aerial bombardment operations.

This dynamic positively affected law's application in two meaningful ways. First of all, because intelligence officers and targeteers effectively internalized the legal requirements applicable to these operations, there were many more "sets of eyes" that understood the basic requirements of proportionality and military necessity considering and balancing the military value of the targets with the potential civilian harm. This internalization of legal concerns by targeting and intelligence officers was already quite evident in the preparation of target lists for the 1996 "Desert Strike" air strikes on Iraq. From a legal perspective, this beneficial dynamic has become even more pronounced in the use of air power during the war on terror.[9]

Perhaps even more important, however, was the effect that this consensus among these supporting groups had on the aircrew performing these missions. In the aviation community, the vast majority of strike missions are flown by junior officers.[10] The individuals at the top of their influence hierarchy are tactically proficient mid-grade aviation officers.[11] While there is appropriate and necessary deference shown to more senior officers (aviators and non-aviators alike), when the junior officers want clarification on operational issues they turn to the tactically proficient mid-grade officers for answers.[12] The strong interaction within the targeting cell among legal, intelligence, and targeting personnel was particularly effective at bridging the understanding gap with this influential group of tactically proficient mid-grade officers, because the targeteers were former pilots assigned to a staff role. To the extent that these targeteers internalized the legal considerations involved in targeting decisions, it made it far more likely that the current pilots at the top of the influence hierarchy would buy in to the importance of the legal

---

[9] *Id.* These points also were made in a 1998 interview by Professor Lewis with LCOL Tony Montgomery, the senior Air Force JAG officer for the Desert Strike operations against Iraq in 1996; and in a 2008 interview by Professor Lewis with COL Gary Brown, the senior JAG at the Air Force operations center in Afghanistan.

[10] In this context, junior officers are defined as O-2s through O-4s, which are Air Force, Army, and Marine Corps First Lieutenants, Captains, and Majors, and Navy Lieutenant(jg)s, Lieutenants, and Lieutenant Commanders.

[11] Mid-grade officers are defined as senior O-4s and O-5s, which are Air Force, Army, and Marine Corps senior Majors and Lieutenant Colonels, and Navy senior Lieutenant Commanders and Commanders. These are the squadron commanders and senior flight leads or mission commanders. Although rank is important, the perception of the tactical proficiency of the mid-grade officers, which is generally based upon their combat experience and reputation, had more to do with whether their opinions influenced junior officer interpretation of the ROE.

[12] *See* Denny Interview, *supra* note 2.

considerations that influenced target and weapon selection. Unlike the legal and intelligence officers who could be viewed by aircrews as independent experts from other fields without operational insight or perspective, the targeteers possessed an instant credibility with the pilots they were assigning missions to that no lecture or rank could duplicate.

2. CRITICISMS AND RESPONSES

The overall success that law achieved in embedding itself within the aerial bombardment planning process before 9/11 did not mean that the conduct in this area of combat was without its legal critics. In fact, the legality of "effects-based targeting" strategies was strongly questioned after the 1991 Gulf War. Further, the scrutiny in this area became even more intense as air power's ability to limit the risk of American casualties made it the "force of choice" after the 1993 debacle in Somalia.[13] The force used in response to events in Iraq in both 1996 and 1998 was a combination of air strikes and cruise missile strikes. This same combination was used in Afghanistan and Sudan after the U.S. Embassy bombings in Kenya and Tanzania in 1998. In addition to these very limited operations, there was the far more extensive bombing campaign conducted by NATO against Serbia and Serb forces in Kosovo in 1999. The legality of all of these operations was challenged on IHL grounds, based on the claim that the harm done to civilians and civilian infrastructure was disproportionate to the military advantage gained by the strikes.

The military responded to these criticisms by developing different weapons, improving the accuracy of existing weapons, and creating more sophisticated damage assessment models. For example, in response to the criticism that targeting electricity during the 1991 Gulf War caused extensive civilian suffering both during and after the war because the generating facilities were so severely damaged, a new type of air-dropped weapon was developed. The carbon-fiber bomb, which releases thousands of thin carbon filaments over electrical transmission lines and generating facilities, short circuits the electrical systems.[14] This weapon was used extensively during NATO's 1999 Serbia/Kosovo campaign. It poses little risk to human beings and shuts down electrical power for hours (or at most a few days) rather than for weeks or months, as happened in Iraq during the 1991 Gulf War after the generator halls were destroyed.

---

[13] *See* RICHARD W. STEWARD, THE UNITED STATES ARMY IN SOMALIA 1992–1994 (U.S. Army Ctr. Mil. Hist. Spec. Pub. 70-81-1) 23 (2002), *available at* http://www.history.army.mil/brochures/Somalia/Somalia.pdf (during operations in Somalia on October 3–4, 1993, the use of U.S. ground forces in an attempt to capture key lieutenants of General Muhammed Farah Aideed of the Habr Gidr subclan in Mogadishu resulted in the deaths of 18 U.S. soldiers and numerous other casualties.

[14] *See* descriptions of the CBU-94 and BLU-114/B munitions, *available at* http://www.globalsecurity.org/military/systems/munitions/blu-114.htm (last visited June 25, 2014).

3. AIR SUPPORT AND THE WAR ON TERROR

Since 9/11, the expansion of legal awareness in the aviation community that began with the 1991 Gulf War has continued apace. Its effectiveness in reducing civilian casualties has occurred in two stages across the 13 years since the conflict with al-Qaeda began. The first stage saw the consolidation of the legal gains at the planning level, where lawyers, pilots, and targeteers continued their cooperation to minimize casualties in preplanned strikes. The second stage was a set of steps taken (as described below) to minimize casualties from strikes that were not pre-planned.

Mission planners took advantage of technological advances that improved the accuracy of existing weapons and of new weapons designed to curtail the effect on the civilian population.[15] The planners also benefited from the vast increase in available information. The widespread use of unmanned aerial vehicles (UAVs) such as the Predator and Global Hawk provided strike planners with a wealth of information that was undreamed of 20 years ago.[16] The planners used this information for a variety of purposes, from assessing air defenses to improving delivery profiles and weapon selection to assessing target activity.

This information improved the accuracy of target identification and selection and also helped to improve the accuracy of proportionality analyses. Intelligence and targeting used this information to develop increasingly sophisticated collateral damage estimation computer models.[17] These models not only accounted for the weapon type, delivery method, and fuse settings, but also for observed patterns of civilian behavior. This modeling influenced the timing of preplanned strikes to minimize both the likely civilian presence and the likelihood of mission failure. These efforts resulted in an acknowledgement by Human Rights Watch that by 2008, "civilian casualties rarely occur during planned airstrikes on suspected Taliban targets."[18] Considering the weapons used, and

---

[15] Such "technological advances" in weapons are not always as profound as the "carbon fiber" bomb described above. In Afghanistan, many bombs have had their heads filled with concrete to allow for greater penetration before detonation, thereby reducing the blast radius and fragmentation effect.

[16] Critics of the Coalition's air strikes in the 1991 Gulf War, particularly the strike on the Al-Firdos intelligence bunker that also served as an air raid shelter for the family members of Iraq's Mukhabarat secret police, cited the failure of Coalition forces to conduct adequate prestrike reconnaissance that might have revealed the dual-use nature of the bunker. See, e.g., MIDDLE EAST WATCH, NEEDLESS DEATHS IN THE GULF WAR 140–43 (1991). However, the reconnaissance assets available at that time were severely limited. Less than 3 percent of the total sorties flown during Desert Storm were dedicated reconnaissance sorties. See Gulf War, supra note 7, at 504. Today, long endurance UAVs ensure that preplanned attacks almost never take place without detailed prestrike reconnaissance, and in many cases they provide several days of continuous surveillance prior to an attack.

[17] See Gregory McNeal, Are Targeted Killings Unlawful? A Case Study in Empirical Claims without Empirical Evidence, in TARGETED KILLINGS, LAW AND MORALITY IN AN ASYMMETRICAL WORLD (Claire Finkelstein, Jens David Ohlin & Andrew Altman eds., 2012).

[18] HUMAN RIGHTS WATCH, "TROOPS IN CONTACT": AIRSTRIKES AND CIVILIAN DEATHS IN AFGHANISTAN 3–4 (2008). This is not to say that air strikes no longer cause civilian casualties in

the uncertainties that remain in any combat environment, this was an exceptional achievement. But it was only the first stage of the civilian casualty reduction. As the same Human Rights Watch report emphasized, much more still needed to be done to reduce civilian casualties in reactive uses of air power.[19]

When Gen. Stanley McChrystal took command of ISAF (International Security Assistance Force) in Afghanistan in 2009, he emphasized the need to continue reducing civilian casualties outside the realm of preplanned strikes. He assigned teams of civilian and military leaders to conduct root cause analyses on all civilian casualties in theater and tasked them with developing protocols to eliminate such casualties. In the aviation realm, this meant improving battlefield communications between forward air controllers (FACs) and manned aircraft and allowing greater commander control of weapons release decisions through the use of drones.[20]

I. MANNED AIRCRAFT

The integration of legal and intelligence perspectives into the strike planning process effectively reduced civilian casualties in preplanned missions in Afghanistan. But to take the next step and further reduce civilian casualties in spontaneous strikes that were supporting troops on the ground or going after targets of opportunity required pilots to change their mindset and ground troops to become more integrated in weapons release decisions.

The restrictive rules of engagement (ROE)[21] imposed by McChrystal changed the mindset from aggressively engaging the enemy at every possible opportunity (any situation in which the anticipated incidental civilian casualties would not be "excessive in relation to the concrete and direct military advantage" gained)[22] to one that emphasized

---

Afghanistan. The report goes on to say that more needs to be done to reduce civilian casualties during rapid response strikes that are carried out in support of ground troops under insurgent attack. *Id.* at 7–8.

[19] *Id.* at 37–39 (listing recommendations).

[20] Interviews by Professor Lewis with Dr. Larry Lewis of McChrystal's staff and senior Air Force officers involved in the drone program.

[21] ROE are "rules of engagement" promulgated by commanders to their forces as a way of directing their behavior. They govern such things as what criteria must be met before lethal force may be resorted to, what types of weapons should be employed in given circumstances, and any temporal or geographic restrictions on weapons employment the commander wishes to impose. Although the ROE are informed by the laws of armed conflict, ROE and law are not the same thing. The laws of armed conflict must be obeyed under all circumstances and represent basic requirements and precautions that cannot be altered by commanders. ROE must include these precautions, but may include other more restrictive requirements and precautions that the commander includes for policy reasons. For example, "no artillery shells may be fired if they are expected to land within 500 meters of a civilian structure" is an example of ROE that is more restrictive than the requirements of the law of war. A commander could lift this restriction and allow such shots, but could not lift the requirement that every use of artillery must comply with the law-of-war principles of proportionality and military necessity.

[22] AP I art. 51(5)(b).

the importance of picking one's spots and engaging only when the risk of civilian casualties was extremely low. This meant that on many occasions air power had to sit by while troops on the ground weathered an attack, and at times took casualties in doing so. This resulted in a very low percentage of air missions actually delivering ordnance. In 2011, for example, NATO aircraft dropped ordnance or conducted strafing runs on only 5.8 of their missions.[23]

It should be emphasized that this more restrictive ROE was *not* based upon an assessment that the LOAC required such restrictions. Rather, it was reflective of a policy judgment that placing greater restrictions upon the use of lethal force was the best way to improve mission success. Because it was a policy judgment, it was one that could be reversed at the discretion of the commander at any time.

The other step that further reduced the civilian casualties caused by unplanned strikes was increased integration between pilots and ground troops. Aircraft crews had a variety of means to ensure that they and the soldiers on the ground were talking about the same building, copse of trees, or rock outcropping. One option was to downlink the pilot's view of a target to soldiers on the ground so that they can see it with a portable laptop-like device. Another option at night is for the aircraft to shine an infrared beam on the intended target and receive confirmation from infrared-equipped troops that the beam is located on the right target.[24] This increased communication between ground forces requesting air support and aircrews in high stress, time-critical situations helped to avoid civilian casualties in a number of instances in Afghanistan.[25]

a. Drones

No weapon is more closely identified with the ongoing conflict with al-Qaeda and its associated forces than the armed drone. Although the first armed drone strike occurred in Yemen in 2002,[26] drones were not used extensively outside of the reconnaissance role until the tail end of the Bush administration.[27] As the conflict in Iraq wound down and more resources were sent to Afghanistan where cross-border attacks from Pakistan were becoming an increasing problem, the unique capabilities of the armed drone became relevant. After their value was demonstrated in the counterinsurgency in the Afghanistan/Pakistan (Af/Pak) region between 2008 and 2010, drones also took on a major role in the conflict in Yemen against al-Qaeda in the Arabian Peninsula (AQAP) and Ansar

---

[23] *See* C.J. Chivers, *Afghan Conflict Losing Air Power as US Pulls Out*, N.Y. TIMES, July 6, 2012, *available at* http://www.nytimes.com/2012/07/07/world/asia/in-dwindling-afghan-war-air-power-has-become-a-way-of-life.html?pagewanted=all&_r=0.

[24] *See id.*

[25] *Id.*

[26] Dana Priest, *U.S. Citizen among Those Killed in Yemen Predator Missile Strike*, THE TECH (online edition), Nov. 8, 2002, *available at* http://tech.mit.edu/V122/N54/long4-54.54w.html (reprinting WASH. POST article).

[27] DANIEL KLAIDMAN, KILL OR CAPTURE 118–21 (2012).

al-Sharia (AAS) in 2010–2011. Although the frequency of strikes in both Pakistan and Yemen decreased in 2012–2013, drones remain active in both regions.[28]

b. Why Are Drones Used?

The first answer that most people offer to this question is that drones have the advantage of keeping pilots out of harm's way. Although this is a benefit of their use, it is a very minor one in the context of the conflicts with al-Qaeda. No ISAF fixed wing aircraft have been shot down in Afghanistan, so the risk reduction associated with using drones rather than manned aircraft has been negligible.

Other factors drove the increasing reliance on drones in the Af/Pak region beginning in 2008–2009, including their loiter time, the size of their weapons, and the increased commander control of weapons employment decisions that they offered. The capability of drones such as the MQ-9 Reaper to fly unrefueled missions of over 20 hours meant that they could loiter over an area of interest or a target for many hours at a time, providing continuous, real-time coverage. A couple of drones could follow a potential target for days or even weeks at a time to create a "pattern-of-life" analysis that assisted in determining whether the target was engaged in hostile activities. Such pattern-of-life analysis is critical to confirming the intelligence that provides the basis for much of the targeting in counterinsurgencies. It would take three or four manned aircraft along with continuous dedicated airborne tanker support to provide the same coverage.

The weapon most commonly used by drones is the Hellfire missile. Originally developed for use on helicopters, Hellfires weigh 100 pounds with a warhead of approximately 35 pounds. In contrast, the Maverick air-to-surface missile weighs 450–800 pounds (depending upon the variant) and carries a warhead of 125–300 pounds, and the smallest laser-guided bomb in the U.S. inventory (the GBU-39) weighs 250 pounds. and carries a warhead of 50 pounds.[29] In the context of a counterinsurgency in which ever-present concerns about collateral damage and civilian casualties were in the front of every commander's mind, the fact that a drone can deliver a weapon such as the Hellfire that was one-quarter to one-half the size of other standard ordnance was a great advantage.

---

[28] The three credible sources of publicly available information, the New America Foundation (http://natsec.newamerica.net/about), the Long War Journal (http://www.longwarjournal.org/pakistan-strikes.php), and The Bureau of Investigative Journalism (http://www.thebureauinvestigates.com/category/projects/drones/) all indicate declining but continuing drone operations in both Yemen and Pakistan as of September 2013.

[29] *Compare* AGM-114 Hellfire specifications, *available at* http://www.globalsecurity.org/military/systems/munitions/agm-114-specs.htm *with* AGM-65 Maverick specifications, *available at* http://www.globalsecurity.org/military/systems/munitions/agm-65-specs.htm*and with* GBU-39 specifications, *available at* http://www.globalsecurity.org/military/systems/munitions/sdb.htm (it should be noted that the GBU-39 was developed in 2006, largely for the purpose of collateral damage mitigation, and that it was half the size of the laser-guided bomb it replaced) (last visited each of these links, June 26, 2014).

The increased control over weapons employment decisions provided by drones was also very appealing to commanders. Manned aircraft are typically flown by junior officers (primarily O-3s and O-4s)[30] who make weapons employment decisions based upon the LOAC training they receive. Although commanders are able to emphasize aspects of the ROE in preflight briefings, the decision to actually release any weapons from manned aircraft is ultimately in the hands of one or two junior officers. Although drones are also operated by junior officers (and in some cases enlisted personnel), these personnel typically have very restrictive weapons release authority.[31] In most cases, drone operators may only employ their weapons with the approval of senior officers who have access to the same sensor feeds (optical and/or infrared). Before such approval, the senior officers are able to consult with others in the chain of command, as well as with legal and intelligence officers who can provide additional input into the validity of the strike. As the inclusion of intelligence and legal officers in the strike planning process in the early 1990s enhanced laws' impact on the battlefield, these additional sets of eyes also greatly improved the likelihood that weapons released by drones complied with both the law of war and the ROE.[32] The potential for additional levels of scrutiny and control prior to launching an attack is another advantage of using drones.

c. Drones and Civilian Casualties

There is very little debate that drones are legal weapons of war. The laws that govern them are the same as the laws governing manned aircraft.[33] But in spite of this broad acknowledgment of their legality, drones are frequently criticized by commentators,

---

[30] As previously stated, *supra* notes 10 and 11, O-3s and O-4s are Captains and Majors in the Army, Air Force, and Marines, and Lieutenants and Lieutenant Commanders in the Navy.

[31] Drone operators are often authorized to employ weapons at their own discretion in situations where allied forces are under direct attack and their sensors can clearly identify the individuals firing upon the allied forces. Any other weapons release decision must be approved by more senior officers. (Professor Lewis interviews with drone operators).

[32] According to testimony by Defense Department officials given in May 2013 before the Senate Armed Services Committee regarding the Authorization for the Use of Military Force, the level of senior oversight for drone strikes conducted outside Afghanistan is even greater. Each strike not only requires approval at the four-star level, but also has to be approved by the Secretary of Defense after consultation with the Joint Chiefs of Staff and other civilian leadership. *Department of Defense Joint Statement for the Record on Law of Armed Conflict, the Use of Military Force and the 2001 Authorization for the Use of Military Force*, May 16, 2016, at 5, *available at* http://www.lawfareblog.com/wp-content/uploads/2013/05/Taylor-Sheehan-Nagata-Gross_05-16-13.pdf.

[33] *See, e.g., Rise of the Drones II: Examining the Legality of Unmanned Targeting: Hearing Before the Subcomm. on Nat'l Sec. & Foreign Affairs of the H. Comm. on Oversight & Gov't Reform*, 111th Cong. 46 (2011) [hereinafter *Drones II*] (written testimony of William C. Banks), *available at* https://www.fas.org/irp/congress/2010_hr/drones2.pdf (describing how legal authority for use of drones in targeting can be found in existing law governing armed conflict but urging modernization of policy and law); *Drones II*, (written statement of Michael W. Lewis, Professor of Law, Ohio Northern University), *available at* http://oversight.house.gov/wp-content/uploads/2012/01/LewisDrones.pdf ("In circumstances where a strike by a helicopter or an F-16 would be legal, the use of a drone would be equally legitimate"); *Rise of the*

politicians, and human rights activists alike for causing excessive civilian casualties. In many cases, these criticisms are accompanied by calls for their curtailment or outright prohibition,[34] particularly outside of "hot" battlefields.[35]

All armed conflicts result in civilian casualties, and most modern conflicts have memorable examples of civilian casualties that have been caused by all kinds of weapons systems being deployed against military targets. The 1991 Gulf War had the Al-Firdos bunker airstrike that killed up to 400 civilians. The Kosovo campaign included air strikes that hit the Chinese Embassy in Belgrade and struck a civilian train crossing a bridge over the Grdelica gorge. Major civilian casualty incidents occurred in the Afghanistan and Iraq Wars. A cruise missile strike in 2009 killed approximately 35 civilians at al-Majalah in Yemen.[36] Like all these other weapons systems, drones have killed civilians. And like any weapons system there was a learning curve associated with their use.

Drones: Unmanned Systems and the Future of War: Hearing Before the Subcomm. on Nat'l Sec. & Foreign Affairs of the H. Comm. on Oversight & Gov't Reform, 111th Cong. 23 (2011) (written testimony of Kenneth Anderson, Professor of Law, Washington College of Law Am. Univ. and Member, Hoover Task Force on Nat'l Sec. & Law), *available at* http://www.fas.org/irp/congress/2010_hr/drones1.pdf (noting that "use of drones is functionally identical to the use of [a] missile fired from a standoff fighter plane").

[34] *See, e.g.,* David Luban, *What Would Augustine Do? The President, Drones and Just War Theory*, Bos. Rev., June 6, 2012, *available at* http://bostonreview.net/david-luban-the-president-drones -augustine-just-war-theory; Peter Finn, *A Future for Drones: Automated Killing*, WASH. POST, Sept. 19, 2011, *available at* http://articles.washingtonpost.com/2011-09-19/national/35273383_1_drones-hu man-target-military-base; BBC News Asia, *US Drone Strikes "Raise Questions"—UN's Navi Pillay*, June 8, 2012, *available at* http://www.bbc.co.uk/news/world-asia-18363003; *Drones II, supra* note 33, at 20 (written testimony of Mary Ellen O'Connell, Robert and Marion Short Chair in Law, Univ. of Notre Dame) (arguing that unmanned drones are "battlefield weapons," and as such should not be used outside of "combat zones"); LA Times Editorial Board, *A Closer Look at Drones*, L.A. TIMES, Sept. 25, 2011, *available at* http://articles.latimes.com/2011/sep/25/opinion/la-ed-drones-20110925; Sudarsan Raghavan, *In Yemen, US Airstrikes Breed Anger, and Sympathy for al Qaeda*, WASH. POST, May 29, 2012, *available at* http://www.washingtonpost.com/world/middle_east/in-yemen-us-airstrikes-breed-anger-and-symp athy-for-al-qaeda/2012/05/29/gJQAUmKI0U_story.html; *Report of the Special Rapporteur on extrajudicial, summary or arbitrary executions, Philip Alston*, U.N. Human Rights Council, 14th Sess., Agenda Item 3, at 25, ¶85, U.N. Doc. A/HRC/14/24/Add. 6, May 28, 2010, *available at* http://www2.ohchr.org/ english/bodies/hrcouncil/docs/14session/A.HRC.14.24.Add6.pdf [hereinafter Alston report]; Murray Wardrop, *Unmanned Drones Could Be Banned, Says Senior Judge*, TELEGRAPH, July 6, 2009, *available at* http://www.telegraph.co.uk/news/uknews/defence/5755446/Unmanned-drones-could-be-banned-s ays-senior-judge.html (quoting Lord Bingham, a former Law Lord, who cited civilian casualties as a possible justification for banning the use of armed drones).

[35] The term "hot battlefield" appears frequently in discussions of the geographical scope of IHL. For U.S. forces, it is generally taken to encompass the conflict in Iraq prior to the U.S. withdrawal and the continuing conflict in Afghanistan. Most commentators would also probably consider Yemen in 2012–2013 to constitute a "hot battlefield," based upon the internal conflict between the Yemeni government and the insurgency there. Whether the term is understood to be based upon the application of the threshold factors that describe a noninternational armed conflict, as recognized by the International Criminal Court for the Former Yugoslavia in the seminal mid-1990s' case of *Prosecutor v. Tadic*, is not clear.

[36] Richard Spencer, *US Cluster Bombs "Killed 35 Women and Children,"* TELEGRAPH, June 7, 2010, *available at* http://www.telegraph.co.uk/news/worldnews/middleeast/yemen/7806882/US-cluster-bombs-killed-35- women-and-children.html.

i. Compound Strikes

Drones were used to watch, and then strike, individual members of al-Qaeda and their associated forces in Af/Pak and later in Yemen. These strikes targeting individual leaders were termed "personality strikes." Although quite effective in degrading al-Qaeda's leadership, "personality strikes" were often criticized for causing civilian casualties, with some justification. This was because a high percentage of personality strikes in the first few years of the drone program targeted leaders in their compounds. Targeting compounds greatly increased the likelihood that the right individual was being targeted while reducing the likelihood that members of the general civilian population would be harmed. However, it also greatly increased the likelihood that members of the target's family and the families of his bodyguards and close associates would be harmed. Even with active surveillance it is extremely difficult to know precisely who is in a compound at any given time and whether family member and friends are in the same building or same room as a target.

ii. Vehicle Strikes

For this reason, the root cause analysis of civilian casualties undertaken by General McChrystal's staff led to a reduction in compound strikes in favor of targeting vehicles. Although vehicle strikes ran a greater risk of target misidentification, increasing surveillance and pattern-of-life analysis mitigated that risk. The pattern-of-life analysis also allowed drone operators to predict when a target vehicle would likely be in a sufficiently remote area to greatly reduce the likelihood of other civilian casualties. In most cases, the only casualties other than the target would be the target's driver and others riding in the vehicle with him. Pattern-of-life analysis would usually be used to confirm that the others in the vehicle were also members or associates of al-Qaeda, the Taliban, or associated forces.

iii. "Soda Straws"

Another criticism leveled against the drone program was the claim that drones were being used to target rescuers. On several occasions in both Pakistan and Yemen an initial drone strike was followed by a pause during which people went to help those who had been killed or wounded by the strike. Then another missile struck the area in which the rescuers had begun to gather. Based on these events, several organizations concluded that the drones were targeting the rescuers.[37] A number of major news organizations repeated this charge without doing any significant further investigation into its factual underpinnings.[38] As a result, the narrative that the United States "uses drones to target rescuers" is frequently repeated although it is factually incorrect.

---

[37] *See* Chris Woods & Christina Lamb, *CIA Tactics in Pakistan include Targeting Rescuers and Funerals*, Feb. 4, 2012, *available at* http://www.thebureauinvestigates.com/2012/02/04/obama-terror-drones-cia-tactics-in-pakistan-include-targeting-rescuers-and-funerals/ [hereinafter Rescuers].

[38] *See, e.g.*, Scott Shane, *U.S. Said to Target Rescuers at Drone Strike Sites*, N.Y. TIMES, Feb. 5, 2012, *available at* http://www.nytimes.com/2012/02/06/world/asia/us-drone-strikes-are-said-to-target-rescuers.html?_

General McChrystal's team determined the cause of these civilian casualties. The process and mechanics of a typical vehicle strike illustrate how these incidents happened. After the target was positively identified, the final approval process would begin. A proportionality analysis was done based upon the information available to the drone operators, their commanders, and the JAGs assessing the strike. When approval was given, the weapon was released. As the weapon neared its target the drone operator's field of view narrowed to allow him or her to make a series of small aimpoint corrections (particularly necessary when targeting a moving vehicle). After the strike, they would maintain the close-up field of view to conduct a battle damage assessment. Was the target killed? One disadvantage of using a missile as small as a Hellfire is that unless it scores almost a direct hit, it may not kill the target. If operators assessed that the first missile missed, they would maintain the close-up field of view (often analogized to "looking through a soda straw") to fire a second missile at the target. Unfortunately, while the results of the first missile were being analyzed and the second missile was being fired, rescuers who were outside the drone's narrow field of view may begin approaching the vehicle. The flight time of the missile was sufficient for rescuers to get close enough to the vehicle to be harmed by the second missile even if they did not enter the operator's narrow field of view. Once this phenomenon was understood, new procedures were developed to prevent it from recurring. These were then disseminated to the various commands involved in drone strikes in Yemen and Pakistan. In an organization the size of the military, the process of identifying a problem, proposing and approving new operating procedures that address it, and communicating those procedures to the necessary commands is not an instantaneous one. As a result, a number of these "soda straw" incidents occurred before this problem was corrected.[39]

iv. Signature Strikes

Another controversial type of strike that was conducted with some frequency between 2007 and 2012 was the so-called "signature strikes." Unlike "personality strikes" that targeted specific individuals, signature strikes were conducted against groups whose specific identities were unknown. The groups were targeted based upon behavior that suggested they were members of al-Qaeda, the Taliban, or associated forces.[40] Critics

---

r=0; Azmat Khan, *New Study Asserts Drones Strikes in Pakistan Target Rescuers, Funerals*, PBS FRONTLINE: THE SECRET WAR, Feb. 6, 2012, *available at* http://www.pbs.org/wgbh/pages/frontline/afghanistan-pakistan/secret-war/new-study-asserts-drone-strikes-in-pakistan-target-rescuers-funerals/.

[39] *See* Rescuers, *supra* note 37. (The Bureau of Investigative Journalism reports that as many as 15 such incidents have occurred although it has only confirmed roughly 10 of them. Some of these incidents were not vehicle strikes and may have involved strikes on training camps or other areas in which those nearby rescuers were likely to be members of al-Qaeda, the Taliban. or associated forces.)

[40] Examples of such behavior might include a number of armed men boarding several vehicles and driving along a road to a border crossing point between Pakistan and Afghanistan frequented by al-Qaeda and Taliban fighters. It might include a group of men engaged in group weapons training, particularly if this included heavier weapons.

of such strikes claimed, with some justification, that such strikes incorrectly targeted civilian gatherings such as tribal councils, causing significant civilian casualties on some occasions.[41] Although the United States has not definitively stated that signature strikes will never occur in the future, President Obama, in his speech at the National Defense University in May 2013, stated that future drone strikes would be conducted only if there was "near-certainty that no civilians would be killed or injured."[42] Although there was also language in the speech that left some possibility for further signature strikes,[43] it would seem that if this policy remains in place it is likely that signature strikes will become increasingly infrequent.

d. Current Trends in Civilian Casualties

The intense focus on reducing civilian casualties has been particularly successful with drones. The best indication of this can be found by looking at the three organizations that have attempted to aggregate casualties caused by drones. The three sites are the New America Foundation,[44] the Long War Journal,[45] and The Bureau of Investigative Journalism (TBIJ).[46] Of these three, the TBIJ site has generally reported the highest number of civilian casualties in both Yemen and Pakistan. Although none of these sites can be completely accurate in assessing casualties in regions that are beyond the control of the central governments in Sana'a (Yemen) and Islamabad (Pakistan), even TBIJ estimates confirm that the civilian casualties caused by drones have plummeted in the last couple of years.

According to TBIJ, between January 2012 and June 2013 there were approximately 60 drone strikes in Pakistan, which TBIJ estimates to have killed a minimum of 283 people. Of these casualties, TBIJ estimates that seven were civilians. This would amount to a civilian casualty rate of less than 2.5 percent, meaning that only 1 in 40 casualties caused by drones over that 18-month period was a civilian. When compared with civilian casualty rates in other conflicts such as the 1999 NATO air campaign in Kosovo, the 2006 Israeli conflict with Hezbollah, the 1999 Russian conflict with Chechen rebels, and the final stages of the conflict between Sri Lanka and the Liberation Tigers of Tamil Eelam (LTTE) (in all of which more civilians than combatants were killed), it becomes apparent how remarkably low this number is. This is particularly true for a conflict in which the enemy routinely hides among the civilian population. Even when TBIJ's cumulative

---

[41] See Chris Woods, *Analysis: Obama Embraced Redefinition of "Civilian" in Drone Wars*, THE BUREAU OF INVESTIGATIVE JOURNALISM, May 29, 2012, *available at* http://www.thebureauinvestigates. com/2012/05/29/analysis-how-obama-changed-definition-of-civilian-in-secret-drone-wars/.

[42] *As Delivered: Obama's Speech on Terrorism*, WALL ST. J. (Washington Wire website), May 23, 2013, *available at* http://blogs.wsj.com/washwire/2013/05/23/prepared-text-obamas-speech-on-terrorism/.

[43] See Andrew Rosenthal, *The "Signature Strikes" Program*, N.Y. TIMES, May 29, 2013, *available at* http://takingnote.blogs.nytimes.com/2013/05/29/the-signature-strikes-program/.

[44] *See* http://natsec.newamerica.net/about.

[45] *See* http://www.longwarjournal.org/pakistan-strikes.php.

[46] *See* http://www.thebureauinvestigates.com/category/projects/drones/.

results for the drone program in Pakistan over the past nine years is considered, it estimates that overall approximately 1 in 5 casualties caused by drones were civilians.

Given how much the changes in targeting practices over the last couple of years have reduced the civilian casualties caused by drones, there is beginning to be a recognition that drones appear to be lowering civilian casualties to levels never before seen in the history of warfare. As a result, some previous critics of drones have gone so far as to ask whether humanitarian considerations should *require* that drones be used for certain kinds of conflicts.[47]

e. Drones as "Video Games"

Another often repeated narrative about drones that is deeply flawed is the claim that drone operators can come to regard their actions as little more than glorified video games. In his 2009 official report as UN Special Rapporteur on extrajudicial, summary, or arbitrary executions, Philip Alston irresponsibly advanced this narrative by citing a risk that drone operators are "developing a 'Playstation' mentality to killing."[48]

In fact it has been a matter of public record since 2008 that drone operators suffer the same kind of post-traumatic stress disorder symptoms as combat forces in Iraq and Afghanistan.[49] This is not surprising when one considers what drone operators actually do. Far from "playing a video game," drone operators are asked to follow a target for days or even weeks to establish a pattern of life. As discussed above, this pattern of life is critical to supporting any targeting decision and confirming the intelligence that made the individual a potential target in the first place. This surveillance is not a 9 to 5 job: it is continuous. This means that drone operators observe their targets for days or weeks doing normal human activities. They watch them having meals with friends, coming home to their wives and families, and playing with their children. If the surveillance also shows them meeting with bomb makers, transporting or planting improvised explosive devices (IEDs), conducting weapons training, or visiting known al-Qaeda/Taliban strongholds for meetings with leaders of those groups, then the drone operators and analysts will examine the pattern-of-life analysis to find a likely opportunity to strike their targets. Then they will follow the target's vehicle into a remote area and kill that person whose habits and family they have come to know. After doing so, the operators zoom in to take a detailed look at the wreckage and the dismembered bodies to make sure they killed their target. Far from depersonalizing warfare, drone operators know more about the people they are killing than almost any other warriors in history. Other than special

---

[47] *See* Scott Shane, *The Moral Case for Drones*, N.Y. TIMES, July 15, 2012, at SR4.

[48] *See* Alston report, *supra* note 34, at 25 ¶ 84.

[49] *See Remote-Control Warriors Suffer War Stress*, NBCNEWS.COM, Aug. 7, 2008, *available at* http://www.nbcnews.com/id/26078087/ns/us_news-military/t/remote-control-warriors-suffer-war-stress/#. U4VZm2dOXrc; *see also* Elisabeth Bumiller, *Air Force Drone Operators Report High Levels of Stress*, N.Y. TIMES, Dec. 19, 2011, at A8.

forces and some ground troops that have been involved in close quarters combat, they also see their handiwork in as much graphic detail as any other combatants.[50]

Critics such as Alston who make and then repeat claims that there is a Playstation mentality problem associated with drones do everyone involved in this debate a great disservice, as do the scholars and news organizations that uncritically repeat such statements without making any attempt to verify their accuracy. Because this narrative reinforces other misconceptions about drones, it was easy to spread and will be particularly difficult to dislodge. But over time the facts on the ground will hopefully overcome these misconceptions, and the debate about drones might proceed in a more fact-based manner.

2. GROUND FORCES

a. Indirect Fires (Artillery)

Among ground forces the legal oversight of artillery fire missions most closely resembles that described in the aviation section above. This is not surprising because the law governing aerial bombardment grew out of the 1907 Hague Conventions that regulated artillery and naval bombardment in the pre-WWI era.[51] Much like the regulation of aerial bombardment described above, the integration of targeting, intelligence, and legal personnel has resulted in legal considerations being embedded in the decision-making processes of many non-legal officers. This is particularly true of preplanned artillery fire missions, which, like preplanned airstrikes, usually have the benefit of aerial reconnaissance. This real-time (or near real-time) reconnaissance information often allows legal officers to recheck their proportionality assumptions just seconds before weapons are employed, and to call off the fire mission if the situation in the target area changes unexpectedly.

The indirect fire card pictured below (Figure 7.1) illustrates the considerations that enter into any decision to employ artillery. Although it is not suggested that such a card is filled out before each artillery shell is fired, it is fair to say that each of the factors listed on the card is considered before firing begins.

As the conflict in Iraq evolved into an insurgency relying primarily on guerilla tactics, the use of artillery in that conflict became more restricted. Its relative inaccuracy[52] meant that it was difficult for artillery to be proportionally employed in urban or suburban

---

[50] These observations are based on interviews by Professor Lewis with drone operators.

[51] *See* Hague IV arts. 23–27; Hague IX arts. 1–7.

[52] The CEP (circular error probable) is the standard measure of weapon accuracy that describes the distance from the intended aimpoint that 50 percent of the weapons will impact. Data on this accuracy is available for all types of weapons and all standard delivery modes. For reference the CEP of "dumb" bombs used during Vietnam was well over 100 meters. This was considered to be quite accurate for the aircraft and munitions being used and was achieved in part through low release altitudes in many attacks. By contrast, many precision-guided munitions have a CEP of around 5 meters or less, even when dropped from much higher altitudes. The CEP for a 155mm shell is approximately 100 meters and for a 105mm shell is approximately

FIGURE 7.1[53] Indirect Fire Card.

Commanders are responsible for assessing proportionality before authorizing indirect fire into a populated area or protected place (NFA/RFA). Refer to ROE; seek legal advice; copy SJA, G5 and FSE.

POPULATED AREA TARGETING RECORD
(Military Necessity - Collateral Damage - Proportionality Assessment)

I. MILITARY NECESSITY - What are we shooting at and why?

1. DTG of mission: _____
2. Location - Grid Coordinates: _____
3. Enemy Target (WMD, CHEM, SCUD, ARTY, ARMOR, C2, LOG)
    a. Type and Unit: _____
    b. Importance to Mission: _____
4. Target Intel:
    a. How Observed: UAV, FIST, SOF, other: _____
    b. Unobserved: Q36, Q37, ELINT, other: _____
    c. Last Known DTG of Observation or Detection: _____
5. Other Concerns as applicable:
    a. US Casualties: Number: _____ Location: _____
    b. Receiving Enemy Fire: Unit: _____ Location: _____

II. COLLATERAL DAMAGE - Who or what is there now?

6. City: _____ Original Population: _____
7. Estimated Population Now in Target Area (if known): _____
8. Cultural, Economic, or Other Significance and Effects:
    _____

III. MUNITIONS SELECTION - Mitigate civilian casualties and civilian property
     destruction

9. Available Delivery Systems Within Range:
    155, MLRS, ATACMS, AH64, CAS, other: _____
10. Munitions: DPICM, Precision-Guided Munitions (PGM),
    other: _____

IV. COMMANDER'S AUTHORIZATION TO FIRE - Proportionality anaysis

11. Legal Advisor's Rank and Name: _____
12. Civil Affairs/G5 Advisor: _____
13. Is the anticipated loss of life and damage to civilian property acceptable in relation
    to the military advantage expected to be gained? _____ Yes/No _____
14. Commander or Representative's Rank, Name, and Position:
    _____

15. Optional Comments:_____
16. DTG of Decision: _____

---

65 meters, compared with <10 meters for precision-guided bombs. The exception to this are the Excalibur fin-stabilized, GPS-guided munitions that also have a CEP of <10 meters.

[53] This card was developed by lawyers for the U.S. Army's Third Infantry Division during Operation Iraqi Freedom. It is reprinted in Mike Newton, *The Military Lawyer: Nuisance or Necessity?, in* INT'L INST. HUMANITARIAN L., CURRENT PROBLEMS OF INTERNATIONAL HUMANITARIAN LAW: PROCEEDINGS OF THE 28TH ROUND TABLE, SANREMO, 2–4, Sept. 2004, at 114, 122, *available at* http://www.iihl.org/iihl/Documents/e2c3a585-a190-4eaf-9665-37fdb682c01d.pdf.

environments. Therefore, it was principally employed as counter-fire, responding to enemy mortar or rocket fire, in rural areas. Because counter-fire missions allow little time for reflection and no time to fill out cards, mentally or otherwise, the legal direction for counter-fire missions is given by developing predetermined rules for weapon employment. Counter-fire may be limited to smaller caliber weapons, or may be forbidden entirely in certain geographical areas because of the population density. In other areas where counter-fire is less restricted, the ROE create a predetermined decision matrix that is completed before responding with counter-fire. Because counter-fire is, by definition, employed in self-defense, the "reasonably necessary" standard underlying this matrix is somewhat more relaxed than the formal proportionality analyses that are conducted for preplanned fire missions. The decision matrix considers, among other things, the reliability of the target identification and verification information, the type of weapon that will be employed, and the geographical area into which the fire will be directed. These factors determine the proper level of approval authority for employing counter-fire.

In contrast to the de-emphasis of artillery in Iraq as the conflict wore on, artillery continues to play an important role in Afghanistan. Artillery units based in the river valleys provide support for infantry units that patrol the surrounding mountainous terrain. When patrols require support after coming into contact with enemy forces, they call for support at the company or battalion level. The approval structure for authorizing artillery is one way that commanders attempt to enhance law's influence on the battlefield.

Mortars are infantry company-level assets that can generally be employed with the approval of an Army or Marine captain. Larger artillery pieces such as 105mm and 155mm howitzers may only be employed with battalion-level approval that would come from a major or lieutenant colonel. A further elevation of approval is required for any artillery rounds that are expected to land within a certain predetermined distance of civilian structures. Such shots require brigade-level approval by a colonel. Increasing the level of authority required to employ either larger caliber artillery or artillery in circumstances in which legal considerations would more likely come into play serves to ensure that the most potentially problematic firing decisions are made at increasingly higher levels of responsibility. The mere fact that the final firing authority comes from a colonel instead of a captain does not guarantee that the decision will be legally correct. What it does do is put the decision in the hands of an officer who has had a great deal more training and exposure to legal considerations and is therefore more likely to have fully internalized the legal issues related to the firing decision.

To understand the challenges faced by artillerymen and the JAGs that advise them, it is worth understanding what it takes to fire a 15 kilogram shell over a distance of 10 kilometers to within ~60 meters of a given target.[54] The target location has to be

---

[54] The maximum range of the larger (105 and 155mm) howitzers is much greater, but most rounds are fired from ranges of 5–10 km with an approximate CEP of 60 m.

communicated to the artillery battery by troops that, in a counter-fire operation, are presumably under fire. The sense of urgency on both sides of this communication is significant because infantry units are generally rather circumspect about getting artillery involved.[55] Once the call for support comes in, the artillery battery must begin plotting a firing solution while requesting the necessary level of approval. Atmospheric factors such as wind, air temperature, and humidity all influence the flight of the artillery round, as does the temperature of the propellant, which needs to be measured accurately to ensure the range is correct. As the target location is verified and the atmospheric information is updated, final firing approval is sought. Part of this approval is the completion of a proportionality analysis in which the accuracy of the weapon and the anticipated damage footprint of the munition are combined with available intelligence about the target, to determine whether there is a risk of civilian casualties associated with a given shot.

Consider a situation in which the CEP[56] of the weapon indicates that rounds are expected to fall within 75 meters of the target and the anticipated blast radius of the munition is an additional 75 meters. If there are no civilians or civilian structures within 150 meters of the intended target then no further proportionality analysis is required because there is no expectation that firing the weapon will have any impact on the civilian population.[57]

The sense of urgency, the need for precision in both identifying the target location and measuring the external factors that contribute to the accuracy of the shot, and the need to clearly communicate the situation to the proper approving authority make the ~10 minutes between the initial call for support and the first round in the air very hectic. In Afghanistan, the topography further complicates matters. The river valleys in which much of the heavy artillery is located are, in most cases, surrounded by steep-sided mountains. Firing at a target on the reverse slope of steeply sided mountains is particularly difficult because a round that only overshoots the intended target by 25 meters could actually land well over 500 meters from the target if the slope falls away steeply enough.[58] For artillerymen and JAGs who had not served in Afghanistan before, the need to take topography into account in conducting proportionality analyses was not intuitively obvious. In some cases, the need to do so was only learned from hard

---

[55] In interviews with Professor Lewis, infantry officers indicated that a certain degree of incoming fire is tolerated, and it is only when the incoming fire has become particularly intense or is coming from a heavy weapon of some kind that artillery support will be sought.

[56] *See* note 53, *supra*, for the definition of CEP.

[57] Obviously common sense trumps mathematics in these sorts of analyses. If there were a civilian structure 170 or 180 meters from the intended target in this hypothetical, serious questions would be asked about the advisability of such a shot and would probably require brigade- rather than battalion-level approval. Serious consideration would also be given to moving the intended target to create a much larger buffer around the civilian structure.

[58] Interview by Professor Lewis with a U.S. Army artillery officer who served in Afghanistan.

experience.[59] Those operating on both sides of the conflict in Afghanistan learned to use the topography. Experienced artillerymen became comfortable firing at a target within 75 meters of friendly forces if the target was on a facing slope because such a shot effectively decreases the CEP of the weapon as long rounds impact closer to the target when they land on an upslope. Not surprisingly, the Taliban appear to have figured this out and conduct most attacks while on a reverse slope relative to known artillery positions.[60] This phenomenon was not one universally understood by all artillerymen, let alone by JAG officers, and is an illustration of the sort of unanticipated complexity that needs to be passed on within the military community in a reliable manner.

b. Ground Maneuver

For legal officers advising infantry (including mechanized units) in the war on terror, the task of providing simple and clear legal direction is far more difficult because these combatants, by their very nature, face much more complex compliance challenges than their counterparts in aviation. This is because the decision-making in aviation is binary: either release the weapon or bring it home. Any nuances concerning the purpose of the strike or its intended lethality are dealt with by preselecting different weapons, different fuse settings, or different aimpoints. In contrast, the fluid situations that routinely confront infantry forces require that the combatants themselves select different weapons, and determine their aimpoints and their intended lethality in response to rapidly changing situations and threats.

The legal complexity confronting infantry units is even greater in the war on terror because most of the combat has been, and for the foreseeable future will be, a series of low-intensity engagements involving insurgent or guerilla activity that is fought in close proximity to the civilian population. In such circumstances, the questions can seem endless. What weapons should be employed—air strikes, artillery support, machine guns, grenades (which kind? fragmentation, concussion, stun, etc.) or rifles? Is the objective to capture or kill the target? At what point is the target so incapacitated as to not pose a threat, thereby requiring capture? In an environment in which women and teenagers have been suicide bombers, are the other people nearby threats, willing participants, hostages, or something in-between? What else does the unit have to do before it can leave the area and return to the relative security of its base? The existence of so many complex decision trees that can neither be passed up the chain of command nor

---

[59] On at least one occasion, the topography caused an otherwise minor overshoot to land over one-half a kilometer long, resulting in civilian casualties. *Id.*

[60] In several interviews with Professor Lewis, U.S. artillery and infantry officers from Afghanistan shared the observation that over time it appeared to them that Taliban attacks were increasingly conducted from the reverse slope away from large fixed U.S. artillery pieces such as the 105mm and 155mm howitzers based in the river valleys.

adequately resolved by referencing a simple number, a single rule, or a predetermined matrix presents difficulties for both the combatants and the legal officer attempting to advise them. Not only does this complexity undermine the goals of simplicity and clarity, but it can also challenge the legal officer's ability to achieve buy-in from the ground forces.

Like aviation, the combatants' internalization of the ROE is driven by the attitudes toward the ROE requirements of those at the top of each combatant's influence hierarchy. As a combatant's role becomes more personal, it more likely results in face-to-face confrontation with the enemy, and for such combatants the combat experience of their leaders plays a large role in shaping their influence hierarchy. This is not to say that rank is not important, but junior combat officers' opinions on how an operation should be conducted are more strongly influenced by the inputs of combat-experienced enlisted personnel with good combat reputations than by those of combat-inexperienced senior officers who have no combat reputation. For this junior group to buy in to the restrictions imposed by the ROE, it is necessary to demonstrate to them how the ROE improves the outcome of their missions, and to secure the support of the combat-experienced personnel who will influence this junior group.

Legal officers answer these complex challenges, and improve buy-in from critical influencers, with a combination of simplification and persuasion. Given the limitless number of potential scenarios that ground forces face, and the narrow "bandwidth" they have available for legal considerations, legal officers are always required to condense and simplify legal rules into easily understood, and easily recalled, principles. Although legal officers might engage in an informational discussion on the concepts of proportionality and military necessity with combatants, the principles that will actually influence behavior in combat are much more basic. Numerical examples that relate to specific scenarios that are likely to occur might be discussed, but given the fluidity of most ground combat scenarios, legal considerations are most effectively injected into this environment through the repetition of broad principles and the use of thought exercises.

For example, "humane treatment" is a basic guiding principle for custody operations. While its repetition is one method of reinforcement, the internalization of this principle can be enhanced with a thought exercise, directed at senior NCOs and junior officers and including such questions as: "Would you find it acceptable if the people under your command were treated this way by the enemy if they were taken into custody?" Similarly, admonitions to be "reasonable" (i.e., proportional) in the use of force in close proximity to civilians are more effective if supported by another thought exercise: "When you are choosing what force to employ, ask yourself if you could explain that choice to your grandmother." Although neither of these examples accurately articulates the legal standard applicable to the situation, they are an effective means of influencing the actions of combatants in the field in a way that enhances legal compliance.

Another tool developed by the U.S. Army's Center for Army Lessons Learned (CALL) is a Handbook of ROE Vignettes that was promulgated in 2011.[61] Although the Handbook is not a definitive statement of the U.S. interpretation of the laws of armed conflict in each situation, and is intended to be a guide to the application of ROE that may be more restrictive than the LOAC, it provides general guidance for soldiers and the JAGs that advise them in how to deal with complicated and confusing situations. The Handbook provides 50 vignettes dealing with a wide range of situations that ground forces may confront. Most of the vignettes are set at the checkpoint, squad, or platoon level. They attempt to strike an appropriate balance between encouraging restraint in the presence of civilians while reaffirming the right of self-defense that allows the use of lethal force even when there remains some uncertainty about the target's intentions.[62]

Matching Mindset with Operational Objectives

Another very important tool that commanders have at their disposal for improving legal outcomes is properly matching the mindset of their forces with the operational objectives. This is particularly true in the low-intensity conflicts that continue to characterize the war on terror. While matching forces with objectives is a basic tenet of military operations, and is widely recognized as improving the safety and operational effectiveness of combatants, the effect that it can have on legal outcomes may be underappreciated. An example from the United Kingdom's experience combating the Irish Republican Army (IRA) illustrates how a mismatch between the mindset of the forces utilized and the objectives sought can result in a legally undesirable outcome.

In 1995, the European Court of Human Rights heard the case of *McCann v. the United Kingdom*, in which the families of IRA members killed by the British military sued the United Kingdom for unlawful killings.[63] Although the claims were based upon an alleged violation of the European Human Rights Convention, not IHL, the legal issues discussed should resonate with legal officers involved in the war on terror.

In 1988, British intelligence had information indicating that three suspected IRA members had arrived in Gibraltar to conduct a car bomb attack on a British military installation there. After shadowing the suspects for a while, the British decided to apprehend them. They assigned the apprehension to Special Air Service (SAS)[64] forces. As the SAS moved in to apprehend the suspected IRA members, the IRA members allegedly

---

[61] CENTER FOR ARMY LESSONS LEARNED, RULES OF ENGAGEMENT VIGNETTES HANDBOOK (May 2011), *available at* http://info.publicintelligence.net/USArmy-ROE-Vignettes.pdf.

[62] *See* id.

[63] McCann et al. v. United Kingdom, 21 Eur. Ct. H.R. (ser. A) 97 (1995) [hereinafter McCann].

[64] SAS are British special forces, somewhat comparable to U.S. Navy Seals or U.S. Army Delta Force.

reached for something, either a weapon or detonator, and the SAS forces killed all three of them.[65]

The court did not fault the SAS for the killings. A car full of plastic explosives and four detonators were discovered as a result of items found on one of the bodies, so the intelligence about their intentions was correct. The court did not try to determine whether the IRA members intended to detonate the bomb as they were being apprehended. It held that the soldiers had a reasonable apprehension of harm to either themselves or others and so their actions were not improper. However, the court did find the United Kingdom liable for wrongful killings and ordered the United Kingdom to pay compensation to the IRA members' families. The rationale for this decision was that the U.K. government sent the SAS to apprehend the suspected terrorists. Because the court found that the U.K. government knew that a likely SAS response to a problem with the mission would be the killing of the IRA members, the court concluded that insufficient steps had been taken by the U.K. government to protect the right to life of the IRA members, including by making certain erroneous assumptions in the briefing given to the SAS unit that increased the likelihood that the SAS would respond with deadly force.[66]

Although it is not surprising that properly matching the mindset of the people assigned to conduct a mission with that mission's objective has a great deal to do with the mission's outcome, there is at least some evidence that ground forces in the war on terror have been placed in situations that make this concept a difficult one to apply. The form below (Figure 7.2) is a capture tag that is used by most of the U.S. forces in Afghanistan when taking an individual into custody.

FIGURE 7.2 Capture Tag.

1. Date and time of Capture		2. Serial No.		ENEMY PRISONER OF WAR (EPW) CAPTURE TAG (PART A) For Use of this form, see AR 190-8, the proponent agency is DCSOPS
3. Name		4. Date of Birth		
5. Rank	6. Service No.			Attach this part of tag to EPW (Do not remove from EPW.)
7. Unit of EPW		8. Capturing Unit		1. Search - For weapons, military documents, or special equipment. 2. Silence - Prohibit talking among EPWs for ease of control
9. Location of Capture *(Grid coordinates)*				3. Segregate - By rank, sex, and nationality 4. Safeguard - To prevent harm or escape.
10. Circumstances of Capture	11. Physical Condition of EPW	12. Weapons, Equipment, Documents		5. Speed - Evacuate from the combat zone. 6. Tag - Prisoners and documents or special equipment. DA FORM 5976, JAN 91

---

65 McCann, *supra* note 63, at ¶¶ 61, 62 & 78.

66 *Id.* at ¶¶ 206–213.

The capture tag contains the information required by article 70 of the GPW[67] for the proper acknowledgment of custody by the detaining power, and the notification of the prisoner's relatives. It is an unremarkable document until it is compared with the two-page Coalition Provisional Authority Forces Apprehension Form (Figure 7.3) that the ROE in Iraq required most units to use when documenting a capture.

FIGURE 7.3 Coalition Provisional Authority Apprehension Form.

COALITION PROVISIONAL AUTHORITY FORCES APPREHENSION FORM
YELLOW FIELDS MUST BE FILLED IN, IF APPLICABLE, UPON APPREHENSION

Offense against Civilian(s) [check one] If "other" then describe: _____
- Arson (I.P.C. 342)
- Solicitation of Fornication/Prostitution (I.P.C. 399)
- Rape/indecent/Sexual Assaults/Acts (I.P.C. 393-98, 402)
- Murdar (I.P.C. 405)
- Aggravated Assault/Assault With Intent To Kill (I.P.C. 410)
- Maiming (I.P.C. 412)
- Simple Assault (I.P.C. 415)
- Kidnapping (I.P.C. 421)
- Burglary of Housebreaking (I.P.C. 428)
- Extortion/Communicating Threats (I.P.C. 430)
- Theft (I.P.C. 439)
- Destruction of Property (I.P.C. 477)
- Obstructing a Public Highway/Place (I.P.C. 487)
- Discharging Firearm/Explosive in City/Town/Village (I.P.C. 495)
- Riot of Breach of Peace (I.P.C. 495(3))
- Other

Offense against Coalition Forces [check one] if "Other" then describe: _____
- Violation of Curfew
- Illegal Possession of Weapon
- Assault/Attack on Coalition Forces
- Theft of Coalition Force Property
- Trespass on Military installation or facility
- Photographing/Surveilling Military Installation of Facility
- Obstructing Performance of Military Mission
- Other

| Apprehending Unit: | | Location Grid: | | |

| Date of Incident: (D /M /Y) / / to / / | Time of Incident: hrs to hrs | Date of Report: (D/M/Y) / / | Time of Report: hrs |

| Detainee # _____ | Key Connected Person: ☐ Victim ☐ Witness |

Last Name:	Last Name:
First Name:	Given Name:	First Name:	Given Name:
Hair Color:	Scars/Tattoos/Deformities:	Hair Color:	Scars/Tattoos/Deformities:
Eye-Color:	Weight: lb	Height: in	Eye-Color:	Weight: lb	Height: in
Address:	Address:
Place of Birth:	Place of Birth:

| Ethn/Tribe/Sect: | Sex: ☐ M ☐ F | Phone#: ☐ Moblie DOB D/M/Y: ☐ Regular | Ethn/Tribe/Sect: | Sex: ☐ M ☐ F | Phone#: ☐ Moblie DOB D/M/Y: ☐ Regular |

| ☐ Passport ☐ Dr. license ☐ Other (specify) Document #: | ☐ Passport ☐ Dr. license ☐ Other (specify) Document #: |

Total Number of Persons Involved _____ (list names/identifying into on reverse under "Additional Helpful Information")

☐ Vehicle Information   Vehicle Number _____ of _____ Vehicle(s)

Make:	Color:	License No:	Owner:
Model:	Type:	Plate No:	Number of People in Vehicle:
Year:	Name of People in Vehicle:		
Contraband/Weapons in Vehicle:			

☐ Property/Contraband   ☐ Weapon   Photo Taken of Suspect with Weapon/Contraband: Yes/No

Type	Model:	Color/Caliber:
Serial No:	Quantity:	Make:	Receipt Provided to Owner: Yes/No
Other Details:	Where Found:	Owner:

| Name of Assisting Interpreter: | Email, Phone, or Contact info: |

Detaining Soldier's Name (Print):	Supervising Officer's Name (Print):
Signature:	Last, First MI	Signature:	Last, First MI
Email: Unit Phone:	Date: / /	Email: Unit Phone:	Date: / /

---

[67] It is modeled on the card found in Annex IV B to the GPW.

COALITION PROVISIONAL AUTHORITY FORCES APPREHENSION FORM

Why was this person detained? _____

Who witnessed this person being detained or the reason for detention? Give names, contact numbers, addresses.

How was this person traveling (car, bus, on foot)? _____

Who was with this person? _____

What weapons was this person carrying? _____

What contraband was this person carrying? _____

What other weapons were seized? _____

What other information did you get from this person? _____

Additional Helpful Information: _____

The most troubling aspect of the Coalition Provisional Authority forms is their striking similarity to a police report, and what that similarity implies about the (lack of) clarity of purpose that ground forces in Iraq may have carried into their missions. Evidence collection to support continued detentions may be a necessary task in counterinsurgency/counter-terrorism operations because it represents the best way to incapacitate insurgents/terrorists. However, to the extent that such requirements represent a shift in mission objectives, it is both operationally and legally important to examine the mindset of the units being used for this task.

The *McCann* example illustrates one way in which a striking mismatch between mindset and objectives can go wrong, but even more subtle mismatches or changes have their costs in terms of operational readiness and less than desirable outcomes. When a broad range of forces are tasked with evidence collection, a predictable result occurs. Those units that are more highly trained in personal combat generally do a less thorough job of evidence gathering than units whose expertise lies elsewhere.[68] If a broad range of forces continues to be used for capture operations, two things can occur. The more "kinetic" forces either may continue to produce less complete evidentiary reports, which will presumably lead to fewer long-term detentions, or if they focus on improving their evidence collection skills, they may get better at producing these reports (because they spend more time working on them), but spend less time maintaining their "kinetic" skills. Although an improvement in detention and evidence collection skills may seem positive, it comes at a price to operational readiness that should be considered, including the possible increase in the risk of casualties among U.S. forces.

Because fractions of a second matter in personal combat, and often represent the difference between winning and losing, and between living and dying, forces that engage in such combat have constant training requirements.[69] The time required for such forces to learn to improve their evidence collection procedures would likely come at a price in combat readiness. This price will not be quantifiable, and will likely be minimal if this proves to be a short-term change in the way forces are utilized. But if the changing nature of the conflict anticipates a need for long-term improvement in evidence gathering and report writing, then a careful consideration of the type of unit assigned to these operations should be undertaken.

Conclusions

For IHL to be effective, it must be successfully translated from words on paper into core beliefs and principles that alter behavior on the battlefield. In prosecuting the war on terror, the U.S. military has stayed true to its core belief that, in addition to obeying the law of war, it has a duty to continually improve the protection of civilians in clashes between U.S. forces and the combatant groups they target. Technology has been an important tool in pursuing this goal. By creating weapons that minimize the effects

---

[68] The apprehension forms produced by the U.S. Army's "Stryker" Brigades conducting custody operations in Iraq tended to be less thorough than those produced by less "kinetic" units.

[69] Based on Professor Lewis's experience, it appears true that in air-to-air "personal" combat training (1 v. 1 dogfighting), the pilot who had received the most recent intense 1 v. 1 training usually performed much better than his experience or aircraft type would have predicted. It was generally agreed that recent 1 v. 1 training significantly improved the split-second recognition and reaction process that makes for a successful engagement. This is almost certainly also true for ground forces engaged in house-to-house operations in a generally hostile environment.

on civilians and civilian infrastructure, and by greatly improving the information flow on the battlefield, the U.S. military has consistently acted on the underlying belief that it has a legal obligation to use available technology to improve the outcomes of war-making in terms of reduced harm to civilians.

But an even more important tool in furthering this goal is the mindset of individual combatants, and their *belief* in the value of the restrictions placed upon them by the ROE and the law. It is the first task of legal officers to communicate the core principles of IHL in a manner that increases the likelihood that combatants will *believe* in these restrictions and guidelines rather than just accept them. This is done most effectively by tailoring the message to the right audience—those at the top of the influence hierarchy—and enlisting the aid of other combat support specialties (such as intelligence and targeting) in addressing the target audience's chief concerns.

Index